FOURTH EDITION

KU-708-286

Models
of
Teaching

Bruce Joyce
Marsha Weil
WITH *Beverly Showers*

UNIVERSITY OF WOLVERHAMPTON
LEARNING RESOURCES

Acc No.
2060190

CLASS
371,
3

CONTROL
0205133983

DATE
22.1.97

SITE
Res JOY
AHWL

LIBRARY
SCHOOL OF NURSING

5406/P
311E

NEW
Sept 95

Allyn and Bacon

BOSTON · LONDON · TORONTO
SYDNEY · TOKYO · SINGAPORE

Cover Administrator: Linda Dickinson
Manufacturing Buyer: Louise Richardson
Editorial-Production Service: York Production Services

Due to circumstances beyond my control I was unable to participate substantively in the preparation of this fourth edition of *Models of Teaching*. There are a number of approaches to the subject matter presented in this book, and I do not necessarily subscribe to all revisions reflected in the fourth edition. While any scholar's view of appropriate theoretical or practical emphases can legitimately differ from another's, my commitment to the theory and philosophy that supported *Models of Teaching* for over twenty years remains unchanged.

Marsha Weil

Acknowledgements appear on p. 493, which constitutes a continuation of the copyright page.

Copyright © 1992, 1986, 1980, 1972 by Allyn and Bacon
A Division of Simon & Schuster, Inc.
160 Gould St.
Needham Heights, Massachusetts 02194

All rights reserved. No part of the material protected by this copyright notice may be reproduced or utilized in any form or by any means, electronic or mechanical, including photocopying, recording, or by any information storage and retrieval system, without written permission from the copyright owner.

Library of Congress Cataloging-in-Publication Data

Joyce, Bruce R.
   Models of teaching / Bruce Joyce, Marsha Weil with Beverly
Showers.—4th ed.
     p.   cm.
   Includes bibliographical references (p.) and index.
   ISBN 0-205-13398-3
   1. Educational innovations. 2. Teaching. I. Weil, Marsha.
II. Showers, Beverly. III. Title.
LB1027.3.J69 1992
371.3—dc20   91-38196
                                                  CIP

Printed in the United States of America

10 9 8 7 6 5 4   96 95 94

This book is dedicated to Seamus and all the wonderful young people he represents.
May we be worthy of them.

and to

Joseph P. Kelley, a dear friend and colleague,
whose enthusiasm and devotion
to Models of Teaching
will be remembered always

CONTENTS

CHAPTER 1
TOOLING UP THE COMMUNITY OF LEARNERS 1

Teaching well means helping students learn well. Powerful learners have
expanded repertoires of strategies for acquiring education. Models of
teaching are designed to impart those strategies while helping students
develop as persons, increase their capacity to think clearly and wisely, and
build social skills and commitment. Teaching is the process of building
communities of learners who use their skills to educate themselves.
Powerful learners know how to profit from a wide range of learning
opportunities, from lectures and readings, from collecting and analyzing
information and building concepts and theories, and from working together
cooperatively. Four families of models are introduced with their purposes
and an introduction to the research that supports them. They promise to
increase student academic learning, social development, and self-esteem far
beyond what has been normal in most schools and classrooms.

PART I
THE SOCIAL FAMILY 27

Introduction: These models capitalize on our nature as social creatures to
further learning and to expand our ability to relate productively to one
another. The models range from the simple processes of organizing students
to work together to elaborate models that teach democratic social
organization and the analysis of major social problems and critical social
values and issues.

The simplest forms of cooperative learning organize students to help one
another respond to the cognitive and social tasks presented to them
through the information-processing models of teaching. The synergy is
generated as they work together to memorize, attain and form concepts,
and learn how to build and test hypotheses. Widely used today through the
efforts and research of Robert Slavin, David and Roger Johnson, and their
colleagues, cooperative learning organizations positively affect academic
learning, social development, and the self-esteem of the learner.

v

C H A P T E R 2

PARTNERS IN LEARNING
From Dyads to Group Investigation

Fundamentally, democracy is a way of solving problems through collective learning and action. John Dewey proposed that group investigation should be the basic model for social and academic learning in a democratic society. Herbert Thelen extended the theory and practice of the model. Recent research and practice by Shlomo Sharan and his colleagues affirm and illuminate this broad, complex, and very powerful model.

C H A P T E R 3

ROLE PLAYING
Studying Social Behavior and Values

Fannie and George Shaftel are the designers of a process to help students understand and develop their social values. Role playing of problematic situations is used to open up discussions of values and how they operate in our daily lives. The model permits values to be studied as a core of the developing self—the place where social norms and personal identity and sense of meaning come together.

C H A P T E R 4

JURISPRUDENTIAL INQUIRY
Learning to Think about Social Policy

The making of social policy is a fundamental need in small groups, communities, nations, and even the internation. Built around the analysis of case studies containing problems that can only be solved by clarifying values and resolving conflicts and competing demands, the jurisprudential model introduces policy analysis. Developed by Donald Oliver and James Shaver, the model can be used to design entire social studies courses or to illuminate policy questions within other curriculum areas from science to athletics.

C H A P T E R 5

ADAPTING TO INDIVIDUAL DIFFERENCES
Conceptual Systems Theory

How do we plan the social education of students who are at different stages of development? We use David Hunt's extensions of the conceptual systems theory which he developed with O.J. Harvey and Harold Schroder to select and modify the social tasks we will provide students to maximize their productivity and development. Because conceptual systems theory describes both social and intellectual development we can use it to match the cognitive and social tasks of both the information-processing and social families of models to the developmental stages of the students.

The Social Family: An Additional Note on Expected Effects

PART II
THE INFORMATION-PROCESSING FAMILY
Teaching Students the Skills of
Learning through Thinking   **107**

Introduction: While research on how students learn to think is by no means a completed science, there are a variety of models that increase students' ability to seek and master information, organize it, build and test hypotheses, and apply what they are learning in their independent reading and writing and their exploration of themselves and the world about them. Some of these models induce the students to collect information and build concepts. Others teach them to profit from direct instruction through readings, lectures, and instructional systems.

CHAPTER 6
THINKING INDUCTIVELY
Collecting, Organizing, and Manipulating Data   **113**

Classification is the fundamental higher-order thinking skill and all analytic and synthetic skills depend on the discriminations made through classification. Based on the work of Hilda Taba and a host of others who have concerned themselves with the development of thinking processes, we present the basic classification model, which begins with concept formation and proceeds to the development of generalizations, hypotheses, and inferences about causation.

CHAPTER 7
ATTAINING CONCEPTS
The Basic Skills of Thinking   **141**

Based on the study of classification processes, this model helps students learn categories and study how to learn and apply them. The model also provides teachers with a conceptual alternative to induction, enabling them to control data sets and help students develop precise knowledge of concepts.

CHAPTER 8

MEMORIZATION
Getting the Facts Straight

Recent research on memorization, especially on the use of "link words" to facilitate associations, has produced some dramatic effects on the rate at which students can acquire information and concepts. In some applications the instructors generate the mnemonics. In others the students develop their own. In both uses the students are organized into learning communities who possess knowledge about how to acquire, store, and retrieve information. Research by Joel Levin, Pressley, and their colleagues has stressed the importance of providing students with cognitive control over learning strategies—the "metacognitive" dimension of being a student. In other words, the students are not taught simply to engage in a learning activity. They are taught how to learn and how to use knowledge of learning to increase their effectiveness.

CHAPTER 9

LEARNING FROM PRESENTATIONS
Advance Organizers

Based on research by David Ausubel these models facilitate learning from lectures, readings and other mediated presentations, and courses by increasing the cognitive activity of the students.

CHAPTER 10

INQUIRY TRAINING
From Facts to Theories

This model is the core of a program, first developed by Richard Suchman, to train students to engage in causal reasoning. The training is built around sets of puzzling problems which the students attempt to solve by collecting and verifying data, developing concepts, and building and testing hypotheses.

CHAPTER 11

SYNECTICS
Enhancing Creative Thought

It can be argued that the ability to go beyond the known and synthesize fresh ideas and solutions is the ultimate information-processing skill. It can also be argued that possessing the freedom to create is one of the peaks of personal development. William Gordon has developed a procedure to help people break set and generate fresh solutions to problems, generate more lucid writing and speaking, and coalesce groups around creative problem-solving. Rather than conceiving of creativity as an isolating, inward process, it is developed in groups and increases cohesion and empathy among group members.

CHAPTER 12

THE DEVELOPING INTELLECT
Adjusting Models to Cognitive Development   241

Jean Piaget and his colleagues have developed a model of intellectual development that we can use to organize the information-processing models to facilitate cognitive growth. We select and modify the models to help students increase their levels of conceptual activity.

The Information Processing Family: An Additional Note on Expected Effects

PART III

THE PERSONAL FAMILY
Focus on the Person   259

Introduction: The personalistic models focus on the development of the integrated feeling, thinking self—the personal identity. They shape the environment around the capacity for self-education and the need to develop self-awareness and understanding.

CHAPTER 13

NONDIRECTIVE TEACHING
The Learner at the Center   261

Carl Rogers has been the leading spokesperson for teaching that is oriented around the student's perceptual world. The teacher operates from a counselling stance, helping the students understand themselves, clarify their goals, and accept responsibility for their growth and the direction of their lives. Designed to enhance the growing self, this model is as important too for us as teachers, helping us to reach into the psychological space of the students and to enlist them in the learning-teaching partnership.

The ultimate evidence of whether education has been effective is in the reciprocal relationship of the educated person with their world— contributing to it and profiting from it. We examine a framework for examining the growing self and modelling for our students a self-actualizing way of life.

The Personal Family: An Additional Note on Expected Effects

On the foundation of the work of B.F. Skinner a large number of approaches to learning have been developed, each taking advantage of the human being's ability to modify behavior in response to tasks and feedback. These models are used in a wide variety of applications, from teaching information, concepts, and skills, increasing comfort and relaxation and decreasing phobias, changing habits, and learning to control one's behavior. Our selection includes just a few of the ones with broad potential for uses in school settings.

One of the important applications of behavioral systems theory is in the development of systems that enable learning tasks to be regulated according to the progress of the learners and which teach students to pace themselves for optimal performance. Often these systems organize material to be learned in relatively small, sequenced, instructional "modules" that are presented to the students with assessments of learning embedded in them. These "mastery learning" or "direct-instruction" systems have been employed successfully in a wide variety of areas involving academic, physical, and mental development.

CHAPTER 16
LEARNING SELF-CONTROL
Using Feedback to Modify Behavior

Teaching students how to modify their patterns of behavior using behavioral systems principles, Carl Thoresen and his colleagues have developed procedures for placing control in the hands of the learners by teaching them how patterns of behavior develop and change.

CHAPTER 17
TRAINING AND SELF-TRAINING: LEARNING FROM SIMULATIONS
From the Basic Skills to the Exploration of Space

In industrial, military, athletic, and educational settings researchers have developed procedures for developing skills and enabling those skills to be used effectively in work and education.

CHAPTER 18
THE CONDITIONS OF LEARNING
Focusing Instruction

Robert Gagné and his colleagues have developed a classification of learning goals that enables us to organize objectives and place them in appropriate sequence.

The Behavioral Systems Family: An Additional Note on Expected Effects

PART V
PROFESSIONAL SKILL

CHAPTER 19
HOW TO LEARN A TEACHING REPERTOIRE
The Professional Learning Community

Based on twenty-five years of research on how we acquire teaching skills, we present a framework for organizing ourselves to expand our teaching repertoire.

CHAPTER 20

LEARNING STYLES AND MODELS OF TEACHING
Making Discomfort Productive   391

For our students and for ourselves, reaching out for new learning tools and ideas involves some necessary and exciting discomfort. One of the major challenges of teaching is to build learning communities that represent "safe space" in which students can keep themselves on the move as learners. "At risk" students are those who are trying to stretch too limited a repertoire over too many learning tasks. Our remedy is to design the school as a laboratory for learning how to learn, a place where stretching one's capacity is a way of life.

APPENDIX

PEER COACHING GUIDES   405

These guides are designed to facilitate planning for practice with nine of the most commonly used models of teaching and to provide formats for observing demonstration and peer practice.

FOREWORD

The autumn efflorescence of color annually admired in New England foliage is no less visually exciting or aesthetically satisfying because it is familiar and oft-observed. Neither is a new publication of *Models of Teaching* less intellectually stimulating or professionally rewarding because one has admired earlier editions of the work. Although I now live most of the year in Florida, I never willingly miss an October in Vermont or up-state New York. And while I'm now only an occasional teacher, I could never ignore a fresh, while yet familiar, demonstration of the authors' insights into the mysteries and complexities of teaching.

The essential task of this realization of *Models of Teaching*, 4th edition, as, indeed, of all earlier editions, is to describe a rich variety of approaches to teaching—in sufficient detail and with sufficient illustration of their uses and purposes in real learning situations as to make each model an active, or at least potentially active, part of a teacher's repertoire. No teacher, prospective, neophyte, or veteran, could examine these models without a renewed sense of the multiplicity of educational purposes, the range and diversity of useful teaching behaviors, or the intellectual zest inherent in the craft.

No model is presented didactically. Each is discussed in terms of its underlying theory and of the problematics intrinsic to its use. Research testing the effectiveness of each model is nicely marshalled. Citing such theory and research is clearly not intended to provide closed, static "proofs" of the efficacy of individual models, but to encourage reflection and inquiry about yet unknown aspects of teaching strategy. Readers of this book are never assumed to be passive receptacles of the authors' wisdom.

I am impressed, as I have long been, with the breadth of scholarship, the command of psychological and pedagogical literature, and the sheer professional enthusiasm that *Models of Teaching* exemplifies. It is true that I have grown accustomed to such virtues and have duly noted them in earlier editions of the book. But I still respond, also, to the familiar golds, the reds, the browns, and the persistent greens of New England autumns. Each manifestation, be it of book or foliage, is a uniquely exciting experience.

Robert J. Schaefer
Longboat Key, Florida

PREFACE

As we have worked through the writing and editing of this fourth edition of *Models of Teaching*, we have relived the affection and respect we have for the many teachers, teacher candidates, education professors, and staff development personnel who have labored to bring expended repertoires into the lives of teachers and students.

We are so fortunate to have the privilege of trying to translate some of the most important educational research into a form that can, hopefully, enhance the achievement, self-esteem, and commitment to society that should represent the product of the educational systems of the world. For we have discovered that, wherever models of teaching are found, those that stand the test of research in one cultural setting also do well in others with proper adaptation to the cultural contexts.

Although the work of producing *Models of Teaching* is largely technical, it took place not only in the library but also in the many settings where we have been fortunate enough to work with teachers, teacher candidates, and students. We watch again and again the tapes where we have led students into new modes of learning, not only for what we can learn, but with strong affection for those children. At this point our "home movies" range from children in the United States and Canada to children in Hong Kong, India, Egypt, Finland, and the United Kingdom where we have been lucky enough to have contact with them. These tapes can serve as demonstrations of the various models of teaching that we hope will enhance the learning of children in the United States and all the countries of the world.*

We are in love with teaching, teachers, and students. We could not ask for more.

*These tapes can be ordered from Booksend Laboratories, 652 St. Andrews Drive, Aptos, CA 95003 (408) 685 3719.

TOOLING UP THE COMMUNITY OF LEARNERS

Schools and classes are communities of students, brought together to explore the world and learn how to navigate it productively. We have high aspirations for these little units of our society. We hope their members will become highly literate, that they will read omnivorously and write with skill and delicacy. We hope they will understand their social world, be devoted to its improvement, and develop the dignity, self-esteem, and sense of efficacy to generate personal lives of high quality. These fundamental goals of education are central to the study of teaching.

In this book we describe a variety of approaches to teaching, discuss their underlying theories, examine the research that has tested them, and illustrate their uses. There are many powerful models of teaching designed to bring about particular kinds of learning and to help students become more effective learners. As educators we need to be able to identify these models and to select the ones we will master in order to develop and increase our own effectiveness. To become competent to use these teaching strategies comfortably and effectively requires much study and practice, but by concentrating on one or two at a time we can expand our repertoires quite easily. (Chapter 19 describes the process of acquiring the skill necessary to use new models of teaching.)

Models of teaching are really models of *learning*. As we help students acquire information, ideas, skills, values, ways of thinking, and means of expressing themselves, we are also teaching them how to learn. *In fact, the most important long-term outcome of instruction may be the students' increased capabilities to learn more easily and effectively in the future, both because of the knowledge and skill they have acquired and because they have mastered learning processes.*

How teaching is conducted has a large impact on students' abilities to educate themselves. Successful teachers are not simply charismatic, persuasive, and expert presenters. *Rather, they present powerful cognitive and social tasks to their students and teach the students how to make productive use of them.* For example, although learning to lecture clearly and knowledgeably is highly desirable, it is the learner who does the learning; successful lecturers teach students how to mine the information in the talk and make it their own. Effective learners draw information, ideas, and wisdom from their teachers and use learning resources effectively. Thus, a major role in teaching is to create powerful learners.

The same principle applies to schools. Outstanding schools teach the students to learn. Thus, teaching becomes more effective as the students progress through those schools because, year by year, the students have been taught to be stronger learners. As we will see, we measure the effects of various models of teaching not only by how well they achieve the specific objectives toward which they are directed (e.g., self-esteem, social skill, information, ideas, creativity) but also by how they increase the ability to learn.

All of the models of teaching in this book can enhance the ability of students to achieve various learning objectives. *Thus, in a very real sense, increasing aptitude to learn is one of the fundamental purposes of these models.* Students will change as their repertoire of learning strategies increases, and they will be able to accomplish more and more types of learning more effectively. It is important that we recognize this, for our view of our efficacy as professionals depends on our belief that we have tools that can affect the strength of our learners.

In a recent study of learning through group investigation (See Chapter 2), Shlomo Sharan and Hana Shachar (1988) illustrated how rapidly students can accelerate their learning rates. Their study focused on a problem that exists in many societies—that students whose families are regarded as socially and economically disadvantaged frequently achieve poorly and also receive disadvantaging treatment in the classroom from teachers and other students. Sharan and Shachar prepared social studies teachers to organize their students into learning communities; they then compared the classroom interaction and academic achievement with classes taught by the customary "whole-class" method. In Israel, where the study was conducted, Middle-Eastern origin students generally belong to the "disadvantaged" population, whereas European-origin students generally are more advantaged. Students from both origins were mixed in each class in the study. The research design compared the achievement (see Table 1–1) of the students who were taught using group investigation with students taught by the "whole-class" method most common in Israeli schools. The Middle-Eastern students taught by group investigation achieved average gains nearly two and a half times those of Middle-Eastern students taught by the whole-class method.

These normally disadvantaged students also achieved larger gains than did the European-origin students taught by the more typical whole-class method (35.16 to 21.05) and exceeded them on the post-test. In other words, the "socially disadvantaged" students taught with group investigation learned at rates above those of the "socially advantaged" students

TABLE 1—1   EFFECTS OF COMPLEX COOPERATIVE LEARNING IN A
HISTORY COURSE BY SES

	Cooperative Learning (Treatment)		Whole Class Control	
	High SES	Low SES	High SES	Low SES
Pretest				
M	20.99	14.81	21.73	12.31
SD	9.20	7.20	10.53	7.05
Posttest				
M	62.60	50.17	42.78	27.23
SD	10.85	14.44	14.40	13.73
Mean Gain	41.61	35.36	21.05	14.92

From: S. Sharan and H. Shackar, *Language and Learning in the Cooperative Classroom*. N.Y.: Springer-Verlag, 1988.

taught by teachers who did not have the repertoire provided by group investigation. This model of teaching had enabled them to become more powerful students immediately.

The average gain by the Western-origin students taught with group investigation was *twice* that of their whole-class counterparts. Thus, the model was effective for students from both backgrounds and by a large margin.

This is just an example to get us thinking about making a big difference for our students. As we will see, other models also can help students increase their learning capability, sometimes modestly and sometimes dramatically. The important point is that teaching can make a big difference to students both at the classroom and school levels. Knowing this is the *core* of effective teaching, because effective teachers are confident that they can make a difference and that the difference is made by tooling up their learning community.

Thus, imagine a school where the variety of models of teaching is not only intended to accomplish a range of curriculum goals (learning to read; to compute; to understand mathematical systems; to comprehend literature, science, and the social world; and to engage in the performing arts and athletics) but is also designed to help the students increase their power as learners. As students master information and skills, the result of each learning experience is not only the content they learn, but the increased ability they acquire to approach future learning tasks and to create programs of study for themselves.

In our school the students acquire a range of learning strategies because their teachers use the models of teaching that require them. Our students learn models for memorizing information (described in Chapter 8). They learn how to attain concepts (Chapter 7) and how to invent them (Chapter 6). They practice building hypotheses and theories and using the tools of science to test them. They learn how to extract information and ideas from lectures and presentations (Chapter 9), how to study social issues (Chapter 4), and how to analyze their own social values (Chapter 3).

Our students also know how to profit from training and how to train themselves in athletic, performing arts, mathematical, and social skills (Chapters 15, 16, and 17). They know how to make their writing and problem solving more lucid and creative (Chapter 11). Perhaps most important, they know how to take initiative in planning personal study (Chapter 13), and they know how to work with others to initiate and carry out cooperative programs of inquiry (Chapter 2). These students are both challenging and exhilarating to teach because their expanded learning styles enable us to teach them in the variety of ways that are appropriate for the many goals of education.

Sources of Models of Teaching

The core of the process of teaching is the arrangement of environments within which the student can interact (Dewey, 1916). A model of teaching is a plan or pattern that we can use to design face-to-face teaching in classrooms or tutorial settings and to shape instructional materials—including books, films, tapes, computer-mediated programs, and curricula (long-term courses of study). Each model guides us as we design instruction to help students achieve various objectives.

For the last 25 years we have conducted a continuous search for promising approaches to teaching. We visit schools and classrooms, examine curricula, and study research on teaching. We also look at the work of persons in a variety of teaching roles outside of schools, such as therapists and industrial, military, and athletic trainers. We have found models of teaching in abundance. Some have broad applications while others are designed for very specific purposes. They range from simple, direct procedures that get immediate results to complex strategies that students acquire gradually from patient and skillful instruction.

For inclusion in this book we have selected models that constitute a basic repertoire for schooling—that is, with them we can accomplish most of the common goals of schools. Also, they represent a broad range of approaches to education. They include many, but not all, of the major philosophical and psychological orientations toward teaching and learning. Each of them has a coherent theoretical basis—that is, their creators provide us with a rationale that explains why we expect them to achieve the goals for which they were designed. The selected models also have long histories of practice behind them: They have been refined through experience so that they can be used comfortably and efficiently in classrooms and other educational settings. Furthermore, they are adaptable: They can be adjusted to the learning styles of students and to the requirements of subject matter.

Finally, there is evidence that they work. In addition to experience, all of them are backed by some amount of formal research that tests their theories and their abilities to gain effects. The amount of related research varies from model to model. Some are backed by a few studies while others have a history of literally hundreds of items of research.

We have grouped the models of teaching that we have discovered into four families that share orientations toward human beings and how they learn. These are the social family, the information-processing family, the personal family, and the behavioral systems family. The first four parts of the book present the models selected for each family, with the last chapter of each part dealing with frameworks for modifying the models to account for individual differences in students.

THE SOCIAL FAMILY: BUILDING THE LEARNING COMMUNITY

When we work together we generate a collective energy that we call "synergy." The social models of teaching are constructed to take advantage of this phenomenon by building learning communities. Essentially, "classroom management" is a matter of developing cooperative relationships in the classroom. The development of positive school cultures is a process of developing integrative and productive ways of interacting and norms that support vigorous learning activity. Thus, we begin with the social family.

PARTNERS IN LEARNING (CHAPTER 2)

During the last 15 years, cooperative learning procedures—ways of building communities of learners—have received intensive research and development. The result is a large number of effective means for organizing students to work together. These range from systems for teaching students to carry on simple learning tasks in pairs to very complex models for organizing classes and even schools in learning communities that strive to educate themselves.

Cooperative learning procedures assist learning across all curriculum areas and ages, improving self-esteem, social skill and solidarity, and academic learning from the acquisition of information and skill through the modes of inquiry of the academic disciplines.

In Chapter 2 we begin with the simpler forms of cooperative learning, especially as they are combined with other models of teaching, and end with the most complex model, that of group investigation, which combines preparation for life in a democratic society with academic study.

Group investigation is the direct route to the development of the community of learners. All the simpler forms of cooperative learning are preparation for rigorous, active, and integrative collective action as learners.

John Dewey (1916) developed the idea—extended and refined by a great many teachers and theorists and shaped into powerful definition by Herbert Thelen (1960)—that education in a democratic society should teach democratic process directly. A substantial part of the students' education should be by cooperative inquiry into important social and academic problems. Essentially, the model also provides a social organization within which many other models can be used when appropriate. Group investigation has been used in all subject areas, with children of all ages, and even as the core social model for entire schools (Chamberlin and Chamberlin, 1943). The model is designed to lead students to define problems, explore various perspectives on the problems, and study together to master information, ideas, and skills—simultaneously developing their social competence. The teacher organizes the group process and disciplines it, helps the students find and organize information, and ensures that there is a vigorous level of activity and discourse. Recently Sharan and his associates (Sharan and Hertz-Lazarowitz, 1980; Sharan and Shachar, 1988) explored the dynamics and the effects of the model, and they learned that rigorous implementation builds a more integrative social environment and, as indicated earlier, can have some very positive effects on academic learning.

ROLE PLAYING (CHAPTER 3)

Role playing is included next because it leads students to understand social behavior, their role in social interactions, and ways of solving problems more effectively. Designed by Fannie and George Shaftel (1982) specifically to help students study their social values and reflect on them, role playing also helps students collect and organize information about social issues, develop empathy with others, and attempt to improve their social skills. The model asks students to "act out" conflicts, to learn to take the roles of others, and to observe social behavior. With appropriate adaptation, role playing can be used with students of all ages.

JURISPRUDENTIAL INQUIRY (CHAPTER 4)

As students mature, the study of social issues at community, state, national, and international levels can be made available to them. The jurisprudential model is designed for this purpose. Created especially for secondary students in the social studies, the model brings the case-study method, reminiscent of legal education, to the process of schooling (Oliver and Shaver (1966, 1971). Students study cases involving social problems in areas where public policy needs to be made (on issues of justice and equality, poverty and power, for example). They are led to identify the public policy issues and the options that are available for dealing with them and the values underlying those options. Although developed for the social studies, this model can be used in any area where there are public policy issues, and most curriculum areas abound with them (ethics in science, business, sports, etc.).

In recent years there has been a great deal of development work on cooperative learning, and great progress has been made in developing strategies that help students work effectively together. The contributions of three teams—led respectively by Roger and David Johnson, Robert Slavin, and Shlomo Sharan—have been particularly notable, but the entire cooperative learning community has been active in exchanging information and techniques and in conducting and analyzing research (see, for example, Sharan, 1990). Teaching students to cooperate has paid off nicely for self-esteem, social-skills development, and academic learning, as we will see below.

THE INFORMATION-PROCESSING FAMILY

Information-processing models emphasize ways of enhancing the human being's innate drive to make sense of the world by acquiring and organizing data, sensing problems and generating solutions to them, and developing concepts and language for conveying them. Some models provide the learner with information and concepts; some emphasize concept formation and hypothesis testing; and still others generate creative thinking. A few are designed to enhance general intellectual ability. Many information-processing models are useful for studying the self and society, and thus for achieving the personal and social goals of education.

The seven information-processing models described in Part II are outlined below.

INDUCTIVE THINKING (CHAPTER 6)

The ability to analyze information and create concepts is generally regarded as the fundamental thinking skill. The model presented here is an adaptation from the work of Hilda Taba (1966) and many others (Schwab, 1965; Tennyson and Cocchiarella, 1986) who have studied how to teach students to find and organize information and to create and test hypotheses describing relationships among sets of data. The model has been used in a wide variety of curriculum areas and with students of all ages—it is not confined to the sciences. Phonetic and structural analysis depend on concept learning, as do rules of grammar. The structure of literature is based on classification. The study of communities, nations, and history requires concept learning. Even if concept learning were not so critical in the development of thought, the organization of information is so fundamental to curriculum areas that inductive thinking would be a very important model for learning and teaching school subjects.

CONCEPT ATTAINMENT (CHAPTER 7)

This model, built around the studies of thinking conducted by Bruner, Goodnow, and Austin (1967), is a close relative of the inductive model. Designed both to teach concepts and to help students become more effective at learning concepts, it provides an efficient method for presenting organized information from a wide range of topics to students at every stage of development. The model is placed here because it provides a way of delivering and clarifying concepts and to train students to become more effective at developing concepts.

MNEMONICS (MEMORY ASSISTS) (CHAPTER 8)

Mnemonics are strategies for memorizing and assimilating information. Teachers can use mnemonics to guide their presentations of material (teaching in such a way that students can easily absorb the information), and they can teach devices that students can use to enhance their individual and cooperative study of information and concepts. This model has also been tested over many curriculum areas and with students of many ages and characteristics. As indicated previously, some of the applications of memorization strategies have had dramatic effects. We include variations developed by Pressley, Levin, and Delaney (1981), Levin and Levin (1990), and popular applications by Lorayne and Lucas (1974). Because memorization is sometimes confused with repetitious, rote learning of obscure or arcane terms and trivial information, people sometimes assume that mnemonics deal only with the lowest level of information. That is by no means true. Mnemonics can be used to help people master interesting concepts, and in addition, they are a great deal of fun.

ADVANCE ORGANIZERS (CHAPTER 9)

During the last 55 years this model, formulated by David Ausubel (1963), has become one of the most researched in the information-processing family. It is designed to provide students with a cognitive structure for comprehending material presented through lectures, readings, and other media. It has been employed with almost every conceivable content and with students of every age. It can be easily combined with other models— for example, when presentations are mixed with inductive activity.

INQUIRY TRAINING (CHAPTER 10)

Designed to teach students to engage in causal reasoning and to become more fluent and precise in asking questions, building concepts and hypotheses, and testing them, this model was first formulated by Richard Suchman (1962). Although originally used with the natural sciences, it has been applied in the social sciences and in training programs with personal and social content. It is included here because it has value for teaching students how to make inferences and build and test hypotheses.

SYNECTICS (CHAPTER 11)

Developed first for use with "creativity groups" in industrial settings, synectics was adapted by William Gordon (1961) for use in elementary and secondary education. Synectics is designed to help people "break set" in problem-solving and writing activities and to gain new perspectives on topics from a wide range of fields. In the classroom it is introduced to the students in a series of workshops until they can apply the procedures individually and in cooperative groups. Although it is designed as a direct stimulus to creative thought, synectics has the side effect of promoting collaborative work and study skills and a feeling of warmth among the students.

ADJUSTING TO THE STUDENT: THE DEVELOPING INTELLECT (CHAPTER 12)

Models based on studies of students' intellectual development (Kohlberg, 1976; Piaget, 1952; Sigel, 1969; and Sullivan, 1967) are used to help us adjust instruction to the stage of maturity of an individual student and to design ways of increasing the students' rate of development. These models can be used in all types of educational settings and with all types of content. Curiously, the majority of such developmental models are used with young children, particularly environmentally disadvantaged children, especially when the educational goal is to accelerate their growth (Spaulding, 1970). The applications for older students are, nevertheless, just as important (Purpel and Ryan, 1976).

The long-term goal of all information-processing models is to teach students how to think effectively. They rest on the thesis that students learning more complex intellectual strategies will increase their ability to master information and concepts. Taken together, they represent a full-blown "thinking skills" program: Helping students learn information, concepts, the ability to analyze information and develop hypotheses, and to synthesize new ideas and solutions to problems.

THE PERSONAL FAMILY

Ultimately human reality resides in our individual consciousnesses. We develop unique personalities and see the world from perspectives that are the products of our experiences and positions. Common understandings are a product of the negotiation of individuals who must live and work and create families together.

The personal models of learning begin from the perspective of the selfhood of the individual. They attempt to shape education so that we come to understand ourselves better, take responsibility for our education, and learn to reach beyond our current development to become stronger, more sensitive, and more creative in our search for high-quality lives.

The cluster of personal models pays great attention to the individual perspective and seeks to encourage productive independence, so that people become increasingly self-aware and responsible for their own destinies.

NONDIRECTIVE TEACHING (CHAPTER 13)

Psychologist and counselor Carl Rogers (1951, 1982) has for three decades been the acknowledged spokesperson for models in which the teacher plays the role of counselor. Developed from counseling theory, the model emphasizes a partnership between students and teacher. The teacher endeavors to help the students understand how to play major roles in directing their own educations—for example, by behaving in such a way as to clarify goals and participate in developing avenues for reaching those goals. The teacher provides information about how much progress is being made and helps the students solve problems. The nondirective teacher has to actively build the partnerships that are required and provide the help needed as the students try to work out their problems.

The model is used in several ways. At the most general level (and the least common), it is used as the basic model for the operation of entire educational programs (Neill, 1960). Second, it is used in combination with other models to ensure that contact is made with the students. In this role, it moderates the educational environment. Third, it is used when students are planning independent and cooperative study projects. Fourth, it is used periodically when counseling the students, finding out what they are thinking and feeling, and helping them understand what they are about.

The model has been used with all types of students and across all subjects and teaching roles. Although it is designed to promote self-understanding and independence, it has fared well as a contributor to a wide range of academic objectives (see Aspy and Roebuck, 1973; Chamberlin and Chamberlin, 1943).

ENHANCING SELF-CONCEPT (CHAPTER 14)

The seminal work of Abraham Maslow has been used to guide programs to build self-esteem and self-actualizing capability for forty years. We explore the principles that can guide our actions as we work with our students to ensure that their personal image functions as well as possible.

The personal, social, and academic goals of education are compatible with one another. The personal family of teaching models provides the essential part of the teaching repertoire that directly addresses the students' needs for self-esteem and self-understanding and for the support and respect of other students.

THE BEHAVIORAL SYSTEMS FAMILY

A common theoretical base—most commonly called social learning theory, but also known as behavior modification, behavior therapy, and cybernetics—guides the design of the models in this family. The stance taken is that human beings are self-correcting communication systems that modify behavior in response to information about how successfully tasks are navigated. For example, imagine a human being who is climbing (the task) an unfamiliar staircase in the dark. The first few steps are tentative as the foot reaches for the treads. If the stride is too high, feedback is received as the foot encounters air and has to descend to make contact with the surface. If a step is too low, feedback results as the foot hits the riser. Gradually behavior is adjusted in accordance with the feedback until progress up the stairs is relatively comfortable.

Capitalizing on knowledge about how people respond to tasks and feedback, psychologists (see especially Skinner, 1953) have learned how to organize task and feedback structures to make it easy for human beings' self-correcting capability to function. The result is, for example, programs for reducing phobias, learning to read and compute, developing social and athletic skills, replacing anxiety with relaxation, and learning the complexes of intellectual, social, and physical skills necessary to pilot an airplane or a space shuttle. Because these models concentrate on observable behavior and clearly defined tasks and methods for communicating progress to the student, this family of teaching models has a very large foundation of research.

Behavioral techniques are amenable to learners of all ages and to an impressive range of educational goals. Part IV describes four models that, together, represent a part of the spectrum and provide considerable power to teachers and program and media designers.

MASTERY LEARNING, DIRECT INSTRUCTION, AND SOCIAL LEARNING THEORY (CHAPTER 15)

The most common application of behavioral systems theory for academic goals takes the form of what is called mastery learning (Bloom, 1971) or direct instruction (Becker, et. al. 1981; Glasser, 1969). This model has several characteristics that are similar to Skinner's design for programed instruction. First, material to be learned is divided into units ranging from the simple to the complex. The material is presented to the students, generally working as individuals, through appropriate media (readings, tapes, activities). Piece by piece, the students work their way successively through the units of materials, after each of which they take a test designed to help them find out what they have learned. If they have not mastered any given unit, they can repeat it or an equivalent version until they have mastered the material.

Instructional systems based on this model have been used to provide instruction to students of all ages in areas ranging from the basic skills to highly complex material in the academic disciplines. With appropriate adaptation, they have also been used with gifted and talented students, students with emotional problems, and athletes and astronauts.

LEARNING SELF-CONTROL (CHAPTER 16)

B. F. Skinner is the parent theorist of modern behavioral management, and his concept of operant conditioning has given rise to an entire school of psychological thought. Skinner himself has applied the theory to many educational problems. Many other scholars, developers, and teachers have applied the concept to therapy (Rimm and Masters, 1974) and to education (Thoresen and Mahoney, 1974). The self-control management model relies on teaching students that their behavior is learned, that they should study the effects of their behavior, and that they should manage their environments so that their own behavior becomes more productive. Students are taught, in other words, that they are responsible for their personal and social environments and that they can learn more productive behavior by understanding themselves more fully. For example, a student who is afraid of snakes or is anxious in examinations learns how to change his or her own behavior so that snakes and examinations lose some or all of their menacing quality.

This model is used to teach students to create productive learning environments and to free themselves from aversions and engage positively with the opportunities that education and life in general offer. Disruptive students learn more productive ways of relating to others. Students who have developed fears about various pursuits (mathematics, athletics, reading) learn to replace those fears with affirmative feelings. Used with people of all ages, the model blends with others in teaching students to take charge of their behavior and approach academic and social tasks positively.

TRAINING AND SELF-TRAINING (CHAPTER 17)

Two approaches to training have been developed from the cybernetic group of behavior theorists. One is a theory-to-practice model and the other is simulation. The former mixes information about a skill with demonstrations, practice, feedback, and coaching until the skill is mastered. For example, if an arithmetic skill is the objective, it is explained and demonstrated, practice is given with corrective feedback, and the student is asked to apply it with coaching from peers or the instructor. This variation is commonly used for athletic training.

Simulations are constructed from descriptions of real-life situations. A less-than-real-life environment is created for the instructional situation. Sometimes the renditions are quite elaborate (for example, flight and space flight simulators or simulations of international relations). The student engages in activity to achieve the goal of the simulation (to get the aircraft off the ground, perhaps, or to redevelop an urban area) and has to deal with realistic factors until the goal is mastered.

THE CONDITIONS OF LEARNING (CHAPTER 18)

Over the years Robert Gagné has provided ways of organizing instruction that take into account both the condition of the learner and ways of sequencing instruction so that one activity builds on another.

These models, employed in all areas where skills need to be acquired, are especially useful for the mastery of teaching strategies. With appropriate modification, they can be used with learners of all ages.

The behavioral systems models are well studied and highly polished. They add significantly to the repertoires of teachers and the makers of instructional materials.

COMMON AND UNIQUE FEATURES

The four families of teaching models we have discussed are by no means antithetical or mutually exclusive, although each represents a distinctive approach to teaching. Whereas debates about educational method have seemed to imply that schools and teachers should choose a single approach, students need growth in all areas. To attend to the personal but not the social, or the informational but not the personal, simply does not make sense in the life of the growing student.

Thus, models from the four families can be combined to increase their effects. Cooperative learning can be used with inductive strategies and with simulations. Concept attainment can structure a unit so that it can then be explored with group investigation. A study of content with advance organizers followed by presentations can be succeeded with an analysis of the value issues using role playing or the jurisprudential inquiry model. This available storehouse of models is a flexible resource we can use to organize courses, learning centers, or media-based education. We can amplify the effects of each of them by using it in harmony with the others.

DESCRIBING THE MODELS

Each of the following chapters begin with a scenario of the model in use. Then we describe the goals of the model, its theoretical assumptions, and the principles and major concepts underlying it. Next we analyze each model in terms of four concepts: syntax, social system, principles of reaction, and support system. These descriptions are the operational heart of each model: They tell us what activities should occur and, when appropriate, in what sequence. The section that follows provides information about the use of the model in the classroom. Sometimes this information consists of an illustration for various subject areas, a guide for age-level applications or for curriculum design, or suggestions for combining the model with other models of teaching. Sometimes it is a discussion of particular points that seem to cause teachers difficulty when they implement the model. We conclude with a discussion of the instructional and nurturant effects that can be expected from the model distilled from research and experience.

Describing a Model

We invented four concepts to describe the operations of the model itself as a way of communicating the basic procedures involved in implementing any instructional model. There are its syntax, social system, principles of reaction, and support system.

SYNTAX

The syntax or phasing of the model describes the model in action. For example: How do we begin? What happens next? We describe syntax in terms of sequences of activities we call *phases*; each model has a distinct flow of phases.

For example, one model begins with a presentation to the learner of a concept called an *advance organizer,* which the leader presents to the student verbally, in either written or oral form. In the second phase, data are presented to the learner. He or she reads them, watches a film, or is exposed to the data in some other way. This phase is followed by another in which the learner is helped to relate the material to the organizing concept. In a different model, the first phase of a typical activity includes data collection by the student. The second phase involves organization of the data under concepts the student forms himself or herself, and the third, a comparison of the concepts developed with those developed by other people. As shown in Table 1–2, these two models have very different structures or sets of phases, even though the same type of concept might emerge from both models and they were in fact designed for somewhat different purposes. The first was designed to encourage mastery of material, and the second, to teach students inductive thinking processes.

Comparing the phasing of the two models in Table 1–2 reveals the practical differences between them. An inductive strategy has different activities and a different sequence than a deductive one.

THE SOCIAL SYSTEM

The social system describes student and teacher roles and relationships and the kind of norms that are encouraged. The leadership roles of the teacher vary greatly from model to model. In some models the teacher is a reflector or a facilitator of group activity, in others a counselor of individuals, and in others a taskmaster. In some models the teacher is the center of activity, the source of information, and the organizer and pacer of the situation (high structure). Some models distribute activity equally between teacher and student (moderate structure), whereas others place the student at the center, encouraging a great deal of social and intellectual independence (low structure).

One way to describe a model of teaching, then, is in terms of the degree of structure in the learning environment. As roles, relationships, norms,

TABLE 1–2 PHASING IN TWO MODELS

	Phase One	Phase Two	Phase Three
Model 1	Presentation of concept	Presentation of data	Relating data to concept
Model 2	Presentation of data	Development of categories by student	Identification and naming of concepts

and activities become less externally imposed and more within the students' control, the social system becomes less structured. As we see, some models are inherently more structured than others. However, the structure of all models can be varied greatly to adapt to the skill and personality of the students. We can tighten or loosen the structure considerably.

PRINCIPLES OF REACTION

Principles of reaction tell the teacher how to regard the learner and how to respond to what the learner does. In some models the teacher overtly tries to shape behavior by rewarding certain student activities and maintaining a neutral stance toward others. In other models, such as those designed to develop creativity, the teacher tries to maintain a nonevaluative, equal stance so that the learner becomes self-directing. Principles of reaction provide the teacher with rules of thumb by which to tune in to the student and select model-appropriate responses to what the student does.

SUPPORT SYSTEM

We use this concept to describe not the model itself so much as the supporting conditions necessary for its existence. What are the additional requirements of the model beyond the *usual* human skills, capacities, and technical facilities? For example, the social models may require a trained leader; the nondirective model may require an exceedingly patient, supportive personality. Suppose a model postulates that students should teach themselves and that the roles of teachers should be limited to consultation and facilitation. What support is necessary? Certainly a classroom filled only with textbooks would be limiting and prescriptive. Rather, support in the form of books, films, self-instructional systems, and travel arrangements is necessary, or the model will be empty.

A few examples of the use of the model are given—usually in classroom settings. The examples are not exhaustive but are selected to make real some of the possibilities.

INSTRUCTIONAL AND NURTURANT EFFECTS

The effects of an environment can be *direct*—designed to come from the content and skills on which the activities are based. Or, effects can be *implicit* in the learning environment. One fascinating question about models is the implicit learnings they engender. For instance, a model that emphasizes academic discipline can also (but need not) emphasize obedience to authority. Or one that encourages personal development can (but need not) beg questions about social responsibility. The examination of latent functions can be as exciting and important as the examination of direct functions.

Hence, the description of the effects of models can validly be categorized as the direct or *instructional* effects and the indirect or *nurturant* effects. The instructional effects are those directly achieved by leading the learner in certain directions. The nurturant effects come from experiencing the environment created by the model. For example, high competition toward a goal may directly spur achievement, but the effects of living in a competitive atmosphere may alienate people from each other.

In choosing a model for teaching, for curriculum building, or as a basis for materials, the teacher must balance instructional efficiency, or directness, with the predictable nurturant effects, as shown in Figure 1–1. For example, when beginning the year, a teacher might employ the inductive model with a group of passive students because it nurtures responsibility for collecting and organizing information and should help bring them out of the passive state.

FIGURE 1–1   Instructional and nurturant effects.

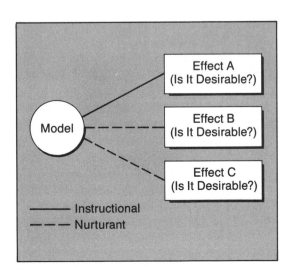

Using the Teaching Repertoire: A Firm Yet Delicate Hand

Although we gain personal satisfaction as teachers by expanding our repertoire of tools, and although teaching is made easier by teaching students strategies of learning, all of the creators of the various models of teaching have designed them to increase student learning and, thus, to help us become more effective professionals.

Thus, as we consider when and how to use various combinations of models and, therefore, which learning strategies will get priority for particular units and lessons and groups of students, we take into account the types and pace of learning that are likely to be promoted. We draw on the research to help us determine the sizes and kinds of effects each model has had in its history so that we can estimate its productivity if we use it properly.

As you study the four families of models of teaching, you will want to accumulate a mental picture of what each model is designed to accomplish and whether, under certain conditions, one is likely to have a larger effect than another.

Sometimes decision making is relatively easy because one model just stands out as though it is crafted for a given purpose. For example, the jurisprudential model is designed to teach students to analyze public issues in the high school. It is not appropriate for use with young children, but then neither is the study of complex national and international political and economic issues. However, a high school course that has the analysis of public issues as a major objective can give major attention to the model, which can actually be used to design a whole course or a part of one. The model serves other objectives (students learn information and concepts while studying issues, and the model promotes cooperative skills), but those are its nurturant rather than its primary objectives.

It is more complicated when there are several models that can achieve the same objective. For example, information can be acquired through inductive inquiry or from readings and lectures developed around advance organizers. Or, the two models can be blended. While a full discussion of the coordination of models with objectives when designing curricula, courses, and activities cannot be thoroughly addressed until the four families have been studied, we need to keep in mind as we study each model that it eventually becomes a part of a repertoire that is drawn on as we design programs of learning.

As we study the research base, we learn to estimate the magnitude of effects we can get when we teach the students one model in comparison with some other possible procedure.

The cognitive and social tasks that are provided to students by each model of teaching are designed to create energy that will result in particular kinds of learning. The *effects* of each model are the types of learning that are prompted by the model in comparison to a condition in which that model or some equivalent one is not being used. For example, we can ask, "Are certain kinds of learning enhanced when students study together *compared* to when they study alone?" Notice that this is a question of comparison. Clearly students can learn under either condition. The question when choosing models is which will probably pay off best in certain courses, units, or episodes. Also, we have to keep in mind that there are many kinds of learning and that some of them may be enhanced through cooperative study whereas others may not.

Placement of models in a program of study is important, as is blending them appropriately. Consider a program to teach students a new language. One of the early tasks when learning a new language is to develop an initial vocabulary. The link-word method has been dramatically successful in initial vocabulary acquisition, in some cases helping students acquire and retain words as much as twice as fast as normal (Pressley, Levin, and Delaney, 1982), making it a good choice for use early in the program. Students need to acquire skills in reading, writing, and conversation which are enhanced by an expanded vocabulary, then other models that generate practice and synthesis can be used.

To make matters more complicated, we have to acknowledge, thankfully, that students are not identical. What helps one person learn a given thing more efficiently may not help another as much. Fortunately, there are very few known cases where an educational treatment that helps a given type of students a great deal has serious damaging effects on another type, but differences in positive effects can be substantial and need to be taken into account when we design educational environments. Thus, we pay considerable attention to the "learning history" of students, how they have progressed academically, how they feel about themselves, their cognitive and personality development, and their social skills and attitudes.

Also, students will change as their repertoire of learning strategies increases. As they become a more powerful learning community, they will be able to accomplish more and more types of learning more effectively. All of the models of teaching in this book can enhance the ability of students to achieve various learning objectives. In a very real sense, increasing aptitude to learn is one of the fundamental purposes of these models.

Thus, in assessing the research, we are concerned with the general educative effects of each model and the specific, "model-relevant" effects for which it was designed. For example, the inductive models were designed to teach students the methods of science. That is their primary, direct mission. Research clearly indicates that those models achieve those effects very well, but that traditional, "chalk-and talk" methods of teaching science are very poor instruments for teaching the scientific method (Bredderman, 1983; El Nemr, 1979). Just as important, scientific inquiry increases the amount of information students learn, encourages their development of concepts, and improves their attitudes toward science.

What is of interest to us is that those models both achieve their primary goals and also have general educational benefits, including gains in student aptitude to learn.

We are satisfied when some models achieve small but consistent effects that accumulate over time. The advance organizer model, which is designed to increase the acquisition and retention of information from lectures and other kinds of presentations such as films and readings, achieves its results when the "organizers" are properly used (Joyce and Showers, 1988). Consider the thousands of hours of presentations and readings to which students are exposed as part of their education: Lectures, written assignments, and films and other media are so pervasive as educational tools that even relatively modest increments of knowledge from specific uses of organizers can add up to impressive increases in learning.

Perhaps the most interesting research has resulted when several models have been combined to attack multifaceted educational problems. Robert L. Spaulding, for example, developed a program for economically poor, socially disruptive, low-achieving children that used social learning theory techniques based on knowledge from developmental psychology and inductive teaching models. That program succeeded in improving students' social skills and cooperative learning behavior, induced students to take more responsibility for their education, substantially increased students' learning of basic skills and knowledge, and even improved students' performances on tests of intelligence (Spaulding, 1970).

Spaulding's work illustrates the importance of combining models in an educational program to pyramid their effects and achieve multiple objectives. Effective education requires combinations of personal, social, and academic learning that can best be achieved by using several appropriate models.

Also, although many models have been designed to promote specific kinds of learning, they do not necessarily inhibit other objectives. For example, because inductive teaching methods are designed to teach students how to form concepts and test hypotheses, it is sometimes assumed that they will inhibit the "coverage" of information. Tests of these models have found that they are also excellent ways of helping students learn information. In addition, the information so learned is likely to be retained longer than that learned by the recitation and drill-and-practice methods that are so common in schools (Worthen, 1968).

Methods designed for particular kinds of content can often be adapted successfully for others. Inductive methods, for example, were designed for academic content in the sciences and social sciences, but they can also be used for studying literature and social values.

However, it would be a mistake to assume that, because a particular model is effective, it should be used exclusively. Inductive models illustrate this point also. If they are used relentlessly for all purposes, they achieve less than optimal results. Creativity is valuable and the creative spirit should pervade our lives. But much learning requires noncreative activity. Memorization is important too, but to build all of education around memorization would be a serious mistake.

A few models of learning can have dramatic effects in specific applications. The link-word method, one of several models that assist memorization, has increased rates of learning two to three times in a series of experiments. Essentially, this means that students learned given amounts of material two to three times more rapidly when they used the link-word methods than they would have if they had used customary procedures for memorizing words (Pressley, Levin, and Delaney 1982). However, such dramatic effects should not lead us to attempt to achieve all objectives with the link-word method. It is one of the models of choice when rapid acquisition of information is the objective, but it is not the sole answer to the problems of education. However, it should not be sold short, either. It has been shown to be useful to teach hierarchies of concepts in science (Levin and Levin, 1990), addressing one of the important and most complex instructional goals in curriculum. It also nurtures academic self-confidence—more rapid and confident learning almost always helps students feel better about themselves.

Thus, as we study the tested alternative models of teaching, we find no easy route to a single model that is superior for all purposes, or even that should be the sole avenue to any given objective. However, we do find powerful options that we can link to the multiple educational goals that constitute a complete educational diet. The message is that the most effective teachers (and designers) need to master a range of models and prepare for a career-long process of adding new tools and polishing and expanding their old ones.

THE CONCEPT OF "EFFECT SIZE"

One of the most important dimensions of educational research is the attempt to learn how much difference it makes to personal, social, and academic growth if we use one teaching strategy rather than another for a particular purpose.

The most direct procedure is to conduct a controlled experiment, take measures of the students at the beginning, assign the students to the control and experimental groups on the basis of the pretests, expose the groups to the procedures, and measure again at the end of the treatment and possibly at intervals thereafter, comparing the distribution of scores of the two groups. A statistic known as "effect size" (Glass, 1982) is then computed. By repeatedly computing the sizes of differences in effects with each study that is conducted, we can arrive at a reasonable picture of the effectiveness of the various teaching and curricular procedures.

To understand the concept we have to understand a number of other concepts that enable us to describe and compare scores on various measures.

We describe distributions of scores in terms of the *central tendencies*, which refer to the clustering of scores around the middle of the distribution, and variance, or their dispersion. Concepts describing central tendency include the *average* or arithmetic mean, which is computed by summing the scores and dividing by the number of scores, and the median or middle score (half of the others are above and half below the median score), and the *mode*, which is the most frequent score (graphically, the highest point in the distribution). In Figure 1–2 the median, the average, and the mode are all in the same place, because the distribution is completely symmetrical.

Dispersion is described in terms of the *range* (the distance between the highest and lowest scores), the rank, which is frequently described in *percentile* (the 20th score from the top in a 100-person distribution is at the 80th percentile because 20 percent of the scores are above and 80 percent are below it), and the *standard deviation*, which describes how widely or narrowly scores are distributed. In Figure 1–3 the range is from 70 (the lowest score) to 150 (the highest score). The 50th percentile score is at the middle (in this case corresponding with the average, the mode, and the median). The standard deviations are marked off by the vertical lines labelled +1 SD, +2 SD, and so on. Note that the percentile rank of the score one standard deviation above the mean is 84 (84 percent of the scores are

FIGURE 1–2   **A sample normal distribution.**

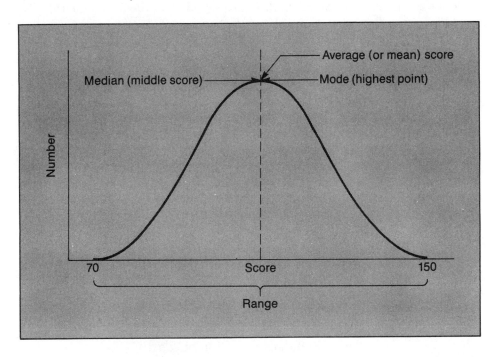

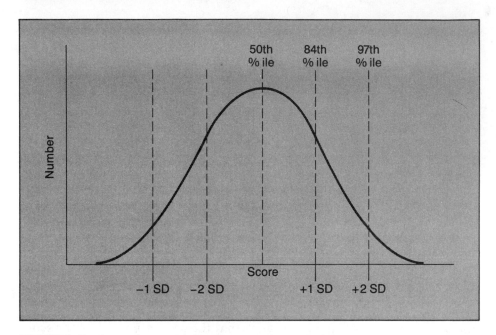

FIGURE 1–3   A sample normal distribution with standard deviations.

below that point); the rank two standard deviations above the mean is 97; and three standard deviations above the mean is 99.

When the mean, median, and mode coincide as in these distributions, and the distribution of scores is as symmetrical as the ones depicted in these figures, the distribution is referred to as *normal*. This concept is very useful in statistical operations, although many actual distributions are not symmetrical, as we will see.

However, to explain the concept of effect size, we will use symmetrical, "normal" distributions before illustrating how the concept works with differently shaped distributions.

Thus, in Figure 1–4 we will convert the results of the study of group investigation that appeared in Table 1–1 to graphical form. Figure 1–4 compares the posttest scores of the low SES students in the "whole class" and "group investigation" treatments. The average score of the "group investigation" treatment corresponds to about the 92nd percentile of the distribution of the "whole class" students. The effect size is computed by dividing the difference between the two means by the standard deviation of the "control" or "whole class" group. The effect size in this case is 1.6 standard deviations using the formula

$$ES = \frac{\text{Average of experimental group } - \text{ Average of control}}{\text{Standard deviation of control}}$$

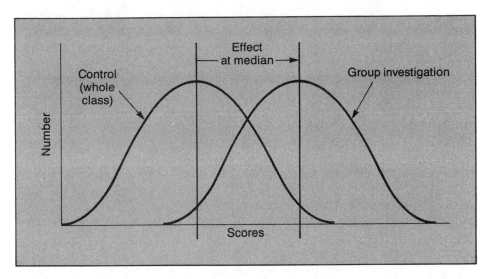

FIGURE 1—4   A sample depiction of effect size: The Sharan–Shachar study.

Throughout the book figures like these will provide an idea about the relative effects one can expect if one teaches students with each model of teaching compared with using the normative patterns of curriculum and instruction. We will create each figure from an analysis of the research base that is currently available and will usually build the figure to depict the average effects from large numbers of studies.

When using the research base to decide when to use a given model of teaching it is important to realize that size of effects is not the only consideration. We have to consider the nature of the objectives and the uses of the model. For example, in Spaulding's study described above, the effect size on ability measures was just 0.5, or about a half standard deviation (see Figure 1–5).

However, ability is a very powerful attribute, and a model or combination of models that can increase ability will have an effect on everything the student does for years to come, increasing learning through those years. The simplest cooperative learning procedures have relatively modest effect sizes, affecting feelings about self as a learner, social skills, and academic learning, *and they are easy to use and have wide applications.* Thus, their modest effect can be felt more regularly and broadly than some models that have more dramatic effect sizes with respect to a given objective.

Some models can help us virtually eliminate dispersion in a distribution. For example, a colleague of ours used mnemonic devices to teach his 4th grade students the names of the states and their capitals. *All* his students learned all of them and remembered them throughout the year. Thus the distribution of his class's scores on tests of their ability to supply all

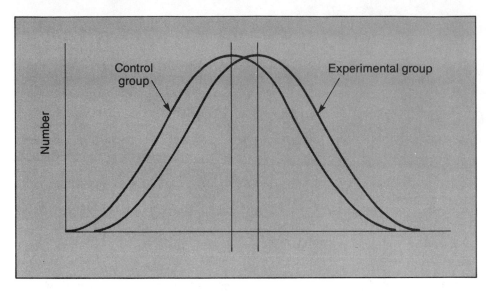

FIGURE 1–5   A sample effect size: Ability scores from Spaulding study.

the names on a blank map had no range at all. The average score was the top possible score. There were no percentile ranks because the students' scores were all tied at the top. For some objectives—basic knowledge about the Constitution of the United States, computation skills, a basic reading vocabulary—we want, in fact, to have a very high degree of success for all our students because anything less is terribly disadvantaging for them.

SCHOOL IMPROVEMENT

School faculties can also use models of teaching as an avenue to school improvement by learning sets of models that can increase the learning capacity of their students. In a recent school improvement project (Joyce, Murphy, Showers, and Murphy, 1989), part of the focus was on a middle school whose students had very poor histories of learning. Only 30 percent of the students achieved promotion at the end of the year before the project began. Scores on standard tests revealed that the average student in the school had gained only about 6 months' achievement for each year in school (10 months is average). The school district had made a number of initiatives to alleviate the situation, including special programs for "at risk" students, lowered class size, increased counseling services, etc., all with no effect. However, as the teachers learned to use several models of teaching designed to increase cooperative activity, teach concepts, teach students to work inductively and to memorize information, the learning rates of the students began to improve dramatically. By the end of the first year, 70 percent achieved the standards required for promotion, and 95 percent achieved promotion at the end of the second year. Judging from the standardized tests administered at the end of the second year, the average students in the school were achieving at a normal rate—that is, gaining 10 months of learning for 10 months of effort when compared to the U.S. population as a whole. We believe that the use of the models of teaching that the teachers added to their repertoire increased the learning rates of the students, reduced off-task behavior, and improved the tone of the social climate of the school. Time lost in disciplinary action decreased dramatically, to about one fifth of the amount lost before the program began. It is unlikely that any one model could have achieved effects of this magnitude, but the combination of models helped students learn a variety of learning strategies which together enabled them to educate themselves more strongly.

Satisfaction from personal and professional growth and exploration should be reason enough for the teacher to set as a goal not one or two basic models to use for all purposes, but a variety which he or she explores for the potential they hold for pupils and teacher alike.

The world we hope to see is one in which children (and older students) will experience many models of teaching and learn to profit from them. As teachers increase their repertoires, so will students increase theirs and become more powerful and multifaceted learners. That is the raison d'etre of *Models of Teaching*.

PART I

THE SOCIAL FAMILY

INTRODUCTION

The social models combine stances toward both learning and society. The position toward learning is that cooperative behavior is stimulating not only socially but also intellectually and, hence, that tasks requiring social interaction can be designed to enhance academic learning. The position toward society is that a central role of education is to prepare citizens to generate integrative democratic behavior both to enhance personal and social life and to ensure a productive democratic social order.

The combination of these two positions has resulted in the development of a large number of models that have great potential for our teaching repertoires. Also, many of the social theorists have not only built rationales for their models, but have raised serious questions about the adequacy of the current dominant patterns of schooling. In most schools the majority of learning tasks are structured by teachers for individuals. Most interaction between teachers and students is in the pattern of recitation—the teacher directs questions about what has been studied, calls on an individual who responds, and then affirms the response or corrects it (Sirotnik, 1983).

Many developers of the social models believe not only that they have developed important additions to the storehouse of models but also that teacher-dominated recitation is actually counter-productive for individuals and for society by depressing learning rates, creating an unnatural and even antisocial climate, and failing to provide opportunities for young people to maximize their potential and that of others by exercising their potential for cooperation.

The ideas of cooperating to learn academic content and of preparing students for citizenship and a satisfying social life are very old ones and can be found in the writings of Aristotle and Plato, the Roman educational philosophers such as Marcus Aurelius, and the Christian educators from the Medieval period, such as Thomas Aquinas, and later in the Renaissance, as John Amos Comenius. The rise of the modern commercial democratic states found expression in the writing of Jean Rousseau in France, John Locke in England, and Thomas Jefferson and Benjamin Franklin in America. During the period of the development of the common school in America, Horace Mann and Henry Barnard argued strongly for an active social component in education.

The concept was announced forcefully by John Dewey throughout the first half of the twentieth century and, with his ideas as the primary rationale, found expression in the development of a number of models for schooling and the activity of the Progressive Education Association, ushering in the current era of research and development of social models of education.

In Chapter 2 we begin with procedures for developing partnerships in learning and proceed to the contemporary versions of the classic group investigation model. In Chapters 3 and 4 we turn to two models designed to focus on values and social problem solving. Role playing can be used with students of all ages, and the jurisprudential inquiry model emphasizes social policies and issues for older students. Finally, we will examine procedures developed from conceptual systems theory for adapting the social models to the learning styles of students.

CHAPTER 2

PARTNERS IN LEARNING
From Dyads to Group Investigation

Mary Hilltepper opens the year in her 10th grade English class by presenting the students with 12 poems that she has selected from a set of 100 poems that represent the works of prominent contemporary poets. She organizes the students into pairs, asks them to read the poems and then classify them by structure, style, and themes. As they classify the poems (see Chapter 6 for the structure of the inductive model), they are to prepare to report their categories to the other students so that the partnerships can compare their classifications with those of the other students. Working together, the class accumulates a list of the ways they have discriminated structure, style, and theme. Then, Ms. Hilltepper presents the pairs of students with another dozen poems which they examine, both fitting them into their existing categories and expanding the categories as necessary. This process is repeated until all students are familiar with four dozen poems. She then gives them several other tasks. One is to decide how particular themes are handled by style and structure and vice versa (whether style and structure are correlated with each other and with themes). Another is to build hypotheses about whether some groups of poems were written by particular authors using distinctive combinations of style, structure, and theme.

Only then does she pass out the anthologies and books of critical analysis that are used as the textbooks of the course, asking students to test their hypotheses about authorship and also to find out if the scholars of poetry employ the same categories they have been developing in their partnerships.

Mary is organizing her class for partnership-based learning and the cognitive tasks of the classification version of the inductive model of teaching have been used to drive the inquiry. In addition to the substance of this opening unit of study she is preparing the students to embark cooperatively on their next unit of study, (writing poetry or studying the short story. Which would you use next? For our answer see Chapter Six.) Before long she will introduce them to the more complex activities of group investigation.

S C E N A R I O   II

As the children enter Kelly Farmer's fifth grade classroom in Savannah Elementary on the first day of the school year, they find the class roster on each desk. She smiles at them and says, "Let's start by learning all our names and one of the ways we will be working together this year. You'll notice I've arranged the desks in pairs, and the persons sitting at each pair will be partners in today's activities. I want each partnership to take our class list and classify the first names by how they sound. Then we will share the groupings or categories each partnership makes. This will help us learn one another's names. It is also to introduce you to one of the ways we will study spelling and several other subjects this year. I know from Mrs. Annis that you have worked inductively last year so you know how to classify, but let me know if you have any problems."

The students *do* know what to do, and within a few minutes they are ready to share their classifications. "We put Nancy and Sally together because they end in 'y'." "We put George and Jerry together because they sound the same at the beginning although they're spelled differently." "We put the three 'Kevin's' together." A few minutes later the pairs are murmuring together as they help one another learn to spell the list of names.

Kelly has started the year by organizing the students into a "cooperative set" by which we mean an organization for cooperative learning. She will teach them to work in dyads and triads which can combine into groups of five or six. (Task or work-groups larger than that generally have much lower productivity.) The partnerships will change for various activities. The students will learn to accept any members of the class as their partners and that they are to work with each other to try to ensure that everyone achieves the objectives of each activity.

She begins with pairs because that is the simplest social organization. In fact, much of the early training in cooperative activity will be conducted in groups of two and three because the interaction is simpler than it is in larger groups. She also uses fairly straightforward and familiar cognitive tasks for the initial training for the same reason—it is easier for students to learn to work together when they are not mastering complex activities at the same time. For example, she will have them change partners and have the new partnerships quiz each other on simple knowledge, such as of the states and their capitals, and tutor one another. She will change partnerships again and ask them to categorize sets of fractions by size. Each student will learn how to work with any and all of the other students in the class over a variety of tasks. Later she will teach the children to respond to the cognitive tasks of the more complex information-processing models of teaching as well as more complex cooperative sets. By the end of October she expects that they will be skillful enough that she can introduce them to group investigation.

Both teachers have embarked on the task of building learning communities. They will teach the students to work together impersonally but positively, to gather and analyze information, to build and test hypotheses, and to coach one another as they develop skills. The difference in maturity between the classes will affect the degree of sophistication of their inquiry, but the basic processes will be the same.

Each of these teachers possesses a variety of strategies for educating their students to work productively together. On their desks are *Circles of Learning* (Johnson and Johnson, 1986) and *Cooperative Learning Resources for Teachers* (Kagan, 1988). Each is studying their students, learning how effectively they cooperate, and deciding how to design the next activities to teach them to work more effectively together.

Purposes and Assumptions

The assumptions that underlie the development of cooperative learning communities are straightforward:

1. The synergy generated in cooperative settings generates more motivation than do individualistic, competitive environments. Integrative social groups are, in effect, more than the sum of their parts. The feelings of connectedness produce positive energy.
2. The members of cooperative groups learn from one another. Each learner has more helping hands than in a structure that generates isolation.
3. Interacting with one another produces cognitive as well as social complexity, creating more intellectual activity that increases learning when contrasted with solitary study.
4. Cooperation increases positive feelings toward one another, reducing alienation and loneliness, building relationships, and providing affirmative views of other people.
5. Cooperation increases self-esteem not only through increased learning but through the feeling of being respected and cared for by the others in the environment.
6. Students can respond to experience in tasks requiring cooperation by increasing their capacity to work productively together. In other words, the more children are given the opportunity to work together, the better they get at it with benefit to their general social skills.
7. Students, including primary-school children, can learn from training to increase their ability to work together.

Recently, interest has been renewed in research on the cooperative learning models. The more sophisticated research procedures that now exist have enabled better tests of their assumptions and more precise estimates of their effects on academic, personal, and social behavior. Work by three groups of researchers is of particular interest. One is led by David and Roger Johnson of the University of Minnesota (Johnson and Johnson, 1974; 1981; 1989). Another is led by Robert Slavin (1983; 1990) of Johns Hopkins University, and the third by Shlomo Sharan of Tel Aviv University (1980; 1990). Using somewhat different strategies, the teams of both the Johnsons and Slavin have conducted sets of investigations that closely examine the assumptions of the social family of teaching models. Specifically, they have studied whether cooperative tasks and reward structures affect learning outcomes positively. Also, they have asked whether group cohesion, cooperative behavior, and intergroup relations are improved through cooperative learning procedures. In some of their investigations they have examined the effects of cooperative task and reward structures on "traditional" learning tasks, in which students are presented with material to master.

Important for us is the question of whether cooperative groups do in fact generate the energy that results in improved learning. The evidence is largely affirmative. Classrooms organized so that students work in pairs and larger groups, tutor each other, and share rewards are characterized by greater mastery of material than the common individual-study cum recitation pattern. Also, the shared responsibility and interaction produce more positive feelings toward tasks and others, generate better intergroup relations, and result in better self-images for students with histories of poor achievement. In other words, the results generally affirm the assumptions that underlie the use of cooperative learning methods (see Sharan, 1990).

Sharan and his colleagues have studied group investigation, and have learned much both about how to make the dynamics of the model work and about its effects on cooperative behavior, intergroup relations, and lower- and higher-order achievement. We will discuss his research as we discuss group investigation later in this chapter.

An exciting use of the cooperative procedures is in combination with models from other families, in an effort to combine the effects of several models. For example, Baveja, Showers, and Joyce (1990) conducted a study in which concept and inductive procedures were carried out in cooperative groups. The effects fulfilled the promise of the marriage of the information-processing and social models, and the treatment generated gains twice those of a comparison group that received intensive individual and group tutoring over the same material. Similarly, Joyce, Murphy, Showers, and Murphy (1989) combined cooperative learning with several other models of teaching to obtain dramatic (30 percent to 95 percent) increases in promotion rates with at-risk students as well as correspondingly large decreases in disruptive activity, an obvious reciprocal of increases in cooperative and integrative behavior.

For those for whom cooperative learning is an innovation, an endearing feature is that it is so very easy to organize students into pairs and triads. And, it gets effects immediately. The combination of social support and the increase in cognitive complexity caused by the social interaction have mild but rapid effects on the learning of content and skills. In addition, partnerships in learning provide a pleasant laboratory in which to develop social skills and empathy for others. Off-task and disruptive behavior diminish substantially. Students feel good in cooperative settings, and positive feelings toward self and others are enhanced.

Another nice feature is that the students with poorer academic histories are benefited so quickly. Partnerships increase involvement, and the concentration on cooperation has the side-effect of reducing self-absorption and increasing responsibility for personal learning. Whereas the effect sizes on academic learning are modest but consistent, the effects on social learning and personal esteem can be considerable when comparisons are made with individualistic classroom organization.

Curiously, we have found that some parents and teachers believe that students who are the most successful in individualistic environments will not profit from cooperative environments. Sometimes this belief is expressed as "gifted students prefer to work alone." A mass of evidence contradicts that belief (Slavin, 1991; Joyce, 1991). Perhaps a misunderstanding about the relationship between individual and cooperative study contributes to the persistence of the belief. Developing partnerships does not imply that individual effort is not required. In the scenario in Ms. Hilltepper's classroom all the individuals read the poems. When classifying poems together, each individual contributed ideas and studied the ideas of others. Individuals are not submerged but are enhanced by partnerships with others. Successful students are not inherently less cooperative. In highly individualistic environments they are sometimes taught disdain for less-successful students, to their detriment as students and people, both in school and in the future.

INCREASING THE EFFICIENCY OF PARTNERSHIPS: TRAINING FOR COOPERATION

For reasons not entirely clear to us, the initial reaction of some people to the proposition that students be organized to study together is one of concern that they will not know how to work together productively. In fact, partnerships over simple tasks are not very demanding of social skills. Most students are quite capable of cooperating when they are clear about what has been asked of them. However, developing more efficient ways of working together is clearly important, and there are some guidelines for helping students become more practiced and efficient: group size, complexity, and practice.

Our initial illustrations are of simple dyadic partnerships over clear cognitive tasks. The reason is that the pair or dyad is the simplest form of social organization. One way to help students learn to work cooperatively is to provide practice in the simpler settings of twos and threes. Essentially, we regulate complexity through the tasks we give and the sizes of groups we form. If students are unaccustomed to cooperative work, it makes sense to use the smallest size groups with simple or familiar tasks to permit them to gain the experience that will enable them to work in groups of larger sizes. However, task groups larger than six persons are clumsy and require skilled leadership which students cannot provide to one another without experience or training. Actually, partnerships of two, three, or four are the most commonly employed.

Practice results in increased efficiency. If we begin learning with partners and simply provide practice for a few weeks, we will find that the students become increasingly productive.

TRAINING FOR EFFICIENCY

There are also methods for training the students for more efficient cooperation and "positive interdependence" (see Johnson and Johnson, 1986, and Kagan, 1990). Simple hand signals can be used to get the attention of busy groups. One of the common procedures is to teach the students that when the instructors raise their hands, anyone who notices is to give their attention to the instructor and raise their hand also. Other students notice and raise their hands, and soon the entire instructional group is attending. This type of procedure is nice because it works while avoiding shouting above the hubbub of the busy partnerships and teaches the students to participate in the management process.

Kagan has developed several procedures for teaching students to work together for goals and to ensure that all students participate equally in the group tasks. An example is what he calls "numbered heads." Suppose that the students are working in partnerships of three. Each member takes a number from one to three. Simple tasks are given ("How many metaphors can you find in this page of prose?"). All members are responsible for mastery of each task. After a suitable interval, the instructor calls out one number, as, "Number twos." The number two persons in all groups raise their hands. They are responsible for speaking for their groups. The instructor calls on one of them. All other persons are responsible for listening and checking the answer of the person who reports. For example, if the response is "seven," the other students are responsible for checking that response against their own. "How many agree? disagree?" The procedure is designed to ensure that some individuals do not become the "learners" and "spokespersons" for their groups while others are carried along for the ride.

Also, for tasks for which it is appropriate, pretests may be given. An example might be a list of words to learn to spell. After the pretest a number of tasks might be given to help the students study the words. Then, an interval might be provided for the students to tutor one another, followed by a posttest. Each group would then calculate their gain-scores (the number correct on the posttest minus the number correct on the pretest), giving all members a stake in everyone's learning. Also, cooperative learning aside, the procedure makes clear that it is learning as expressed in *gain* that is the purpose of the exercise. When posttests only are used, it is not clear whether anyone has actually *learned*—students can receive high marks for a score no higher than they would have achieved in a pretest.

Sets of training tasks can help students learn to be more effective partnerships, to increase their stake in one another, and to work assiduously for learning by all.

TRAINING FOR INTERDEPENDENCE

In addition to practice and training for more efficient cooperative behavior, procedures for helping students become truly interdependent are available. The least complex involve reflection on the group process and discussions about ways of working together most effectively. The more complex involve the provision of tasks that require interdependent behavior. For example, there are card games where success depends on "giving up" valuable cards to another player and communication games where success requires taking the position of another. Familiar games like "Charades" and "Pictionary" are popular because they increase cohesion and the ability to put oneself in the place of the other. There are also procedures for rotating tasks so that each person moves from subordinate to superordinate tasks and where members take turns as coordinators.

The Johnsons (1986) have demonstrated that sets of these tasks can increase interdependence, empathy, and role-taking ability and that students can become quite expert at analyzing group dynamics and learning to create group climates that foster mutuality and collective responsibility. The role-playing model of teaching, discussed in the next chapter, is designed to help students analyze their values and to work together to develop interactive frames of reference.

DIVISION OF LABOR: SPECIALIZATION

A variety of procedures have been developed to help students learn how to help one another by dividing labor. Essentially, tasks are presented in such a way that division of labor increases efficiency. The underlying rationale is that dividing labor increases group cohesion as the team works to learn information or skills while ensuring that all members have both responsibility for learning and an important role in the group. Imagine, for example, that a class is studying Africa and is organized into groups of four. Four countries are chosen for study. One member of each team might be designated a "country specialist." The country specialists from all teams would gather together and study their assigned nation and become the tutors for their original groups, responsible for summarizing information and presenting it to the other members. Or, similarly, when tasks requiring memorization are presented to the class, the group will divide responsibility for creating mnemonics for aspects of the data. Or, teams could take responsibility for parts of the information to be learned.

A procedure known as "jigsaw" (Aronson et al., 1983; Slavin, 1983) has been worked out to develop formal organizations for divisions of labor. It is highly structured and appropriate as an introduction to division-of-labor processes. Whereas individualistic classroom organization allows individuals to exercise their best-developed skills, division of labor procedures require students to rotate roles, developing their skills in all areas.

COOPERATIVE OR COMPETITIVE GOAL STRUCTURES

Some developers organize teams to compete against one another while others emphasize cooperative goals and minimize team competition. Johnson and Johnson (1989) have analyzed the research and argue that the evidence favors cooperative goal-structures while Slavin (1983) argues that competition between teams benefits learning. The fundamental question is whether students are oriented toward competing with one another or with a goal. Recently several of our colleagues have organized whole classes to work cooperatively toward a goal. For example, the science department of a high school began the year in chemistry by organizing the students to master the essential features of the Table of Elements. In teams, they built mnemonics that were used by all teams. Within two weeks, all students knew the table backward and forward, and that information served as the structural organizer (see Chapter 4) for the entire course. In a group of fifth-grade classes the exploration of social studies began with memorization of the states, large cities, river and mountain systems, and other basic information about the geography of the United States. Class scores were computed (for example, 50 states times 30 students is 1,500 items). The goal was for the class as a whole to achieve a perfect score. The classes reached scores over 1,450 within a week, leaving individuals with very few items to master to reach a perfect score for the class.

MOTIVATION: FROM EXTRINSIC TO INTRINSIC?

The issue about how much to emphasize cooperative or individualistic goal structures relates to conceptions of motivation. Sharan (1990) has argued that cooperative learning increases learning partly because it causes motivational orientation to move from the external to the internal. In other words, when students cooperate over learning tasks, they become more interested in learning for its own sake rather than for external rewards. Thus, students engage in learning for intrinsic satisfaction and become less dependent on praise from teachers or other authorities. The internal motivation is more powerful than the external, resulting in increased learning rates and retention of information and skills.

The frame of reference of the cooperative learning community is a direct challenge to the principles which many schools have used to guide their use of tests and rewards to students for achievement. Unquestionably, one of the fundamental purposes of general education is to increase internal motivation to learn and to encourage students to generate learning for the sheer satisfaction in growing. If cooperative learning procedures (among others) succeed partly because they contribute to this goal, then the testing and reward structures that prevail in most school environments may actually retard learning. As we turn to group investigation, a powerful model that radically changes the learning environment, consider how different are the tasks, cooperative structures, and principles of motivation we observe in many contemporary schools.

GROUP INVESTIGATION: BUILDING EDUCATION THROUGH THE DEMOCRATIC PROCESS

S C E N A R I O   III

Debbie Psychoyos' 11th-grade social studies class on world geography has been studying demographic data from the computer program PCGLOBE on the 177 nations of the world. Each of the nine groups of four have analyzed the data on about 20 nations and searched for correlations among the following variables: population, per capita GNP, birth rate, life expectancy, education, health care services, industrial base, agricultural production, transportation systems, foreign debt, balance of payments, women's rights, and natural resources.

The groups reported, and what had begun as a purely academic exercise suddenly aroused the students.

"People born in some countries have a life expectancy 20 years less than folks in other countries."

"We didn't find a relationship between levels of education and per capita wealth!"

"Some rich countries spend more on military facilities and personnel than some large poor ones spend on health care!"

"Women's rights don't correlate with type of government! Some democracies are less liberal than some dictatorships!"

"Some little countries are relatively wealthy because of commerce and industry. Some others just have one mineral that is valuable."

"The United States owes other countries an awful lot of money."

The time is ripe for group investigation. Ms. Psychoyos carefully leads the students to record their reactions to the data. They make a decision to bring together the data on all the countries and find out if the conclusions the groups are coming to will hold over the entire data set. They also decide that they need to find a way of getting in-depth information about selected countries to flesh out their statistical data. But which countries? Will they try to test hypotheses?

One student wonders aloud about world organizations and how they relate to the social situation of the world. They have heard of the United Nations and UNESCO but are vague about how they function. One has heard about the "Committee of Seven," but the others have not. Several have heard of NATO and SEATO but are not sure how they operate. Several wonder about the European Economic Community. Quite a number wonder about the unification of Germany and what it will mean. Several wonder about India and China and how they fit into the picture.

Clearly, deciding priorities for the inquiry will not be easy. However, the conditions for group investigation are present. The students are puzzled. They react differently to the various questions. They need information and information sources are available. Ms. Psychoyos smiles at her brood of young furrowed brows. "Let's get organized. There is information we all need, and let's start with that. Then let's prioritize our questions and divide the labor to get information that will help us."

John Dewey's ideas have given rise to the broad and powerful model of teaching known as group investigation. In it, students are organized into democratic problem-solving groups who attack academic problems and are taught democratic procedures and scientific methods of inquiry as they proceed. The movement to practice democracy in the classroom constituted the first major reform effort in American education and generated a great deal of critical reaction. As schools experimented with democratic-process education, they were subjected to serious criticism during the 1930s and 1940s, and the first items of research produced by the reformers were actually developed in defense—in response to questions raised by concerned citizens about whether such a degree of reliance on social purposes would retard the students' academic development. The studies generally indicated that social and academic goals are not at all incompatible. The students from those schools were not disadvantaged; in many respects, in fact, they outperformed students from competitive environments where social education was not emphasized (Chamberlin and Chamberlin, 1943). The reaction continued, however, a seeming anomaly in a democracy whose political and commercial institutions depend so much on integrative organizational behavior.

Educational models derived from a conception of society usually envision what human beings would be like in a very good, even utopian, society. Their educational methods aim to develop ideal citizens who could live in and enhance that society, who could fulfill themselves in and through it, and who would even be able to help create and revise it. We have had such models from the time of the Greeks. Plato's *Republic* is a blueprint for an ideal society and the educational program to support it (Cornford, 1945). Aristotle also dealt with the ideal education and society (Smith and Ross, 1912). Since their time, many other utopians have produced educational models, including Augustine (*The City of God*, 1931), Sir Thomas More (*Utopia*, 1965), Comenius (*The Great Didactic*, 1907), and John Locke (1927).

It was natural that attempts would be made to use teaching methods to improve society. In the United States, extensive efforts have been made to develop classroom instruction as a model of democratic process; in fact, variations on democratic process are probably more common than any other general teaching method as far as the educational literature is concerned. In terms of instructional models, *democratic process* has referred to organizing classroom groups to do any or all of the following tasks:

1. Develop a social system based on and created by democratic procedures.
2. Conduct scientific inquiry into the nature of social life and processes. In this case the term *democratic procedures* is synonymous with the scientific method and inquiry.
3. Engage in solving a social or interpersonal problem.
4. Provide an experience-based learning situation.

The implementation of democratic methods of teaching has been exceedingly difficult. They require the teacher to have a high level of interpersonal *and* instructional skills. Also, democratic process is cumbersome and frequently slow; parents, teachers, and school officials often fear that it will not be efficient as a teaching method. In addition, a rich array of instructional resources is necessary, and these have not always been available. Probably the most important hindrance is that the school simply has not been organized to teach the social and intellectual processes of democracy. Instead, it has been directed toward and organized for basic instruction in academic subjects; and school officials and patrons have, for the most part, been unwilling to change that direction or organization. Given the positive effects on student learning in all domains, it is a serious mistake not to make group investigation a staple in the repertoire of all schools.

THE PHILOSOPHICAL UNDERPINNINGS

The dominating figure in the effort to develop models for democratic process has been John Dewey, who wrote *How We Think* in 1910. Nearly all of the theoreticians dealing with reflective thinking since that time have acknowledged their debt to him. However, those who have emphasized democratic process have by no means been homogeneous, nor have they followed Dewey in the same ways or even directly. For example, in the 1920s Charles Hubbard Judd emphasized academic scholarship (Judd, 1934). William Heard Kilpatrick, for many years a major spokesperson for the Progressive movement, emphasized social problem solving (Kilpatrick, 1919). George Counts stressed not only problem solving but also reconstruction of society (Counts, 1932). Boyd Bode emphasized the general intellectual processes of problem solving (Bode, 1927).

A well-known statement of this group's concern with the democratic process and societal reconstruction was made in 1961 by Gordon H. Hullfish and Philip G. Smith in *Reflective Thinking: The Method of Education*. These authors stress the role of education in improving the capacity of individuals to reflect on the ways they handle information and on their concepts, their beliefs, their values. A society of reflective thinkers would be capable of improving itself and preserving the uniqueness of individuals. This philosophy contains many ideas or propositions common to democratic-process philosophies. It carefully delineates the ties among the personal world of the individual, his or her intellect, social processes, and the functioning of a democratic society.

Hullfish and Smith see intellectual development and skill in social process as inextricably related. For example, the development of skill in social process requires skill in synthesizing and analyzing the viewpoints of those engaged in social interaction.

Next, they believe that knowledge is constructed and continuously reconstructed by individuals and groups. They stress that knowledge is not conveyed to us merely through our sensory interactions with our environment, but that we must operate on experience to produce knowledge. As a result, knowledge has a personal quality and is unique for each individual. For example, a few hours before writing this, one of the authors stood on a rocky point looking at the Pacific Ocean against the brown of the California coast. He felt a quiet excitement and an appreciation of the sea and the rocks and the great peace of the scene about him. Yet the concept *sea*, the concept *rock*, the concept *wave*, and the excitement, peace, and appreciation he felt were not inherent in the experience themselves. These were constructed by the author in relation to that experience and to others he has had. He created some concepts and borrowed some from others. He generated some feelings and some beliefs and had been given some by imitating other people (the vast majority were borrowed in this way).

Thus, individuals' ways of reflecting on reality are what make their world comprehensible to them and give them personal and social meaning. Therefore, the quality of an individual's ability to reflect on experience becomes a critical factor in determining the quality of the world that individual will construct about himself or herself. Someone who is insensitive to much of his or her experience and does not reflect on it will have a far less richly constructed world than someone who takes in a good deal of experience and reflects fully on it. It becomes critical for education to sensitize the individual to many aspects of the physical and social environment and to increase the individual's capacity to reflect on the environment.

The individual quality of knowledge creates some difficulties, especially when it comes to constructing a society. Nevertheless, Hullfish and

Smith maintain that individual differences are the strength of a democracy, and negotiating among them is a major democratic activity. The more an individual learns to take responsibility for reflecting on experience and developing a valid view of the world and a valid set of beliefs, the more it is likely that the resulting network of information, concepts, and values will be unique to the individual. In other words, the more fully reflective an individual is, the more he or she will develop a personal processing system. A democratic society requires that we work together to understand each other's worlds and develop a shared perspective that will enable us to learn from each other and govern ourselves while preserving a pluralistic reality.

The perception of alternative frames of reference and alternative courses of action is essential to social negotiations. But one must have very great personal development to understand other people's viewpoints. This sharing of perceptions is necessary, however, if a mutual reality is to be constructed (see Berger and Luckman, 1966).

The essence of a functioning democracy is the negotiation of problem definitions and problem situations. This ability to negotiate with others also helps each person negotiate his or her own world. Maintaining a sense of meaning and purpose depends on developing a valid and flexible way of dealing with reality. Failure to make life comprehensible or to negotiate reality with others will result in a feeling of chaos. The ability to continually reconstruct one's value stances and the ability to create value systems that are compatible are both essential to mature development.

Most models of teaching assume that one does something in particular to get a specific outcome from the learner. *On the contrary, models that emphasize democratic process assume that the outcome of any educational experience is not completely predictable.* The democratic-model makers reason that if they are successful in persuading students to inquire into the nature of their experiences, and to develop their own ways of viewing the world, it will be impossible to predict just how they will face any given situation or solve any particular problem. Hence, if the students are taught an academic discipline, it is not so that they will know *exactly* the discipline known by others, but so that this exposure will help each of them create a frame of reference and a unique way of ordering reality.

ORIENTATION TO THE MODEL

GOALS AND ASSUMPTIONS

In *Democracy and Education*, John Dewey (1916) recommends that the entire school be organized as a miniature democracy. Students participate in the development of the social system and, through experience, gradually learn how to apply the scientific method to improve human society. This, Dewey feels, is the best preparation for citizenship in a democracy. John U. Michaelis (1980) has extracted from Dewey's work a formulation specifically for teaching the social studies at the elementary level. Central to his method of teaching is the creation of a democratic group that defines and attacks problems of social significance.

Herbert Thelen is one of the founders of the National Training Laboratory. In many respects Thelen's group investigation model resembles the methods Dewey and Michaelis recommend. Group investigation attempts to combine in one teaching strategy the form and dynamics of the democratic process with the process of academic inquiry. Thelen is reaching for an experience-based learning situation, easily transferable to later life situations and characterized by a vigorous level of inquiry.

Thelen begins with a conception of a social being, "A man [woman] who builds with other men [women] the rules and agreements that constitute social reality" (Thelen, 1960, p. 80). Any view of how people should develop has to refer to the inescapable fact that life is *social*—and a social being cannot act without reference to his or her companions on earth; otherwise in the quest for self-maintenance and autonomy each person may well conflict with other people making similar efforts. In establishing social agreements, each individual helps to determine both prohibitions and freedom for action. Rules of conduct operate in all fields—religious, political, economic, and scientific—and constitute the culture of a society. For Thelen, this negotiation and renegotiation of the social order are the essence of social process:

> Thus in groups and societies a cyclical process exists: individuals, interdependently seeking to meet their needs, must establish a social order (and in the process they develop groups and societies). The social order determines in varying degrees what ideas, values and actions are possible, valid, and "appropriate"! Working within these "rules" and stimulated by the need for rules the culture develops. The individual studies his reactions to the rules and reinterprets them to discover their meaning for the way of life he seeks. Through this quest, he changes his own way of life, and this in turn influences the way of life of others. But as the way of life changes, the rules must be revised, and new controls and agreements have to be hammered out and incorporated into the social order. (Thelen, 1960, p. 80)

The classroom is analogous to the larger society; it has a social order and a classroom culture, and its students care about the way of life that develops there—that is, the standards and expectations that become established. Teachers should seek to harness the energy naturally generated by the concern for creating the social order. The model of teaching replicates the negotiation pattern needed by society. Through negotiation the students study academic knowledge and they engage in social problem solving. According to Thelen, one should not attempt to teach knowledge from any academic area without teaching the social process by which it was negotiated.

Thelen rejects the normal classroom order that develops around the basic values of comfort and politeness or of keeping the teacher happy.

Rather, the classroom group should take seriously the process of developing a social order:

> The teacher's task is to participate in the activities of developing the social order in the classroom for the purpose of orienting it to inquiry, and the "house rules" to be developed are the methods and attitudes of the knowledge discipline to be taught. The teacher influences the emerging social order toward inquiring when he "brings out" and capitalizes on differences in the way students act and interprets the role of investigator—which is also the role of member in the classroom." (Thelen, 1960, p. 8)

Life in classrooms takes the form of a series of "inquiries." Each inquiry starts with a stimulus situation to which students

> can react and discover basic conflicts among their attitudes, ideas, and modes of perception. On the basis of this information, they identify the problem to be investigated, analyze the roles required to solve it, organize themselves to take these roles, act, report, and evaluate these results. These steps are illuminated by reading, by personal investigation, and by consultation with experts. The group is concerned with its own effectiveness, and with its discussion of its own process as related to the goals of investigation. (Thelen, 1960, p. 82)

In their concentration on the overt activities of democratic process, many followers and interpreters of Dewey overlook the underlying spirit that brings the democratic process to life. The activities, if followed by rote, provide only lifeless applications quite unlike the democratic process and scientific method Dewey and Thelen have in mind. The class should become a miniature democracy that attacks problems and, through problem solving, acquires knowledge and becomes more effective as a social group. Many attempts to use democratic process did little to change educational practice because the implementation was superficial, following the form but not the substance of democracy.

BASIC CONCEPTS

The three concepts of (1) inquiry, and (2) knowledge, are central to Thelen's strategy.

Inquiry Inquiry is stimulated by confrontation with a problem, and knowledge results from the inquiry. The social process enhances inquiry and is itself studied and improved. The heart of group investigation lies in its formulation of inquiry. According to Thelen (1960), the concern of inquiry is "to initiate and supervise the processes of giving attention to something; of interacting with and being stimulated by other people, whether in person or through their writing; and of reflection and reorganization of concepts and attitudes as shown in arriving at conclusions, identifying new investigations to be undertaken, taking action and turning out a better product" (p. 85).

The first element of inquiry is an event the individual can react to and puzzle over—a problem to be solved. In the classroom the teacher can select content and cast it in terms of problem situations—for example, "How did our community come to be the way it is?" Simply providing a problem, however, will not generate the puzzlement that is a major energy source for inquiry. The students must add an awareness of self and a desire for personal meaning. In addition, they must assume the dual roles of participant and observer, simultaneously inquiring into the problem and observing themselves as inquirers. Because inquiry is basically a social process, students are aided in the self-observer role by interacting with, and by observing the reactions of, other puzzled people. The conflicting viewpoints that emerge also energize the students' interest in the problem.

Although the teacher can provide a problem situation, it is up to the students as inquirers to identify and formulate the problem and pursue its solution. Inquiry calls for first-hand activity in a real situation and ongoing experience that continually generates new data. The students must thus be conscious of method so that they may collect data, associate and classify ideas recalling past experience, formulate and test hypotheses, study consequences, and modify plans. Finally, they must develop the capacity for reflection, the ability to synthesize overt participative behavior with symbolic verbal behavior. The students are asked to give conscious attention to the experience—to formulate explicitly the conclusions of the study and to integrate them with existing ideas. In this way thoughts are reorganized into new and more powerful patterns.

Let us examine a few examples that Thelen gives us to illustrate the flavor of inquiry and to point out the difference between inquiry and activity. The first example is drawn from a second-grade social studies class dealing with the question, "How do different people live?" The teacher proposed that the students select some group, find out how they live, and put this information in a play they would write themselves. After some discussion the students selected prairie dogs as a focus for their study. Here is an account of their inquiry:

> They started their study by naming the characters for the play they would write, and of course the characters turned out to be baby, chicken, mother, father, farmer's boy, snake, etc. They made lists of questions to be answered: What do prairie dogs eat? Where do they live? What do they do with their time? How big are their families? Who are their enemies? etc. Individuals sought answers to questions from science pamphlets, books, the science teacher, officials of the local zoo, and I have no doubt at least a few of them talked to their parents. They reported their findings in compositions during the writing lessons. The plot of the play gradually took shape and was endlessly modified with each new bit of information. The play centered around family life, and there was much discussion and spontaneous demonstration of how various members of the family would act. Most of these characterizations

actually represented a cross-section of the home lives of seven-year-old children, as perceived by the children. But each action was gravely discussed and
soberly considered, and justified in terms of what they knew about the ecology
of prairie dogs.

They built a stage with sliding curtains and four painted backdrops—more
reference work here to get the field and farm right. The play itself was given
six times, with six different casts, and each child played at least two different
parts. There was never any written script; only an agreement on the line of
action and the part of it to occur in each scene. And after each presentation
the youngsters sat around and discussed what they had been trying to communicate, how it might be improved. (Thelen, 1960, pp. 142–143)

Thelen contrasts this example with one drawn from a high school social studies class in which students were to put on a series of television
programs on the history of the community. As preparation, the students
looked up information and visited historical sites, taking pictures of important evidence:

Harry and Joe took pictures of an Indian mound, left there by original settlers.
They took it from the south because the light was better that way; and they
never discovered the northern slope where erosion had laid bare a burrow full
of Indian relics. Mary and Sue spent two afternoons on a graph of corn production in the region; the graph was in a geography book the teacher gave
them and the time was mostly spent in making a neat elaborately lettered
document for the camera. The narrators were chosen for their handsome appearance, and much of the staging of the show (which used reports mostly)
centered around deciding the most decorative way to seat the students. A lot
of old firearms and household implements were borrowed from a local museum and displayed, a sentence or two of comment for each. (Thelen, 1960, pp.
143–144)

In this latter instance, Thelen acknowledges that the students have
learned something about the region, but he points out that most of the
energy, the measure of success, was the effectiveness of the television as a
blend of entertainment and information giving. The roles in which the
students inquired "were those of a reporter with a keen eye for human
interest angles, rather than the sociologist's or historian's with a disciplined concern for the course of human events" (Thelen, 1960, p. 144).

These two examples illustrate the distinction between activity and inquiry. The actions of the second-grade class investigating prairie dogs contained the elements of inquiry: puzzlement, self-awareness, methodology,
and reflection. In looking at the two examples given, we may ask ourselves: Were there questions? Who formulated them? Who sought their
answers? How was the information obtained? Was the information applied? Were conclusions drawn, and who drew them? Activities are potential channels for inquiry, but inquiry must emanate from the motivations
and curiosity of students. Activities cease to be inquiry when the teacher
is the sole source of the problem identification and the formulation of

plans, or when the end-product of inquiry takes precedence over the inquiry process. That is what happened to the high school group—they attained production, but lost the process on the way.

Knowledge   The development of knowledge is the goal of inquiry, but Thelen uses knowledge in a special way: as the application of the universals and principles drawn from past experience to present experience. In the prairie dog example, the process of discovering knowledge was on center stage at all times; the principles of inquiry were what counted:

> Knowledge is unborn experience; it is the universals incorporated into the nervous system; it is a predisposition to approach the world with inquiry; it is meaningful past experience living within itself; it is the seed of potential internal reorganization through which one keeps in touch with the changing world. Knowledge lies in the basic alternative orientations and the proposition through which new orientations can be built. (Thelen, 1960, p. 51)

In other words, we "try on" various ways of looking at experience, continually reinterpreting experience into workable principles and concepts.

Why should inquiry take place in groups? In addition to the application of scientific method, inquiry has emotional aspects—emotions rising from involvement and growing self-awareness, the seeking of personal meaning and the affect that accompanies conscious reflective behavior. Thus, Thelen views a learning situation as "one which involves the emotions of the learner" (Thelen, 1954, p. 45). The group is both an arena for personal needs (individuals with their anxieties, doubts, and private desires), and also an instrument for solving social problems. As conflicting views impinge on individuals, they find themselves inescapably involved in the social and academic dimensions of inquiry. The individual "is driven by very profound and very pervasive psyche needs for the kind of classroom in which he can survive as a person and find a place for himself in the organization. Algebra may mean less than nothing initially, but self-esteem, freedom of sorts, feelings of growing adequacy and stimulation that provoke him into rewarding activity are important" (Thelen, 1960, p. 147). The social aspects of group investigation provide a route, therefore, to disciplined academic inquiry.

As a group confronts a puzzling situation, the reactions of individuals vary widely, and the assumptive worlds that give rise to these varied reactions are even more different than the reactions themselves. The need to reconcile this difference generates a basic challenge. The newly perceived alternatives extend the student's experience by serving both as a source of self-awareness and as a stimulant to his or her curiosity. Engaged in inquiry with a group, individuals become aware of different points of view that help them find out who they are by seeing themselves projected against the views of others. It also stimulates them: They want to know *why* differences exist and how they affect them.

OVERVIEW OF THE TEACHING STRATEGY

Thelen provides the example of a group of 11 adult women preparing to be elementary school teachers. This group has enough in common to facilitate close relationships but contains enough diversity to generate the differing reactions that energize inquiry. These women were investigating the skills, attitudes, and knowledge necessary to be effective teachers. The initial confrontation centered on seven elementary school classes which the teachers had observed. They were given no instructions as to what to observe but were simply told to report their findings to the group.

Soon, heated arguments developed over the interpretation of a kindergarten teacher's behavior. The discussion revealed a great many attitudes and ideas about teaching and learning as well as many submerged personal concerns about the course. At that point the discussion dissolved into arguments and ceased being informative. Hence, the instructors broke in with the suggestion that the group accept the difference of opinion and more systematically examine the factors that influence classroom activities.

Short filmstrip samples of classroom activities were then presented. The group listed all the factors they could think of to account for the differences among the samples. The purposes of the teacher seemed central.

The next task was to relate the observed behavior of children to the motivations of the teacher. Out of this task grew a checklist for studying the behavior and roles of the students. In other words, the original emotional conflict had led to the collection of new information, more disciplined analysis, and finally the development of an instrument for making judgments more objectively.

The group continued to make and compare its observations. From these discussions individuals were stimulated to pursue aspects of teaching that interested them; then they met on a private, personal basis with each person and developed further individual goals.

But what were to be the next activities of the group as a whole? On the basis of their discussion with their students, the instructors were able to identify broad questions about child development that interested the group. Accordingly, they made a proposal to study the skills, attitudes, and orientations of children at different ages. The group called in resource people, evaluated the children's progress gradually, and took over responsibility for guiding its own action. The original inquiry into different reactions to the behavior of a teacher had been "recycled" into an inquiry into child development.

THE MODEL OF TEACHING

SYNTAX

The model begins by confronting the students with a stimulating problem. The confrontation may be presented verbally, or it may be an actual experience; it may arise naturally, or it may be provided by a teacher. If the students react, the teacher draws their attention to the differences in their reactions—what stances they take, what they perceive, how they organize things, and what they feel. As the students become interested in their differences in reaction, the teacher draws them toward formulating and structuring the problem for themselves. Next, students analyze the required roles, organize themselves, act, and report their results. Finally, the group evaluates its solution in terms of its original purposes. The cycle repeats itself, either with another confrontation or with a new problem growing out of the investigation itself (see Table 2–1).

SOCIAL SYSTEM

The social system is democratic, governed by decisions developed from, or at least validated by, the experience of the group—within boundaries and in relation to puzzling phenomena identified by the teacher as objects to study. The activities of the group emerge with a minimal amount of external structure provided by the teacher. Students and teacher have equal status except for role differences. The atmosphere is one of reason and negotiation.

PRINCIPLES OF REACTION

The teacher's role in group investigation is one of counselor, consultant, and friendly critic. He or she must guide and reflect the group experience over three levels: the problem-solving or task level (What is the

TABLE **2–1**   **SYNTAX OF GROUP INVESTIGATION MODEL**

Phase One	Phase Two
Students encounter puzzling situation (planned or unplanned).	Students explore reactions to the situation.

Phase Three	Phase Four
Students formulate study task and organize for study (problem definition, role, assignments, etc.).	Independent and group study.

Phase Five	Phase Six
Students analyze progress and process.	Recycle activity.

nature of the problem? What are the factors involved?); the group management level (What information do we need now? How can we organize ourselves to get it?); and the level of individual meaning (How do you feel about these conclusions? What would you do differently as a result of knowing about . . . ?) (Thelen, 1954, pp. 52–53). This teaching role is a very difficult and sensitive one, because the essence of inquiry is student activity—problems cannot be imposed. At the same time the instructor must: (1) facilitate the group process, (2) intervene in the group to channel its energy into potentially educative activities, and (3) supervise these educative activities so that personal meaning comes from the experience (Thelen, 1960, p. 13). Intervention by the instructor should be minimal unless the group bogs down seriously. Chapters 16, 17, and 18 of *Leadership of Discussion Groups* by Gertrude K. Pollack (1975) provide an excellent advanced discussion of leadership in groups. Although the material was prepared for persons leading therapy groups, it is written at a very general level and provides much useful advice for persons wishing to build classrooms around group inquiry.

SUPPORT SYSTEM

The support system for group investigation should be extensive and responsive to the needs of the students. The school needs to be equipped with a first-class library that provides information and opinion through a wide variety of media; it should also be able to provide access to outside resources as well. Children should be encouraged to investigate and to contact resource people beyond the school walls. One reason cooperative inquiry of this sort has been relatively rare is that the support systems were not adequate to maintain the level of inquiry.

APPLICATION

Group investigation requires flexibility from the teacher and the classroom organization. Although we assume that the model fits comfortably with the environment of the "open" classroom, we believe it is equally compatible with more traditional classrooms. We have observed successful group-investigation teachers in a context in which other subjects, such as math and reading, are carried out in a more structured, teacher-directed fashion. If students have not had an opportunity to experience the kind of social interaction, decision making, and independent inquiry called for in this model, it may take some time before they function at a high level. On the other hand, students who have participated in classroom meetings and/or self-directed, inquiry-oriented learning will probably have an easier time. In any case, it is probably useful for the teacher to remember that the social aspects of the model may be as unfamiliar to students as the intellectual aspects and may be as demanding in terms of skill acquisition.

Although the examples of the model described here tend to be intellectually and organizationally elaborate, all investigations need not be so complex. With young children or students new to group investigation, fairly small-scale investigations are possible; the initial confrontation can provide a narrow range of topics, issues, information, and alternative activities. For example, providing an evening's entertainment for the school is more focused than resolving the energy crisis. Deciding who will care for the classroom pet and how is even narrower. Of course, the nature of the inquiry depends on the interests and ages of the students. Older students tend to be concerned with more complex issues. However, the skillful teacher can design inquiries appropriate to the students' abilities and to his or her own ability to manage the investigation.

As we indicated in the introduction to the social family of models, three recent lines of research by three teams (led by David and Roger Johnson, Robert Slavin, and Shlomo Sharan) have contributed a good deal of knowledge about how to engineer social models and what their effects are likely to be.

The Johnsons have concentrated on cooperative tasks, cooperative rewards, and peer tutoring. They have made extensive reviews of studies with students of all ages working in many substantive areas. As mentioned earlier, their reviews and studies support the contention that working together increases student energy and that rewarding teams of students for performance is effective, appearing to increase the energy of the teams. (Johnson, Maruyana, Johnson, Nelson, and Skon, 1981). In addition, their work with peer tutoring appears positive as well, and heterogeneous teams (composed of high and low achievers) appear to be the most productive (Johnson and Johnson, 1972).

Slavin's (1983) work generally confirms that of the Johnsons, and he has added some interesting variations. He has explored ways of differentiating tasks when groups are working on projects and has found that differentiating tasks increases the energy of the students. For example, when students are studying a topic in history, individuals can become "specialists" in certain areas of the topic, with the responsibility of mastering certain information and conveying it to the other students. In addition, he has looked at the effects of team composition on learning and attitudes toward self and others. Generally, the more heterogeneous groups learn more, form more positive attitudes toward the learning tasks, and become more positive toward one another (Slavin, 1983).

Sharan has studied group investigation per se. His team has reported that the more pervasive the cooperative climate, the more positive the students toward both the learning tasks and toward each other (Sharan and Hertz-Lazarowitz, 1980). In addition, he has hypothesized that the greater social complexity would increase achievement of more complex learning goals (concepts and theories) and both confirmed his hypothesis and found that it increased the learning of information and basic skills as well.

The purpose of cooperative inquiry is to combine complex social and academic tasks to generate academic and social learning. Properly implemented, it appears to achieve its goals.

INSTRUCTIONAL AND NURTURANT EFFECTS

This model is highly versatile and comprehensive; it blends the goals of academic inquiry, social integration, and social process learning. It can be used in all subject areas, with all age levels, when the teacher desires to emphasize the formulation and problem-solving aspects of knowledge rather than the intake of preorganized, predetermined information.

Provided that one accepts Thelen's view of knowledge and its reconstruction, the group investigation model (Figure 2-1) can be considered a very direct and probably efficient way of teaching academic knowledge as well as social process. It also appears likely to nurture interpersonal warmth and trust, respect for negotiated rules and policies, independence in learning, and respect for the dignity of others.

In deciding whether to use the model, considering the potential nurturant effects may be as important as analyzing the likely direct instructional effects. Another model might be as appropriate for teaching academic inquiry, but a teacher may prefer group investigation for what it might nurture.

FIGURE 2–1 Instructional and nurturant effects: group investigation model.

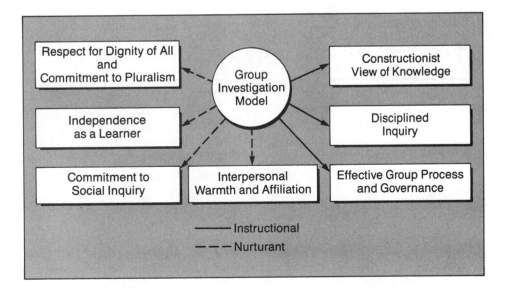

SUMMARY CHART ▶ GROUP INVESTIGATION MODEL

Syntax

Phase One: Encounter Puzzling Situation (planned or unplanned)

Phase Two: Explore Reactions to the Situation

Phase Three: Formulate Study Task and Organize for Study (problem definition, role, assignments, etc.)

Phase Four: Independent and Group Study

Phase Five: Analyze Progress and Process

Phase Six: Recycle Activity

Social System

The system is based on the democratic process and group decisions, with low external structure. Puzzlement must be genuine—it cannot be imposed. Authentic exchanges are essential. Atmosphere is one of reason and negotiation.

Principles of Reaction

Teacher plays a facilitative role directed at group process (helps learners formulate plan, act, manage group) and requirements of inquiry (consciousness of method). He or she functions as an academic counselor.

Support System

The environment must be able to respond to a variety of learner demands. Teacher and student must be able to assemble what they need when they need it.

3

ROLE PLAYING
Studying Social Behavior and Values

S C E N A R I O

We are in a seventh-grade classroom in East Los Angeles, California. The students have returned to the classroom from a recess period and are complaining excitedly to one another. Mr. Williams, the teacher, asks what the matter is and they all start in at once, discussing a series of difficulties that lasted throughout the recess period. Apparently, two of the students began to squabble about who was to take the sports equipment outside. Then all of the students argued about what game to play. Next, there was a dispute about choosing sides for the games. This included a dispute over whether the girls should be included with the boys or whether they should play separately. The class finally began to play volleyball, but very shortly there was a dispute over a line call, and the game was never completed.

At first, Mr. Williams displays his displeasure toward the class. He is angry, not simply over the incidents, but because these arguments have been going on since the beginning of the year. At last he says, "OK, we really have to face this problem. You must be as tired of it as I am, and you really are not acting maturely. So we are going to use a technique that we have been using to discuss family problems to approach our own problems right here in this classroom: We're going to use role playing. Now, what I want you to do is divide into groups and try to identify the types of problems that we've been having. Just take today, for example, and outline the problem situations that got us into this fix.

The students begin with the argument over taking the sports equipment outside, and then outline other arguments. Each is a typical situation that people face all the time and that they must learn to take a stand on. After the separate groups of students have listed their problems, Mr. Williams appoints one of the students to lead a discussion in which each group reports the kinds of problem situations that have come up; the groups agree on a half-dozen problems that have consistently bothered the class.

The students then group the problems according to type. One type concerns the division of labor. A second type deals with deciding principles for selecting teams. A third type focuses on resolving disputes over the particulars of games, such as whether balls have been hit out of bounds, whether players are out or safe, and so on. Mr. Williams then assigns one type of problem to each group and asks the groups to describe situations in which the problems come up. When they have done this, the class votes on which problem to start with. The first problem they select is disputes over rules; the actual problem situation they select is the volleyball game in which the dispute over a line call occurred.

Together, the class talks about how the problem situation develops. It begins when a ball is hit close to the boundary line. One team believes it is in, and the other believes it is out of bounds. The students then argue with one another, and the argument goes on so that the game cannot continue.

Several students are selected to enact the situation. Others gather around and are assigned to observe particular aspects of the role playing that follows. Some students are to look for the particulars of how the argument develops. Some are to study one role player and others another, to determine how they handle the situation.

The enactment is spirited. The students select as role players those who have been on opposite sides during the game, and they become as involved in the argument during the role playing as they were during the actual situation. Finally, they are standing in the middle of the room shouting at one another. At this point, Mr. Williams calls, "Time!" and asks the students to describe what has gone on.

Everyone is eager to talk. The discussion gradually focuses on how the attitude of the participants prevented resolving the problem. No one was listening to the other person. And no one was dealing with the problem of how to resolve honest disputes. Finally, Mr. Williams asks the students to suggest other ways that people could behave in this kind of conflict. Some students suggest giving in gracefully. But others object that if someone believes he or she is right, that is not an easy thing to do. Finally, the students identify an important question to focus on: "How can we develop a policy about who should make calls, and how should others feel about those calls?" They decide to reenact the scene by having all the particpants assume that the defensive team should make the calls only when they see clear evidence that a ball is out and the other team has not seen the evidence.

The enactment takes place. This time, the players attempt to follow the policy that the defensive team has the right to make the call, but the offensive team has the right to object to a call. Once again, the enactment results in a shouting match; however, after it is over, the students who have watched the enactment point out that the role players have not behaved as if there is a resolution to the situation. They recognize that if there are to be games, there has to be agreement about who can make calls and a certain amount of trust on both sides.

They decide to try a third enactment, this time with two new role players inserted as dispute referees. The introduction of referees completely changes the third enactment. The referees insist that the other players pay attention to them, which the players do not want to do. In discussing this enactment, the students point out that there has to be a system to ensure reasonable order and the resolution of disputes. The students also agree that as things stand, they probably are unable to resolve disputes without including a referee of some sort, but that no referees will be effective unless the students agree to accept the referees' decisions as final. They finally decide that in future games, two students will be referees. Those students will be chosen by lot prior to the game; their function will be to arbitrate and to make all calls relevant to the rules of the game, and their decisions will be final. The students agree that they will see how that system works.

The next day Mr. Williams opens up the second set of issues, and the students repeat this process. The exploration of other areas of dispute continues over the next few weeks. At first, many of the notions that are clarified are simply practical ones about how to solve specific problems. Gradually, however, Mr. Williams directs the discussion to a consideration of the basic values governing individual behavior. The students begin to see the problems of communal living; and they develop policies for governing their own behavior, as individuals and as a group. They also begin to develop skills in negotiating. The students who were locked in conflict gradually learn that if they behave in a slightly different way, others may also modify their behavior, and problems become easier to solve.

In role playing, students explore human-relations problems by enacting problem situations and then discussing the enactments. Together, students can explore feelings, attitudes, values, and problem-solving strategies. Several individuals have experimented with role playing, and their treatments of the strategy are remarkably similar. The version we explore here was formulated by Fannie and George Shaftel (1967). We have also incorporated ideas from the work of Mark Chesler and Robert Fox (1966).

Role playing as a model of teaching has roots in both the personal and social dimensions of education. It attempts to help individuals find personal meaning within their social worlds and to resolve personal dilemmas with the assistance of the social group. In the social dimension, it allows individuals to work together in analyzing social situations, especially interpersonal problems, and in developing decent and democratic ways of coping with these situations. We have placed role playing in the social family of models because the social group plays such an indispensable part in human development and because of the unique opportunity that role playing offers for resolving interpersonal and social dilemmas.

ORIENTATION TO THE MODEL

GOALS AND ASSUMPTIONS

On its simplest level, role playing is dealing with problems through action; a problem is delineated, acted out, and discussed. Some students are role players; others observers. A person puts himself or herself in the position of another person and then tries to interact with others who are also playing roles. As empathy, sympathy, anger, and affection are all generated during the interaction, role playing, if done well, becomes a part of life. This emotional content, as well as the words and the actions, becomes part of the later analysis. When the acting out is finished, even the observers are involved enough to want to know why each person reached his or her decision, what the sources of resistance were, and whether there were other ways this situation could have been approached.

The essence of role playing is the involvement of participants and observers in a real problem situation and the desire for resolution and understanding that this involvement engenders. The role-playing process provides a live sample of human behavior that serves as a vehicle for students to: (1) explore their feelings; (2) gain insight into their attitudes, values, and perceptions; (3) develop their problem-solving skills and attitudes; and (4) explore subject matter in varied ways.

These educational goals reflect several assumptions about the learning process in role playing. First, role playing implicitly advocates an experience-based learning situation in which the "here and now" becomes the content of instruction. The model assumes that it is possible to create authentic analogies to real-life problem situations and that through these recreations students can "sample" life. Thus, the enactment elicits genuine, typical emotional responses and behaviors from the students.

A related assumption is that role playing can draw out students' feelings, which they can recognize and perhaps release. This *catharsis,* or release of feeling, is an especially important goal when role playing is used in therapeutic settings in a variation known as *psychodrama.* In psychodrama, the enactment and its emotional and behavioral confrontations are the central activities; discussion and analysis are minimal. Educational uses of role playing, in contrast to therapeutic uses, are oriented to the generation and recognition of feelings. The Shaftels' version of role playing emphasizes the intellectual content as much as the emotional content; analysis and discussion of the enactment are as important as the role playing itself. We, as educators, are concerned that students recognize and understand their feelings and see how their feelings influence their behavior.

Another assumption, similar to an assumption of the synectics models, is that emotions and ideas can be brought to consciousness and enhanced by the group. Problem solving is not stifled by the activity of an overt, public situation, nor is an expert necessary to solve dilemmas or to teach everything. On the contrary, the collective reactions of the peer group can bring out new ideas and provide directions for growth and change. The model deemphasizes the traditional role of teacher and encourages listening and learning from one's peers.

A final assumption is that covert psychological processes involving one's own attitudes, values, and belief system can be brought to consciousness by combining spontaneous enactment with analysis. Furthermore, individuals can gain some measure of control over their belief systems if they recognize their values and attitudes and test them against the views of others. Such analysis can help them evaluate their attitudes and values and the consequences of their beliefs, so that they can revise them if necessary.

THE CONCEPT OF ROLE

Each individual has a unique manner of relating to people, situations, and objects. One person may feel that most people are dishonest and cannot be trusted; someone else may feel that everyone is interesting and may look forward to meeting new people. People also evaluate and behave in consistent ways towards themselves, seeing themselves as powerful and smart, or perhaps afraid and stupid. These feelings about people and situations and about themselves influence people's behavior and determine how they will respond in various situations. Some people respond with aggressive and hostile behavior, playing the part of a bully. Others withdraw and remain alone, playing the part of a shy or sulking person.

These parts people play are called *roles*. A role is "a patterned sequence of feelings, words, and actions. . . . It is a unique and accustomed manner of relating to others" (Chesler and Fox, 1966, pp. 5, 8). Unless people are looking for them, it is sometimes hard to perceive consistencies and patterns in behavior. But they are usually there. Terms such as *friendly, bully, snobby, know-it-all*, and *grouch* are convenient for describing characteristic responses or roles.

The roles individuals play are determined by several factors over many years. The kinds of people someone meets determine his or her general feelings about people. How those people act toward the individual and how the individuals perceive their feelings toward them influence their feelings about themselves. The rules of one's particular culture and institutions help to determine which roles a person assumes and how he or she plays them.

People may not be happy with the roles they have assumed. And they may misperceive the attitudes and feelings of others because they do not recognize *their* role and *why* they play it. Two people can share the same feelings but behave in very different ways. They can desire the same goals, but if one person's behavior is misperceived by others, he or she may not attain that goal.

For a clear understanding of oneself and of others, it is thus extremely important that a person be aware of roles and how they are played. To do this, each person must be able to put himself or herself in another's place, and to experience as much as possible that person's thoughts and feelings. If someone is able to empathize, he or she can accurately interpret social events and interactions. Role playing is a vehicle that forces people to take the roles of others.

The concept of role is one of the central theoretical underpinnings of the role-playing model. It is also a major goal. We must teach students to use this concept, to recognize different roles, and to think of their own and other's behavior in terms of roles. At the same time, there are many other aspects to this model, and many levels of analysis, which to some extent compete with one another. For example, the content of the problem, the solutions to the problem, the feelings of the role players, and the acting itself all serve to involve students in the role play. Therefore, to be a salient part of the role-playing experience, the concept of role must be interwoven, yet kept in the fore throughout all the role-playing activities. It also helps if, prior to using the model, students have been taught this concept directly.

THE MODEL OF TEACHING

SYNTAX

The benefits of role playing depend on the quality of the enactment and especially on the analysis that follows. They depend also on the students' perceptions of the role as similar to real-life situations. Children do not necessarily engage effectively in role playing or role analysis the first time they try it. Many have to learn to engage in role playing in a sincere way so that the content generated can be analyzed seriously. Chesler and Fox suggest pantomimic exercises as a way of freeing inexperienced students (Chesler and Fox, 1966, pp. 64–66). Role playing is not likely to be successful if the teacher simply tosses out a problem situation, persuades a few children to act it out, and then conducts a discussion about the enactment.

The Shaftels suggest that the role-playing activity consist of nine steps: (1) warm up the group; (2) select participants; (3) set the stage; (4) prepare observers; (5) enact; (6) discuss and evaluate; (7) reenact; (8) discuss and evaluate; and (9) share experiences and generalize. Each of these steps or phases has a specific purpose that contributes to the richness and focus of the learning activity. Together, they ensure that a line of thinking is pursued throughout the complex of activities, that students are prepared in their roles, that goals for the role play are identified, and that the discussion afterwards is not simply a collection of diffuse reactions, though these are important too. Table 3-1 summarizes the phases and ac-

TABLE 3–1   SYNTAX OF ROLE PLAYING

Phase One: Warm Up the Group	Phase Two: Select Participants
Identify or introduce problem. Make problem explicit. Interpret problem story, explore issues. Explain role playing.	Analyze roles. Select role players.

Phase Three: Set the Stage	Phase Four: Prepare the Observers
Set line of action. Restate roles. Get inside problem situation.	Decide what to look for. Assign observation tasks.

Phase Five: Enact	Phase Six: Discuss and Evaluate
Begin role play. Maintain role play. Break role play.	Review action of role play (events, positions, realism). Discuss major focus. Develop next enactment.

Phase Seven: Reenact	Phase Eight: Discuss and Evaluate
Play revised roles; suggest next steps or behavioral alternatives.	As in phase six.

Phase Nine: Share Experiences and Generalize
Relate problem situation to real experience and current problems. Explore general principles of behavior.

Based on Fannie Shaftel and George Shaftel, *Role-Playing for Social Values* (Englewood Cliffs, N.J.: Prentice-Hall, Inc., 1967).

tivities of the model, which are discussed and illustrated in the remainder of this section.

Phase one, warm up the group, involves introducing students to a problem so that they recognize it as an area with which everyone needs to learn to deal. The warm-up can begin, for example, by identifying a problem within the group.

> **Teacher:**   Do you remember the other day we had a discussion about Jane's lunch money? Because she had put her money in her pocket and had not given it to me when she came into the room, it was lost. We had quite a talk about finding money: whether to keep it or turn it in. Sometimes it's not easy to decide what to do. Do you ever have times when you just don't know what to do? (Shaftel and Shaftel, 1967, p. 67)

The teacher sensitizes the group to a problem and creates a climate of acceptance, so that students feel that all views, feelings, and behaviors can be explored without retribution.

The second part of the warm-up is to express the problem vividly through examples. These may come from student descriptions of imaginary or real situations that express the problem, or from situations selected by the teacher and illustrated by a film, television show, or problem story.

In *Role Playing for Social Values*, the Shaftels provide a large selection of problem stories to be read to the class. Each story stops when a dilemma has become apparent. The Shaftels feel that problem stories have several advantages. They focus on a particular problem and yet ensure that the children will be able to disassociate themselves from the problem enough to face it. Incidents that students have experienced in their lives or that the group has experienced as a whole, though visually and emotionally involving, can cause considerable stress and therefore be very difficult to analyze. Another advantage of problem stories is that they are dramatic and make role playing relatively easy to initiate. The burden of involving the children in the activity is lightened.

The last part of the warm-up is to ask questions that make the children think about and predict the outcome of the story: "How might the story end?" "What is Sam's problem and what can he do about it?" The teacher in the preceding illustration handled this step as follows:

> **Teacher:**   I would like to read you a story this afternoon about a boy who found himself in just such a spot. His parents wanted him to do one thing, but his gang insisted he do something else. Trying to please everybody, he got himself into difficulty. This will be one of those problem stories that stop, but are not finished.
> **Pupil:**   Like the one we did last week?

Teacher: Yes.
Pupil: Oh! But can't you give us one with an ending?
Teacher: When you get into a jam, does someone always come along and tell you how your problems will end?
Pupil: Oh no! Not very often.
Teacher: In life, we usually have to make our own endings—we have to solve our problems ourselves. That's why I'm reading these problem stories—so that we can *practice* endings, trying out many different ones to see which works the best for us. As I read this story, you might be thinking of what you would do if you were in Tommy Haines's place (Shaftel and Shaftel, 1967, p. 67).

The story is about a boy caught between his father's views and those of his club. He has committed himself financially to a club project his father does not approve of and would not support. Tommy does not have the money and resorts to somewhat devious means of getting it. The problem centers on Tommy's opportunity to clear the debt with his gang. He delivers a package for the druggist and is overpaid $5—enough to clear the debt. Tommy stands outside the customer's door, trying to decide whether to return or keep the money. After reading the story, the teacher focuses the discussion on what might happen next, thus preparing for different enactments of the situation:

Teacher: What do you think Tommy will do?
Pupil: I think he'll keep the money.
Teacher: Oh?
Pupil: Because he needs to pay the club.
Pupil: Oh no he won't. He'll get found out, and he knows it. (Shaftel and Shaftel, 1967, p. 69).

In phase two, select participants, the children and the teacher describe the various characters—what they are like, how they feel, and what they might do. The children are then asked to volunteer to role play; they may even ask to play a particular role. The Shaftels caution us against assigning a role to a child who has been suggested for it, because the person making the suggestion may be stereotyping the child or putting him or her in an awkward situation. A person must want to play a role. Although he or she takes into account the children's preferences, the teacher should exercise some control in the situation.

We can use several criteria for selecting a child for a role. Roles can be assigned to those children who appear to be so involved in the problem that they identify with a specific role, those who express an attitude that needs to be explored, or those who should learn to identify with the role or place themselves in another person's position. The Shaftels warn the teacher not to select children who would give "adult-oriented, socially acceptable" interpretations to the role, because such a quick and superficial resolution of the problem dampens discussion and exploration of the basic issues (Shaftel and Shaftel, 1967, p. 67).

In our illustration, the teacher asks a student to be Tommy and then asks the student what roles need to be filled. He answers that he'll need someone to be the customer and some student to be the gang. The teacher asks several children to fill these roles.

In phase three, set the stage, the role players outline the scene but do not prepare any specific dialogue. They simply sketch the setting and perhaps one person's line of action. The teacher may help set the stage by asking the students a few simple questions about where the enactment is taking place, what it is like, and so on. It is necessary only that a simple line of action be identified and a general setting clarified so that participants feel enough security in the roles to begin to act.

The setting is arranged so that one corner of the classroom becomes the school where the gang is waiting for Tommy to bring the money; in another corner, a chair is used to represent the door of the customer's house. The teacher asks the boy playing Tommy where in the action he wants to begin, and the boy decides to start with the scene where he is delivering the packages.

In phase four, prepare the observers, it is important that the observers become actively involved so that the entire group experiences the enactment and can later analyze the play. The Shaftels suggest that the teacher involve observers in the role play by assigning them tasks, such as evaluating the realism of the role playing, commenting on the effectiveness and the sequences of the role players' behavior, and defining the feelings and ways of thinking of the persons being portrayed. The observers should determine what the role players are trying to accomplish, what actions the role players took that were helpful or not helpful, and what alternative experiences might have been enacted. Or they can watch one particular role to define the feelings of that person. The observers should understand that there will be more than one enactment in most cases, and if they would have acted out a certain role in a different way, they may have a chance to do so.

In our illustration, the teacher prepares the observers as follows:

Teacher: Now you people, as you watch, consider whether you think Jerry's way of ending the story could really happen. How will people feel? You may want to think of what will happen next. Perhaps you'll have different ideas about it; and when Jerry's finished, and we've talked about it, we can try your ideas. (Shaftel and Shaftel, 1967, p. 69)

At phase five, enact, the players assume the roles and "live" the situation spontaneously, responding realistically to one another. The role playing is not expected to be a smooth dramatization, nor is it expected that each role player will always know how to respond. This uncertainty is part of life, as well as part of feeling the role. A person may have a general idea of what to say or do but not be able to enact it when the time comes. The action now depends on the children and emerges according to what happens in the situation. This is why the preparatory steps are so important.

The Shaftels suggest that enactments be short. The teacher should allow the enactment to run only until the proposed behavior is clear, a character has developed, a behavioral skill has been practiced, an impasse is reached, or the action has expressed its viewpoint or idea. If the follow-up discussion reveals a lack of student understanding about the events or roles, the teacher can then ask for a reenactment of the scene.

The purpose of the first enactment is simply to establish events and roles, which in later enactments can be probed, analyzed, and reworked. In our illustration, the boy playing Tommy chooses not to tell the customer that he has overpaid. During the initial enactment, the players of the major role can be changed to demonstrate variety of the role and to generate more data for discussion.

In phase six, discuss and evaluate, if the problem is an important one and the participants and the observers are intellectually and emotionally involved, then the discussion will probably begin spontaneously. At first, the discussion may focus on different intepretations of the portrayal and on disagreements over how the roles should have been carried out. More important, however, are the consequences of the action and the motivations of the actors. To prepare for the next step, a teacher should focus the discussion on these aspects.

To help the observer think along with the role players, the teacher can ask questions such as, "How do you suppose John felt when he said that?" The discussion will probably turn to alternatives, both within the roles and within the total pattern of action. When it does, the stage is set for further enactments in which role players change their interpretations, playing the same roles in a different way.

In our illustration, the discussion of the first enactment goes like this:

Teacher: Well, Jerry has given us one solution. What do you think of it?
Pupil: Uh-uh! It won't work!
Jerry: Why not?
Pupil: That man is going to remember how much money he had. He'll phone the druggist about it.
Jerry: So what? He can't prove anything on me. I'll just say he didn't overpay me.
Pupil: You'll lose your job.
Jerry: When they can't prove it?
Pupil: Yes, even if they can't prove it.

Teacher: Why do you think so, John?

Pupil: Because the druggist has to be on the side of his customer. He can fire Tommy and hire another boy. But he doesn't want his customers mad at him.

Pupil: He's going to feel pretty sick inside, if he keeps the money.

Teacher: What do you mean?

Pupil: Well it bothers you when you know you've done something wrong.

Teacher: Do you have any other way to solve this problem?

Pupil: Yes. Tommy should knock on the door and tell the customer about being overpaid. Maybe the man'll let Tommy keep the money.

Teacher: All right, let's try it your way, Dick. (Shaftel and Shaftel, 1967, p. 71)

In phase seven, reenact, the reenactment may take place many times. The students and the teacher can share new interpretations of roles and decide whether new individuals should play them. The activity alternates between discussion and acting. As much as possible, the new enactments should explore new possibilities for causes and effects. For example, one role may be changed so that everyone can observe how that change causes another role player to behave. Or at the critical point in the enactment, the participants may try to behave in a different way and see what the consequences are. In this way, the role playing becomes a dramatic conceptual activity.

In our illustration, a second enactment produces the solution in which Tommy alerts the man to his overpayment and gets to keep the money for being so honest.

In the discussion that follows the second enactment—phase eight, discuss and evaluate—students are willing to accept the solution, but the teacher pushes for a realistic solution by asking whether they think this ending could really happen. One student has had a similar experience but was overpaid only $1.25, which he was allowed to keep. The teacher asks the class whether they think it might be different with $5. She asks for another solution, and it is suggested that Tommy consult his mother. There follows some discussion of Tommy's father, concepts about family, and parental roles. The teacher suggests that this third solution be enacted. Here's what happens in the third enactment:

Tommy: Mom, I'm in an awful jam!

Mother: What's the trouble, Tommy?

Tommy: (tells his mother the whole story)

Mother: Why, Tommy, you should have told me sooner. Here, you pay the money (opens purse), and we'll talk this over with Dad when he comes home. (Shaftel and Shaftel, 1967, p. 73)

During the discussion of this enactment, the teacher asks what will happen next, and someone suggests that Tommy will get a licking. The students feel that his punishment will relieve Tommy's guilt.

Phase nine, share experiences and generalize, should not be expected to result immediately in generalizations about the human-relations aspects of the situation. Such generalizations require much experience. The teacher should, however, attempt to shape the discussion so that the children, perhaps after long experience with the role-playing strategy, begin to generalize about approaches to problem situations and the consequences of those approaches. The more adequate the shaping of the discussion, the more general will be the conclusions reached, and the closer the children will come to hypothetical principles of action they can use in their own lives.

The initial goal, however, is to relate the problem situation to the children's experiences in a nonthreatening way. This goal can be accomplished by asking the class members if they know someone who has had a similar experience. In our illustration with Tommy and the money, the teacher asks if anyone in the class knows of an instance in which a boy or girl was in a situation like Tommy's. One student describes an experience with his father. The teacher then asks about parental attitudes and the role of fathers with respect to their children's money.

From such discussions emerge principles that all students can articulate and use. These principles may be applied to particular problems, or they can be used by the children as a springboard for exploring other kinds of problems. Ideally, the children will gradually master the strategy so that when a problem comes up, either within their group or from a topic they have studied, they will be able to use role playing to clarify and gain insight into the problem. Students might, for example, systematically use role playing to improve the quality of classroom democracy.

THE SOCIAL SYSTEM

The social system in this model is moderately structured. Teachers are responsible, at least initially, for starting the phases and guiding students through the activities within each phase; however, the particular content of the discussions and enactments is determined largely by the students.

The teachers' questions and comments should encourage free and honest expression of ideas and feelings. Teachers must establish equality and trust between themselves and their students. They can do this by accepting all suggestions as legitimate and making no value judgments. In this way, they simply reflect the children's feelings or attitudes.

Even though teachers are chiefly reflective and supportive, they assume direction as well. They often select the problem to be explored, lead the discussion, choose the actors, make decisions about when the enactments are to be done, help design the enactments, and most significant, decide what to probe for and what suggestions to explore. In essence, the teachers shape the exploration of behavior by the types of questions they ask and, through questioning, establish the focus.

PRINCIPLES OF REACTION

We have identified five principles of reaction that are important to this model. First, teachers should accept student responses and suggestions, especially their opinions and feelings, in a nonevaluative manner. Second, teachers should respond in such a way that they help the students explore various sides of the problem situation, recognizing and contrasting alternative points of view. Third, by reflecting, paraphrasing, and summarizing responses, the teacher increases students' awareness of their own views and feelings. Fourth, the teacher should emphasize that there are different ways to play the same role and that different consequences result as they are explored. Fifth, there are alternative ways to resolve a problem; no one way is correct. The teacher helps the students look at the consequences to evaluate a solutions and compare it with alternatives.

THE SUPPORT SYSTEM

The materials for role playing are minimal but important. The major curricular tool is the problem situation. However, it is sometimes helpful to construct briefing sheets for each role. These sheets describe the role or the character's feelings. Occasionally, we also develop forms for the observers that tell them what to look for and give them a place to write it down.

Films, novels, and short stories make excellent sources for problem situations. Problem stories or outlines of problem situations are also useful. Problem stories, as their name implies, are short narratives that describe the setting, circumstances, actions, and dialogue of a situation. One or more of the characters faces a dilemma in which a choice must be made or an action taken. The story ends unresolved.

Many resource materials now commercially available include stories or problem stories whose endings can be omitted or changed. Books by the Shaftels and by Chesler and Fox each contain a section of problem stories.

APPLICATION

The role-playing model is extremely versatile and applicable to several important educational objectives. Through role playing, students can increase their abilities to recognize their own and other people's feelings; they can acquire new behaviors for handling previously difficult situations; and they can improve their problem-solving skills.

In addition to its many uses, the role-playing model carries with it an appealing set of activities. Because students enjoy both the action and the acting, it is easy to forget that the role play itself is a vehicle for developing the content of the instruction. The stages of the model are not ends in themselves, but they help expose students' values, feelings, attitudes, and solutions to problems, which the teacher must then explore.

ROLE PLAYING AND THE CURRICULUM

There are two basic reasons why a teacher might decide to use role playing with a group of children. One is to begin a systematic *program of social education* in which a role-playing situation forms much of the material to be discussed and analyzed; for this purpose, a particular kind of problem story might be selected. The second reason is to counsel a group of children to deal with an *immediate human-relations problem*; role playing can open up this problem area to the students' inquiry and help them solve the problem.

Several types of social problems are amenable to exploration with the aid of this model, including:

1. *Interpersonal conflicts.* A major use of role playing is to reveal conflicts between people so that students can discover techniques for overcoming them.
2. *Intergroup relations.* Interpersonal problems arising from ethnic and racial stereotyping or from authoritarian beliefs can also be explored through role playing. These problems involve conflict that may not be apparent. Role playing situations of this type might be used to uncover stereotypes and prejudices or to encourage acceptance of the deviant.
3. *Individual dilemmas.* These arise when a person is caught between two contrasting values or between his or her own interests and the interests of others. Such problems are particularly difficult for young children to deal with, since their moral judgment is still relatively egocentric. Some of the most delicate and difficult uses of role playing make this dilemma accessible to the child and help him or her understand why it occurs and what to do about it. Individual dilemmas that might be explored are ones in which a person is caught between the demands of the peer group and those of his or her parents, or between the pressures of the group and his or her own preferences.
4. *Historical or contemporary problems.* These include critical situations, past or present, in which policy makers, judges, political leaders, or statespeople have to confront a problem or person and make a decision.

Regardless of the particular type of social problem, students will focus naturally on the aspects of the situation that seem important to them. The students may concentrate on the feelings that are being expressed, the attitudes and values of the role players as seen through their words and actions, the problem solution, or the consequences of behavior. It is possible for the teacher to emphasize any or all of these areas in the enactments and discussions. In-depth curriculum sequences can be based on each of the following focuses:

> Exploration of feelings
> Exploration of attitudes, values, and perceptions
> Development of problem-solving attitudes and skills
> Subject-matter exploration

We have found that a single role-playing session is often extremely rich. Discussion can go in many directions—toward analyzing feelings, consequences, the roles themselves and ways to play them, and alternative solutions. After several years of working with this model, we have come to believe that if any one of these ideas, or objectives, is to be developed adequately, the teacher must make a concerted effort to explore one particular emphasis. Because all these aspects tend to emerge in the role-playing process, it is easy to consider them only superficially. One difficulty we are faced with, then, is that an in-depth treatment of any one focus requires time. Especially in the beginning, when students are getting accustomed to the model and to exploring their behavior and feelings, we feel it is

TABLE 3–2   POSSIBLE FOCUSES OF A ROLE PLAYING SESSION

I. Feelings
   A. Exploring one's own feelings
   B. Exploring others' feelings
   C. Acting out or releasing feelings
   D. Experiencing higher-status roles in order to change the perceptions of others and one's own perceptions
II. Attitudes, values, and perceptions
   A. Identifying values of culture or subculture
   B. Clarifying and evaluating one's own values and value conflicts
III. Problem-solving attitudes and skills
   A. Openness to possible solutions
   B. Ability to identify a problem
   C. Ability to generate alternative solutions
   D. Ability to evaluate the consequences to onseself and others of alternative solutions to problems
   E. Experiencing consequences and making final decisions in light of those consequences
   F. Analyzing criteria and assumptions behind alternatives
   G. Acquiring new behaviors
IV. Subject matter
   A. Feelings of participants
   B. Historical realities: historical crises, dilemmas, and decisions

important to select one major focus, or perhaps two, for any one session. Other aspects, of course, may also need to be considered in the development of ideas, but their place should be secondary. For example, the feelings of the characters will be discussed even when the teacher is trying to get the students to concentrate on alternative solutions to the problem; but, in this case, the feelings will tie in to a consideration and evaluation of the solutions.

By choosing one or perhaps two emphases for the role play, carefully questioning and responding to students' ideas, and building on the ideas of the previous phases, the teacher gradually develops each phase so that it supports the particular objectives that have been selected for that session. This is what we mean by developing a focus (see Table 3–2 on previous page).

SELECTING A PROBLEM SITUATION

The adequacy of the topic depends on many factors, such as the age of the students, their cultural background, the complexity of the problem situation, the sensitivity of the topic, and the students' experience with role playing. In general, as students gain experience with role playing and develop a high degree of group cohesiveness and acceptance of one another, as well as a close rapport with the teacher, the more sensitive the topic can be. The first few problem situations should be matters of concern to the students but not extremely sensitive issues. Students themselves may develop a list of themes or problems they would like to work on. Then, the teacher can locate or develop specific problem situations that fit the themes.

The sex of the students and their ethnic and socioeconomic backgrounds influence their choice of topic and, according to Chesler and Fox (1966), their expectations for the role play. Different cultural groups experience different sets of problems, concerns, and solutions. Most teachers account for these differences in their curricula all the time. Problems that are typical for a particular ethnic or age group, sex, or socioeconomic class can become the basis of problem situations.

Other ideas for problem situations can be derived from: (1) the age and developmental stage of the student, such as personal and social concerns; (2) value (ethical) themes, such as honesty, responsibility; (3) problem behaviors, such as aggression, avoidance; (4) troublesome situations—for example, making a complaint at a store, meeting someone new; and (5) social issues, such as racism, sexism, labor strikes. These various sources of problem situations are summarized in Table 3–3.

Another consideration in choosing a problem situation is its complexity, which may be a result of the number of characters or the abstractness of the issues. There are no definite rules about levels of difficulty in problem situations, but intuitively it seems that the following sequence is a reasonable guide: (1) one main character; (2) two characters and alterna-

TABLE 3–3   SOURCES OF PROBLEM SITUATIONS

1. Issues arising from developmental stages
2. Issues arising from sexual, ethnic, or socioeconomic class
3. Value (ethical) themes
4. Difficult emotions
5. Scripts or "games people play"
6. Troublesome situations
7. Social issues
8. Community issues

tive solutions; (3) complex plots and many characters; (4) value themes, social issues, and community issues.

INSTRUCTIONAL AND NURTURANT EFFECTS

Role playing is designed specifically to foster: (1) the analysis of personal values and behavior; (2) the development of strategies for solving interpersonal (and personal) problems; and (3) the development of empathy toward others. Its nurturants are the acquisition of information about social problems and values, and comfort in expressing one's opinions (see Figure 3-1).

FIGURE 3–1   Instructional and nurturant effects: role playing model.

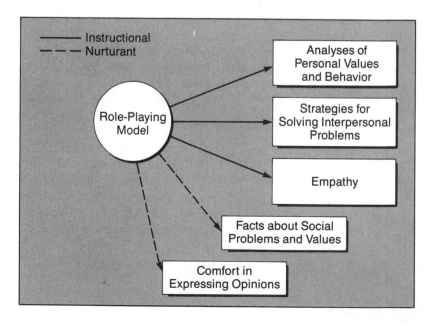

SUMMARY CHART ▶ ROLE-PLAYING MODEL

Syntax

Phase One: Warm Up the Group
　　Identify or introduce problem.
　　Make problem explicit.
　　Interpret problem story, explore issues.
　　Explain role playing.

Phase Two: Select Participants
　　Analyze roles.
　　Select role players.

Phase Three: Set the Stage
　　Set line of action.
　　Restate roles.
　　Get inside problem situation.

Phase Four: Prepare the Observers
　　Decide what to look for.
　　Assign observation tasks.

Phase Five: Enact
　　Begin role play.
　　Maintain role play.
　　Break role play.

Phase Six: Discuss and Evaluate
　　Review action of role play (events, positions, realism).
　　Discuss major focus.
　　Develop next enactment.

Phase Seven: Reenact
　　Play revised roles.
　　Suggest next steps or behavioral alternatives.

Phase Eight: Discuss and Evaluate
　　As in phase six.

Phase Nine: Share Experience and Generalize
　　Relate problem situation to real experience and current problems.
　　Explore general principles of behavior.

Social System

The model is moderately structured. The teacher is responsible for initiating the phases and guiding students through the activities within each phase. The particular content of the discussions and enactments is determined largely by the students.

Principles of Reaction

Accept all student responses in a nonevaluative manner. Help students explore various sides of the problem situation and compare alternative views.

Increase students' awareness of their own views and feelings by reflecting, paraphrasing, and summarizing their responses.

Use the concept of role, and emphasize that there are different ways to play a role.

Emphasize that there are alternative ways to resolve a problem.

Support System

Role playing is an experience-based model and requires minimal support material outside of the initial problem situation.

4

JURISPRUDENTIAL INQUIRY
Learning to Think about Social Policy

Mrs. Giaretto's senior civics class is examining current cases before the United States Supreme Court. One morning one of the students brings in an article from the *New York Times* discussing the Bakke case. (This case dealt with admission to higher education institutions. Bakke claimed that special preference given to minority candidates had discriminated against him.)

"This case bothers me personally," comments Tammy. "You know a number of us are applying for colleges, and my college board scores aren't too high. It seems to me, though, the important thing is that the actual scores I have are changed depending on how I'm looked at. If I'm looked at as an anonymous person, then my scores are what they are. In some colleges I would be looked at as a woman, and the scores would be higher if they wanted to increase the number of women. In some other places they would be lower because I don't belong to a minority group."

"Wait a minute," says one of the other students, "the Bakke case involved a law student. Are the same kind of issues involved in undergraduate college admissions?"

"You bet they are," comments one of the black students. "We've been shut out of a lot of private universities for years."

"Do medical schools do this kind of thing?" asks another. "Do they admit unqualified doctors?"

"Now just a minute," says one of the other students, "just because some groups are given a break doesn't mean that they are unqualified."

"Well, what *is* the story on test scores?" asks another.

"OK, OK," says Mrs. Giaretto. "This is obviously going to be a compli-cated case. It's important in so many ways. I think we'd better sort out the public issues and see where we stand on them."

"Well, how do we begin?" asks Miguel.

"I think we ought to begin by collecting some information. Let's have one group find an abstract of the case to see how it was argued in the lower courts. You can go up to the law library at the university, and I'll call the reference librarian before you get there. Then let's have another group col-lect what the newspapers have said about it since the case first came to public attention. A third group can collect editorials from the newspapers. I think it would be worthwhile if a fourth group talked to the counselors to find out what information they have about college admissions. Another group might arrange to have one of the college admissions officers talk with us about how they handle scores. Can anybody think of anything else?"

"Yes," adds Sally. "Do the people who sell tests have representatives we can talk to?"

"That's a wonderful idea," says Mrs. Giaretto. "Now let's organize our-selves into those groups and begin to get the facts. Then each group can take the material they've collected and start identifying some of the issues. I think it's going to take us quite a long time just to get the issues identi-fied. Then we can proceed to identify the value questions that underlie those issues. Finally we can look at the implications for public policy and try to come up with a statement about where we stand as individuals and possibly as a group."

For the senior civics class at Mervyn Park High School, this discussion initiates exposure to jurisprudential inquiry, which the class later used to resolve their differences over the dance program. During the intervening months, Mrs. Giaretto exposed the class to several more important public issues and taught them the framework for jurisprudential inquiry.

Donald Oliver and James P. Shaver (1966/1974) created the jurispru-dential inquiry model to help students learn to think systematically about contemporary issues. It requires them to formulate these issues as public policy questions and to analyze alternative positions about them. Essen-tially, it is a high-level model for citizenship education.

As our society undergoes cultural and social changes, the jurispruden-tial inquiry model is especially useful in helping people rethink their po-sitions on important legal, ethical, and social questions. The citizenry needs to understand the current critical issues and share in the formula-tion of policy. By giving them tools for analyzing and debating social is-sues, the jurisprudential approach helps students participate forcefully in the redefinition of social values.

ORIENTATION TO THE MODEL

GOALS AND ASSUMPTIONS

This model is based on a conception of society in which people differ in their views and priorities and in which social values legitimately conflict with one another. Resolving complex, controversial issues within the context of a productive social order requires citizens who can talk to one another and successfully negotiate their differences.

Such citizens can intelligently analyze and take a stance on public issues. The stance should reflect the concepts of justice and human dignity, two values fundamental to a democratic society. Oliver and Shaver's image of a skillful citizen is very much that of a competent judge. Imagine for a moment that you are a Supreme Court justice hearing an important case. Your job is to listen to the evidence that is presented, analyze the legal positions taken by both sides, weigh these positions and the evidence, assess the meaning and provisions of the law, and finally, to make the best possible decision. This is the role students are asked to take as they consider public issues.

To play the role, three types of competence are required. The first is familiarity with the values of the American creed, as embedded in the principles of the Constitution and the Declaration of Independence. These principles form the *values framework*—the basis for judging public issues and for making legal decisions. If policy stances are to be truly derived from ethical considerations, one must be aware of and understand the key values that form the core of our society's ethical system.

The second area of competence is a set of skills for clarifying and resolving issues. Usually, a controversy arises because two important values conflict or because public policies, when examined closely, do not adhere to the core values of our society. Whenever a conflict of value arises, three kinds of problems are likely to be present:

> The first kind of problem (*value problem*) involves clarifying which values or legal principles are in conflict, and choosing among them. The second kind of problem (*factual problem*) involves clarifying the facts around which the conflict has developed. The third kind of problem (*definitional problem*) involves clarifying the meanings or uses of words which describe the controversy. (Oliver and Shaver, 1966/1974, p. 89)

The process of clarifying and resolving issues involves clarifying definitions, establishing facts, and identifying the values important to each issue.

The third area of competence is knowledge of contemporary political and public issues, which requires that students be exposed to the spectrum of political, social, and economic problems facing American society. Although a broad understanding of the history, nature, and scope of these problems is very important, in the jurisprudential inquiry model, students explore issues in terms of a specific legal case rather than in terms of a general study of values.

OVERVIEW OF THE TEACHING STRATEGY

Oliver and Shaver's work encompasses many ideas: They present us with a model of society, a conception of values, and a conception of productive dialogue. They also detail curriculum and pedagogical considerations (see Oliver and Shaver, 1971, p. 7). It is possible to extrapolate several models of teaching from their work. However, to us, the strategy that seems most reflective of their goals and thinking is one built around a confrontational, or Socratic, mode of discussion. In Socratic dialogue, the students take a position and the teacher challenges the position with questions. The teacher's questions are designed to push students' thinking about their stance and to help them learn:

> Does it hold up well against positions reflecting alternative values?
> Is it consistent across many situations?
> Are the reasons for maintaining the position relevant to the situation?
> Are the factual assumptions on which the position is based valid?
> What are the consequences of this position?
> Will the student hold on to this stance in spite of its consequences?

In the sample Socratic discussion that follows, students have been examining a voting rights issue. The policy question is: Should the federal government compel southern states to give Negroes equal voting rights? The setting for this session is a ninth-grade public school classroom in Philadelphia in 1962. The teacher has oriented the class to the case, and the students have identified the values in conflict as states' rights versus equality of opportunity. One student, Steve, has volunteered to state his position and defend it. His position is that blacks should have the right to vote. The teacher and students are exploring Steve's stance; throughout the discussion the teacher uses several patterns of reasoning to challenge his position.

T: What do you think, Steve?

S: I think that the police power of local government can go only so far, that the constitutional rights of voting— maybe the Negroes should have them.

Steve takes a position.

T: Negroes should have the right to vote even though there may be all kinds of violence and resistance? We should send troops into the South and protect every individual's right to vote?

Teacher explores the stance by pointing out undesirable consequences of the position (Pattern 3).

S: I'm not saying that. I don't think that we would have to send down troops.

Steve qualifies his position.

T: But what if it did go that far?

Teacher continues probing.

S: Probably, yes.

T: Suppose people called the Negroes who intended to vote on the phone and said, "If you vote tomorrow, something might very well happen to your kids." Do you think we should send the FBI down there to investigate these intimidations?

Teacher checks to determine the point at which the value is violated (Pattern 1).

S: No.

T: Why not?

S: If the threat is carried out, then I would send down troops or the FBI.

Steve establishes the point at which the value is violated.
Teacher checks consistency of Steve's position (Principle of Reaction).

T: After something has happened to the courageous Negro's family, then you would send someone down to stop it? You don't go along with the notion that, if there is an atmosphere of fear and intimidation, we should do something to change the atmosphere so that people will be free to vote? We shouldn't do anything until there is actual violence?

S: In the case of Negroes, yes.

T: Why?

S: Because I don't want to give them complete power to vote. This is taking a little of it away.

Steve changes his position.

T: You want to deny some Negroes the right to vote, a right you are willing to give to whites?

Teacher tests the new position for consistency (Principle of Reaction).

S: Yes.

T: Why?

S: Because I feel that Negroes are inferior to whites.

Steve gives underlying assumption for his position.

T: In what respect?

S: In intelligence, in health, in crime rates.

T: You are suggesting that if a person is tubercular or sick, you should deny him the right to vote?

S: No.

T: But if a Negro is sick, we don't let him vote?

S: Let him vote, sure. It is just that they are inferior for these reasons. I'm not saying because of these reasons I'm not going to let him vote.

T: Then for what reasons aren't you going to let him vote?

S: Because I think they are inferior because of these reasons. (Student then laughs, self-consciously, aware of his inconsistency.) (Oliver and Shaver, 1966/1974, pp. 150–152)

Teacher uses an analogy to test Steve's position (Pattern 2).

By having to take a stand and defend a position, students usually become emotionally involved in the analysis, making the discussions intense and personal. It is hoped that with more practice, their positions will become more complex and well formulated.

MAJOR CONCEPTS

SOCRATIC DIALOGUE

In the Socratic style, the teacher asks the students to take a position on an issue or to make a value judgment, and then he or she challenges the assumptions underlying the stand by exposing its implications. For example, if a student argues for freedom in some situation, the teacher will test whether the argument is meant to apply to *all* situations. The function of the teacher is to probe the students' positions by questioning the relevance, consistency, specificity, and clarity of the students' ideas until they become more clear and more complex.

Most characteristic of the Socratic style is the *use of analogies* as a means of contradicting students' general statements. For example, if a student argues that parents should be fair with children, the teacher may wonder if the parents' function is being compared to that of a court. Analogous situations that test and define the logic and limits of positions are chosen.

PUBLIC POLICY ISSUES

Public controversies tend to fill many pages of our newspapers and many hours of television coverage. A public policy issue is a way of synthesizing a controversy or case in terms of a decision for action or choice.

> A PUBLIC POLICY ISSUE is a question involving a choice or a decision for action by citizens or officials in affairs that concern a government or community.
>
> Policy issues can be phrased as general questions: "Should the United States stay in Vietnam?" "Should capital punishment be abolished?" "Should Government regulate automobile design?"
>
> Public policy issues can also be phrased as choices for personal action: "Should I write my Congressman to protest the draft laws?" "Should I petition the Governor to commute a criminal's death sentence?" "Should I write a candidate asking him to pledge support for auto design regulations?" (Oliver and Newman, 1967, p. 29)

One of the most difficult tasks for the teacher is to assist students in integrating the details of a case into a public policy question.

A FRAMEWORK OF VALUES

Political and social values, such as personal freedom, equality, and justice, concern Oliver and Shaver in their strategy because these are "the major concepts used by our government and private groups to justify public policies and decisions" (Oliver and Shaver, 1966/1974, p. 64). When we speak of a framework of values for analyzing public issues, we imply the *legal-ethical* framework that governs American social policies and decisions. A partial list of these principles of American government as found in the Declaration of Independence and the Constitution of the United States) is shown in Table 4–1.

Resolving a controversy involves screening the details of the case through this legal-ethical framework, identifying the values and policies in question. Social values help us to analyze controversial situations because they provide a common framework that transcends any one particular controversy. However, in most controversial situations, two general rules of ethical conduct conflict with each other. Thus although a framework of social values permits us to speak of diverse conflict situations in common terms, it does not tell us how to go about resolving controversies.

Recent years have witnessed many social problems, frequently involving conflicting values. Some of these problem areas and their underlying value conflicts are listed in Table 4–2. As you read over these topics, note that although the values are identified, the controversies remain. Alternative policy stances are possible on any topic, and most issues can be argued on a number of grounds.

TABLE 4–1   THE LEGAL-ETHICAL FRAMEWORK: SOME BASIC SOCIAL VALUES

Rule of law. Actions carried out by the government have to be authorized by law and apply equally to all people.

Equal protection under the law. Laws must be administered fairly and cannot extend special privileges or penalties to any one person or group.

Due process. The government cannot deprive individual citizens of life, liberty, or property without proper notice of impending actions (right to a fair trial).

Justice. Equal opportunity.

Preservation of peace and order. Prevention of disorder and violence (reason as a means of dealing with conflict).

Personal liberty. Freedom of speech, right to own and control property, freedom of religion, freedom of personal associations, right of privacy.

Separation of powers. Checks and balances among the three branches of government.

Local control of local problems. Restriction of federal government power and preservation of states' rights.

TABLE 4–2   SOME GENERAL PROBLEM AREAS

Problem Areas	Sample Unit Topics	Conflicting Values[a]
Racial and ethnic conflict	School desegregation Civil rights for nonwhites and ethnic minorities Housing for nonwhites and ethnic minorities Job opportunities for nonwhites and ethnic minorities Immigration policy	Equal protection Due process Brotherhood of man v. Peace and order Property and contract rights Personal privacy and association
Religious and ideological conflict	Rights of the Communist party in America Religion and public education Control of "dangerous" or "immoral" literature Religion and national security: oaths, conscientious objectors Taxation of religious property	Freedom of speech and conscience v. Equal protection Safety and security of democratic institutions

TABLE **4–2** *Continued*

Problem Areas	Sample Unit Topics	Conflicting Values[a]
Security of the individual	Crime and delinquency	Standards of freedom Due process v. Peace and order Community welfare
Conflict among economic groups	Organized labor Business competition and monopoly "Overproduction" of farm goods Conservation of natural resources	Equal or fair bargaining Power and competition General welfare and progress of the community v. Property and contract rights
Health, education, and welfare	Adequate medical care: for the aged, for the poor Adequate educational opportunity Old-age security Job and income security	Equal opportunity Brotherhood of man v. Property and contract rights
Security of the nation	Federal loyalty-security programs Foreign policy	Freedom of speech, conscience, and association Due process Personal privacy v. Safety and security of democratic institutions

[a]The *v.* in the listing of values suggests that the top values conflict with the bottom values. Although this is generally true, there are, of course, many exceptions. One can argue, for example, that a minimum-wage law violates property and contract rights and that it is also against the general welfare. *Source:* Donald Oliver and James P. Shaver, *Teaching Public Issues in the High School* (Boston: Houghton Mifflin Company, 1966), pp. 142–143.

Definitional Value and Factual Problems   Most arguments center on three types of problems: definitional, values, and factual. Participants in a discussion need to explore these three kinds of assumptions in one another's position to assess the strength of alternative stances. The process of clarifying and resolving issues by solving these problems is called *rational consent*.

A basic problem in discussions of social issues is the ambiguous or confusing use of words. Unless we recognize common meaning in the words we use, discussion is very difficult and agreement on issues, policies, or actions is virtually impossible. To resolve these definitional disagreements, it is necessary first to determine whether participants in a discussion are using the same term in a different way or different terms for the same referent, and second to establish a common meaning for terms. Then, to clarify communication, participants may: (1) appeal to common usage by finding out how most people use a word or by consulting a dictionary, (2) stipulate the meaning of the word for purposes of discussion by listing the agreed criteria, and/or (3) obtain more facts about an example to see if it meets the agreed criteria for a definition.

Valuing means classifying things, actions, or ideas as good or bad, right or wrong. If we speak of something as a value (such as honesty), we mean that it is good. As people make choices throughout their lives, they are constantly making value judgments, even if they cannot verbalize their values. The range of items or issues over which each of us makes value judgments is vast—art, music, politics, decoration, clothes, and people. Some of these choices seem less important than others, and the degree of importance has something to do with what we mean by a value. Choices that are not so important are personal preferences, not values. Value issues such as art or the physical environment involve artistic taste or judgment of beauty, and many such choices of ideas, objects, or actions do become subjects of discussion in our society and communities.

People make decisions on issues involving values because they believe: (1) certain consequences will occur, (2) other consequences will be avoided, or (3) important social values will be violated if the decision is not made. In a values conflict there is often disagreement about the predicted consequences, which can be partially resolved by obtaining evidence to support the prediction; however, to some extent it is always a matter of speculation. "Affirmative action laws will equalize employment opportunity" is an example of predicted consequences. Although there is some evidence that equal employment opportunity results from affirmative action, this is partly a prediction based on logical grounds.

When two *values* conflict, Oliver and Shaver suggest that the best solution is one in which each value is compromised somewhat, or put another way, each value is violated only minimally (see the following section on balancing values). When the value issues conflict because of predicted consequences, then the disagreement becomes a *factual* problem.

The reliability of a factual claim can be established in two ways: (1)

by evoking more specific claims, and (2) by relating it to other general facts accepted as true (Oliver and Shaver, 1966/1974, pp. 103–104). In both approaches, evidence is used to support the truth of a factual claim. For example, suppose we claim that lowering the speed limit will reduce accidents and save gas. The first way we might support the statement is to look at more *specific* claims. We might find that:

1. In cities that have adopted the 55 mile-per-hour speed limit, accidents have decreased.
2. Gasoline consumption decreased under the 55-mile-per-hour speed limit, while the number of miles driven remained the same.

The greater the number of specific claims we can identify to support the conclusion we are trying to prove, the more reliable the conclusion becomes.

A second way to support the claim is to relate it to other general facts accepted as true. In this example, we might find that cars traveling at 55 miles per hour can stop 25 percent faster than cars traveling at 65 miles per hour.

Balancing Values: The Best Policy Stance   Oliver and Shaver emphasize that values can be used on a *dimensional* as well as an *ideal* basis. If social values are constructed as ideals, they have to be dealt with on an *absolute* basis; either one lives up to a value or one does not. For example, if you approve of equality of all races before the law in the ideal sense, you feel it either has or has not been achieved. If you see values on a dimensional basis, then you judge *degrees* of desirable conditions on a continuum. For example, you can accept a compromise that ensures some, but not all, possible racial equality. Politically, you might choose such a position, hoping to gain more in the future.

Using the example of free speech, Oliver and Shaver suggest that if we see free speech as a total ideal—something to be preserved at all costs and in all situations—then we are unable to cope with situations in which it might be desirable to abrogate free speech temporarily in deference to public safety. For instance, a speaker might be prevented from continuing a speech before a hostile crowd about to turn on him violently. In such a case, one might restrict his free speech to provide for his safety and prevent the crowd from destructive action. The *dimensional* basis enables such a policy to be considered, although citizens may well prefer an ideal basis.

Oliver and Shaver feel that the best stance on an issue is to maintain a *balance of values* in which each value is only minimally compromised. To achieve such a balance, each party in a controversy should try to understand the reasons and assumptions behind the other's position. Only by rational consent can useful compromises be reached.

THE MODEL OF TEACHING

SYNTAX

Although the exploration of students' stances through confrontational dialogue is the heart of the jurisprudential inquiry model, several other activities are especially important, such as helping students *formulate* the stance they eventually defend and helping them *revise* their position after the argumentation. The basic model includes six phases: (1) orientation to the case; (2) identifying the issues; (3) taking positions; (4) exploring the stances underlying the positions taken; (5) refining and qualifying positions; and (6) testing assumptions about facts, definitions, and consequences (see Table 4-3).

In phase one, the teacher introduces the students to case materials by reading a story or historical narrative out loud, watching a filmed incident depicting a value controversy, or discussing an incident in the lives of the students, school, or community. The second step in orienting students to the case is to review the facts by outlining the events in the case, analyzing who did what and why, or acting out the controversy.

In phase two, the students synthesize the facts into a public issue, characterize the values involved (for example, freedom of speech, protecting the general welfare, local autonomy, or equal opportunity), and *identify conflicts between values*. In the first two phases, the students have not been asked to express their opinions or take a stand.

In phase three, they are asked to articulate positions on the issue and state the basis for their positions. In a school finance case, for example, a student might take the position that the state should not legislate how much each school district can spend on each pupil because this would constitute an unacceptable violation of local autonomy.

In phase four, the positions are explored. The teacher now shifts to a confrontational style as he or she probes the students' positions. In enacting the Socratic role, the teacher (or a student) may use one of four patterns of argumentation:

1. Asking the students to identify the point at which a value is violated.
2. Clarifying the value conflict through analogies.
3. Asking students to prove desirable or undesirable consequences of a position.
4. Asking students to set value priorities: asserting priority of one value over another *and* demonstrating lack of gross violation of the second value.

Phase five consists of refining and qualifying the positions. This phase often flows naturally from the dialogue in phase four, but sometimes the teacher may need to prompt students to restate their positions.

While phase five clarified the reasoning in a value position, phase six further tests the position by identifying the factual assumptions behind it

TABLE 4-3 SYNTAX OF JURISPRUDENTIAL INQUIRY MODEL

Phase One: Orientation to the Case	Phase Two: Identifying the Issues
Teacher introduces materials. Teacher reviews facts.	Students synthesize facts into a public policy issue(s). Students select one policy issue for discussion. Students identify values and value conflicts. Students recognize underlying factual and definitional questions.

Phase Three: Taking Positions	Phase Four: Exploring the Stance(s), Patterns of Argumentation
Students articulate a position. Students state basis of position in terms of the social value or consequences of the decision.	Establish the point at which value is violated (factual). Prove the desirable or undesirable consequences of a position (factual). Clarify the value conflict with analogies. Set priorities. Assert priority of one value over another *and* demonstrate lack of gross violation of second value.

Phase Five: Refining and Qualifying the Positions	Phase Six: Testing Factual Assumptions Behind Qualified Positions
Students state positions and reasons for positions, and examine a number of similar situations. Students qualify positions.	Identify factual assumptions and determine if they are relevant. Determine the predicted consequences and examine their factual validity (will they actually occur?).

and examining them carefully. The teacher helps the students to check whether their positions hold up under the most extreme conditions imaginable.

The six phases of the jurisprudential inquiry model can be divided into analysis (phases one, two, and three) and argumentation (phases four, five, and six). The analysis activities, which occur in the form of careful discussion of values and issues, prepare the material for exploration. The argumentation, carried out in a confrontational style, seeks to produce the strongest possible stance.

SOCIAL SYSTEM

The structure in this model ranges from high to low. At first, the teacher initiates the phases; moving from phase to phase, however, is dependent on the students' abilities to complete the task. After experience with the model the students should be able to carry out the process unassisted, thereby gaining maximum control of the process. The social climate is vigorous and abrasive.

PRINCIPLES OF REACTION

The teacher's reactions, especially in phases four and five, are not evaluative in the sense of being approving or disapproving. They probe substance: The teacher reacts to students' comments by questioning relevance, consistency, specificity or generality, and definitional clarity. The teacher also enforces continuity of thought, so that one thought or line of reasoning is pursued to its logical conclusion before other argumentation begins.

To play this role well, the teacher must anticipate student value claims and must be prepared to challenge and probe. In the Socratic role, the teacher probes one student's opinion at length before challenging other students. Because a Socratic dialogue can easily become a threatening cross-examination or a game of "guess what the teacher's right answer is," the teacher must make it clear that the clarification of issues and the development of the most defensible position are the objectives. The questioning of evidence and assumptions must be tempered with supportiveness. The merits of the case, not of the students, are the basis for evaluation.

SUPPORT SYSTEM

The major material support for this model are source documents that focus on a problem situation. There are some published case materials, but it is relatively easy to develop one's own case materials. The distinguishing feature of this approach is that the cases are accounts of real or hypothetical situations. It is essential that all pertinent facts of the situation be included in the case material so the case will not be vague and frustrating.

A controversial case describes a specific situation that has conflicting ethical, legal, factual, or definitional interpretations. The case may consist of a classic historical or legal situation, such as *Plessy v. Ferguson* in race relations, or the Wagner Act or the Kohler strike in labor relations; or it may be a short story or fictionalized account of a social controversy, such as Orwell's *Animal Farm*. Generally, each page of the daily newspaper contains three or four articles that either explicitly or implicitly present an important public policy question. Usually some facts of the situation are presented, but the original situation that provoked the controversy is not described in full detail.

APPLICATION

In developing their alternative framework for teaching social studies courses in high schools, Oliver and Shaver were concerned with both the *substance* of what is taught and the *methods* of teaching it. Consequently, the model provides a framework for developing contemporary course *content* in public affairs (cases involving public issues) and for developing a *process* to deal with conflict in the public domain, leading students to an examination of values.

The model is tailored to older students and must be modified considerably for use at the junior high school and middle school levels, even with the most able students. We have successfully carried out the model with extremely able seventh- and eighth-grade students but have had little success with younger children.

The confrontational dialogue that surrounds the argumentation of social issues is apt to be very threatening at first, especially to less verbal students. We have had small groups (three or four students) formulate a stand and collectively argue the stand with another small group. The format allows for time out, reevaluating the stance with one's group, and discussing the issue again. Initially, we presented the case; and, after students had selected the policy issue, we asked them to take an initial stand. On this basis we divided them into small groups and told each group to come up with the strongest possible case. The students understood that regardless of the group they were in at first, they might well choose a different stance at the end of the discussion.

Neither the skills of reasoning nor the confidence to take a stance and discuss it are acquired easily or quickly. Teachers should let a single case continue for a long period of time, giving students the opportunity to acquire information, reflect on their ideas, and build their courage. It is self-defeating to set up short, one-time debates over complex questions. Formal instructional sessions teaching students directly about analytic and argumentative techniques may be useful, but these should be introduced naturally and slowly. The initial case materials should be relatively simple and require little previous background. Some should be drawn from the students' experiences, perhaps in the classroom or at home.

For many years instructors have organized social studies courses around cases; the jurisprudential inquiry model heightens the vigor and intensity with which such cases are studied. Of course, cases must have public issues or value conflicts embedded in them to lend themselves readily to the jurisprudential approach. But unless social studies courses deal with values, both personal and public, they will have missed the vital mainstream of social concern.

Once students become fluent in the use of the jurisprudential inquiry

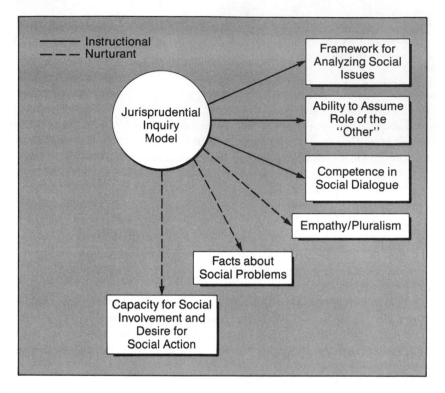

FIGURE 4–1 Instructional and nurturant effects: jurisprudential inquiry model.

model, they can apply it to conflicts that occur in and around their own lives. The scenario at the beginning of this chapter is an example of students' exploration of an issue that touched their own concerns. Without such application, we speculate that the study of public issues, even vigorously pursued, can seem abstract and irrelevant to the lives of students. Because students live in communities where issues abound, their study of values should not be confined to cases far removed from them, but should be applied to the dynamics of their own lives and the community around them.

AGE-LEVEL ADAPTATION

This model is not easily applied below the junior high level. It does seem possible to introduce some highly verbal upper-elementary students to aspects of the model, such as identifying issues and alternative value positions.

LEARNING ENVIRONMENT ADAPTATIONS

Initially, the jurisprudential inquiry model requires a fair amount of teacher-directed activity and direct instruction. Gradually, as students become competent, the phases of the model should blend into student-directed discussions.

INSTRUCTIONAL AND NURTURANT EFFECTS

Mastery of the framework for analyzing issues is the major direct learning outcome. This includes skill in identifying policy questions; application of social values to policy stances; the use of analogies to explore issues; and ability to identify and resolve definitional, factual, and value problems.

The ability to carry on forceful dialogue with others is another important outcome. It nurtures the capacity for social involvement and arouses the desire for social action.

Finally, the model nourishes the values of pluralism and a respect for the point of view of others. It also advocates the triumph of reason over emotion in matters of social policy, although the strategy itself strongly brings into play the students' emotional responses (see Figure 4–1).

At the Ontario Institute for Studies in Education, a number of faculty members, particularly Malcolm Levin and John Isenberg, have developed interesting cases for use with the jurisprudential inquiry model. Many of these cases are set in Canada and can be quite exciting for students not only because the issues are excellent but because of the somewhat different context and legal system. In addition, their publication, *Ethics in Education*, covers a large number of issues which can stimulate the development of cases and the study of public issues.

Syntax

Phase One: Orientation to the Case
  Introduce materials.
  Review facts.

Phase Two: Identifying the Issues
  Synthesize facts into a public policy issue or issues.
  Select one policy issue for discussion.
  Identify values and value conflicts.
  Recognize underlying factual and definitional questions.

Phase Three: Taking Positions
  Articulate a position.
  State the basis of the position in terms of the social value or consequences of the decision.

Phase Four: Exploring the Stance(s). Patterns of Argumentation
  Establish the point at which value is violated (factual).
  Prove the desirable or undesirable consequences of a position (factual).
  Clarify the value conflict with analogies.
  Set priorities. Assert priority of one value over another *and* demonstrate lack of gross violation of second value.

Phase Five: Refining and Qualifying the Positions
  State position and reasons for position, and examine a number of similar situations.
  Qualify position.

Phase Six: Testing Factual Assumptions behind Qualified Positions
  Identify factual assumptions and determine if they are relevant.
  Determine the predicted consequences and examine their factual validity (will they actually occur?).

Social System

The model has moderate to high structure, with the teacher initiating and controlling the discussion; however, an atmosphere of openness and intellectual equality prevails.

Principles of Reaction

Maintain a vigorous intellectual climate where all views are respected; avoid direct evaluation of students' opinions.

See that issues are thoroughly explored.

Probe the substance of students' thinking through questioning relevance, consistency, specificity, generality, definitional clarity, and continuity.

Maintain dialectical style: Use confrontational dialogue, questioning students' assumptions and using specific instances (analogies) to contradict more general statements.

Avoid taking a stand.

Support System

Source documents that focus on a problem situation are needed.

CHAPTER 5

ADAPTING TO INDIVIDUAL DIFFERENCES
Conceptual Systems Theory

Up to this point our emphasis has been on describing the social models, what they are good for, and how they work. Well-executed, they work well and they provide positive learning environments for a large range of students. However, they work best when they are adapted to the characteristics of the students. In this chapter we turn our attention to individual differences and present a framework that can be used to understand some of the important ways that students respond differently to the social (and some other) models. This framework also provides guidelines for adapting the environment to make it more likely that individual differences will be capitalized on rather than being hindrances to learning.

Conceptual systems theory was developed by David Hunt and his associates (Harvey, Hunt, and Schroder, 1961; Schroder, Driver, and Streufert, 1967). The theory describes human development in terms of increasingly complex systems for processing information about people, things, and events. Growth is "an interactive function of the person's level of personality development (or stage) and the environmental conditions he encountered" (Hunt, 1970, p. 4).

Optimal development occurs when the environment facilitates the "conceptual work necessary for the person's conceptual growth. When environmental conditions are not optimal, then some form of arrestation is assumed to occur" (Hunt, 1970, p. 4). In other words, as the individual becomes more complex, the environment needs to change with him or her if growth is to continue at an optimal rate. One of Hunt's purposes is to help us plan environments to keep people growing conceptually. Second, since people at different stages of development respond differently to various models of teaching, he wants to help us shape teaching strategies to match the learner's development. Theoretically, the closer a teaching strategy is tailored to the learner's conceptual level, the more learning will take place (Hunt, 1970, p. 2).

The focus of conceptual systems theory is on the learner's cognitive complexity (the complexity of his or her information-processing system). Our first task is to examine the construct of conceptual level (CL). Then we explore its implications for the identification of optimal training environments. Finally, we discuss how to select and modify models of teaching according to the theory.

This information-processing view of personality development focuses on the structures—that is, the programs or sets of rules—by which individuals relate to their environment. Some individuals relate to the environment through relatively few lenses—they see fewer dimensions of a situation, and those few are not very well integrated with one another. At the opposite end of the continuum are individuals who view the environment through many dimensions and manifest a high level of integrative complexity in their relationships to it. The more dimensions one has available, the more likely integration is present. Highly integrated information-processing systems have many more conceptual connections between rules—that is, "they have more schemata for forming new hierarchies, which are generated as alternative perceptions, or further rules for comparing outcomes. High integration structures contain more degrees of freedom, and are more subject to change as complex changes occur in the environment" (Schroder, Driver, and Streufert, 1967, p. 7).

By the conceptual systems view, therefore, we can discriminate individuals in terms of the number of dimensions they use for relating to the environment and the interrelationships of these dimensions. For example, Figure 5–1 illustrates the relationships among rules in situations of low and high integration (Schroder, Driver, and Streufert, 1967, p. 8). Individual A obtains information through three dimensions but reduces them to one integrated dimension. Individual B also uses three dimensions but processes the data he or she receives in complex ways.

To illustrate concretely, let us consider an interpersonal-relations situation. Natalie would tend to respond to ideas that conflict with hers either by incorporating them into her own as if there were no difference, or by rejecting them completely. Will would dissect the ideas, balancing them against his own, perhaps rejecting portions and accepting others,

FIGURE 5–1   Variation in level of conceptual structure. (From Schroder, Driver, and Streufert, *Human Information Processing* © 1967 by Holt, Rinehart & Winston. Reprinted by permission of the publisher and authors.)

A. Low Integration Index

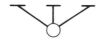

B. High integration Index

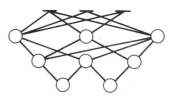

perhaps modifying his own. Thus, it is easier for Will to be productive in complex social models, for he can more easily receive ideas from others and more easily adapt his expressions to meet the frame of reference of the others. Natalie will need much more guidance to develop the capacity that Will has come by through natural development.

Four levels of INTEGRATIVE COMPLEXITY

Particular behavior patterns are characteristic of different levels of integrative complexity. Schroder, Driver, and Streufert identify and describe four levels: low complexity, moderate complexity, moderately high complexity, and high complexity.

LOW COMPLEXITY

Categorical, black-white thinking. The discrimination of stimuli along dimensions is minimally graduated; for example, if a person holds an extremely concrete attitude toward an ethnic group, that group will be "lumped" into one category (for example, "bad") and contrasted with others. A structure that depends upon a single fixed rule of integration reduces the individual's ability to think in terms of relativeness, of "grays" and "degrees."

Minimizing conflict. Stimuli either fit into a category or are excluded from consideration. There is no conceptual apparatus that can generate alternatives; the result is fast "closure" in choice or conflict situations (Schroder, Driver, and Streufert, 1967, pp. 16–17).

MODERATE COMPLEXITY

The major characteristics of this second structural level are: The presence of a conceptual apparatus that is able to generate alternate organizations of dimensions. That is, if there are three dimensions, such a structure would provide at least two possible rules for combining these dimensions.

This moderately low level of organization is characterized by the delineation of several alternative ways of structuring the world. Although such conceptual properties are not effective for relating or organizing differentiated sets of rules for decision-making processes, they do usher in the problem of choice and probability.

Some of the consequences of moderately low structural properties include: A movement away from absolutism. Because of the availability of alternate schemata, "right" and "wrong" are not fixed as they were in structures with low integration index (Schroder, Driver, and Streufert, 1967, p. 19).

A good deal of negativism is also present, because the individual is struggling against his or her old rules and, hence, against those who expose them. He or she especially resents parents and authority figures or any other controlling figures.

MODERATELY HIGH COMPLEXITY

Moderately high complexity is described as follows:

The system is less deterministic. Combining and using two alternate systems of interpretation greatly increase the number of alternative resolutions that can be generated. Even when the individual closes on a particular decision, he is still open to a number of alternative pressures. At this level, abstractness (that is, lack of fixity) becomes a formal rule of the system. . . .

The environment can be tracked in many more ways. While moderately low integration index structure permits different ways of tracking or interpreting an environment at different times, moderately high integration index structure can vary combinations of alternate schemata. A person who is functioning at this level may view a social situation in terms of two points of view, see one in relationship to the other, perceive the effects of one upon the other. He is able to generate strategic adjustment processes, in which the effects of behavior from one standpoint are seen as influencing the situation viewed from another vantage point. This implies, for example, that a person can observe the effects of his own behavior from several points of view; he can simultaneously weigh the effects of taking different views. The adaptive utilization of alternate schemata here is much less compartmentalized than at moderately low levels. (Schroder, Driver, and Streufert, 1967, pp. 21, 23)

HIGH COMPLEXITY

High level structure includes additional and more complex potentialities for organizing additional schemata in alternate ways. At the fourth level, comparison rules can be further integrated. Alternate complex combinations provide the potential for relating and comparing different systems of interacting variables. As with other system differences, the difference between the moderately high and the high levels is one of degree. In the latter, the potential to organize different structures of interacting schemata opens up the possibility of highly abstract function. . . .

This very abstract orientation should be highly effective in adapting to a complex, changing situation. It is certainly much more effective than a structure that is dependent upon external conditions for building rules and upon past experiences for predicting events. (Schroder, Driver, and Streufert, 1967, pp. 22, 23)

In using the social models one of our goals is to help students progress toward greater integrative complexity. To facilitate this, we modify the environment to increase the probability that development will take place.

Optimal environments

The best procedure for inducing an individual to progress toward complexity and flexibility is to match that person's present stage of personality development to an environment tailored to the characteristics of that stage, but in such a way as to pull the individual toward the next stage of development (Harvey, Hunt, and Schroder, 1961). The following chart summarizes the four conceptual levels described earlier and indicates in general terms the matching training environment:

CHARACTERISTICS OF STAGE

I. This stage is characterized by extremely fixed patterns of response. The individual tends to see things evaluatively—that is, in terms of rights and wrongs—and he or she tends to categorize the world in terms of stereotypes. The individual prefers unilateral social relationships—that is, those which are hierarchical and in which some people are on top and others are on the bottom. The individual also tends to reject information which does not fit in with his or her present belief system or to distort the information in order to store it in his or her existing categories.

II. In this stage the individual is characterized by a breaking away from the rigid rules and beliefs which characterized his or her former stage. He or she is in a state of active resistance to authority and tends to resist control from all sources, even nonauthoritative ones. This person still tends to dichotomize the environment. He or she has difficulty seeing the points of view of others, and difficulty in maintaining a balance between task orientation and interpersonal relations.

OPTIMAL ENVIRONMENT

In order to produce development from this stage, the environment needs to be reasonably well structured, because this kind of person will become even more concrete and rigid in an overly open social system. At the same time, however, the environment has to stress delineation in such a way that the individual begins to see him- or herself as distinct from his or her beliefs and begins to recognize that different people, including him- or herself, have different vantages from which they look at the world, and that the rights and wrongs in a situation and the rules in a situation can be negotiated. In summary, the optimal environment for this individual is supportive, structured, and fairly controlling, but with a stress on self-delineation and negotiation.

The delineation of self which is suggested is now taking place, and the individual needs to begin to reestablish ties with others, to begin to take on the points of view of others, and to see how they operate in situations. Consequently, the environment needs to emphasize negotiation in interpersonal relations and divergence in the development of rules and concepts.

U.M.C. DUDLEY LIBRARY

III. At this stage, the individual is beginning to reestablish easy ties with other people and to take on the point of view of the other. In his or her newfound relationships with other people, this person has some difficulty maintaining a task orientation because of his or her concern with the development of interpersonal relations. He or she is, however, beginning to balance alternatives and to build concepts which bridge differing points of view and ideas which apparently contradict each other.

The environment at this point should strengthen the reestablished interpersonal relations, but an emphasis should also be placed on tasks in which the individual as a member of the group has to proceed toward a goal as well as maintain him- or herself with other individuals. If the environment is too protective at this point, the individual could be arrested at this stage, and although he or she might continue to develop skills in interpersonal relations, would be unlikely to develop further skill in conceptualization or to maintain himself or herself in task-oriented situations.

IV. The individual is able to maintain a balanced perspective with respect to task orientation and the maintenance of interpersonal relations. He or she can build new constructs and beliefs, or belief systems, as these are necessary in order to adapt to changing situations and new information. In addition, this individual is able to negotiate with others the rules or conventions that will govern behavior under certain conditions, and he or she can work with others to set out programs of action and to negotiate with them conceptual systems for approaching abstract problems.

Although this individual is adaptable, he or she no doubt operates best in an interdependent, information-oriented, complex environment.

CONCEPTUAL DEVELOPMENT AND THE SOCIAL MODELS OF TEACHING

Thus, we can search for the amount of structure the student needs, and *we can modify models to increase or decrease their structure to fit the level at which the student operates best.* Thus, the teacher has three important tasks in relation to the conceptual system of the child. First, is to learn to discriminate children according to levels of development. Second, inasmuch as individuals of varying levels of integrative complexity perform very differently in different environments, the teacher must create an environment that is *matched* to the complexity of the student. Third, environmental prescriptions can be made to *increase* the integrative complexity of the individual—that is, the optimal environments for *growth* in personality can be identified.

Let us look closely at each of these three tasks. Discriminating the conceptual level of individuals is extremely important because of the effect of conceptual level on the perceptual world. The "real" world of a person of low complexity (who regards his or her environment as fixed, prefers hierarchical relationships, is evaluative, and becomes rigid under even moderate stress) is very different from the real world of a person of high complexity (who can generate many alternative avenues for dealing with stress and opposition, accepts the responsibility for creating rules in new situations, and can easily build conceptual bridges between himself or herself and problem situations). The first individual is not likely to be adaptive or flexible, whereas the latter individual is likely to have the capacity to generate new solutions to problems and to adapt to changing conditions. This would be true whether the individual is young or old. For example, mature physicists of about equal knowledge who differ greatly in integrative complexity could be expected to face problem situations very differently. Similarly, an elementary school youngster of very low complexity would be expected to perceive civil disorder differently from an individual of high complexity (Hunt and Hardt, 1967).

The very different performance of individuals who differ in conceptual complexity under different conditions makes the second task—creating an environment matched to the student's complexity—an interesting challenge for the teacher. For example, when Hunt divided groups of youngsters according to their levels of integrative complexity, teachers found that the groups of low complexity had difficulty carrying on discussions. A discussion technique simply was not appropriate for individuals who view the world as fixed and rules as unchanging and permanent. On the other hand, individuals of moderate structure who were engaged in delineating themselves sharply from authority were very easy to engage in debate, although the debate was terribly vigorous and difficult to control.

In other words, for optimal growth in complexity, the student needs to be exposed to an environment matched to the characteristics of his or her world. An environment in which a complex individual will flourish would create unbearable stress for a person of low complexity. There are considerable implications here for educational theory and practice. Hunt's research on the Upward Bound programs in the United States validated the position that personality and training environment should be related. Hunt examined a sample of Upward Bound programs and found that when environment and trainee personality were matched (high structure with low complexity, and vice versa) the greatest growth took place (Hunt and Hardt, 1967).

The third task is to provide environments that will help individuals become more complex, and the hypothesis that makes the most sense at this time is to attempt to lead the person's present state of development slightly—that is, when an individual is at a low level of complexity, one would want to have a moderate amount of complexity in the environment, but not too much. The tasks presented to the individual, for example, should involve some negotiating about rules, but not total negotiation as, for example, under Rogerian conditions.

Hunt's model is really a plan for changing social systems to match the complexity of the learner—that is, it suggests principles for behaving in relation to the student, depending on the kind of person he or she is. For students of low conceptual level, tasks or educational approaches of low complexity, with high sequence and a clear establishment of rules, would be indicated. For students of high complexity, a very emergent structure, with higher task complexity and an interdependent social system, would be indicated. For students of low conceptual level, we need to provide structure, be clear in directions, supportive but fairly direct. When dealing with students of high conceptual level, the teacher needs to be much more interdependent and mutual, placing much more of the burden for learning on the students, and helping them develop their own structure.

Thus, a social studies teacher who can match students and environment should be more effective at teaching the social studies and have a more comfortable time in managing the students than a teacher who does not make such a match. For example, students with a high preference for structure could be very uncomfortable under conditions of low structure and might not learn as much as they would in highly structured environments.

Hunt, Joyce, and others have engaged in a series of investigations to determine the relationship between conceptual level and student response to a variety of teaching models. These are described in some detail in a series of papers by Hunt and in a lengthy review (Joyce, Peck, and Brown, 1981). In most of the investigations, students who varied considerably in conceptual level were taught using models of teaching representing different structures. It was expected, for example, that the high CL students would perform more effectively at first in the relatively unstructured models such as group investigation than would the low CL students. Generally speaking, the results of Hunt's theories were confirmed by these investigations. Conceptual level definitely affects student behavior when different models of teaching are used, and the directions of the differences in behavior generally confirmed conceptual systems theory. Student learning from various models of teaching is also affected by conceptual level. For example, in experiments with the inductive thinking model, students of higher conceptual level formed more concepts, but factual learning was about equal. Apparently, more flexible students function more effectively as the cognitive demands of the model increase, resulting in the development of greater conceptual activity and hence increased numbers of concepts learned.

Hunt takes the optimistic view that even though conceptual level may predict student responsiveness, the differences in responsiveness can be compensated for to some extent by effective training and by modifying the teaching strategy. From this point of view, differences in conceptual level help to identify needed types of training rather than prohibit students from participating in certain kinds of education (see Hunt and Sullivan, 1974).

Skill Training for Specific Models of Teaching

Hunt's optimism led us to consider how we can increase the range of models from which students can profit. It is surely true that students react quite differently to various models of teaching, and everybody finds that there are certain ways of learning most comfortable for him or her. But nearly everyone learns something from each model of teaching; there are very few students whose characteristics are so pronounced that they cannot profit to some extent from any given model. And, just as important, students need to learn to profit from a wider range of environments. A student needs to learn how to exploit the social models in order to profit from them in terms of self esteem, social skills, academic achievement, and the ability to study social values and issues.

Some students, however, experience discomfort when first exposed to complex social models. Equally, others are somewhat uneasy if there is too much control of their behavior, such as the conditions that prevail in game-type simulations and training models.

Rather than excluding students from experiences with those models, we find that we can adapt the teaching strategy so that most students can be relatively comfortable using them. We should be optimistic about students' abilities to learn from a variety of models of teaching. A major goal of education is to help students develop the skills they need to react productively to an increasingly broad spectrum of approaches to learning.

Thus, a considerable portion of our energy when we are teaching is directed toward helping students learn "how to learn" so that they will become increasingly independent, versatile, and productive. We take the position that the ability to respond productively to any model of teaching is more a matter of skills on the part of the learner than it is a matter of any kind of immutable characteristic. Our task as teachers is to identify the skills necessary to use the model productively, find out which ones our students possess, and teach them the others. For example, role playing requires the ability to analyze a problem situation, to take the part of another in the enactment, and to empathize with alternative points of view. In addition it requires skill in expressing one's value position and in developing concepts that build bridges between one's own values and those of others.

Some of the instruction in model-relevant skills can take place in the course of using a given model. Inquiry training, for example, is built on the premise that students need to learn skills of inquiry. We do not expect a high level of performance the first time students attempt to engage in the inquiry process. However, those early attempts provide us with the opportunity to learn which skills the students need so that we can teach them directly. Also, students learn through practice. For example, when engaging in the enactments of role playing for the first time, students are often "stagey" and artificial. With successive enactments, however, they learn that role playing depends on involvement, and they begin to overcome their awkwardness and shyness and play the roles more spontaneously.

Generally speaking, the more complex the social action required by a model and the more demanding its intellectual tasks, the more initial difficulty students will have with that approach to teaching. Unfamiliarity also increases initial difficulty. For example, students who have never engaged in directing their own learning activities will have considerable difficulty with group investigation as the teacher relinquishes control and increasingly asks the students to direct their own educational activities. After a time, however, the students will become more accustomed to taking responsibility and learn the skills of setting their own objectives, reflecting on their own experiences and accepting feedback from the teacher. Thus, practice with the model gives the students a chance to learn some of the skills it requires. Those not acquired by practice we can teach directly.

The skills involved in accepting responsibility for growth, such as setting goals, making personal plans, and reflecting on them are critical. Similarly, skills in stating needs are crucial, for if individuals are unable to make their needs known, it is difficult for them to set goals or make realistic plans. At the same time, the skill of analyzing one's own behavior has to be developed if the student is to come to the increasing self-awareness necessary to conduct his or her own education.

The skills in the social models include practical interpersonal skills such as negotiating goals and plans with others, but also include the far more complex skills necessary to clarify one's values, analyze one's role in group situations, and take the view of others. There are also substantive skills involved in debating alternatives and in negotiating goals and plans. Until the learner has skill in perceiving his or her own behavior in the group, social models are not very satisfying.

Additional skills important to group investigation include collecting and organizing information, generating and testing hypotheses and theories, and moving back and forth from data to more abstract concepts and ideas. Unless these skills are developed, the student is extremely dependent on the teacher. At certain times within teaching episodes, skills are concentrated on and practiced. It is not difficult to present the students with relatively simple problems and then demonstrate to them how one follows up another person's line of inquiry. Many basic skills can be taught simply by interrupting the sequence of activities and concentrating on a particular skill.

Training sessions can be organized for students who have special skill needs. An experiment to verify a hypothesis may be easy for some students and not for others. We can provide time to work more closely with the students whose skill deficits are greatest and ease them through the early stages of training.

ADAPTING THE MODEL

Similarly, the teacher can take a more active role in structuring activities in the areas in which students are having difficulty. Nearly all learners, from children to adults, are unaccustomed to engaging in the problem-solving activities characteristic of group investigation. Thus, when students are first learning to engage in group investigation we can provide more structure, taking a more active leadership role, so that students are not asked to engage in activities beyond their independent capabilities. As they become more familiar with the model, we simply loosen the structure, turning increasing amounts of control over to the learners. Throughout the process, we continuously adjust the activities to the ability levels of the students as they gradually learn the model.

In all models, the teacher should be open with the students. Part of their task is not simply to learn the material under consideration but to become increasingly capable of directing their own activities. The students, in other words, gradually learn the model itself.

LEVELS OF STRUCTURE

In general, then, we work to help students develop the skills necessary to profit from the approaches to teaching that we use, and we gradually teach them to assume control. The first time that students are exposed to partnerships we make elaborate preparations to acquaint them with the process, its purpose, and its rules, and we lead them step by step through the activities. After several such experiences, students should take an active role in orienting themselves, identifying the goals and rules, and governing their own activities.

Classroom discipline is thus a matter of teaching students how to relate to instruction and helping them assume greater responsibility for their own learning. In the best-disciplined classrooms, students know what they are doing, how to go about it, and how to govern themselves. Until this stage has been achieved, we cannot say that *discipline* is complete, in any sense of the word that relates to the purposes of the school. Thus, we begin with relatively high levels of structure. Gradually we reduce that structure as the students become increasingly capable of governing their own affairs.

As indicated earlier, the best way to identify the skills students need is to let them practice with the method and observe their behavior. In partnerships engaged in inductive teaching, for example, if students are having trouble collecting data, instruction can be provided to help them become more effective. Similarly, students working with group investigation may be relatively good at negotiating goals and fairly poor at clarifying values. We can teach much more effectively if we take the time to diagnose the skills our students need to carry out the models of instruction being employed.

THE SOCIAL FAMILY: AN ADDITIONAL NOTE ON EXPECTED EFFECTS

The social models have several purposes—increasing social skill, providing strategies for the study of social values, developing self-esteem, and facilitating academic learning.

Judging the effects on all these is a complicated business, especially since the social models are generally used in combination with other models, so it is difficult to assign causes. Also, many people have difficulty recognizing the validity of personal and social achievement, like self-esteem, social skill, and the study of values unless these are also accompanied by increases in the amounts of information learned by the students. Yet, the role-playing and jurisprudential models, designed to facilitate the study of social values and public issues, have validity in that they enable students to engage in study directed toward those goals. They do not decrease amounts of information learned, but they *change* the content in the direction of social values and the study of public issues and thus are appropriate when those goals are sought. They should not be compared with instructional approaches that *avoid* the study of values, because they will always exceed them with respect to the purposes for which they are designed.

With respect to general cooperative approaches to teaching, we can ask whether they increase self-esteem (they do) and the learning of integrative social skills (they do) and also whether they increase lower-order and higher-order academic learning when, which is often, they are used to teach academic content. When illustrating the concept of *effect-size* in Chapter 1, we used the recent dramatic research on group investigation to illustrate how much students can benefit when a very powerful social model is used. Group investigation literally immerses students in a cooperative environment. What happens when students are taught to work cooperatively but are not fully immersed in a democratic classroom or school, but where cooperative groups are used selectively in the teaching of academic subjects? Judging from several hundred relevant studies, we can expect an effect size of from .25 to .50, as depicted in Figure 5–2.

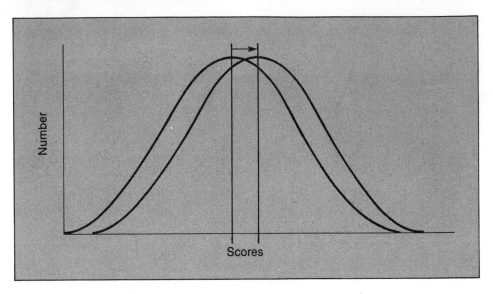

FIGURE 5–2   Effect size in a typical cooperative learning study.

At the middle of the distribution, the median student, working selectively in cooperative groups, places at about the 57th to the 67th percentile of students working where interdependence is not stressed. Also, *all* students benefit. Thus, failure is reduced and outstanding achievement is facilitated.

Over the years, the effects will be cumulative. The increases in learning will build on one another, with each modest gain increasing the base of knowledge and self-confidence of the students.

THE INFORMATION-PROCESSING FAMILY

Teaching Students the Skills of Learning Through Thinking

Old fencing masters used to tell their students that you grip the sword as you would hold a sparrow. If you hold it too tightly, it cannot breathe. If you hold it too loosely, it will fly away.

Good thinking bears analogy to the fencer's grip. It combines discipline with flexibility. If we are to nurture it we must master that paradox, and create environments that offer strength without strangulation.

We are dreaming about creating a school where the study of human thought is a central mission, where the cultivation of the intellect is comfortably woven with the study of values, the mastery of information, and training in the basic subjects.

In our school, science and social sciences are taught with the methods of their parent disciplines. Reading, literary analysis, and writing draw on criticism and nurture productive thinking. Theater introduces the craft and special metaphors of the stage. Domestic and international perspectives are illuminated by philosophy. The atmosphere draws talent into bloom as naturally and inexorably as springtime leads the daffodil towards its lovely fate.

The core of good thinking is the ability to solve problems. The essence of problem solving is the ability to learn in puzzling situations. Thus, in the school of these particular dreams, learning how to learn pervades what is taught, how it is taught, and the kind of place in which it is taught (Downey, 1967).

Through the ages our dream has had different forms in the minds of our most powerful thinkers. The variety of embodiments of just a few of them is wonderful to think about. Plato and Aristotle spun different webs around the subject. In the Middle Ages, Aquinas created his version out of Catholic philosophy; it was echoed later, in Renaissance terms, by John Amos Comenius. With secular logic Newton wove his discipline of thought. Martin Luther spoke for the Reformation; Jefferson, Franklin, and Rousseau for the democratic revolution. Dewey and James pulled the methods of science toward the psychology of thought. The distinctive orientations of Montessori, De Beauvoir, Hutchins, Adler, Bruner, Schwab, and the other academic reformers followed and are now mixed with the current arguments about how to bring electronic technology into play. The world views embraced by these people have a wide span. They emphasize different aspects of thinking and recommend different ways of teaching it. But they all agree that there is life after school and that learning to think (learning to learn) is what school is all about.

As we enter a period where this theme is again being made prominent, this time with an emphasis on the skills of thinking, we need to ponder why something so universally affirmed has so rarely become a dream fulfilled in the realities of education.

We believe that a serious bad habit shares the majority of the blame. (The enemy, as usual, is us.) It is the habit of setting different approaches against each other and persuading ourselves that they are incompatible.

THE UNNECESSARY DICHOTOMIES

The most familiar wrangles are between the emphasis on basic school subjects, most commonly the "basic skills," and on the direct teaching of thinking. The argument is usually carried on as if to do one would sacrifice the other. Otherwise reasonable people argue that if we teach the sciences inductively, we will lose coverage of the subjects, or that we will undermine values if we teach students to think about them, or even that drill and practice will always and surely dull the mind. These arguments reductio ad absurdum, riding on deeply felt emotions and expressed in hyperbole, are hangers-on from the poverty of our past, when it seemed almost too much to afford the barest education. Now, when any but the fullest education will deprive our children of important parts of the achievements of this new worldwide civilization, we must put away the luxury of dichotomous thinking. The skills of reading, the study of values, the analytic tools of scholars, and the nurture of intuition are compatible, and we can and should teach them simultaneously. As we enter this period of renewed emphasis on the teaching of thinking, let us not pit the cultivation of the mind against the acquisition of skills and knowledge as if these goals were adversaries.

We also have a firm foundation of methods for teaching thinking on which we can build—we do not have to start from scratch. We have also much experience with the teaching of thinking from which we can profit. Thus, let us now discuss that storehouse of models for teaching thinking and some of the experiences we have had with them, especially how children acquire various modes of thinking and how teachers can acquire thinking-oriented teaching models.

As Bereiter (1984) points out, it is possible to pervade the curriculum with intellectual activity so that the teaching of thinking is an important component of every activity. The reasons for adopting a pervasive approach are:

1. We have a substantial storehouse of models of teaching that directly teach both content and intellectual process. Although we always need to invent more, the existing storehouse is more than adequate to create programs that will develop many of the most powerful ways of thinking that have been discovered.
2. These models of teaching result in more effective teaching of the basic school subjects, both elementary and secondary, than the methods generally employed to teach them (Joyce, Showers, Beaton, and Dalton, 1984).
3. Teaching the basic subjects in such a way that thinking is enhanced avoids the traditional dichotomies between the content of education and intellectual activity.

There is no inherent conflict between teaching the fundamentals of citizenship in a democratic society, learning to read, write, analyze literature, engage in scientific inquiry, participate in the performing arts or athletics, on the one hand, and learning how to think on the other. The schools of thought identified earlier all have some educational truth in them, and each is enhanced by the other. To teach the basic subjects without teaching thinking simultaneously not only neglects thinking but is also inefficient. Students learn more traditional substance when mastery is generated by models that also produce intellectual growth. Similarly, the development of citizenship is enhanced by the analysis of social values and the clarification of social issues. Learning how to be a committed and self-aware person is enhanced by learning to think about one's growing self and to analyze one's development and social milieu.

MODELS OF TEACHING, THINKING SKILLS, AND CURRICULUM

Various kinds of thinking are enhanced by particular models of teaching. Some models, for instance, are designed to teach students to:

Attack problems inductively (concept formation models)

Attain concepts and analyze their thinking strategies (concept attainment models)

Analyze social issues and problems (jurisprudential and role-playing models)

Break set and think divergently (synectics and group investigation models)

Other models are designed to teach students to:

Work together to generate and test hypotheses (group investigation and scientific inquiry models)

Reason causally (inquiry training, scientific inquiry, synectics, group investigation, simulation models)

Master complex bodies of information (memory, scientific inquiry, group investigation models)

This is just part of the storehouse of models and the types of intellectual growth the models can stimulate. Some of them are designed to teach particular types of thinking; others are designed to teach thinking skills that are applicable in many types of situations. For maximum effect, they are generally used in combination; when they are, the results can be very impressive. Some single models, used intensively, have also had impressive results. Well-implemented scientific inquiry models, for example, have achieved substantial informational and conceptual outcomes, have successfully taught methods of scientific inquiry, and have also produced increases in intelligence test scores (Bredderman, 1983).

Models are combined not only to pyramid their effects but also to address the different kinds of objectives and thinking that we wish to engender. For example, learning how to memorize is an important intellectual skill, but we do not expect a memory model to be the only foundation of creative thinking. Likewise, creative thinking models, although they enhance memory, are not the only ones we would use to do so.

USING MODELS TO TEACH THINKING TO CHILDREN

First of all, the core outcome of using a model of teaching is that students learn how to learn (reason) in a certain fashion. When we use a model to enhance memory, we teach students to think in such a way that they will increase their ability to memorize. Similarly, when we use inductive models, we teach students how to learn inductively by thinking inductively. When we use group investigation, we teach students to work together to gather information, set and test hypotheses, and balance one another's perspectives for approaching a problem area.

Second, to teach students how to think and learn in a certain way, we have to establish a program to use on a regular basis. If in social studies we wish to teach strategies for analyzing social issues, then we have to use the appropriate model over time and handle it in such a way that the students become increasingly able to analyze social issues independently. In other words, we teach the model to the students. This takes patience. The first time that students are exposed to a method for attaining concepts, they are likely to be inefficient. With practice and instruction they become more competent. Finally, they are able to attain concepts and analyze their thinking strategies effectively and comfortably. Teachers and administrators are often concerned that students first exposed to a model appear slow and uncomfortable with its processes. They worry that valuable instructional time is being lost. If they persist, however, they find that the students become more powerful. In the early stages, then, we provide more structure and explicit instruction in the skills necessary to learn from and use a model. As the students become more skillful, less and less instruction is necessary (Joyce, 1984).

Third, by teaching students how to reason independently, we increase their power to teach themselves and thus to share power in the instructional situation. As students reach out and build new ideas, we can guide them so that they develop better and better ideas. However, we cannot teach students to reason inductively and then reject the ideas they develop. Encouraged to think creatively, students will develop solutions we have not thought of. We have to expect this and learn to love the uncertainty it creates for us.

Fourth, strategies for thinking do not come in fragments. We cannot teach their elements as isolated skills—for example, "how to observe objectively." Rather we teach thinking strategies that include particular skills, such as how to observe, but the observations are used in relation to other skills.

Teaching thinking requires a commitment to solid instruction in the models of teaching that engender those types of thinking and the willingness to persist until the students become effective in their use. Thinking strategies are most effectively taught in conjunction with appropriate content. It is not difficult to use synectics to teach students to use metaphors and analogies more skillfully in their writing unless we try to teach the use of metaphor separately from the acts of writing. It is not difficult to teach students to form concepts when they read unless we separate concept formation from the act of reading.

Thus, teaching thinking requires that we teach the core subjects of the school in a different fashion, using the appropriate models systematically over time until they are a part of the students' natural repertoires.

6

THINKING INDUCTIVELY
Collecting, Organizing, and Manipulating Data

S C E N A R I O **I**

At the Motilal Nehru School of Sports in the state of Haryana, India, two groups of 10th-grade students are engaged in the study of a botany unit that focuses on the structure of plant life. One group is studying the textbook with the tutorial help of their instructor, who illustrates the structures with plants found on the grounds of the school. We will call this group the presentation-cum-illustration group. The other group, which we will call the inductive group, is taught by Bharati Baveja, an instructor at Delhi University. This group is presented with a large number of plants that are labeled with their names. Working in pairs, the students build classifications of the plants based on the structural characteristics of their roots, stems, and leaves. Periodically, the pairs share their classifications and generate labels for them. Occasionally, Mrs. Baveja employs concept attainment to introduce a concept designed to expand the students' frame of reference and induce more complex classification. She also supplies the scientific names for the categories the students invent. Eventually Mrs. Baveja presents the students with some new specimens and asks them to see if they can predict the structure of one part of the plant from the observation of another part (as predicting the root structure from the observation of the leaves). Finally, she asks them to collect some more specimens and fit them to the categories they have developed so they can determine how comprehensive their categories have become. They discover that most of the new plants will fit into existing categories but that new categories have to be invented to hold some of them.

After two weeks of study, the two groups take a test over the content of the unit and are asked to analyze some more specimens and name their structural characteristics.

The inductive group has gained twice as much on the test of knowledge and can correctly identify the structure of eight times more specimens than the presentation-cum-illustration group.

S C E N A R I O   II

Jack Wilson is a first-grade teacher in Lincoln, Nebraska. He meets daily for reading instruction with a group of children who are progressing quite well. He is concerned, however, that they have no trouble attacking new words unless they are unable to figure out the meaning from context. If they are able to figure out what the word means from the rest of the sentence, they seem to have no difficulty using principles they have learned to sound the words out. He has concluded that they don't have full control over phonetic and structural analysis concepts and principles. He plans the following activity, which is designed to help them develop concepts of how words are structured and to use that knowledge in attacking words unknown to them.

Jack prepares a deck of cards with one word on each card. He selects words with particular prefixes and suffixes, and he deliberately puts in words that have the same root words but different prefixes and suffixes. He picks prefixes and suffixes because they are very prominent structural characteristics of words—very easy to identify. (He will later proceed to more subtle phonetic and structural features.) Jack plans a series of learning activities over the next several weeks using the deck of cards as a data base. Here are some of the words:

| set | reset | heat | preheat | plant | replant |
| run | rerun | set | preset | plan | preplan |

When the group of students convenes on Monday morning, Jack gives several cards to each student. He keeps the remainder, counting on gradually increasing the amount of information students get. Jack has each student read a word on one of the cards and describe something about the word. Other students can add to the description. In this way the structural properties of the word are brought to the students' attention. The discussion surfaces features like initial consonants (begins with an "s," vowels, pairs of consonants ("pl"), and so on.

After the students have familiarized themselves with the assortment of words, Jack asks them to put the words into groups. "Put the words that go together in piles," he instructs. The students begin studying their cards, passing them back and forth as they sort out the commonalities. At first the students' card groups reflected only the initial letters or the meanings of the words, such as whether they referred to motion or warmth. Gradually, they noticed the prefixes, how they were spelled, and looked up their meanings in the dictionary, discovering how the addition of the prefixes affected the meanings of the root words.

When the students finished sorting the words, Jack asked them to talk about each category, telling what the cards had in common. Gradually, because of the way Jack had selected the data, the students could discover the major prefixes and suffixes and reflect on their meaning. Then he gave them sentences in which words not in their deck began and ended with those prefixes and suffixes and asked them to figure out the meanings of those words, applying the concepts they had formed to help them unlock these meanings.

The inductive activity was continued many times as, by selecting different sets of words, Jack led the students through the categories of consonant and vowel sounds and structures they would need to attack unfamiliar words.

S C E N A R I O   III

Eight-year-old Seamus is apparently playing in his kitchen. In front of him are a number of plates. On one is a potato, cut in quarters. Another contains an apple, similarly cut. The others contain a variety of fruits and vegetables. Seamus pushes into the segments of potato a number of copper and zinc plates which are wired together. He notes with satisfaction that a tiny light bulb lights up, then disconnects the bulb and attaches a voltmeter, examines it briefly, and then reattaches the bulb. He repeats the process with the apple, examining the bulb and voltmeter once again. Then come the raspberries, lemon, carrot, and so on. His father enters the room and Seamus looks up. "I was right about the raspberries," he says, "We can use them as in a battery. But, some of these things . . ."

Seamus is, of course, classifying fruits and vegetables in terms of whether they can interact with the metals to produce electric current.

S C E N A R I O   IV

Diane Schuetz has provided her first-grade students with sets of tulip bulbs which they classify according to size, whether two are joined together ("Some have babies on them."), whether they have "coats," or have the beginnings of what look like roots. Now they are planting them, trying to find out whether the variation in attributes will affect how they will grow. ("Will the big ones grow bigger?" "Will the babies grow on their own?", etc., etc.) She has designed the science curriculum area around the basic processes of building categories, making predictions, and testing their validity.

S C E N A R I O   V

Dr. Makibbin's social studies class is examining data from a large demographic base on the nations of the world. One group is looking at the base on Africa, another is studying Latin America, and the others are pouring over the data from Asia and Europe. They are searching for correlations among variables, such as trying to learn whether per-capita income is associated with life expectancy and whether educational level is associated with rate of increase in population, and so on. As they share the results of their inquiry, they will compare the continents, trying to learn whether the correlations within each are comparable to the other.

TEACHING THINKING

Probably nothing has been more consistently pursued yet remained more elusive than has the teaching of thinking. From the earliest days of schooling, teachers have searched for ways of helping students become more effective in processing information and solving problems. Thus, there are many models for teaching students to collect and process information. In this chapter, we consider part of the work of the late curriculum theorist, Hilda Taba, who developed a series of teaching strategies designed to help develop inductive mental processes, especially the ability to categorize and to use categories. We also examine curricula developed to teach students to think as scientists do as they analyze data and create and test theories and hypotheses.

LEARNING TO CLASSIFY

We begin with models that teach students to classify data and thus form categories, because it is generally believed that concept formation is the basic higher-order thinking skill and that all other analytic and synthetic skills depend on the development of the distinctions that result in categories.

ORIENTATION TO THE MODEL

Twenty five years ago, Taba was largely responsible for popularizing the term *teaching strategy*, and her work in the Contra Costa, California, schools provided a first-rate example of a teaching strategy designed to improve the student's ability to handle information. In fact, her strategy formed the backbone of an entire social studies curriculum (Taba, 1966), enabling the design of courses, units of study, and lessons where the teaching of thinking was integrated with the study of content.

THINKING PROCESSES

She built her approach around three assumptions:

1. *Thinking can be taught.* There is evidence for and against this postulate, but we do not debate it here.
2. *Thinking is an active transaction between the individual and data.* This means that in the classroom setting, the materials of instruction become available to the individual when he or she performs certain cognitive operations on them—organizing facts into conceptual systems; relating points in data to each other and generalizing from these relationships; making inferences and generalizing from known facts to hypothesize, predict, and explain unfamiliar phenomena. Mental operations cannot be taught directly in the sense of being "given by a teacher" or be acquired by absorbing someone else's thought products. The teacher can, however, *assist* the processes of internalization and conceptualization by stimulating the students to perform complex mental processes and by offering progressively less direct support.
3. *Processes of thought evolve by a sequence that is "lawful."* Taba postulates that, in order to master certain thinking skills, certain earlier ones must be mastered first, and this sequence cannot be reversed. Therefore, "this concept of lawful sequences requires teaching strategies that observe these sequences." (Taba, 1966, pp. 34, 35)

In other words, Taba concludes that thinking skills should be taught using specific teaching strategies designed to elicit those skills. Furthermore, these strategies need to be used sequentially, because one thinking skill builds on the others. One can argue with this assumption, but she built a very logical series of strategies by applying it.

THREE TEACHING STRATEGIES

Taba identifies three inductive thinking tasks and then develops three teaching strategies to induce those tasks. Each task represents a stage in the inductive thinking process as Taba describes it. The first is *concept formation* (the basic teaching strategy), the second is *interpretation of data,* and the third is the *application of principles.*

CONCEPT FORMATION

This stage involves: (1) identifying and enumerating the data that are relevant to a topic or problem; (2) grouping these items into categories whose members have common attributes; and (3) developing labels for the categories. To engage students in each of these activities, Taba invented teaching moves in the form of tasks given to the students. For example, asking students to "look up the data on per capita income and population growth for 12 countries from each of the major regions of the world" will induce the students to create a data file. The task "Decide which countries are most alike" is likely to cause people to group those things that have been listed. The question, "What would we call these groups?", begins a task likely to induce people to develop labels or categories.

An illustration of the concept formation strategy is the second-grade unit of Taba's Contra Costa social studies curriculum. The unit attempts to develop the main idea that a supermarket needs a place, equipment, goods, and services (Taba, 1967). The unit opens by asking the students to visit supermarkets and study what is found there. The children can be expected to identify individual food items, stock people, cashiers, equipment, a building (or place), deliveries of food. Their responses can be recorded and the listing continued until several categories are represented. After the enumerated list has been completed, the children are asked, perhaps on another day, to group the items on the basis of similarity. "What belongs together?" Presumably, if the enumeration is rich enough, the children will identify "things the market sells" and "things done for the supermarket owner." These concepts can then be labeled *goods* and *services*.

The purpose of this strategy is to induce students to expand the conceptual system with which they process information. In the first phases, they are required to group the data, an activity requiring them to alter or expand their capacity for handling information. In other words, they have to form concepts they subsequently can use to approach new information they encounter.

Each overt activity elicited by the teaching strategy reflects mental operations that are hidden from view, which Taba referred to as "covert." Table 6–1 illustrates the relationship between the overt activities in the concept-formation model, the mental operations that the students pre-

TABLE **6–1**   **CONCEPT FORMATION**

Overt Activity	Covert Mental Operations	Eliciting Questions
1. Enumeration, listing	Differentiation (identifying separate items)	What did you see? hear? note?
2. Grouping	Identifying common properties, abstracting	What belongs together? On what criterion?
3. Labeling, categorizing	Determining the hierarchical order of items super- and subordination.	How would you call these groups? What belongs to what?

SOURCE: Hilda Taba, *Teacher's Handbook for Elementary Social Studies* (Reading, Mass.: Addison-Wesley Publishing Co., Inc., 1967), p. 92.

sumably perform during the activity, and the eliciting questions teachers use to lead the students through each activity.

INTERPRETATION OF DATA

Taba's second teaching strategy (interpretation of data) is built around the mental operations she refers to as *interpreting, inferring,* and *generalizing.* Table 6–2 shows the overt and covert activities involved in the interpretation of data and the questions a teacher can use to elicit the activities. Essentially, students build hypotheses about relationships, inferring causation, and explore these to build generalizations.

In the first phase, the teacher's questions lead students to identify critical aspects of the data. For example, after students classify countries as described above, they might read about their economic and political systems and try to identify their salient aspects (as which ones depend on a few agricultural or mining products, which ones depend on commerce or manufacturing, and which ones combine all of these).

Second, students are to explore relationships. Here the teacher asks questions concerning causes and effects. For example, he or she might simply ask, "Do you think the differences in the economic systems are related to differences in per capita income or educational levels?"

APPLICATION OF PRINCIPLES

The third cognitive task around which Taba builds a teaching strategy is that of applying principles to explain new phenomena (predicting con-

TABLE **6–2**   **INTERPRETATION OF DATA**

Overt Activity	Covert Mental Operations	Eliciting Questions
1. Identifying critical relationships	Differentiating	What did you notice? see? find?
2. Exploring relationships	Relating categories to each other Determining cause-and-effect relationships	Why did this happen?
3. Making inferences	Going beyond what is given Finding implications, extrapolating	What does this mean? What picture does it create in your mind? What would you conclude?

SOURCE: Hilda Taba, *Teacher's Handbook for Elementary Social Studies* (Reading, Mass.: Addison-Wesley Publishing Co., Inc., 1967), p. 101.

sequences from conditions that have been established, as predicting which countries have similar interests that might affect how they would vote on relevant issues in the United Nations Assembly). This strategy follows the first two: A unit or course would lead the students from concept formation activities to activities requiring interpretation of data and then to activities requiring application of principles. At each stage, students would be required to expand their capacities to handle information, first developing new concepts, then developing new ways of applying established principles in new situations. Table 6–3 describes the overt activities, covert mental operations, and the eliciting questions for this teaching strategy.

The first phase of the strategy requires students to predict consequences, explain unfamiliar data, or hypothesize. We might continue our previous example by asking students to predict how the numbers of people sharing various cultures are likely to be altered when population growth data are considered.

In the second phase, students attempt to explain or support the predictions or hypotheses. For example, if someone feels that a fixed currency rate for all countries should be established and held for a long time, that person would attempt to explain why he or she thought this system would work and how it would fare with such factors as the relative prosperities or production ratios within the countries. In the third phase, students verify these predictions or identify conditions that would verify the predictions.

TABLE 6–3   APPLICATION OF PRINCIPLES

Overt Activities	Covert Mental Operations	Eliciting Questions
1. Predicting consequences, explaining unfamiliar phenomena, hypothesizing	Analyzing the nature of the problem or situation, retrieving relevant knowledge	What would happen if . . . ?
2. Explaining and/or supporting the predictions and hypotheses	Determining the causal links leading to prediction or hypothesis	Why do you think this would happen?
3. Verifying the prediction	Using logical principles or factual knowledge to determine necessary and sufficient conditions	What would it take for this to be generally true or probably true?

SOURCE: Hilda Taba, *Teacher's Handbook for Elementary Social Studies* (Reading, Mass.: Addison-Wesley Publishing Co., Inc., 1967), p. 109.

THE MODEL OF TEACHING

SYNTAX

These three teaching strategies strongly resemble each other. Each is built around a mental operation: concept formation, interpretation of data, application of principles or ideas. In each case, the strategy involves overt activities that assume students must go through certain covert operations to perform the activities. Thus, the sequence of activities forms the syntax of the teaching strategies and is presumably accompanied by underlying mental processes. In each case, the teacher moves the strategy along by means of eliciting questions to guide the student from one phase of activity into the next, at the appropriate time. In the case of concept-formation strategy, for example, the grouping of data would be premature if the data had not been identified and enumerated. But to delay too long before moving to the next phase would be to lose opportunities and interest.

To teach students to respond to the model, we advise teachers to begin by leading the students through activities based on data sets that are presented to them and in later lessons teaching the students how to create and organize data sets.

SOCIAL SYSTEM

In all three strategies, the atmosphere of the classroom is cooperative, with a good deal of pupil activity. Since the teacher is generally the initiator of phases, and the sequence of the activities is determined in advance, he or she begins in a controlling, though cooperative, position. However, as the students learn the strategies, they assume greater control.

PRINCIPLES OF REACTION

Taba provides the teacher with rather clear guidelines for reacting and responding within each phase. When using cognitive tasks within each strategy, the teacher must be sure that the cognitive tasks occur in optimum order, and also at the "right" time. Regulating the tasks requires that studying the data set is done thoroughly before categorization proceeds, that seeking for relationships follows thorough categorization. The teacher's primary mental task in the course of the strategies is to monitor how students are processing information and then to use appropriate eliciting questions. The important task for the teacher is to sense the students' readiness for new experience and new cognitive activity with which to assimilate and use those experiences.

SUPPORT SYSTEM

These strategies can be used in any curricular area that has large amounts of raw data that need to be organized. For example, in studying the economic aspects of various nations, students would need large quantities of data about the economics of those countries and statistics about world affairs. Then the teacher's job is to help them process the data in increasingly complex ways and, at the same time, to increase the general capacities of their systems for processing data.

APPLICATION

Since each of Taba's teaching strategies is built on a particular mental, or cognitive, task, the primary application of the model is to develop thinking capacity. However, in the course of developing thinking capacity, the strategies obviously require students to ingest and process large quantities of information. The model can be used in every curriculum area and in the grades from kindergarten through high school. The third strategy, by inducing students to go beyond the given data, is a deliberate attempt to increase productive or creative thinking. Inductive processes thus include the creative processing of information, as well as the convergent use of information to solve problems.

The concept-formation strategy is especially applicable to the education of young children. Although many early childhood teachers have their students engage in grouping activities, few understand this process from the points of view of Taba and Bruner (concept formation and concept attainment). Concept formation, like concept attainment, can be a vehicle for helping students understand the nature of a concept. It is a strategy especially suited to philosophies of education and instruction that call for *active* learning and require manipulable materials. The strategy is also beneficial to students in upper grades who must learn and process masses of information. Concept formation is a means of pulling discrete items together into larger conceptual schemes.

The model causes students to collect information and examine it closely, to organize it into concepts, and to learn to manipulate those concepts. Used regularly, the strategy increases the students' abilities to form concepts efficiently and also the perspectives from which they can view information.

For example, if a group of students regularly engage in inductive activity, the group can be taught increasing numbers of sources of data. The students can learn to examine data from many sides and to scrutinize all aspects of objects and events. For example, imagine students studying communities. We can expect that at first their data will be superficial, but their increasingly sophisticated inquiry will turn up more and more attributes that they can use for classifying the data. Also, if a classroom of students works in groups to form concepts and data, and then the groups share the categories they develop, they will stimulate each other to look at the information from different perspectives. The instructor can use the concept-attainment strategy to open up still more perspectives to them.

Also, the students can learn to categorize categories. Imagine students who have classified poems or short stories. They can build concepts that further cluster those categories.

Another example may serve to pull these ideas together in practical terms. As we have discussed, sometimes we create and organize data sets for our students to classify, and sometimes we help them create and organize sets. In the following example we have organized a set from writing samples produced by the students themselves.

S C E N A R I O   **VI**

ADVERBS: AN INDUCTIVE EXERCISE OVER STUDENT WRITING

The students have watched a scene from the film *Out of Africa* in which three new friends amuse themselves with witty conversation and telling anecdotes and stories. Then the students were instructed to create a sentence about the scene, beginning each sentence with an adverb. (They are studying the use of adverbs because it was discovered that they are more awkward using adverbs than they are with adjectives.)

They opened their sentences in the following ways (the rest of the sentences are omitted to create a focus on the use of adverbs in openings):

1. Profoundly looking into one another's eyes . . .
2. Intently listening to one another's words . . .
3. Wonderingly and as if by magic the love began to flow
4. With relaxed and forthright honesty they shared a part of themselves . . .
5. Anxiously the husband watched as his normally taciturn wife . . .
6. Passionately I gazed at my two companions . . .
7. Playfully at first, but with growing intensity . . .
8. Tentatively, like three spiders caught in the vortex of the same web, . . .
9. With heated anticipation, the three formed a web of mystery and emotion.
10. Quietly listening they were engulfed by the tale.
11. With awe and a certain wonderment . . .

12. Tenderly, in the midst of warm candlelight, they . . .

13. Skillfully she met the challenge . . .

14. Boldly they teased one another with their mutual love of language.

15. Effortlessly her practiced mind . . .

16. Awkwardly, like children just learning to walk . . .

17. Softly, slowly, but glowing like the candles about them, they negotiated . . .

18. Boldly she drew them into the fabric of her story.

19. Suspended by the delicate thread of her tale . . .

20. Instinctively she took his cue . . .

Before reading further, read the passages and make notes about the attributes of the writing. Then classify the sentences. (If you are alone or in a small group studying the model, classify them independently. If you are in a group of eight or more, classify them with a partner. Then share your classifications, discussing the basis each of you used and the attributes you focused on.)

Now, let's turn to some of the categories developed by our class.

One group classified them by the form of the adverbs, placing single words together (as "profoundly" from number 1, "anxiously" from 5), phrases together (as "with relaxed and forthright honesty" from 4) and the single clause (number 19) by itself. A second group reported that it had classified them according to the mood or tone that was evoked. For example, numbers 12, 17, 19, 11, 3, and 7 were placed together because the group members decided that they all shared the creation of a gentle, loving mood, whereas 5 and 16 emphasized the awkwardness of strangers.

The class then used their categories to experiment with writing, changing single words into phrases and clauses and vice versa, substituting words in order to change the mood evoked, and so on. For example, one pair experimented with 6, trying "with passion," and "passion flowed as I gazed. . . ." Another changed number 8 to "tentatively and spiderlike . . ." and decided the change reduced the creation of the mood. One changed "boldly" to "skillfully" in number 18 and judged that it helped the development of the mood.

The episode was followed by a foray into several books of short stories and the members of the class created a data set of sentences in which authors had made use of adverbs. Classifying them, they proceeded to create categories of adverb use by expert writers and to experiment with them in their own writing.

Thus, the phases of the model built on one another to generate increasingly complex mental activity and increase the likelihood that the study of language would have a yield for their skill in writing; and the second inductive activity built on the first as the students added the study of expert writers and tried to learn from them.

RESEARCH ON INDUCTIVE MODELS

The research on the effects of inductive teaching strategies has explored, first, whether students can learn inductive processes, and, second, what are the effects of these processes on the acquisition of information and concepts. The answer to the first question appears to be affirmative (Bredderman, 1981; El Nemr, 1979). Also, when compared to drill-and-practice methods that typify instruction in most schools, induction appears to increase both the amount of information learned and the concepts that are developed to organize it. Worthen (1968) hypothesized that inductive processes would increase the retention of information and found that it did. Apparently the process of forming concepts enabled the students to develop mental structures that "held" the information better than structures that were provided to them. Hunt and Joyce (1981) explored inductive processes with both relatively rigid and flexible students; they found that both groups were able to engage in the inductive process but that the more flexible students made the greatest gains initially. More important, they found that practice and training increased effectiveness and that the students could learn to carry on inductive activity independently.

The accompanying summary chart outlines elements of the concept formation strategy. All the strategies have relatively clear syntaxes, with the reactions of the teacher coordinated with the phases, a cooperative but (at first) teacher-centered social system, and support systems that require ample sources of raw ungrouped data. Their applicability is extremely wide, and the classroom teacher should consider a repertoire of basic inductive strategies such as these to be an essential tool.

S C E N A R I O   **VII**

BIOLOGICAL SCIENCE INQUIRY MODEL

APPROACHES BUILT ON THE RESEARCHER'S TOOLS

In London, Ontario, Mr. Hendricks's fourth-grade students enter their classroom after lunch to find an array of glasses, bottles, bells, wooden boxes of different sizes (with holes in them), tuning forks, xylophones, and small wooden flutes. These objects are spread about the room, and the students spend a few minutes playing with them, creating a most horrendous sound. Mr. Hendricks watches.

After a few minutes the students begin to settle down and one of them asks, "What's going on here, Mr. Hendricks? It looks like you've turned the place into an orchestra."

SUMMARY CHART ► INDUCTIVE-THINKING MODEL

Syntax

Strategy One: Concept Formation
  Phase One: Enumeration and listing
  Phase Two: Grouping
  Phase Three: Labeling, categorizing

Strategy Two: Interpretation of Data
  Phase Four: Identifying critical relationships
  Phase Five: Exploring relationships
  Phase Six: Making inferences

Strategy Three: Application of Principles
  Phase Seven: Predicting consequences, explaining unfamiliar phenomena, hypothesizing
  Phase Eight: Explaining and/or supporting the predictions and hypotheses
  Phase Nine: Verifying the prediction

Social System

The model has high to moderate structure. It is cooperative, but the teacher is initiator and controller of activities.

Principles of Reaction

Teacher matches tasks to students' level of cognitive activity, determines students' readiness.

Support System

Students need raw data to organize and analyze.

Instructional and Nurturant Effects

The inductive thinking model (Figure 6–1) is designed to instruct students in concept formation and, simultaneously, to teach concepts. It nurtures attention to logic, to language and the meaning of words, and to the nature of knowledge.

"Well, in a way," he smiles. "Actually, for the next few weeks this is going to be our sound laboratory." He moves across the room and picks up an instrument made of wood and wires and plucks one of the wires. At the same time he uses a spoon to strike a soft drink bottle on the desk next to him. "Do you notice anything about these sounds?" he asks, and repeats his plucking and striking.

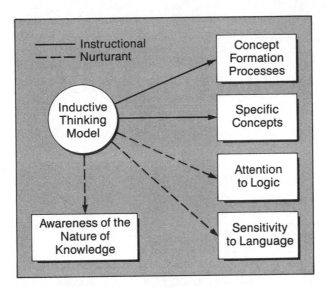

FIGURE 6–1   Instructional and nurturant effects: inductive thinking model.

"Hey," says one of the girls, "they sound the same, but different."

"Do it again," suggests one of the students, and Mr. Hendricks obliges. Soon all of the students have noticed that the sound is at the same pitch or level.

"Your problem," explains Mr. Hendricks, "is to find out what makes sound vary and to describe that variation. Given the limitations of the devices we have in this room, I want you to organize yourselves to conduct some experiments and present me with sets of principles that you think describe the variations. When you're finished, I want you to be able to describe to me how you would design an instrument with certain capabilities. I'll tell you what I want the instrument to be able to do, and you can tell me how to make it. Then we'll begin to test your ideas. Now, I think we ought to organize ourselves into groups and decide how we're going to go about this. Does anybody have any ideas?"

"Well," Sally ventures, "I've noticed that the things are made out of five different kinds of materials. Maybe we could get into five groups and each group would experiment with those for awhile. Then we could share what we've learned and trade around and check out the thinking of the other groups. After that we could decide what to do next."

Someone joins in with another suggestion, and the class spends the next half hour planning how the study will begin.

From the early 1950s to the late 1960s, innovation in American education was propelled mainly by the Academic Reform movement, an effort to revise the conventional curriculum areas of the school around conceptions of the major ideas and research methods of the academic disciplines. In the area of mathematics, for example, the curriculum designers attempted to influence the way students would think about mathematics, both the major ideas and the methods they would use to inquire into mathematics. Similarly, the science curricula reflected both the major ideas of the sciences and the research methods and attitudes of the scientific community. In other words, curricula were built around the information-processing systems of the academic disciplines.

Two straightforward examples were the Biological Sciences Curriculum Study (BSCS) (Schwab, 1965), which produced curricular and instructional patterns for use in high school biology, and the Social Science Curriculum project, which teaches the use of social psychology methods to study human relations (Lippit, Fox, and Schaible, 1969). In this chapter we use the BSCS model to represent the group of models.

ORIENTATION TO THE MODEL

The essence of the BSCS approach is to teach students to process information using techniques similar to those of research biologists—that is, by identifying problems and using a particular method to solve them. BSCS emphasizes content and process. The first emphasis is on human behavior in the ecology of earth: "The problems created by growing human populations, by depletion of resources, by pollution, by regional development, and the like, all require intelligent government or community action. These are, in part at least, biological-ecological problems, and every citizen should have some awareness of their background" (Schwab, 1965, p. 19). The second emphasis is on scientific investigation:

> Although one of the major aims of this version (of the course) is to describe the major contributions modern molecular biology has made to the general understanding of scientific problems, a second aim will also be apparent. Measured by almost any standard, science has been and continues to be a powerful force in our society. A difficulty has arisen, however. This difficulty, expressed by C.P. Snow in his book, *Two Cultures*, arises from the fact that although many people may understand the *products* of science, at the same time they may be very ignorant of the nature of science and its methods of inquiry. It is probably a safe generalization to say that the understanding of the *products* of science cannot be attained unless the process is also understood. It is apparent that in a free society such as ours, much will depend on the average citizen's evaluation of science. (Schwab, 1965, pp. 26–27)

To help students understand the nature of science, the strategies developed by the BSCS committees introduce students to the methods of biology at the same time that they introduce them to the ideas and facts. The committee put it rather pungently:

> If we examine a conventional high school text, we find that it consists mainly or wholly of a series of unqualified, positive statements. "There are so many

kinds of mammals." "Organ A is composed of three tissues." "Respiration takes place in the following steps." "The genes are the units of heredity." "The function of A is X."

This kind of exposition (the statement of conclusions) has long been the standard rhetoric of textbooks even at the college level. It has many advantages, not the least of which are simplicity and economy of space. Nevertheless, there are serious objections to it. Both by omission and commission, it gives a false and misleading picture of the nature of science.

By commission, a rhetoric of conclusions has two unfortunate effects on the student. First, it gives the impression that science consists of unalterable, fixed truths. Yet, this is not the case. The accelerated pace of knowledge in recent years has made it abundantly clear that scientific knowledge is revisionary. It is a temporary codex, continuously restructured as new data are related to old.

A rhetoric of conclusions also tends to convey the impression that science is complete. Hence, the fact that scientific investigation still goes on, and at an ever-accelerated pace, is left unaccounted for to the student.

The sin of omission by a rhetoric of conclusions can be stated thus: It fails to show that scientific knowledge is more than a simple report of things observed, that it is a body of knowledge forged slowly and tentatively from raw materials. It does not show that these raw materials, data, spring from planned observations and experiments. It does not show that the plans for experiments and observations arise from problems posed, and that these problems, in turn, arise from concepts which summarize our earlier knowledge. Finally, of great importance, is the face that a rhetoric of conclusions fails to show that scientists, like other men, are capable of error, and that much of inquiry has been concerned with the correction of error.

Above all, a rhetoric of conclusions fails to show that our summarizing concepts are tested by the fruitfulness of the questions that they suggest, and through this testing are continually revised and replaced.

The essence, then, of a teaching of science as inquiry, would be to show some of the conclusions of science in the framework of the way they arise and are tested. This would mean to tell the student about the ideas posed, and the experiments performed, to indicate the data thus found, and to follow the interpretation by which these data were converted into scientific knowledge. (Schwab, 1965, pp. 39–40)

The BSCS uses several techniques to teach science as inquiry. First, it uses many statements that express the tentative nature of science, such as, "We do not know." "We have been unable to discover how this happens." and "The evidence about this is contradictory." (Schwab, 1965, p. 40). Current theories, it is pointed out, may be replaced by others as time goes by. Second, in place of a rhetoric of conclusions, BSCS uses what is called a "narrative of inquiry" in which the history of major ideas in biology is described and the course of inquiry in that area is followed. Third, the laboratory work is arranged to induce students to investigate problems, rather than just to illustrate the text. As they put it, "They (scientists) treat problems for which the text does not provide answers. They create situations in which the students can participate in the inquiry" (Schwab 1965, p. 40). Fourth, the laboratory programs have been designed in blocks that involve the student in an investigation of a real biological problem. At first students may be presented with materials already familiar to scientists and problems whose solutions are already disclosed, but "as the series of problems progresses, they come nearer and nearer to the frontier of knowledge" (Schwab, 1965, p. 41). Thus, the student simulates the activity of the research scientist. Finally, there is the use of what are called "Invitations to Enquiry." Like the functioning of the laboratory, the Invitations to Enquiry involve the student in activities that enable him or her to follow and participate in the reasoning related to a frontline item of investigation or to a methodological problem in biology.

In this chapter we present the Invitations to Enquiry as the model of teaching drawn from the BSCS materials.

INVITATIONS TO ENQUIRY

Credited to Schwab, this strategy was designed:

> To show students how knowledge arises from the interpretation of data . . . to show students that the interpretation of data—indeed, even the search for data—proceeds on the basis of concepts and assumptions that change as our knowledge grows . . . to show students that as these principles and concepts change, knowledge changes too . . . to show students that though knowledge changes, it changes for a good reason—because we know better and more than we knew before. The converse of this point also needs stress: The possibility that present knowledge may be revised in the future does *not* mean that present knowledge is false. Present knowledge is science based on the best-tested facts and concepts we presently possess. It is the most reliable, rational knowledge of which man is capable. (Schwab, 1965, p. 46)

Each Invitation to Enquiry (or lesson) is a case study illustrating either a major concept or method of the discipline. Each invitation "poses example after example of the process itself. Second, *it engaged the participation of the student in the process*" (Schwab, 1965, p. 47).

In each case a real-life scientific study is described. However, omissions, blanks, or curiosities are left uninvestigated, which the student is invited to fill. "This omission may be the plan of an experiment, or a way to control one factor in an experiment. It may be the conclusion to be drawn from given data. It may be an hypothesis to account for data given" (Schwab, 1965, p. 46). In other words, the format of the invitation ensures that the student sees biological inquiry in action and is involved in it, because he or she has to perform the missing experiment or draw the omitted conclusion.

The sets of invitations are sequenced in terms of difficulty to gradually lead the students to more sophisticated concepts. We can see this sequencing in the first group of Invitations to Enquiry, which focus on topics related to methodology—the role and nature of general knowledge, data, experiment, control, hypothesis, and problems in scientific investigation. The subjects and topics of the invitations in Group 1 appear in Table 6–4.

TABLE 6–4 INVITATIONS TO ENQUIRY, GROUP 1, SIMPLE ENQUIRY:
THE ROLE AND NATURE OF GENERAL KNOWLEDGE, DATA,
EXPERIMENT, CONTROL, HYPOTHESIS, AND PROBLEMS IN
SCIENTIFIC INVESTIGATION

Invitation	Subject	Topic
1	The cell nucleus	Interpretation of simple data
2	The cell nucleus	Interpretation of variable data
3	Seed germination	Misinterpretation of data
4	Plant physiology	Interpretation of complex data
Interim Summary 1, Knowledge and Data		
5	Measurement in general	Systematic and random error
6	Plant nutrition	Planning of experiment
7	Plant nutrition	Control of experiment
8	Predator-prey; natural populations	"Second-best" data
9	Population growth	The problem of sampling
10	Environment and disease	The idea of hypothesis
11	Light and plant growth	Construction of hypotheses
12	Vitamin deficiency	"If . . . , then . . . ." analysis
13	Natural selection	Practice in hypothesis
Interim Summary 2, The Role of Hypothesis		
14	Auxins and plant movement	Hypothesis; interpretation of abnormality
15	Neurohormones of the heart	Origin of scientific problems
16	Discovery of penicillin	Accident in inquiry
16A	Discovery of anaphylaxis	Accident in inquiry

SOURCE: Joseph J. Schwab, supervisor, BSCS, *Biology Teachers' Handbook* (New York: John Wiley & Sons, Inc., 1965), p. 52. By permission of the Biological Sciences Curriculum Study.

Invitation 3 in Group 1, an example of this model, leads students to deal with the problem of misinterpretation of data.

INVITATION 3

(Subject: Seed Germination)

(Topic: Misinterpretation of Data)

(It is one thing to take a calculated risk in interpreting data. It is another thing to propose an interpretation for which there is no evidence—whether based on misreading of the available data or indifference to evidence. The material in this Invitation is intended to illustrate one of the most obvious misinterpretations. It also introduces the role of a clearly formulated *problem* in controlling interpretation of the data from experiments to which the problem leads.)

To the student: (a) An investigator was interested in the conditions under which seeds would best germinate. He placed several grains of corn on moist blotting paper in each of two glass dishes. He then placed one of these dishes in a room from which light was excluded. The other was placed in a well-lighted room. Both rooms were kept at the same temperature. After four days the investigator examined the grains. He found that all the seeds in both dishes had germinated.

What interpretation would you make of the data from this experiment? Do not include facts that you may have obtained elsewhere, but restrict your interpretation to those from *this experiment alone*.

(Of course the experiment is designed to test the light factor. The Invitation is intended, however, to give the inadequately logical students a chance to say that the experiment suggests that moisture is necessary for the sprouting of grains. Others may say it shows that a warm temperature is necessary. If such suggestions do not arise, introduce one as a possibility. Do so with an attitude that will encourage the expression of unwarranted interpretation, if such exists among the students.)

(If such an interpretation is forthcoming, you can suggest its weakness by asking the students if the data suggest that corn grains require a glass dish in order to germinate. Probably none of your students will accept this. You should have little difficulty in showing them that the data some of them thought were evidence for the necessity of moisture or warmth are no different from the data available about glass dishes. In neither case are the data evidence for such a conclusion.)

To the student: (b) What factor was clearly *different* in the surroundings of the two dishes? In view of your answer, remembering that this was a deliberately planned experiment, state as precisely as you can the specific problem that led to this particular plan of experiment.

(If it has not come out long before this, it should be apparent now that the experiment was designed to test the necessity of light as a factor in germination. As to the statement of the problem, the Invitation began with a very general question: "Under what conditions do seeds germinate best?" This is not the most useful way to state a problem for scientific inquiry, because it does not indicate where and how to look for an answer. Only when the "question" is made specific enough to suggest what data are needed to answer it does it become an immediately useful scientific problem. For example, "Will seeds germinate better with or without light?" is a question pointing clearly to what data are required. A comparison of germination in the light with germination in the dark is needed. So we can say that a general "wonderment" is converted into an immediately useful problem when the question is made sufficiently specific to suggest an experiment to be performed or specific data to be sought. We do not mean to suggest that general "wonderments" are bad. On the contrary, they are indispensable. The point is only that they must lead to something else—a solvable problem.)

To the student: (c) In view of the problem you have stated, look at the data again. What interpretation are we led to?

(It should now be clear that the evidence indicates that light is *not* necessary for the germination of *some* seeds. You may wish to point out that light is necessary for some other seeds [for example, Grand Rapids Lettuce] and may inhibit the germination of others [for example, some varieties of onion].)

(N.B.: This Invitation continues to deal with the ideas of data, evidence, and interpretation. It also touches on the new point dealt with under paragraph (b), the idea of a *problem*. It exemplifies the fact that general curiosity must be converted into a specific problem.)

(It also indicates that the problem posed in an inquiry has more than one function. First, it leads to the design of the experiment. It converts a wonder into a plan of attack. It also guides us in interpreting data. This is indicated in (c) where it is so much easier to make a sound interpretation than it is in (a), where we are proceeding without a clear idea of what problem led to the particular body of data being dealt with.)

(If your students have found this Invitation easy or especially stimulating, you may wish to carry the discussion further and anticipate to some extent the topic of Invitation 6 [planning an experiment]. The following additions are designed for such use.) (Schwab, 1965, pp. 57–58)

The format of this investigation is fairly typical. The students are introduced to the problem the biologist is attacking, and they are given some information about the investigations that have been carried on. The students are then led to interpret the data and to deal with the problems of warranted and unwarranted interpretations. Next, the students are led to try to design experiments that would test the factor with less likelihood of data misinterpretation. This syntax—to pose a problem about a certain kind of investigation, and then to induce students to attempt to generate ways of inquiring that will eliminate the particular difficulty in the area— is used throughout the program.

Let's look at another Invitation to Enquiry—this time, with a more concept-oriented topic. The following illustration is from the Invitation to Enquiry group dealing with the concept of *function*. The topic has been structured so that it is approached as a methodological problem. How can we infer the function of a given part from its observable characteristics (what is the evidence of function)? In this model the question is not posed directly. Rather the student is guided through an area of investigation, which in this invitation has been framed to embed the methodological concern and the spirit of inquiry. Questions are then posed so that the student himself or herself identifies the difficulty and later speculates on the ways to resolve it.

INVITATION 32
(Subject: Muscle Structure and Function)
(Topic: Six Evidences of Function)

(We concluded Interim Summary 3 by pointing out that the concept of causal lines has no place for the organism as a whole. Instead, the concept treats the organism simply as a collection of such causal lines, not as an organization of them. Each causal line, taken separately, is the object of investigation. The web formed by these lines is not investigated. The conception of function is one of the principles of inquiry which brings the web, the whole organism, back into the picture.)

(This Invitation introduces the student to the idea of *function*. This concept involves much more than the idea of causal factor. It involves the assumption that a given part (organ, tissue, and so on) encountered in an adult organism is likely to be so well suited to the role it plays in the life of the whole organism that this role can be inferred with some confidence from observable characteristics of the part (its structure, action, and so on). As we shall indicate later, this assumption, like others in scientific research is a *working* assumption only. We do not assume that organs are invariably perfectly adapted to their functions. We do assume that most or many of the organs in a living organism are so well adapted (because of the process of evolution) that we proceed farther in studying an organ by assuming that it is adapted to its function than by assuming that it is not.)

To the student: (a) Which of the various muscle masses of the human body would you say is the strongest?

(Students are most likely to suggest the thigh muscles, or the biceps, on the grounds that they are the largest single muscle in the body. If not, suggest the thigh muscle yourself, and defend your suggestion on grounds of size.)

To the student: (b) We decided that the thigh muscle was probably the strongest of our body muscles, using *size* as our reason for choosing it. Hence size seems to be the datum on which we base this decision. But why size, rather than color or shape? Behind our choice of size as the proper criterion, are there not data of another sort, from common experience, that suggest to us that larger muscles are likely to be stronger muscles?

(In considering this question students should be shown that their recognition and acceptance of this criterion of muscle strength is derived from associations from common experience. A drop-kick sends a football farther than a forward pass, a weight lifter has bulkier musculature than a pianist, and so on.)

To the student: (c) Now a new point using no information beyond common experience. What can you say happens to a *muscle* when it contracts?

(The question here is *not* what a muscle does to other parts of the body, but what the muscle itself does—its change of shape in a certain way—becoming shortened, thicker, firmer by contraction. Have the students feel their arm muscles as they lift or grasp.

To the student: (d) To the fact that the motion of muscle is as you have found it to be, add two further facts: Many muscles are attached to some other parts of the body, and many such muscles are spindle-shaped, long, narrow, and tapering. From these data alone, what do you think muscles do?

(The motion, attachment, and shape taken together suggest that muscles in general move one or all of the other parts of the body to which they may be attached. Such inferences about function are only probable. But so are practically all inferences in science. In (e) and later queries, we shall make a point of the doubtful character of functional inference.) (Schwab, 1965, pp. 174–76)

The example continues in this vein.

THE MODEL OF TEACHING

The essence of the model is to involve students in a genuine problem of inquiry by confronting them with an area of investigation, helping them identify a conceptual or methodological problem within that area of investigation, and inviting them to design ways of overcoming that problem. Thus, they see knowledge in the making and are initiated into the community of scholars. At the same time, they gain a healthy respect for knowledge and will probably learn both the limitations of current knowledge and its dependability.

SYNTAX

The syntax takes a number of forms. Essentially it contains the following elements or phases, although they may occur in a number of sequences (also see Table 6–5): In phase one, an area of investigation is posed to the student, including the methodologies used in the investigation. In phase two, the problem is structured so that the student identifies a difficulty in the investigation. The difficulty may be one of data interpretation, data

TABLE 6–5   SYNTAX OF BIOLOGICAL SCIENCE INQUIRY MODEL

Phase One	Phase Two
Area of investigation is posed to student.	Students structure the problem.

Phase Three	Phase Four
Students identify the problem in the investigation.	Students speculate on ways to clear up the difficulty.

generation, the control of experiments, or making inferences. In phase three, the student is asked to speculate about the problem, so that he or she can identify the difficulty involved in the inquiry. In phase four, the student is then asked to speculate on ways of clearing up the difficulty, either by redesigning the experiment, organizing data in different ways, generating data, developing constructs, and so on.

SOCIAL SYSTEM

A cooperative, rigorous climate is desired. Because the student is to be welcomed into a community of seekers who use the best techniques of science, the climate includes a certain degree of boldness as well as humility. The students need to hypothesize rigorously, challenge evidence, criticize research designs, and so on. In addition to the necessity for rigor, students must also recognize the tentative and emergent nature of their own knowledge as well as that of the discipline, and in doing so develop a certain humility with respect to their approach to the well-developed scientific disciplines.

PRINCIPLES OF REACTION

The teacher's task is to nurture the inquiry by emphasizing the process of inquiry and inducing the students to reflect on it. The teacher needs to be careful that the identification of facts does not become the central issue and should encourage a good level of rigor in the inquiry. He or she should aim to turn the students toward the generation of hypotheses, the interpretation of data, and the development of constructs, which are seen as emergent ways of interpreting reality.

SUPPORT SYSTEM

A flexible instructor skilled in the process of inquiry, a plentiful supply of "real" areas of investigation and their ensuing problems, and the necessary data sources from which to conduct inquiry into these areas provide the necessary support system for this model.

APPLICATION

A number of models for teaching the disciplines as processes of inquiry exist, all built around the concepts and methods of the particular disciplines.

The Michigan Social Science Curriculum Project, directed by Ronald Lippitt and Robert Fox, is based on an approach that is potentially very powerful but is startling in its simplicity. The strategy is to teach the research techniques of social psychology directly to children using human relations content, including their own behavior. The result presents social psychology as a living discipline whose concepts and method emerge through continuous application to inquiry into human behavior. Another result is a direct demonstration of the relevance of social science to human affairs. This curriculum illustrates how elementary school children can use scientific procedures to examine social behavior.

Both the conception of social psychology held by these curriculum makers and their teaching strategy, which is essentially to lead the children to practice social psychology, are probably best illustrated by looking at their materials and the activities they recommend. They have prepared seven "laboratory units" developed around a resource book or text and a series of project books. The seven units begin with an exploration of the nature of social science, "Learning to Use Social Science," and proceed to a series of units in which the students apply social science procedures and concepts to human behavior: "Discovering Differences," "Friendly and Unfriendly Behavior," "Being and Becoming," "Influencing Each Other."

The first unit is structured to introduce students to social science methods such as:

1. "What is a behavior specimen?" (How do we obtain samples of behavior?)
2. "Three ways to use observation" (Introduces the children to description, inference, and value judgment, and the differences among them.)
3. "Cause and Effect" (Introduces the inference of cause, first in relation to physical phenomena, then in relation to human behavior.)
4. "Multiple Causation" (Teaches how to deal with several factors simultaneously. For example, the children read and analyze a story in which a central character has several motivations for the same action.) (Lippitt, Fox, and Schaible, 1969, pp. 24–25)

The children compare their analyses of the samples so that they check observations and inferences against one another and come to realize problems of obtaining agreement about observations. They also learn how to analyze interaction through the technique of circular analysis.

Finally, a series of activities introduces the children to experiments by social psychologists that have generated interesting theories about friendly and unfriendly behavior and cooperation and competition.

This approach focuses the children's study on human interaction, provides an academic frame of reference and techniques for delineating and carrying out inquiry, and involves the student in the observation of his or her own behavior and that of those around him. The overall intention is that he or she will take on some of the characteristics of the social scientist. Thus, the instructional values are in the interpersonal as well as the academic domain.

This model has wide applicability, but unfortunately it is dependent on inquiry-oriented materials (areas of investigation), which are rare in most classrooms, since the didactic text is the standard. However, every subject area has at least one text series that is inquiry-oriented or one that is easily adapted to this model. An instructor with a clear understanding of the model will easily discern instructional material that, with a little rearrangement, might provide suitable areas for investigation. Instructors who are quite knowledgeable in their particular disciplines can probably construct their own materials.

INSTRUCTIONAL AND NURTURANT EFFECTS

The biological science inquiry model (Figure 6–2) is designed to teach the processes of research biology, to affect the ways that students process information, and to nurture a commitment to scientific inquiry. It probably also nurtures open-mindedness and an ability to suspend judgment and balance alternatives. Through its emphasis on the community of scholars, it also nurtures a spirit of cooperation and an ability to work with others.

Scientific-inquiry models have been developed for use with students of all ages, from preschool through college. The core purpose is to teach the essential process of science and, concurrently, major concepts from the disciplines along with the information from which these have been developed.

Research on these models has usually focused on entire curriculums

FIGURE 6–2   Instructional and nurturant effects: biological science inquiry model.

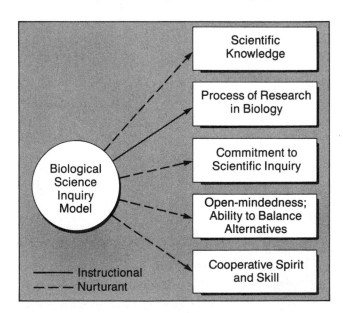

that have been implemented for one or more years, using the models consistently with appropriate materials of instruction. Two types of findings are of particular interest to us. The first is that teachers who would use them need to engage in intensive study both of the academic substance and of these models of teaching. Otherwise, they tend to withdraw from inquiry-based instruction. The second is that where these models have been well implemented with adequate attention to the teachers' study of academic content and teaching process, the results have been impressive (Bredderman, 1981; El Nemr, 1979). The students have learned the scientific process, have mastered the major concepts of the disciplines, have acquired basic information about science, and developed positive views toward science.

S U M M A R Y ► **BIOLOGICAL SCIENCE INQUIRY**
C H A R T   **MODEL**

Syntax

Phase One: Pose Area of Investigation to Students
Phase Two: Students Structure the Problem
Phase Three: Students Identify the Problem in the Investigation
Phase Four: Students Speculate on Ways to Clear Up the Difficulty

Social System

The model has moderate structure and a cooperative, rigorously intellectual climate.

Principles of Reaction

Teacher nourishes inquiry, turning students toward inquiry process rather than identification efforts.

Support System

The model requires a flexible instructor skilled in the process of inquiry and a supply of problem areas of investigation.

THE FUTURE OF INDUCTIVE MODELS
OF TEACHING

A number of lines of inquiry are currently in progress that will probably advance thinking about how students can learn to build categories, make inferences, and develop more effective causal reasoning and synthesizing skills. Papert and others are experimenting with a number of nascent strategies. Theories about "multiple intelligence" may give rise to more alternative ways of thinking about thinking.

Computers are making large databases available to students that will enable much more complex types of concept formation easier to research and will permit the development of more intricate and, probably, more powerful support systems.

Research on how to help students organize data, build categories, generate hypotheses and understand how science works has provided us with a rich array of tools. Using these tools we can help students accelerate and sophisticate their learning substantially.

CHAPTER 7

ATTAINING CONCEPTS
The Basic Skills of Thinking

We happen on a classroom in Hong Kong. Dr. Ora Kwo is teaching a lesson on English to her students. She has a chart in the front of the room. We will follow her as she leads her students through an exercise that employs it. The headings on the chart are:

Positive Exemplars   Negative Exemplars

She puts the following two words under the headings on the chart:

   clean   help

"Take a look at these two words. How are they alike and how are they different? *Clean* has the attributes of our category. *Help* does not." She places cards containing two more words on the chart.

   clear   trim

"Now examine this pair. *Clear* has the attributes we are concerned with. *Help* does not. What do *clear* and *clean* have in common that *help* and *trim* do not?"

She asks the students to work singly during this phase of the exercise. She presents two more words and asks the students to compare and contrast them, trying to discover what the positive exemplars have in common that they do not share with the negative exemplars.

   clip   hip

"Now, what do you see? Please write down your hypothesis at this point. What do you think are the attributes that the 'positive' words have in common that they do not share with the words I have identified as 'negative.'" After a few seconds, she proceeds to the next pair of words.

clap   lap

"Did any of you have to change your ideas." She looks around the room and finds that several did. Then, in the same fashion, she presented several other pairs of words:

cling   ring
climb   limb
club   tree

Ora continued until she had presented a dozen more pairs. Then she presented a word and asked the students whether they believed, on the basis of their hypothesis, that it was positive or negative.

lip

Of the students, 30 correctly identified the word as a negative exemplar. Six did not. She inferred that the 30 were concentrating on the "cl" while the others were still not sure whether having either a "c" or an "l" would qualify it. Therefore, she presented to them the following series:

clue   flue
clarify   rarify
clack   lack

Then, she asked the question again. "What do you think of this one?"

crack

All the students identified the word as negative. Thus, she presented the next one.

clank

They all identified it as positive. She proceeded to present them with a half-dozen positive and negative exemplars and, when they could identify them correctly, asked them to share their current hypotheses. ("The positives begin with 'cl' and sound like [imagine the sound].") She had them identify what was *not* critical (meanings, endings, etc.) and then asked them how they would make negatives positive (Transforming "an" to "clan" and so forth until she was satisfied that the idea was clear).

Ora then sent them to scour a couple of stories, looking for positive exemplars, and gave them a list of words to classify on the basis of the attributes of the category.

We have, of course, looked in on a phonics lesson for students for whom English is a second language. The lesson is designed with the concept attainment model of teaching and teaches concepts useful in both writing and spelling.

S C E N A R I O   **II**

Mrs. Stern's eighth-grade class in Houston, Texas, has been studying the characteristics of the 14 largest cities in the United States. They have collected data on size, ethnicity of population, types of industry, location, and proximity to natural resources.

Working in committees, the students have collected information and summarized it on a series of charts now pasted up around the room. One Wednesday in November, Mrs. Stern says, "Today let's try a series of exercises designed to help us understand these cities better. I have identified a number of concepts that help us compare and contrast them. I am going to label our charts either *yes* or *no*. If you look at the information we have and think about the populations and the other characteristics, you will identify the ideas that I have in mind. I'm going to start with the city that's a *yes* and then one that's a *no*, and so forth. Think about what the yeses have in common. Then write down after the second yes the idea that you think connects those two places, and keep testing those ideas as we go along." "Let's begin with our own city," she says. "Houston is a yes."

The students look at the information about Houston, its size, industries, location, ethnic composition. Then she points to Baltimore, Maryland.

"Baltimore is a no," she says. Then she points to San Jose, California. "Here is another yes," she comments.

The students look for a moment at the information about San Jose. Two or three raise their hands.

"I think I know what it is," one offers.

"Hold on to your idea," she replies. "See if you're right." She then selects another yes—Seattle, Washington; Detroit, Michigan, is a no. Miami, Florida, is a yes. She continues until all students think they know what the concept is, and then they begin to share concepts.

"What do you think it is, Jill?"

"The yeses all have mild climates," says Jill. "That is, it doesn't get very cold in any of them."

"It gets pretty cold in Salt Lake City," objects another.

"Yes, but not as cold as in Chicago, Detroit, or Baltimore," another student counters.

"I think the yeses are all rapidly growing cities. Each one of them increased more than 10 percent during the last 10 years." There is some discussion about this.

"All the yeses have lots of different industries," volunteers another.

"That's true, but almost all of these cities do," replies another student.

Finally the students decide the yeses are all cities that are growing very fast and have relatively mild climates.

"That's right," agrees Mrs. Stern. "That's exactly what I had in mind. Now let's do this again. This time I want to begin with Baltimore, Maryland, and now it is a yes."

The exercise is repeated several times. Students learn that Mrs. Stern has grouped the cities on the basis of their relationship to waterways, natural resources, ethnic composition, and several other dimensions.

The students are beginning to see patterns in their data. Finally she says, "Now, each of you try to group the cities in a way that you think is important. Then take turns and lead us through this exercise, helping us to see which ones you place in which category. Then we'll discuss the ways we can look at cities and how we can use different categories for different purposes. Finally, we'll use the inductive model and you can see how many relationships you can find."

In this scenario Mrs. Stern is teaching her students how to think about cities. At the same time she is teaching them about the process of *categorizing*. This is their introduction to the model of teaching we call *concept attainment*.

CATEGORIZING, CONCEPT FORMATION, AND CONCEPT ATTAINMENT

Concept attainment is "the search for and listing of attributes that can be used to distinguish exemplars from nonexemplars of various categories" (Bruner, Goodnow, and Austin, 1967, p. 233). Whereas *Concept formation*, which is the basis of the inductive model described in the previous chapter, requires the students to decide the basis on which they will build categories, concept attainment requires a student to figure out the attributes of a category that is already formed in another person's mind by comparing and contrasting examples (called exemplars) that contain the characteristics (called attributes) of the concept with examples that do not contain those attributes. To create such lessons we need to have our category clearly in mind. As an example let us consider the concept *adjective*. Adjectives are words, so we select some words that are adjectives (these become the positive exemplars) and some that are not (these become "negative" exemplars—the ones that do not have the attributes of the category *adjective*). We present the words to the students in pairs. Consider the following four pairs:

triumphant	triumph
large	chair
broken	laugh
painful	pain

It is probably best to present the words in sentences to provide more information, because adjectives function in the context of a sentence. For example:

YES: Our triumphant team returned home after winning the state championship.

NO: After his triumph, Senator Jones gave a gracious speech.

YES: The broken arm healed slowly

NO: His laugh filled the room.

YES: The large truck backed slowly into the barn.

NO: He sank gratefully into the chair.

YES: The painful separation had to be endured.

NO: He felt a sharp pain in his ankle.

To carry on the model, we need about 20 pairs in all—we would need more if the concept were more complex than our current example, *adjectives*.

We begin the process by asking the students to scrutinize the sentences and to pay particular attention to the underlined words. Then we instruct them to compare and contrast the functions of the positive and negative exemplars. "The positive exemplars have something in common in the work they do in the sentence. The negative exemplars do different work."

We ask the students to make notes about what they believe the exemplars have in common. Then we present more sets of exemplars and ask them whether they still have the same idea. If not, we ask what they now think. We continue to present exemplars until most of the students have an idea they think will withstand scrutiny. At that point we ask one of the students to share his or her idea and how he or she arrived at it. One possible response is as follows: "Well, at first I thought that the positive words were longer. Then some of the negatives were longer, so I gave that up. Now I think that the positive ones always come next to some other word and do something to it. I'm not sure just what."

Then other students share their ideas. We provide some more examples. Gradually the students agree that each positive exemplar adds something to the meaning of a word that stands for an object or a person, or qualifies it in some way.

We continue by providing some more sentences and by asking the students to identify the words that belong to our concept. When they can do that, we provide them with the name of the concept (*adjective*) and ask them to agree on a definition.

The final activity is to ask the students to describe their thinking as they arrived at the concepts and to share how they used the information that was given.

For homework we ask the students to find adjectives in a short story we assign them to read. We will examine the exemplars they come up with to be sure that they have a clear picture of the concept.

This process ensures that the students learn the attributes that define a concept (the defining attributes) and can distinguish those from other important attributes that do not form the definition. All the words, for example, are composed of letters. But the presence of letters does not define the parts of speech. Letters are important characteristics of all items in the data set, but are not critical in defining the category we call "adjective." The students learn that it is the function of the word that is the essence of the concept, not what it denotes. *Pain* and *painful* both refer to trauma, but only one is an adjective.

As we teach the students with this method, we help them become more efficient in attaining concepts. They learn the rules of the model.

Let us look at another example, this time language study for beginning readers.

TEACHER: (Presents 6-year-old students with the following list of words labeled *yes* or *no*.)

fat	Yes
fate	No
mat	Yes
mate	No
rat	Yes
rate	No

I have a list of words here. Notice that some have "yes" by them and some have "no" by them. (Children observe and comment on the format. Teacher puts the list aside for a moment.) Now, I have an idea in my head, and I want you to try to guess what I'm thinking of. Remember the list I showed you. (Picks up the list.) This will help you guess my idea because each of these is a clue. The clues work this way. If a word has a *yes* by it (points to first word), then it is an example of what I'm thinking. If it has a *no* by it, then it is not an example.

(The teacher continues to work with the students so that they understand the procedures of the lesson and then turns over the task of working out the concept to them.)

TEACHER: Can you come up with the name of my idea? Do you know what my idea is? (The students decide what they think the teacher's idea is. She continues the lesson.)

TEACHER: Let's see if your idea is correct by testing it. I'll give you some examples, and you tell me if they are a *yes* or a *no*, based on your idea. (She gives them more examples. This time the students supply the *nos* and *yeses*.)

kite   (No)
cat   (Yes)
hat   (Yes)

Well you seem to have it. Now think up some words you believe are *yeses*. The rest of us will tell you whether your example is right. You tell us if we guessed correctly. (The exercise ends with the students generating their own examples and telling how they arrived at the concept.)

In this lesson if the children simply identified the concept as the *at* vowel-consonant blend and correctly recognized *cat* and *hat* as a yes, they had attained the concept on a simple level. If they verbalized the distinguishing features (essential attributes) of the *at* sound, they attained the concept on a harder level. Bruner outlines these different levels of attainment: Correctly distinguishing examples from nonexamples is easier than verbalizing the attributes of the concept. Students will probably be able to distinguish examples correctly before they will be able to explain verbally either the concept name or its essential characteristics.

Concept teaching provides a chance to analyze the students' thinking processes and to help them develop more effective strategies. The approach can involve various degrees of student participation and student control, and material of varying complexity.

RATIONALE

We have used terms such as *exemplar* and *attribute* to describe categorizing activity and concept attainment. Derived from Bruner's study of concepts and how people attain them, each term has a special meaning and function in all forms of conceptual learning, especially concept attainment.

EXAMPLARS

Essentially the examplars are a subset of a collection of data or a data set. The category is the subset or collection of samples that share one or more characteristics that are missing in the others. It is by comparing the positive examplars and contrasting them with the negative ones that the concept or category is learned.

ATTRIBUTES

All items of data have features, and we refer to these as *attributes*. Nations, for example, have areas with agreed on boundaries, people, and governments that can deal with other nations. Cities have boundaries, people, and governments also, but they cannot independently deal with other countries. Distinguishing nations from cities depends on locating the attribute of international relations.

Essential attributes are those that are critical to the domain under consideration. Exemplars of a category have many other attributes that may not be relevant to the category itself. For example, nations have trees and flowers also, but these are not relevant to the definition of nation; although they, too, represent important domains and can also be categorized and subcategorized. However, with respect to the category "nation," trees and flowers are not essential.

Another important definition is that of *attribute value*. This refers to the degree to which an attribute is present in any particular example. For example, everyone has some rationality and irrationality mixed together. The question is when is there enough rationality that we can categorize someone as "rational" or enough irrationality that "irrational" is appropriate. For some types of concepts—triangle, for example—attribute values are not a consideration. For others, they are. When creating a data set for instruction, it is wise to begin with exemplars where the value of the attribute is high, dealing with the more ambiguous ones after the concept has been well established. Thus, when classifying nations according to wealth, beginning with the very rich and the very poor makes it easier for the students. Thus, as we categorize things, we have to deal with the fact that some attributes are present to various degrees. We have to decide whether any amount of presence of an attribute is sufficient to place something in a particular category and what the range of density is that qualifies something to belong to a category. For example, consider the category *poisonous*. We put chlorine in water precisely because chlorine is poison. Yet, we judge the amount that will kill certain bacteria and still not harm us. So tap water in a city is not an exemplar of poisonous water because it does not contain enough poison to harm us. But, if we added enough chlorine, it would affect us. In this case, if the value of the attribute is low enough, its presence does not give the water membership in the category *poisonous to humans*.

Now consider the category *short person*. How short is short enough to be so categorized? People generally agree on a relative value, just as they do for *tall*. When is something cold? Hot? When is a person friendly? Hostile? These are all useful concepts, yet the categorization issue turns on matters of degree, or what we call *attribute value*.

In other cases, value is not a consideration. To be a telephone an instrument simply must have certain characteristics. Yet, there are degrees or quality. A question such as, "When is a sound machine a high-fidelity instrument?" puts us back into the consideration of attribute values.

Once a category is established, it is named so that we can refer to it symbolically. As the students name the categories, they should do so in terms of attributes. Thus, in the scenario at the very beginning of the chapter, they will describe the category as words beginning with "cl" and sounding like (imagine the sound of cl at the beginning of a word). Then, if there is a technical term (*adjective* in one of the other examples above), we supply it. However, the concept attainment process is not one of guessing names. It is to get the attributes of a category clear. Then the name can be created or supplied. Thus, the name is merely the term given to a category. *Fruit, dog, government, ghetto* are all names given to a class of experiences, objects, configurations, or processes. Although the items commonly grouped together in a single category may differ from one another in certain respects (dogs, for example, vary greatly), the common features cause them to be referred to by the same general term. Often we teach ideas that students already know intuitively without knowing the name itself. For instance, young children often put pictures of fruit together for the reason that they are "all things you can eat." They are using one characteristic to describe the concept instead of the name or label. If students know a concept, however, they can easily learn the name for it, and their verbal expressions will be more articulate. Part of knowing a concept is recognizing positive instances of it and also distinguishing closely related but negative examples. Just knowing terms will not suffice for this. Many people know the terms *metaphor* and *simile* but have never clarified the attributes of each well enough to tell them apart or apply them. One can not knowingly employ metaphoric language without a clear understanding of its attributes.

Multiple attributes are another consideration. Concepts range from cases in which the mere presence of a single attribute is sufficient for membership in a category to those in which the presence of several attributes is necessary. Membership in the category *red-haired boys* requires the presence of maleness and red hair. *Intelligent, gregarious, athletic red-haired boys* is a concept that requires the presence of several attributes simultaneously. In literature, social studies, and science we deal with numerous concepts that are defined by the presence of multiple attributes, and sometimes attribute value is a consideration also. Consider the theatrical concept *romantic comedy*. A positive example must be a play or film, must have enough humorous values to qualify as a comedy, and must be romantic as well. Negative exemplars include plays that are neither funny nor romantic, are funny but not romantic, and are romantic but not funny.

To teach a concept, we have to be very clear about its defining attributes and about whether attribute values are a consideration. We must also select our negative exemplars so that items with some but not all the attributes can be ruled out.

We call concepts defined by the presence of one or more attributes *conjunctive* concepts. The exemplars are joined by the presence of one or more characteristics. Two other kinds of concepts need to be considered. *Disjunctive* concepts are defined by the presence of some attributes and the absence of others. Inert gases, for example, have the properties of all other gases but are missing the property of being able to combine with other elements. Bachelors, for example, have the characteristics of other men and women, but are identified by an absence of something—a spouse.

Lonely people are defined by an absence of companionship. Prime numbers are defined by the absence of a factor other than the one and the number itself.

Finally, some concepts require connection between the exemplar and some other entity. Parasites, for example, have hosts, and the relationship between the parasite and its host is crucial to its definition. Many concepts of human relationships are of this type. There are no uncles without nephews and nieces, no husbands without wives, and no executives without organizations to lead.

STRATEGIES FOR CONCEPT ATTAINMENT

What goes on in the minds of students when they are comparing and contrasting sets of exemplars? What kinds of hypotheses occur to them in the early stages and how do they modify and test them? To answer these questions, three factors are important to us. First, we can construct the concept attainment exercises so that we can study how our students think. Second, the students can not only describe how they attain concepts but they can learn to be more efficient by altering their strategies and learning to use new ones. Third, by changing the way we present information and by modifying the model slightly, we can affect how students will process information.

The key to understanding the strategies students use to attain concepts is to analyze how they approach the information that is available in the exemplars. In particular, do they concentrate on just certain aspects of the information (partistic strategies), or do they keep all or most of the information in mind (holistic strategies)? To illustrate, suppose we are teaching concepts for analyzing literary style by comparing passages from novels and short stories. The first set of positive exemplars includes the following passage:

> A new country seems to follow a pattern. First come the openers, strong and brave and rather childlike. They can take care of themselves in a wilderness, but they are naive and helpless against men, and perhaps that is why they went out in the first place. When the rough edges are worn off the new land, businessmen and lawyers come in to help with the development—to solve problems of ownership, usually by removing the temptations to themselves. And finally comes culture, which is entertainment, relaxation, transport out of the pain of living. And culture can be on any level, and is. (Steinbeck, *East of Eden*, 1952, p. 249)

The students know that this passage will be grouped with the others to come, on the basis of one or more attributes pertaining to style.

Some students will concentrate on just one kind of attribute, say the use of declarative sentences or the juxtaposition of contrasting ideas about the opening of the frontier. Others will scan the details of the passage, noting the presence or absence of metaphors, the use of evocative language, the author's stance of being an observer of the human scene, and so on.

When comparing this passage with another positive one, a partist, someone who focuses on just one or two aspects of the use of language, will in some sense appear to have an easier task—just looking to see if the attribute present in the first is also present in the second, and so on. However, if the student's focus does not work out, he or she must return to the earlier examples and scan them for something else on which to concentrate. A holist, on the other hand, has to keep many attributes in mind and has to eliminate nondefining elements one at a time. However, the holistic strategy places the learner in a good position to identify multiple attribute concepts and the loss of a single attribute is not as disruptive to the overall strategy.

There are two ways that we can obtain information about the way our students attain concepts. After a concept has been attained, we can ask them to recount their thinking as the exercise proceeded—by describing the ideas they came up with at each step, what attributes they were concentrating on, and what modifications they had to make. ("Tell us what you thought at the beginning, why you thought so, and what changes you had to make.") This can lead to a discussion in which the students can discover one another's strategies and how they worked out.

Older students can write down their hypotheses, giving us (and them) a record we can analyze later. For example, in a study of the classification of plants conducted by Baveja, Showers, and Joyce (1985), students worked in pairs to formulate hypotheses as pairs of exemplars (one positive and one negative) where presented to them. They recorded their hypotheses, changes they made, and the reasons they made them. The students who operated holistically, painstakingly generated multiple hypotheses and gradually eliminated the untenable ones. The students who selected one or two hypotheses in the early stages needed to review the exemplars constantly and revise their ideas in order to arrive at the multiple attribute concept that was the goal. By sharing their strategies and reflecting on them, the students were able to try new ones in subsequent lessons and to observe the effect of the changes.

If we provide students with a large number of labeled exemplars (ones identified as positive and negative) to commence a lesson, they are able to scan the field of data and select a few hypotheses on which to operate. If we provide the exemplars pair by pair, however, the students are drawn toward holistic, multiple-attribute strategies.

Many people, on first encountering the concept attainment model, ask about the function of the negative exemplars. They wonder why we should not simply provide the positive ones. Negative exemplars are very important because they help the students identify the boundaries of the concept. For example, consider the concept *impressionism* in painting. Impressionistic styles have much in common with other painting styles. It is important for students to "see" examples which have no traces of impressionism for them to be absolutely certain about the defining attributes. Likewise, to identify a group of words as a prepositional phrase, we need to be able to tell it from a clause. Only by comparing exemplars that contain and do not contain certain attributes can we identify the characteristics of the attributes precisely, and over time. The concept attainment model is designed to produce long-term learning. Having struggled our way, for example, to precise definitions of *prime number, element, developing nation, irony,* and so on, we should recognize members of their categories positively and surely when we encounter them in the future.

Tennyson and his associates (Tennyson and Cocchiarella, 1986) have conducted important research into concept learning and developed a number of models that can be used to improve instructional design. In the course of their explorations, they have dealt with a number of questions that can help us understand the model that we are presenting in this chapter. They have compared treatments where students induce attributes and definitions much as we have been describing the process with conditions where the definition is discussed before the list of exemplars is presented. In both cases the students developed clearer concepts and retained them longer when the examination of the exemplars *preceded* the discussion of attributes and definitions. Tennyson and Cocchiarella also discovered that the first positive exemplars presented should be the *clearest possible prototypes*, especially with multiple-attribute concepts. In other words, the teacher should not try to "fake out" the students with vague exemplars, but should take care to facilitate concept learning by arranging the data sets so that less clear exemplars are dealt with in the phases where the principles are applied.

Tennyson and his associates also have concluded that students develop procedural knowledge (how to attain concepts) with practice, and also that the more procedural knowledge the students possess, the more effectively they attain and can apply conceptual knowledge. Thus, the analysis of thinking to facilitate learning the metacognitions of concept attainment appears to be very important.

The idea of learning concepts and then clarifying attributes and definitions runs counter to much current teaching practice. We have learned that some teachers, when first using concept attainment, have an urge to provide definitions and lists of attributes, and it is important to remember that the appropriate time for clarification is *after* the students have abstracted the concepts.

Data are presented to the students in the form of sets of items called "exemplars," for example, a set of poems. These are labeled "positive" if they have characteristics or attributes of the concept to be taught (for example, the sonnet form). The exemplars are labeled "negative" if they do not contain the attributes of the concept (for example, poems that do not have all the attributes of "sonnet").

By comparing the positive and negative exemplars, the students develop hypotheses about the nature of the category. They do not, however, share their hypotheses at this point. When most of the students have developed a hypothesis, some unlabeled exemplars are presented to them and they indicate whether they can successfully identify positive exemplars. They may be asked to produce some of their own (as by scanning a set of poems and picking out some positive and negative ones).

Then they are asked to share their hypotheses and describe the progression of their ideas during the process. When they have agreed on the hypotheses that appear most likely, they generate labels for them. Then the teacher supplies the technical label, if there is one (*sonnet*, for example).

To consolidate and apply the concept, the students then search for more items of the class (poems, in this case) and find which ones most closely match the concept they have learned.

TABLE 7–1   **SYNTAX OF THE CONCEPT ATTAINMENT MODEL**

Phase One: Presentation of Data and Identification of Concept	Phase Two: Testing Attainment of the Concept
Teacher presents labeled examples. Students compare attributes in positive and negative examples.	Students identify additional unlabeled examples as yes or no.
Students generate and test hypotheses.	Teacher confirms hypotheses, names concept, and restates definitions according to essential attributes.
Students state a definition according to the essential attributes.	Students generate examples.

Phase Three: Analysis of Thinking Strategies
Students describe thoughts. Students discuss role of hypotheses and attributes. Students discuss type and number of hypotheses.

THE MODEL OF TEACHING

The phases of the concept attainment model are outlined in Table 7–1.

SYNTAX

Phase one involves presenting data to the learner. Each unit of data is a separate example or nonexample of the concept. The units are presented in pairs. The data may be events, people, objects, stories, pictures, or any other descriminable units. The learners are informed that there is one idea that all the positive examples have in common; their task is to develop a hypothesis about the nature of the concept. The instances are presented in a prearranged order and are labeled "yes" or "no." Learners are asked to compare and justify the attributes of the different examples. (The teacher or students may want to maintain a record of the attributes.) Finally, they are asked to name their concepts and state the rules or definitions of the concepts according to their essential attributes. (Their hypotheses are not confirmed until the next phase; students may not know the names of some concepts, but the names can be provided when the concepts are confirmed.)

In phase two, the students test their attainment of the concept, first by correctly identifying additional unlabeled examples of the concept and then by generating their own examples. After this, the teacher (and students) confirm or disconfirm their original hypotheses, revising their choice of concepts or attributes as necessary.

In phase three, students begin to analyze the strategies by which they attain concepts. As we have indicated, some learners initially try broad constructs and gradually narrow the field; others begin with more discrete constructs. The learners can describe their patterns; whether they focused on attributes or concepts, whether they did so one at a time or several at once, and what happened when their hypotheses were not confirmed. Did they change strategies? Gradually, they can compare the effectiveness of different strategies.

SOCIAL SYSTEM

Prior to teaching with the concept attainment model, the teacher chooses the concept, selects and organizes the material into positive and negative examples, and sequences the examples. Most instructional materials, especially textbooks, are not designed in a way that corresponds to the nature of concept learning as described by educational psychologists. In most cases teachers will have to prepare examples, extract ideas and materials from texts and other sources, and design them in such a way that the attributes are clear and that there are, indeed, both positive and negative examples of the concept. When using the concept attainment model, the teacher acts as a recorder, keeping track of the hypotheses (concepts) as they are mentioned and of the attributes. The teacher also supplies additional examples as needed. The three major functions of the teacher during concept-attainment activity are to record, prompt (cue), and present additional data. In the initial stages of concept attainment, it is helpful for the examples to be very structured. However, cooperative learning procedures can also be used successfully (see Part I).

PRINCIPLES OF REACTION

During the flow of the lesson, the teacher needs to be supportive of the students' hypotheses—emphasizing, however, that they are hypothetical in nature—and to create a dialogue in which students test their hypotheses against each others'. In the later phases of the model, the teacher must turn the students' attention toward analysis of their concepts and their thinking strategies, again being very supportive. The teacher should encourage analysis of the merits of various strategies rather than attempt to seek the one best strategy for all people in all situations.

SUPPORT SYSTEM

Concept attainment lessons require that positive and negative exemplars be presented to the students. It should be stressed that the students' job in concept attainment is not to invent new concepts, but to attain the ones that have previously been selected by the teacher. Hence, the data sources need to be known beforehand and the attributes visible. When students are presented with an example, they describe its characteristics (attributes), which can then be recorded.

APPLICATION

The use of the Concept Attainment Model determines the shape of particular learning activities. For instance, if the emphasis is on acquiring a new concept, the teacher will emphasize through his or her questions or comments the attributes in each example (particularly the positive examples) and the concept label. If the emphasis is on the inductive process, the teacher might want to provide fewer clues and reinforce students for participating and persevering. The particular content (concept) may be less important than participating in the inductive process; it may even be a concept the students already know (as it was in Bruner's original experiments). If the emphasis is on the analysis of thinking, a short sample concept attainment exercise might be developed so that more time can be spent on the analysis of thinking.

The concept attainment model may be used with children of all ages and grade levels. We have seen teachers use the model very successfully with kindergarten children, who love the challenge of the inductive activity. For young children the concept and examples must be relatively simple, and the lesson itself must be short and heavily teacher-directed. The typical curriculum for young children is filled with concrete concepts that readily lend themselves to concept attainment methodology. The analysis-of-thinking phase of the strategy (phase three) is not possible with very young children, though most upper elementary students will be responsive to this kind of reflective activity.

When the model is used in early childhood education, the materials for examples are often available and require little transformation for their use as examples. Classroom objects, cuisinaire rods, pictures, and shapes can be found in almost any early childhood classroom. Although helping children work inductively can be an important goal in itself, the teacher should also have more specific goals to obtain by using this model.

As with all models, we encourage teachers to take the essence of this model and incorporate its features into their natural teaching styles and forms. In the case of concept attainment, it is relatively easy (and intellectually powerful) to incorporate Bruner's ideas about the nature of concepts into instructional presentations and assessment activities. We have seen our own students make these ideas a natural part of their concept teaching.

The concept attainment model is an excellent evaluation tool when teachers want to determine whether important ideas introduced earlier have been mastered. It quickly reveals the depth of students' understanding and reinforces their previous knowledge.

The model can also be useful in opening up a new conceptual area by initiating a sequence of individual or group inquiries. For example, a unit exploring the concept of culture could begin with a series of concept attainment lessons followed by a simulation activity, in which students experience the problems that persons of one culture have when they are first introduced to members of a different culture. From this experience, students would be prepared to read about different cultures.

Thus, the concept attainment model can not only introduce extended series of inquiries into important areas, but it can also augment ongoing inductive study. Concept attainment lessons providing important concepts in social studies units—concepts such as *democracy, socialism, capitalism,* and *due process*—can be interjected periodically into units that otherwise depend on student reading and reporting. If a concept is controversial, the teacher can present several interpretations of it, which the student can then debate. Debates are usually great motivators for further inquiry into any subject matter in question.

INSTRUCTIONAL AND NURTURANT
EFFECTS

The concept attainment strategies can accomplish several instructional goals depending on the emphasis of the particular lesson. They are designed for instruction on specific concepts and on the nature of concepts. They also provide practice in inductive reasoning and opportunities for altering and improving students' concept-building strategies. Finally, especially with abstract concepts, the strategies nurture an awareness of alternative perspectives, a sensitivity to logical reasoning in communication, and a tolerance of ambiguity (see Figure 7–1).

Robert Gagne's 1965 article thoroughly discusses a similar approach to concept attainment. Merrill and Tennyson (1977) describe a similar approach without, however, an extensive analysis of the thinking processes. McKinney, Warren, Larkins, Ford, and Davis (1983) have reported a series of interesting studies comparing the Merrill/Tennyson approaches with that of Gagne's and a recitation procedure. Their work illustrates the complexity of designing studies to meaningfully compare sets of models built on the same premises but differing in details of execution. However, the differences in approach and the research to build better models are probably of less importance to teachers than the fact that there are models that do a good job of teaching concepts—ones more powerful than the way concepts have traditionally been taught—and therefore represent useful additions to the teaching/learning repertoire. The model we have been discussing is one of them.

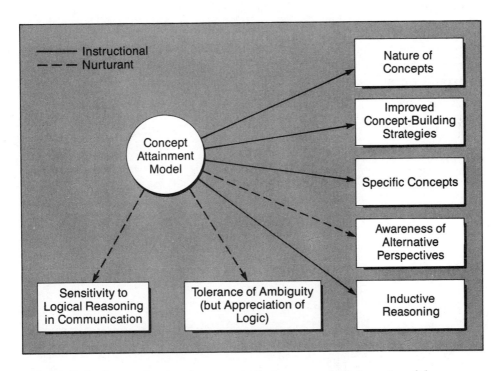

FIGURE 7–1   Instructional and nurturant effects: concept attainment model.

THE CONCEPT ATTAINMENT MODEL

Syntax

The syntax proceeds from presentation of the exemplars to testing and naming concepts to application.

Social System

The model has moderate structure. Teacher controls the sequence, but open dialogue occurs in the latter phases. Student interaction encouraged. Relatively structured with students assuming more initiative for inductive process as they gain more experience with the model (other concept attainment models are lower in structure).

Principles of Reaction

1. Give support but emphasize hypothetical nature of discussion.
2. Help students balance one hypothesis against another.
3. Focus attention on specific features of examples.
4. Assist students in discussing and evaluating their thinking strategies.

Support System

Support consists of carefully selected and organized materials and data in the form of discrete units to serve as examples. As students become more sophisticated, they can share in making data units, just as in phase two they generate examples.

CHAPTER 8

MEMORIZATION
Getting the Facts Straight

Imagine a group of students who are presented with the task of learning the names of the presidents of the United States and the order in which they served. Previously, the students have learned to count from 1 to 40 mnemonically. That is, each number is represented by a rhyming word that has an image attached to it. "One" is "bun," "two" is "shoe," and so on. Also, each set of number decades (1 to 10, 11 to 20) is connected to a location or setting. The decade 1 to 10 is represented by a spring garden scene, 11 to 20 by a summer beach scene, 21 to 30 by a fall football scene, and 31 to 40 by a winter snow scene.

Now, capitalizing on this system of number associations, the name and order of each president is presented to the students in terms of the scene, the mnemonic for the number, and a word, called a *link-word*, associated with the president's name. Thus Lincoln (link), number sixteen (sticks), is presented with an illustration of a sand castle on a beach encircled by a set of sticks which are linked together. Similar illustrations are used for the other presidents. The students study the pictures and the words. They are given a test right after they study and again 60 days later.

How effective was this experience? Did the students learn more than other students who tried to memorize the names and their order using the usual procedures for the same length of time? The answer is "yes." In this and other studies, students are being taught unfamiliar material much more quickly than usual through the application of various mnemonic devices (Pressley, Levin, and Delaney, 1982, p. 83).

S C E N A R I O   II

The Phoenix High School social studies department has developed a set of mnemonics that are combined with inductive activities to teach the students the names and locations of the Planet Earth's 177 countries plus basic demographic knowledge about each of them—population, per capita GNP, type of government, and life expectancy. The students work in groups using mnemonics like the following one, which is designed to teach the names and locations of the Central American countries.

The exercise begins with the blank map of Central America with the countries numbered. The leader describes an imaginary tour they are about to take:

"Imagine that we're about to take a tour of Central America. Our group has learned that there has been a great deal of Spanish influence on the language and the dissemination of a religion based on the Christian Saviour—thus, we will see many signs in Spanish and will see mission churches with their distinctive bell towers. We know that the Spanish came for riches and that they expected to find a *rich coast*. We also know we will have to be careful about the water, and we will carry a lot of *nickels* that we will use to buy bottled water. We are going to drive little Hondas, rather than taking a bus, and we will wear Panama hats for identifying our tour group members."

Then, the leader points to the first country, Panama, shows the first cartoon, and says, "The link word for Panama is *Panama hat*." The group repeats the link word. The leader then points to the second country and shows the second cartoon, saying "This country stands for the rich coast the Spanish were looking for, which is Costa Rica. The link word for Costa Rica is *rich coast*." The group repeats the link word and the names of the countries as the leader points to them: "Panama, Panama hat, Costa Rica, rich coast." The exercise continues. The link word for Nicaragua is "nickel water" or "nickel agua" (see the third cartoon), and El Salvador is "Saviour." (See the fourth cartoon.) The group repeats the names of the countries and the link words in order as the leader points to the country.

The leader proceeds to introduce the link word for Honduras by saying, "We get bored a little and decide to have a 'Honda Race' in our little cars." (See the fifth cartoon.) He proceeds to Guatemala by pointing out that it has the largest population in Central America and that the link word is "gotta lotta." (See the sixth cartoon.) Finally, pointing to the seventh country, he reminds them about the bell towers and that the sound from them is "belleeeezzz." The group then names the countries and the link words as the leader points to them in turn.

Over the next couple of days the group members study the map, the names of the countries, and the link words until they know them backward and forward. They also consult a data base containing information on pop-

THE TOUR

Imagine that we're about to take a tour of Central America. Our group has learned that there has been a great deal of Spanish influence that has affected the language and the religion based on the Christian savior (we will see mission churches with their distinctive bell towers). We also know that they came for riches. We also know that we have to be careful about the water, except in Panama, and we will carry nickels we will use to buy bottled water. We are going to drive little Hondas and wear Panama hats for identification.

Thus
1. Panama—Panama hat
2. Costa Rica—rich coast
3. Nicaragua—nickel water
4. El Salvador—savior
5. Honduras—Honda race
6. Guatemala—gotta lotta
7. Belize—belleeeeeezzz

CENTRAL AMERICA

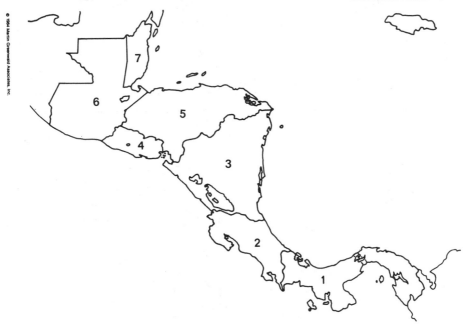

SOURCE: Developed by Beverly Showers and Bruce Joyce with the Richmond County, Georgia, Staff Development Cadre. Drawings on this page and on pages 162, 163, 168, 169, 170, 174, and 175 are by Jenna Beard, Eugene, Oregon.

5.

6.

7.

ulation, birth and death rates, per capita income, health care, and such, and classify the countries seeking correlations among those variables. (Are level of education and life expectancy correlated? and so forth.)

In this way they proceed to examine the regions of the world, comparing and contrasting the countries and learning the names and locations of enough of them that the Atlas will seem a familiar place. Eventually, of course, the study goes beyond names, locations, and demographics and proceeds to rich information about a sample of the countries.

The humble task of memorizing is with us throughout our lives. From the moment of birth, a world of new artifacts and events is presented to us and has to be sorted out. Moreover, many of the elements of our world have been named by those who have come before us. We have to learn large quantities of words, and we have to learn to connect them to the objects, events, actions, and qualities that they represent. In other words, we have to learn a meaningful language.

In any new area of study, a major task is learning the important words and definitions—the languages, if you will—that pertain to the area. To deal with chemistry we have to learn the names of the elements and their structural properties. To study a continent we have to learn the names of its countries, its major geographical features, the important events in its human history, and so on. Initial foreign-language learning involves developing a vocabulary of words that look and sound unfamiliar.

The study of memory has a long history. Although "the goal of a unified coherent and generally satisfying theory of human memory" (Estes, 1976, p. 11) has not yet been achieved, progress has been made. A number of instructional principles are being developed whose goals are both to teach memorization strategies and to help students study more effectively.

For instance, the material on which a particular teacher chooses to focus will affect what information the students retain. "Many items are presented to an individual in a short time, and only those to which attention is directed enter into memory, and only those receiving rehearsal are maintained long enough to secure the processing necessary to establish a basis for long-term recall" (Estes, 1976, p. 7). In other words, if we do not pay attention to something, we are not likely to remember it. Second, we need to attend to it in such a way that we are rehearsing later recall of it. For example, as we wander through a forest, if we do not look carefully at the tree trunks, we are unlikely to remember them, although some visual images may be retained in a haphazard fashion. Second, even if we notice them, we need to use the information, for example by comparing different trees, in order to remember it. When we rehearse, we develop *retrieval cues*, which are the basis for sorting through our memories at later times and locating information.

Short-term memories are often associated with *sensory* experiences of various kinds. When we are exposed to the wine called *Chablis*, we may remember it as straw-colored and tasting a certain way. For long-term recall we may associate things according to *episodic* cues—that is, having to do with the sequences of experience to which we have been exposed. We may remember Andrew Johnson, for example, as the president who followed Abraham Lincoln. They are connected in time, and their episodes in history are connected to one another. *Categorical* cues, on the other hand, involve conceptualizations of the material. When we compare tree trunks, for example, we form concepts that provide a basis for describing the individual trunks in relation to one another. In other words, we replace specific items with categories, and this categorization provides us with the basis for memory.

Both scholarly and popular sources agree that the ability to remember is fundamental to intellectual effectiveness. Far from being a passive, trivial activity, memorizing and remembering are active pursuits. The capacity to take information, to integrate it meaningfully, and later to retrieve it at will is the product of successful memory learning. Most important, individuals can improve this capacity to memorize material so that they can recall it later. That is the objective of this model.

ORIENTATION TO THE MODEL

GOALS AND ASSUMPTIONS

Our recollection of our early years in school usually includes an image of struggles to master lists of unstructured material such as new words, new sounds, the days of the week, the fifty states, and the nations of the world. Some of us became effective at memorizing. Some did not. As we look back, it is easy to dismiss much of this information as trivial. However, imagine for a moment what our world would be like without the information we acquired in those years of school. We *need* information.

One of the most effective forms of personal power comes from competence based on knowledge; it is essential to success and a sense of well-being. Throughout our lives, we need to be able to memorize skillfully. To improve this ability increases learning power, saves time, and leads to a better storehouse of information.

THE LINK-WORD METHOD

Over the last 10 years an important line of research has been conducted on what is termed the link-word method. The result is a considerable advance in knowledge about memorization as well as the development of a system that has practical implications for the design of instructional materials, for classroom teaching and tutoring, and for students.

The method has two components, assuming that the learning task is to master unfamiliar material. The first component provides the students with familiar material to link with the unfamiliar items. The second provides an association to establish the meaning of the new material. For example, when the task involves new foreign-language words, one link ties the sounds to those of words in English. The second ties the new word to a representation of its meaning. For example, the Spanish word *carta* (postal letter) might be linked to the English word *cart* and a picture showing a letter inside a shopping cart (Pressley, Levin, and Delaney, 1981, p. 62).

An important finding from the research is that people who master material more quickly and who retain it longer generally use more elaborate strategies for memorizing material. They use mnemonics—assists to memorization. The less-effective memorizers generally use "rote" procedures. They "say" what is to be memorized over and over again until they believe it is implanted in their memories.

A second important finding is that devices like the link-word method are even more elaborate than the methods used by the better "natural" memorizers—that is, they require more mental activity than do the rote procedures. When first confronted by the presidential illustrations discussed earlier, many teachers respond, "But why add all the extra stuff? Isn't it hard enough to master the names of the presidents and their order? Why add words like "link" and "stick" and pictures of sand castles on a summer beach?"

The answer is that the additional associations provide a richer mental context and the linking process increases the cognitive activity. The combination of activity and associations provides better "anchors" within our information-processing systems.

Does the key-word method help students who are ordinarily good, poor, and average memorizers? Apparently so (Pressley and Dennis-Rounds, 1980). Further, it appears to help students who are below average in verbal ability, who might have been expected to have greater difficulty with complex learning strategies. In addition, as students use the method, they seem to transfer it to other learning tasks. In other words, mnemonics can be taught so that students can use them independently of the teacher. The students, in other words, can develop systems for making up their own links.

Finally, even young (kindergarten and first-grade) students can profit from mnemonics (Pressley et al., 1981). Obviously, they have greater difficulty generating their own links, but they can benefit when links are provided to them.

The effect sizes from this research are impressive. Even in Atkinson's (1975) early studies the link-word method was about 50 percent more effective than conventional rote methods. That is, students learned half-again more material in the same time period as students not using link words. In some of the later studies, it has been twice as efficient or more (Pressley, 1977; Pressley, Miller, and Levin, 1981). Just as important, retention has been facilitated. That is, more is remembered longer when link words are used.

As we stated earlier, there are two obvious uses of this research in teaching. The first is to arrange instruction so as to make it as easy as possible for students to make associations and to discourage isolated rote drill. The second is to teach students to make their own links when they are studying new material.

Some of the other models can help us here. Concept attainment provides categories that associate exemplars on the basis of attributes and induce students to make contrasts with the nonexemplars. Inductive teaching causes students to build associations on the basis of common characteristics. Advance organizers provide an "intellectual scaffolding" that ties material together and comparative organizers link the new with the old. The scientific inquiry methods provide an experiential base for terms and an intellectual structure to "glue" material together.

In a very interesting recent study, Levin and Levin (1990) applied the method to teach what are generally considered "higher-order" objectives—in this case, a hierarchical system for classifying plants. They compared the effectiveness of using links to familiar concepts with a traditional graphic representation, with the hierarchy presented in a chart featuring boxes connected by lines. The links not only facilitated the learning and remembering of the hierarchical scheme, but also affected problem solving.

For the teacher, the major labor for this method is in its preparation. Generating the links, and in some cases creating visual materials or working with students to create them, are the chief activities involved. Once the presentations have been prepared, the delivery is rather straightforward. Let us look at an example that is accompanied by cartoon figures.

This exercise is similar to the one described in Scenario Two at the beginning of the chapter and is part of a global literacy program. The link words are phonetic and are created in a sequence following a made-up story of a career woman in the United States. We begin with the map of the Middle East with seven of the countries numbered in the order in which they will be memorized.

Our career woman is recounting the beginning of her day. "I got up," she says, and "*I ran* downstairs." The *I ran* and its accompanying cartoon are the links to Iran. Then she says, "I took the dishes from the *rack*." *Rack*, with its accompanying cartoon, are links to Iraq. She continues, "I fixed the children bowls of *Serios*." *Serios*, with the accompanying cartoon, are links to Syria. "I fixed myself some English muffins and took out the *jar of jam*." *Jar of jam*, with its cartoon, are the links to Jordan. "I also fixed myself a cup of tea and sliced a *lemon* for it." *Lemon* is the link, with its cartoon, for Lebanon.

"Finally, I ran for the *rail*road train." *Rail*road, with its cartoon, is the link for Israel.

"When I got to my office, I was so hot and thirsty I ran straight to the vending machine and got a *soda* to pick me up." *Soda (sody)* is the link for Saudi Arabia (See cartoon).

These are phonetic links, which, with the illustrations, help the students connect the words (new to them) with known words and phrases and visualizations to help anchor the new material in association with familiar words, pictures, and actions. The somewhat humorous and absurd tone helps make the links vivid.

OTHER MEMORY-ASSIST SYSTEMS

A number of popular "memory systems" have been developed; none of them backed by the research that Pressley, Levin, and their associates have generated. However, some of these systems use sensible principles that are congruent with that research. Lorayne and Lucas's *The Memory Book*

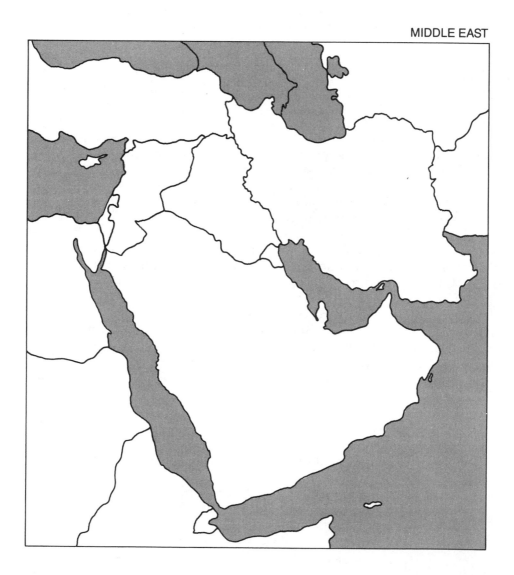

MIDDLE EAST

(1974) is one such, and we have drawn on it for some suggestions of procedures to use with children.

We repeat first the important maxim, that before we can remember something we must first attend to it. An effective memory model must induce attention to what is to be learned. Because entities we can see, feel, touch, smell, or taste generate powerful associations for remembering, we remember best those ideas that are represented to several of our sensory channels. Each channel contains old material we can associate with the new. If we "see" a flower, for example, as a visual image, something that feels a certain way, has a distinctive smell, and makes a crunchy noise when its stem is cut, we are linked to it through several types of perception. The likelihood of remembering it (or its name) is greater than if we observe it through one sense only. Lorayne and Lucas quote Aristotle:

> It is the image-making part of the mind which makes the work of the higher processes of thought possible. Hence the mind never thinks without a mental picture. The thinking faculty thinks of its form in pictures. (Lorayne and Lucas, 1974, p. 22)

Lorayne and Lucas built their model to increase (1) *attention* to what is to be learned; (2) the *senses* involved in attending; and (3) the *associations* we make between the new material and things that have previously been learned. A sense of how this is done can be seen in the following vignette:

Boris, who is running for student body president of the elementary school, has prepared a speech to deliver before his schoolmates. But he is having difficulty remembering his speech, so he appeals to his teacher for help and support. The teacher encourages him to use the memory strategies they have applied to other seemingly simple learning tasks such as learning new words and the names of African and Latin American countries. Informally, she guides him through the stages of the model much the same way Lorayne and Lucas do with their clients.

First, the teacher has Boris identify (attend to) the main thoughts of his speech. He carefully numbers each different and main idea. Next she has him identify one word from each main idea that reminds him of the entire thought. One by one Boris isolates ideas and underlines a *key word* (one that can stand for the point to be made).

Next the teacher has Boris identify familiar words that have vivid meaning for him and connect those words with the key words. He picks his sister Kate for the term *qualifications* and *pear* for peer. To help him remember those two ideas she asks him to imagine them in any silly way he can. Boris thinks for a minute and then relays the picture of a gigantic pear chasing his sister Kate. He is on his way to remembering! With each pair of key words and substitute words, Boris imagines some outrageous event combining the two.

After he has gone through all of the key thoughts and generated appropriate images, the teacher has Boris repeat words and describe the images several times. Then she asks him to test his memory by giving the whole speech. He is able to go through it comfortably. He has *attended* to his major points, *visualized* the key words and substitutes, and *associated* the key points with vivid sensory images.

If Boris had been learning a new vocabulary or important science concepts, the teacher would have asked him to relate the new material to other *related* material he had learned previously, and she would have suggested that he put the new material to use immediately. This active repetition in a natural setting would assist Boris in retaining the material over the long term. However, Boris's speech is a one-time activity requiring only short-term retention, so it is necessary only to review the associations and test his memory by giving the speech several times.

CONCEPTS ABOUT MEMORY

The following concepts are essentially principles and techniques for enhancing our memory of learning material.

AWARENESS

Before we can remember anything we must give attention to, or concentrate on, the things or idea to be remembered. "Observation is essential to original awareness" (Lorayne and Lucas, 1974, p. 6). According to Lorayne and Lucas, anything of which we are originally aware cannot be forgotten.

ASSOCIATION

The basic memory rule is, "You Can Remember Any New Piece of Information if It Is Associated to Something You Already Know or Remember" (Lorayne and Lucas, 1974, p. 7). For example, to help students remember the spelling of *piece*, teachers will give the cue a *piece* of *pie*, which helps with both spelling and meaning.

The major limitation of these devices is that they apply only to one specific thing. We can't use the phrase *a piece of pie* for more than the spelling of *piece*. In addition, we usually need to remember a number of ideas. To be broadly applicable, a memory system should apply more than once and should link several thoughts or items.

LINK SYSTEM

The heart of the memory procedure is connecting two ideas, with the second idea triggering yet another one, and so on. Although generally we only expend energy to learn meaningful material, an illustration with material that is not potentially useful helps us see how the method works. Suppose, for example, you want to remember the following five words in order: *house, glove, chair, stove, tree.* (There is no earthly reason why you would want to.) You should imagine an unusual picture, first with a house and a glove, then with a glove and a chair. For example, in the first picture you might imagine a glove opening the front door of a house, greeting a family of gloves. The second picture might be a huge glove holding a tiny chair. Taking the time to concentrate making up these images and then to visualize them will develop associations that link them in order.

Many memory problems deal with the association of two ideas. We often want to associate names and dates or places, names and ideas, words and their meaning, or a fact that establishes a relationship between two ideas.

RIDICULOUS ASSOCIATION

Even though it is true that association is the basis of memory, the strength of the association is enhanced if the image is vivid and ridiculous, impossible, or illogical. A tree laden with gloves and a family of gloves are examples of ridiculous association.

There are several ways to make an association ridiculous. The first is to apply the rule of substitution. If you have a car and a glove, picture the glove riding along driving the car. Second, you can apply the out-of-proportion rule—make small things gigantic or large things miniature—for example, a gigantic baseball glove driving along. The third means is the rule of exaggeration, especially by number. Picture millions of gloves parading down the street. Finally, get action into the association. In the examples discussed earlier, the glove is *ringing* the doorbell and *parading* down the street. Imagining ridiculous associations is not at all difficult for us when we are young children, but making these images gets harder for us as we get older and more logical.

SUBSTITUTE-WORD SYSTEM

The substitute-word system is a way of making "an intangible, tangible and meaningful" (Lorayne and Lucas, 1974, p. 21). It is quite simple. Merely take any word or phrase that seems abstract and "think of something . . . that sounds like, or reminds you of, the abstract material and can be pictured in your mind" (Lorayne and Lucas, 1974, p. 22). Remember when you used to say "I'll ask her"in order to remember the state of Alaska. If you want to remember the name *Darwin* you might visualize a dark wind. The concept of force can be represented by a fork. The pictures you construct represent words, thoughts, or phrases. On the next two pages there are two examples of substitute link words and graphics that we use when introducing students to the names of the European countries.

KEY WORD

The essence of the key-word system is to select one word to represent a longer thought or several subordinate thoughts. Boris's speech is an ex-

FINS

FINLAND

ample of one word's being used to trigger many verbal statements. Boris
chose key-word qualifications to represent a list of his superior qualities.
If, as in his case, the key word is abstract, is it necessary to use the substitute-word system before inventing a memorable image.

THE MODEL OF TEACHING

The model of teaching that we have developed from the work of Pressley,
Levin, and their associates includes four phases: attending to the material,
developing connections, expanding sensory images, and practicing recall.
These phases are based on the principle of attention and the techniques
for enhancing recall (see Table 8–1).

SYNTAX

Phase one calls for activities that require the learner to concentrate on
the learning material and organize it in a way that helps that learner remember it. Generally, this includes focusing on what needs to be remembered—the major ideas and examples. Underlining is one way to do this.
Listing the ideas separately and rephrasing them in one's own words is
another task that forces attention. Finally, reflecting on the material, comparing ideas, determining the relationship among the ideas is a third attending activity.

Once the material to be learned has been clarified and evaluated, several memory techniques should be used to develop connections with what
is to be learned. Phase two includes using such techniques as the link

TABLE 8–1   SYNTAX OF MEMORY MODEL

Phase One: Attending to the Material	Phase Two: Developing Connections
Use techniques of underlining, listing, reflecting.	Make material familiar and develop connections using key-word, substitute-word, and link-word system techniques.

Phase Three: Expanding Sensory Images	Phase Four: Practicing Recall
Use techniques of ridiculous association and exaggeration. Revise images.	Practice recalling the material until it is completely learned.

words, substitute words (in the case of abstractions), and key words for long or complex passages. The notion is to connect the new material to familiar words, pictures, or ideas, and to link images or words together.

Once the initial associations have been identified, the images can be enhanced (phase three) by asking the student to associate with more than one sense and by generating humorous dramatizations through ridiculous association and exaggeration. At this time the images can be revised for greater recall power.

In phase four the student is asked to practice recall of the material.

SOCIAL SYSTEM

The social system is cooperative; the students and teacher work as a team to shape the new material for commitment to memory.

PRINCIPLES OF REACTION

The teacher's role in this model is to help the student work the material. Working from the student's frame of reference, the teacher assists him or her to identify key items, pairs, and images.

SUPPORT SYSTEM

Pictures, concrete aids, films, and other audiovisual materials are especially useful for increasing the sensory richness of the associations. However, no special support system is required for this model.

APPLICATION

The memory model is applicable to all curriculum areas where material needs to be memorized. It can be used with groups (a chemistry class mastering the table of elements) or individuals (a student learning a poem, story, speech, or part in a play).

Although it has many uses in teacher-led "memory sessions," it has its widest application after students have mastered it and can use it independently. Thus, the model should be taught so that dependence on the teacher is decreased and students can use the procedures whenever they need to memorize.

INSTRUCTIONAL AND NURTURANT EFFECTS

The memory model is specifically designed to increase the capacity to store and retrieve information. It should nurture a sense of intellectual power—a growing consciousness of the ability to master unfamiliar ma-

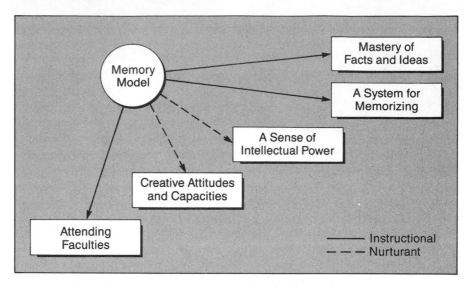

FIGURE 8–1 Instructional and nurturant effects: memory model.

terial, as well as imagery skills and attention to one's environment (See Figure 8–1).

One of the most important outcomes of the model is the students' recognition that learning is not a mysterious, innate process over which they have no control. As Ian Hunter (1964) points out:

> The mastery of some simple mnemonic system may lead some people to realize, for the first time, that they can control and modify their own mental activities. And this realization may encourage them to undertake that self-critical experimentation with their own learning and remembering procedures which is such an important part of intellectual development. (p. 302)

Thus, awareness of how to learn and how to improve learning results in a sense of mastery and control over one's future.

A second outcome is the improvement of imaging capacity and the realization that creative forms of thinking are an essential part of more convergent, information-oriented learning. In training for imagery, creativity is nourished, and ease with playful, creative thought is encouraged.

Imaging requires that we observe and attend to the world around us. Consequently, the use of imaging as part of memory work disciplines us to attend to our surroundings automatically.

Finally, of course, our capacity for remembering particular material is strengthened by this model—we become more effective memorizers.

SUMMARY
CHART ▶ **MEMORY MODEL**

Syntax

Phase One: Attending to the Material
  Use techniques of underlining, listing, reflecting

Phase Two: Developing Connections
  Make material familiar and develop connections using key-word, substitute-word, and link-word system techniques.

Phase Three: Expanding Sensory Images
  Use techniques of ridiculous association and exaggeration. Revise images.

Phase Four: Practicing Recall
  Practice recalling the material until it is completely learned.

Social System

The social system is cooperative. Teacher and students become a team working with the new material together. The initiative should increasingly become the students' as they obtain control over the strategy and use it to memorize ideas, words, and formulas.

Principles of Reaction

The teacher helps the student identify key items, pairs, and images, offering suggestions but working from the students' frames of reference. The familiar elements must be primarily from the students' storehouse of material.

Support System

All of the customary devices of the curriculum areas can be brought into play. Pictures, concrete aids, films, and other audiovisual materials are especially useful for increasing the sensory richness of the associations.

LEARNING FROM PRESENTATIONS
Advance Organizers

S C E N A R I O   I

A guide, beginning a tour of an art museum with a group of high school students, says, "I want to give you an idea that will help you understand the paintings and sculpture we are about to see. The idea is simply that art, although it is a personal expression, reflects in many ways the culture and times in which it was produced. This may seem obvious to you at first when you look at the differences between Oriental and Western art. However, it is also true that, within each culture, as the culture changes, so the art will change—and that is why we can speak of *periods* of art. The changes are often reflected in the artists' techniques, subject matter, colors, and style. Major changes are often reflected in the forms of art that are produced." The guide then points out examples of one or two changes in these characteristics. She also asks the students to recall their elementary school days and the differences in their drawings when they were five and six, and when they were older. She likens the different periods of growing up to different cultures.

In the tour that follows, as the students look at paintings and sculpture, the guide points out to them the differences that result from changing times. "Do you see here," she asks, "that in this painting the body of the person is almost completely covered by his robes, and there is no hint of a human inside his clothes? In medieval times, the church taught that the body was unimportant and that the soul was everything." Later she remarks, "You see in this painting how the muscularity of the man stands out through his clothing and how he stands firmly on the earth. This represents the Renaissance view that man was at the center of the universe and that his body, his mind, and his power were very important indeed."

The art teacher is using an *advance organizer*—in this case, a powerful concept used by art historians. This organizer contains many subordinate ideas that can be linked to the particular characteristics of the art objects being viewed. In this scenario, the teacher has thus provided students with what David Ausubel calls an "intellectual scaffolding" to structure the ideas and facts they encounter during their lesson.

S   C   E   N   A   R   I   O   II

Wendy and Keith open their course on chemistry by using a combination of inductive and mnemonics models to teach their students the table of elements. The students learn the names of the elements, their atomic weights, and categorize them in terms of their states at 10 degrees Celsius. They learn the concepts *element*, *atomic weight*, and *chemical bond*.

These concepts and the knowledge of the table itself serve as the conceptual structure of their course. The information to be studied will be linked to this structure and the concepts themselves will be refined and extended as the course proceeds.

S   C   E   N   A   R   I   O   III

Kelly Young is introducing his students to the difference between the literal and figurative meanings of words, or the difference between *denotative and connotative language.* He begins by presenting an organizer, which is simply to point out that words both represent things, actions, states of beings, and so on, and, while doing so, often *suggest* things. He uses examples. The word *puppy* refers to a young dog, but it also suggests playfulness and cuddliness because we think of puppies as playful and cuddly. *Limousine* refers to a car, but it suggests status, wealth, and perhaps snobbishness and conspicuous consumption.

He then presents students with a set of short stories and asks them to read them and pick out words that have, in their opinion, only literal or referential meanings and words that also suggest things they do not refer to directly. They develop lists of words and then discuss why some words have only literal and others have literal and figurative meanings. They build categories and then continue their exploration, looking at the works of favorite authors and continuing to develop their lists.

David Ausubel is an unusual educational theorist. First, he directly addresses the goal of learning subject matter. Second, he advocates the improvement of *presentational* methods of teaching (lectures and readings) at a time when other educational theorists and social critics are challenging the validity of these methods and finding fault with the "passiveness" of expository learning. In contrast to those who advocate discovery methods of teaching, "open education," and experience-based learning, Ausubel stands unabashedly for the mastery of academic material through presentation.

Ausubel is also one of the few educational psychologists to address himself simultaneously to learning, teaching, and curriculum. His theory of meaningful verbal learning deals with three concerns: (1) how knowledge (curriculum content) is organized; (2) how the mind works to process new information (learning); and (3) how teachers can apply these ideas about curriculum and learning when they present new material to students (instruction).

ORIENTATION TO THE MODEL

GOALS AND ASSUMPTIONS

Ausubel's primary concern is to help teachers organize and convey large amounts of information as meaningfully and efficiently as possible. He believes that the acquisition of information is a valid, indeed an essential, goal of schooling, and that certain theories can guide teachers in their job of transmitting bodies of knowledge to their students. His stance applies to situations in which the teacher plays the role of organizer of subject matter and presents information through lectures, readings, and providing tasks to the learner to integrate what has been learned. In his approach, the teacher is responsible for organizing and presenting what is to be learned. The learner's primary role is to master ideas and information. Whereas inductive approaches lead the students to discover or rediscover concepts, the advance organizers provide concepts and principles to the students directly.

The advance organizer model is designed to strengthen students' *cognitive structures*, a term Ausubel uses for a person's knowledge of a particular subject matter at any given time and how well organized, clear, and stable it is (Ausubel, 1963, p. 27). In other words, cognitive structure has to do with what kind of knowledge of a field is in our minds, how much of it there is, and how well it is organized.

Ausubel maintains that a person's existing cognitive structure is the foremost factor governing whether new material will be meaningful and how well it can be acquired and retained. Before we can present new material effectively, we must increase the stability and clarity of our students' structures. This is done by presenting to them concepts that govern the information to be presented to them. The example above in the art gallery, where the docent presented the idea that art reflects culture and cultural change is intended to provide the intellectual scaffolding which will enable the students to see the information in the paintings more clearly. The example of opening the chemistry course as did Wendy and Keith is another example—the students have little knowledge of chemistry, so the organizing concepts provide a conceptual structure on which the course can be built. Strengthening students' cognitive structure in this way facilitates their acquisition and retention of new information. Ausubel rejects the notion that learning through listening, watching, or reading is necessarily rote, passive, or nonmeaningful. It can be, of course, but won't be if the students' minds are prepared to receive and process information. If the mind is not prepared, the student must fall back to learning by rote (repeating material over and over), which is arduous and highly subject to forgetting. Any poorly executed teaching methods can lead to rote learning. Expository teaching is no exception. Well done, it promotes the active processing of information.

WHAT IS MEANINGFUL?

According to Ausubel, whether or not material is meaningful depends more on the preparation of the learner and on the organization of the material than it does on the method of presentation. If the learner begins with the right "set," and if the material is solidly organized, then meaningful learning can occur.

IS RECEPTION LEARNING PASSIVE?

Ausubel says "No!," provided the proper conditions are set up. During a lecture or other form of expository teaching, the listeners' or watchers' minds can be quite active. But they must be involved in relating material to their own cognitive structure. Ausubel speaks about the learners' struggle with the material—looking at it from different angles, reconciling it with similar or perhaps contradictory information, and finally translating it into their own frame of reference and terminology. However, this does not happen automatically.

ORGANIZING INFORMATION: THE STRUCTURE OF THE DISCIPLINE AND COGNITIVE STRUCTURE

According to Ausubel there is a parallel between the way subject matter is organized and the way people organize knowledge in their minds (their cognitive structures). He expresses the view that each of the academic disciplines has a structure of concepts (and/or propositions) that are organized hierarchically (Ausubel, 1963, p. 18). That is, at the top of each discipline are a number of very broad, abstract concepts that include the more concrete concepts at lower stages of organization. Figure 9–1 illustrates the hierarchical structure of the discipline of economics, with the more abstract concepts at the top of the pyramid of concepts.

Like Jerome Bruner, Ausubel believes that the structural concepts of each discipline can be taught to students, for whom they become an information-processing system for them—that is, they become an intellectual map that students can use to analyze particular domains and to solve problems within those domains. For example, students can use economic

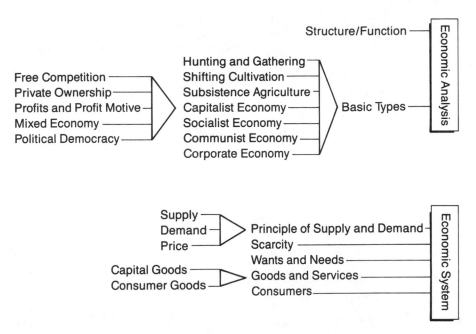

FIGURE 9–1   Structure of the discipline of economics. Based on Clinton Boutwell, *Getting It All Together* (San Rafael, Calif.: Leswing Press, 1972).

concepts to analyze events from an economic point of view. Suppose we present filmed case studies depicting activities on a farm, in a grocery store, in a suburban household, and in a brokerage house. Each case contains many pieces of information. The students see people engaged in various activities, observe many behaviors, and listen to several conversations. If the students were then to make an economic analysis of these cases, they would catalog the behaviors and activities of the people in terms of such concepts as supply and demand, wants and needs, goods and services, consumers and producers. These concepts help in several ways. They enable students to make sense of large amounts of data and to compare the four case studies, discovering the underlying commonalities in the apparent differences.

Ausubel describes the mind as an information-processing and information-storing system that can be compared to the conceptual structure of an academic discipline. Like the disciplines, the mind is a hierarchically organized set of ideas that provides anchors for information and ideas and that serves as a storehouse for them. Figure 9–2 shows the hierarchy of cognitive structure in the discipline of economics. The shaded concepts are the most inclusive. They have been "learned" and exist presently in a hypothetical learner's cognitive structure. The unshaded concepts are potentially meaningful because they can be *linked* to the existing concepts. The

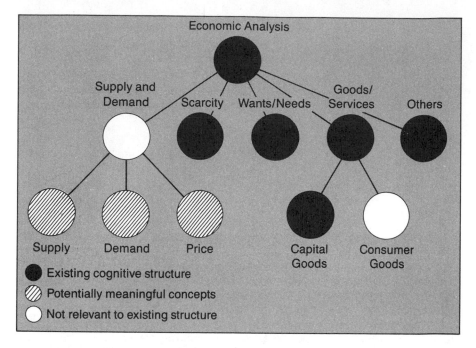

FIGURE 9–2 An individual's cognitive structure with respect to economics. Based on Clinton Boutwell, *Getting It All Together* (San Rafael, Calif.: Leswing Press, 1972, pp. 180–280).

black circles are not yet potentially meaningful concepts because suitable anchors for them are not yet incorporated into the cognitive structure. As this information-processing system acquires new information and new ideas, it reorganizes itself to accommodate those ideas. Thus, the system is in a continuous state of change.

Ausubel maintains that new ideas can be usefully learned and retained only to the extent that they can be related to already available concepts or propositions that provide ideational anchors. If the new material conflicts too strongly with the existing cognitive structure *or* is so unrelated that no linkage is provided, the information or ideas may not be incorporated or retained. To prevent this from occurring, the teacher must sequence the material to be learned and present it in such a way that the ideational anchors are provided. In addition, the learner must actively reflect on the new material, think through these linkages, reconcile differences or discrepancies, and note similarities with existing information.

IMPLICATIONS FOR CURRICULUM

Ausubel's ideas about subject matter and cognitive structure have important and direct implications for the organization of curriculum and for instructional procedures. He uses two principles, *progressive differentiation* and *integrative reconciliation*, to guide the organization of content in the subject fields in such a way that the concepts become a stable part of a student's cognitive structure and to describe the student's intellectual role.

Progressive differentiation means that the most general ideas of the discipline are presented first, followed by a gradual increase in detail and specificity. *Integrative reconciliation* simply means that new ideas should be consciously related to previously learned content. In other words, the sequence of the curriculum is organized so that each successive learning is carefully related to what has been presented before. If the entire body of material has been conceptualized and presented according to progressive differentiation, then integrative reconciliation follows naturally, though it requires the learner's active cooperation. Gradually, as a result of both principles, the discipline is built into the mind of the learner.

It must be remembered that both the discipline and the sequence of instruction are built from the top down, with the most inclusive concepts, principles, and propositions presented first. Ausubel points out that the organization of most textbooks puts each topic into a separate chapter or subchapter, all at the same level of abstraction and generality. "Thus, in most instances students are required to learn the details of new and unfamiliar disciplines before they have acquired an adequate body of relevant subsumers at an appropriate level of inclusiveness" (Ausubel, 1968, p. 153).

IMPLICATIONS FOR TEACHING

Advance organizers are the primary means of strengthening cognitive structure and enhancing retention of new information. Ausubel describes advance organizers as introductory material presented ahead of the learning task and at a higher level of abstraction and inclusiveness than the learning task itself. Their purpose is to explain, integrate, and interrelate the material in the learning task with previously learned material (and also to help the learner discriminate the new material from previously learned material) (Ausubel, 1968, p. 148). The most effective organizers are those that use concepts, terms, and propositions that are already familiar to the learners, as well as appropriate illustrations and analogies.

Suppose, for example, a teacher wants students to acquire information about current energy problems. The teacher provides learning material containing data about possible power sources, general information about United States economic growth and technology, and alternative policies on the energy crisis and future planning. The learning material is in the form of newspaper articles, a lecture, and perhaps a film. The learning task for the students is to internalize the information—that is, to remember the central ideas and perhaps the key facts. Before introducing students to the learning material, however, the teacher provides introductory material in the form of an advance organizer to help them relate to the new data.

In this example, the concept of energy might be used as the basis of the organizer, and related concepts such as energy efficiency and energy conservation can provide auxiliary organizers. Other possibilities are the concept of ecology and its various subsystems dealing with the environment, the economy, the political arena, and social structures. This second set of organizers would focus students' attention on the *impact* of old and new energy sources on the subsystems of our ecological system, whereas, the first set would encourage them to process the data through a consideration of energy efficiency and energy conservation.

The organizer is important content in itself and needs to be taught. It may be a concept or a statement of relationship. In either case, time must be taken to explain and develop the organizer, because only when it is fully understood can it serve to organize the subsequent learning material. For example, students must fully understand the concept of *culture* before the teacher can use it effectively to organize factual information about different culture groups. Advance organizers are generally based on the major concepts, propositions, generalizations, principles, and laws of a discipline. For example, a lesson or text describing the caste system in India might be preceded by an organizer based on the concept of social stratification. Similarly, the generalization, "Technological changes can produce major changes in society and culture," could be the *basis* for an organizer preceding the study of several historical periods and places.

Usually, the organizer is tied closely to the material it precedes. However, the organizer can also be created from an analogy from another field in order to provide a new perspective. For instance, the concept of balance or form, though generic to the arts, may be applied to literature, to mathematics, to the functioning of the branches of government, or even to our daily activities. A study of churches can be viewed under the rubric of many different organizers: those focusing on the economic implications of the church, cultural or sociological perspectives, or architectural perspectives.

There are two types of advance organizers—*expository* and *comparative*. *Expository organizers* provide a basic concept at the highest level of abstraction and perhaps some lesser concepts. These represent the intellectual scaffold on which the student will "hang" the new information as it is encountered. Expository organizers are especially helpful because they provide ideational scaffolding for *unfamiliar* material. Thus the basic concepts of economics would be presented prior to the study of the economic condition of a city.

Comparative organizers, on the other hand, are used most with relatively familiar material. They are designed to discriminate between the old and new concepts in order to prevent confusion caused by their similarity. For example, when the learner is being introduced to long division, a comparative organizer might be used to point out the similarities and differences between division facts and multiplication facts. Whereas in multiplication, the multiplier and multiplicand can be reversed without changing the product—that is, 3 times 4 can be changed to 4 times 3—the divisor and dividend cannot be reversed in division without affecting the quotient—that is, 6 divided by 2 is not the same as 2 divided by 6. The comparative organizer can help the learner see the relationship between multiplication and division and clarify the differences between the two. The learner can then borrow from knowledge about multiplication when learning division without being confused by the differences.

Ausubel and others have conducted a variety of studies exploring the general theory, especially the use of advance organizers. In the early 1960s Ausubel and Fitzgerald (1962) presented research that supported the theory, and Ausubel and other colleagues followed with a series of studies that confirmed the original findings (Ausubel, 1968; Ausubel, Stager, and Gaite, 1968; Barron, 1971). However, in many studies the effects were small (Clauson and Barnes, 1973).

In 1977 Joseph T. Lawton reported a very careful and complex investigation of whether the use of advance organizers would affect the learning of social studies materials and also facilitate logical thinking in 6- and 10-year-old children (see the developmental model for a more complete discussion of children's development and thinking) (Lawton, 1977). The investigation provides support for a theory of meaningful verbal learning, both with respect to learning and retention of material and also with respect to its potential for influencing logical operations—that is, thinking in general. However, the effects are much stronger for the older children, especially with regard to transfer of thinking ability.

In general, Lawton's study seems to support the notion that what is taught will be learned. If we present material to students, some of it will be learned. If it is presented with an organizing structure, somewhat more will be learned. If we use a process that helps students develop certain ways of thinking, then some of those ways of thinking will be learned. Thus, if we avoid using those models of teaching that provide certain intellectual structures and employ certain thinking processes, we decrease the chances of those structures and thinking processes being acquired. Generally speaking, the development of an *intellectual structure*—whether through presentational or inductive methods—increases the probability that students will learn those structures and the thinking processes associated with them, and that they will retain material more fully.

THE MODEL OF TEACHING

The model of teaching developed here is based on Ausubel's ideas about subject matter, cognitive structure, active reception learning, and advance organizers.

SYNTAX

The advance organizer model has three phases of activity. Phase one is the presentation of the advance organizer; phase two is the presentation of the learning task or learning material; and phase three is the strengthening of cognitive organization. Phase three tests the relationship of the learning material to existing ideas to bring about an active learning process. A summary of the syntax appears in Table 9–1.

The activities are designed to increase the clarity and stability of the new learning material so that fewer ideas are lost, confused with one another, or left vague. The students should operate on the material as they receive it by relating the new learning material to personal experience and to their existing cognitive structure, and by taking a critical stance toward knowledge.

Phase one consists of three activities: clarifying the aims of the lesson, presenting the advance organizer, and prompting awareness of relevant knowledge.

Clarifying the aim of the lesson is one way to obtain students' attention and to orient them to their learning goals, both of which are necessary to

TABLE 9–1   SYNTAX OF THE ADVANCE ORGANIZER MODEL

Phase One: Presentation of Advance Organizer	Phase Two: Presentation of Learning Task or Material

Clarify aims of the lesson.
Present organizer:
  Identify defining attributes.
  Give examples.
  Provide context.
  Repeat.
Prompt awareness of learner's relevant knowledge and experience.
	Present material.
	Maintain attention.
	Make organization explicit.
	Make logical order of learning material explicit.

Phase Three: Strengthening Cognitive Organization
Use principles of integrative reconciliation. Promote active reception learning. Elicit critical approach to subject matter. Clarify.

facilitate meaningful learning. (Clarifying aims is also useful to the teacher in planning a lesson.)

As mentioned earlier, the organizer is not just a brief, simple statement; it is an idea in itself and, like the learning material, must be explored intellectually. It must also be distinguished from introductory comments, which are useful to the lesson but are not advance organizers. For instance, when we teach, many of us begin our instruction by asking students to recall what we did last week or last year or by telling them what we are going to do tomorrow. In this way, we give them a context or orientation for our presentation. Or we may ask students to recall a personal experience and then acknowledge that what we are about to say resembles that situation or will help students understand a previous experience. We may also tell them the objectives of the session—what we hope they will get out of the presentation or discussion. *None of the just-described techniques are advance organizers.* However, all of them are part of a well-organized presentation, and some of them reflect principles that are central to Ausubel's theory of meaningful verbal learning and are part of the model of teaching.

The actual organizer, however, is built around the major concepts and/or propositions of a discipline or area of study. First, the organizer has to be constructed so that the learner can perceive it for what it is—an idea distinct from and more inclusive than the material in the learning task itself. The chief feature of an organizer is thus that it is at a higher level of abstraction and generality than the learning material itself. This higher level of abstraction is what distinguishes organizers from introductory overviews, which are written (or spoken) at the same level of abstraction as the learning material because they are, in fact, previews of the learning material.

Second, whether the organizer is expository or comparative, the essential features of the concept or proposition must be pointed out and carefully explained. Thus, the teacher and students must explore the organizer as well as the learning task. To us, this means citing the essential features, explaining them, and providing examples. The presentation of an organizer need not be lengthy, but it must be perceived (the learner must be aware of it), clearly understood, and continually related to the material it is organizing. This means the learner must already be familiar with the language and ideas in the organizer. It is also useful to illustrate the organizer in multiple contexts and to repeat it several times, particularly any new or special terminology.

Finally, it is important to prompt awareness of the learner's prior knowledge and experiences that might be relevant to this learning task and organizer.

Following the presentation of the advance organizer in phase one, in phase two the learning material is presented in the form of lectures, discussions, films, experiments, or reading. During the presentation the organization of the learning material needs to be made explicit to the students so that they have an overall sense of direction and can see the logical order of the material and how the organization relates to the advance organizer.

The purpose of phase three is to anchor the new learning material in the students' existing cognitive structure—that is, to strengthen the student's cognitive organization. In the natural flow of teaching, some of these procedures may be incorporated into phase two; however, we want to emphasize that the reworking of new material is a separate teaching task with its own set of activities and skills. Ausubel identifies four activities: (1) promoting integrative reconciliation, (2) promoting active reception learning, (3) eliciting a critical approach to subject matter, and (4) clarification.

There are several ways to facilitate reconciliation of the new material with the existing cognitive structure. The teacher can: (1) remind students of the ideas (the larger picture), (2) ask for a summary of the major attributes of the new learning material, (3) repeat precise definitions, (4) ask for differences between aspects of the material, and (5) ask students to describe how the learning material supports the concept or proposition that is being used as organizer.

Active learning can be promoted by: (1) asking students to describe how the new material relates to the organizer, (2) asking students for additional examples of the concept or propositions in the learning material, (3) asking students to verbalize the essence of the material, using their own terminology and frame of reference, and (4) asking students to examine the material from alternative points of view.

A critical approach to knowledge is fostered by asking students to recognize assumptions or inferences that may have been made in the learning material, to judge and challenge these assumptions and inferences, and to reconcile contradictions among them.

It is not possible or desirable to use all these techniques in one lesson. Constraints of time, topic, and relevance to the particular learning situation will guide their use. However, it is important to keep in mind the four goals of this phase and specific techniques for effective expository teaching.

Ideally, the initiation of phase three is shared by teachers and students. At first, however, the teacher will have to respond to the students' need for clarification of some area of the topic and for integration of the new material with existing knowledge.

Essentially, Ausubel has provided us with a method for improving not only presentations, but also students' abilities to learn from them. The more we teach students to become active—to *look* for organizing ideas, reconcile information with them, and generate organizers of their own (engaging in inductive activity while reading or watching)—the greater their potential for profiting from presentations becomes.

SOCIAL SYSTEM

In this model the teacher retains control of the intellectual structure, as it is continually necessary to relate the learning material to the organizers and to help students differentiate new material from previously learned material. In phase three, however, the learning situation is ideally much more interactive, with students initiating many questions and comments. The successful acquisition of the material will depend on the learners' desire to integrate it with prior knowledge, on their critical faculties, and on the teacher's presentation and organization of the material.

PRINCIPLES OF REACTION

The teacher's solicited or unsolicited responses to the learners' reactions will be guided by the purpose of clarifying the meaning of the new learning material, differentiating it from and reconciling it with existing knowledge, making it personally relevant to the students, and helping to promote a critical approach to knowledge. Ideally, students will initiate their own questions in response to their own drives for meaning.

SUPPORT SYSTEM

Well-organized material is the critical support requirement of this model. The effectiveness of the advance organizer depends on an integral and appropriate relationship between the conceptual organizer and the content. This model provides guidelines for building (or reorganizing) instructional materials.

APPLICATION

INSTRUCTIONAL USES

The advance organizer model is especially useful to structure extended curriculum sequences or courses and to instruct students systematically in the key ideas of a field. Step by step, major concepts and propositions are explained and integrated, so that at the end of a period of instruction, the learners should gain perspective on the entire area being studied.

We would expect an increase, too, in the learners' grasps of factual information linked to and explained by the key ideas. For example, the concept of socialization can be drawn on recurrently in the study of socialization patterns in different cultures and subcultures. This advance organizer thus aids in expanding students' knowledge about cultures.

The model can also be shaped to teach the *skills* of effective reception learning. Critical thinking and cognitive reorganization can be explained to the learners, who receive direct instruction in orderly thinking and in the notion of knowledge hierarchies. Ultimately, they can apply these techniques independently to new learning. In other words, this model can increase effectiveness in reading and watching films, and in other "reception" activities.

Other models are also useful for evaluating or applying the material presented by the advance organizer. For example, the advance organizer model, after introducing new material in a deductive, presentational way, can be followed by inductive concept attainment activities that reinforce the material or that informally evaluate students' acquisition of the material.

INSTRUCTIONAL AND NURTURANT EFFECTS

The probable instructional values of this model seem quite clear—the ideas themselves that are used as the organizer are learned, as well as information presented to the students. The ability to learn from reading, lectures, and other media used for presentations is another effect, as are an interest in inquiry and precise habits of thinking. (See Figure 9–3.)

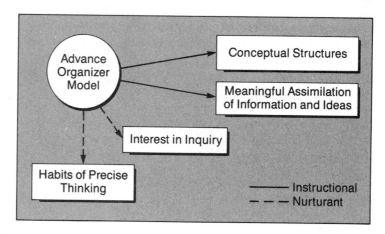

FIGURE 9–3   Instructional and nurturant effects: advance organizer model.

S U M M A R Y ▶ **ADVANCE ORGANIZER**
C H A R T

Syntax

Phase One: Presentation of Advance Organizer
    Clarify the aims of the lesson.
    Present organizer:
        Identify defining attributes.
        Give examples or illustrations where appropriate.
        Provide context.
        Repeat.
    Prompt awareness of learner's relevant knowledge and experience.

Phase Two: Presentation of Learning Task or Material
    Present material.
    Make logical order of learning material explicit.
    Link material to organizer.

Phase Three: Strengthening Cognitive Organization
    Use principles of integrative reconciliation.
    Elicit critical approach to subject matter.
    Clarify ideas.
    Apply ideas actively (as testing them).

Social System

Highly structured.
However, requires active collaboration between teacher and learner.

Principles of Reaction

1. Negotiation of meaning.
2. Responsively connecting organizer and material.

Support System

Data-rich, well-organized material.
    (Caution: Many textbooks do not feature conceptually-organized material).

CHAPTER 10

INQUIRY TRAINING
From Facts to Theories

One morning, as Mrs. Harrison's fourth-grade class is settling down to their arithmetic workbooks, she calls their attention. As they raise their eyes toward her, a light bulb directly over Mrs. Harrison's desk blows out and the room darkens.

"What happened?" asks one child.

"Can't you see?" remarks another. "The light bulb blew out."

"Yeah," inquires another, "but what does that mean?"

"What do you mean, 'What does that mean?'"

"Just that we have all seen a lot of light bulbs blow out, but what does that really mean? What happens?"

Mrs. Harrison unscrews the light bulb and holds it up. The children gather around, and she passes it among them. After she receives it, she says, "Well, why don't you see if you can develop a hypothesis about what happened?"

"What's inside the glass?" asks one of the children.

"I'm afraid I can't answer that," she replies. "Can you put it another way?"

"Is there air inside the glass?" one questions.

"No," says Mrs. Harrison.

"Is there a gas inside?" asks another.

"Yes," says Mrs. Harrison. The children look at one another in puzzlement. Finally, one asks, "Is it inert?"

"Yes," nods Mrs. Harrison.

"What is that little wire made of?" asks another student.

"I can't answer that," says Mrs. Harrison. "Can you put it another way?"

"Is the little wire made of metal?"

"Yes," she responds.

Asking questions such as these, the children gradually identify the materials that make up the light bulb and the events that took place. Finally, they begin to venture hypotheses about what happened. After they have generated four or five of these, they search through reference books in an effort to verify them.

Mrs. Harrison's class has been prepared to carry out a model of teaching that we call *inquiry training*. Normally, the class uses inquiry training to explore preselected areas. That is, either Mrs. Harrison organizes a unit of instruction, or the children identify a topic that they are going to explore. In this case, the children used the techniques of inquiry training to formulate theories about an event that was familiar to all of them and yet puzzled them, for none of them had previously developed ideas about what really went on when a light bulb blew out.

Inquiry training was developed by Richard Suchman to teach students a process for investigating and explaining unusual phenomena. Suchman's model takes students through miniature versions of the kinds of procedures that scholars use to organize knowledge and generate principles. Based on a conception of scientific method, it attempts to teach students some of the skills and language of scholarly inquiry (Suchman, 1962).

Suchman developed his model by analyzing methods employed by creative research personnel, especially physical scientists. As he identified the elements of their inquiry processes, he built them into the instructional model called "inquiry training."

RESEARCH

Inquiry training is designed to bring students directly into the scientific process through exercises that compress the scientific process into small periods of time. What are the effects? Schlenker (1976) reported that inquiry training resulted in increased understanding of science, productivity in creative thinking, and skills for obtaining and analyzing information. He reported that it was not more effective than conventional methods of teaching in the acquisition of information, but that it was as efficient as recitation or lectures accompanied by laboratory experiences. Ivany (1969) and Collins (1969) reported that the method works best when the confrontations are strong, arousing genuine puzzlement, and when the materials the students use to explore the topics under consideration are especially instructional. Both elementary and secondary students can profit from the model (Voss, 1982). In an intriguing study, Elefant (1980) successfully carried out the model with deaf children, which suggests that the method can be powerful with students who have severe sensory handicaps.

ORIENTATION TO THE MODEL

GOALS AND ASSUMPTIONS

Inquiry training originated in a belief in the development of independent learners; its method requires active participation in scientific inquiry. Children are curious and eager to grow, and inquiry training capitalizes on their natural energetic explorations, giving them specific directions so that they explore new areas more forcefully. The general goal of inquiry training is to help students develop the intellectual discipline and skills necessary to raise questions and search out answers stemming from their curiosity. Thus, Suchman is interested in helping students inquire independently, but in a disciplined way. He wants students to question why events happen as they do and to acquire and process data logically, and he wants them to develop general intellectual strategies that they can use to find out why things are as they are.

Inquiry training begins by presenting students with a puzzling event. Suchman believes that individuals faced with such a situation are *naturally* motivated to solve the puzzle. We can use the opportunity provided by natural inquiry to teach the procedures of disciplined searching.

Like Bruner and Taba, Suchman believes that students can become increasingly conscious of their process of inquiry and that they can be taught scientific procedures directly. All of us often inquire intuitively; however, Suchman feels we cannot analyze and improve our thinking unless we are conscious of it.

Suchman believes, further, that it is important to convey to students the attitude that *all knowledge is tentative*. Scholars generate theories and explanations. Years later, these are pushed aside by new theories. There are no permanent answers. We can always be more sophisticated in our explanations, and most problems are amenable to several plausible explanations. Students should recognize and be comfortable with the ambiguity that genuine inquiry entails. They should also be aware that the point of view of a second person enriches our own thinking. The development of knowledge is facilitated by help and ideas from colleagues if we can learn to tolerate alternative points of view. Thus, Suchman's theory is that:

1. Students inquire naturally when they are puzzled.
2. They can become conscious of and learn to analyze their thinking strategies.
3. New strategies can be taught directly and added to the students' existing ones.
4. Cooperative inquiry enriches thinking and helps students to learn

about the tentative, emergent nature of knowledge and to appreciate alternative explanations.

OVERVIEW OF THE TEACHING STRATEGY

Following Suchman's belief that individuals have a natural motivation to inquire, the inquiry training model is built around intellectual confrontations. The student is presented with a puzzling situation and inquires into it. Anything that is mysterious, unexpected, or unknown is grist for a discrepant event. Because the ultimate goal is to have the students experience the creation of new knowledge, the confrontation should be based on discoverable ideas. In the following example, bending a metallic strip held over a flame begins the inquiry cycle.

> The strip is made of a lamination of unlike strips of metal (usually steel and brass) that have been welded together to form a single blade. With a handle at one end it has the appearance of a narrow knife or spatula. When this apparatus is heated, the metal in it expands, but the rate of expansion is not the same in the two metals. Consequently, half of the thickness of this laminated strip becomes slightly longer than the other half and since the two halves are attached to each other the internal stresses force the blade to assume a curve of which the outer circumference is occupied by the metal which has expanded the most. (Suchman, 1962, p. 28)

Suchman deliberately selects episodes that have sufficiently surprising outcomes to make it difficult for students to remain indifferent to the encounter. Usually things that are heated do not bend into a big curve. When this metal strip does, the students *naturally* want to know *why*. The learners cannot dismiss the solution as obvious; they have to work to explain the situation, and the products of that work are a new insight, concepts, and theories.

After the presentation of the puzzling situation, the students ask the teacher questions. The questions, however, must be answered by yeses or nos. Students may not ask the teacher to explain the phenomenon to them. They have to focus and structure their probes to solve the problem. In this sense, each question becomes a limited hypothesis. Thus, the student may not ask, "How did the heat affect the metal?" but must ask, "Was the heat greater than the melting point of the metal?" The first question is not a specific statement of what information is wanted; it asks the teacher to do the conceptualizing. The second question requires the student to put several factors together—heat, metal, change, liquid. The student had to ask the teacher to verify the hypothesis that he or she has developed (the heat caused the metal to change into a liquid).

The students continue to ask questions. Whenever they phrase one that cannot be answered by a yes or a no, the teacher reminds them of the rules and waits until they find a way of stating the question in proper form. Comments such as "Can you restate this question so that I can answer it with a yes or a no?" are common teacher responses when students slip out of the inquiry mode.

Over time, the students are taught that the first stage in inquiry is to verify the facts of the situation—the nature and identity of the objects, the events, and the conditions surrounding the puzzling event. The question "Was the strip made of metal?" helps verify the facts—in this case, a property of the object. As the students become aware of the facts, hypotheses should come to mind and guide further inquiry. Using their knowledge about the behavior of the objects, students can turn their questions to the relationships among the variables in the situation. They can conduct verbal or actual experiments to test these causal relationships, selecting new data or organizing the existing data in new ways to see what will happen if things are done differently. For example, they could ask, "If I turn the flame down, will the bend still occur?" Better yet, they could actually do this! By introducing a new condition or altering an existing one, students isolate variables and learn how they affect one another.

It is important for students and teachers to recognize the difference between questions that attempt to verify "what is" and questions or activities that "experiment" with the relationships among variables. Each of these is essential to theory development, but fact gathering should precede hypothesis raising. Unless sufficient information about the nature of the problem situation and its elements is verified, students are likely to be overwhelmed by the many possible causal relationships.

> If the child immediately tries to hypothesize complex relationships among all the variables that seem relevant to him, he could go on testing indefinitely without any noticeable progress, but by isolating variables and testing them singly, he can eliminate the irrelevant ones and discover the relationships that exist between each relevant independent variable (such as the temperature of the blade) and the dependent variable (which in this case is the bending of the blade). (Suchman, 1962, pp. 15–16)

Finally, the students try to develop hypotheses that will fully explain what happened. (For instance, "The strip was made of two metals that were fastened together somehow. They expand at different rates; and when they were heated, the one that expanded the most exerted pressure on the other one so that the two bent over together.") Even after lengthy and rich verification and experimentation activities, many explanations may be possible, and the students are encouraged not to be satisfied with the first explanation that appears to fit the facts.

Inquiry cannot be programmed, and the range of productive inquiry strategies is vast. Thus, students should

> experiment freely with their own questions, structuring and sequencing [the inquiry session]. . . . Nevertheless, inquiry can be divided into broad phrases which, on the whole, should be taken in logical order simply because they build upon one another. Failure to adhere to this order leads either to erro-

neous assumptions or to low efficiency and duplication of effort. (Suchman, 1962, p. 38)

The emphasis in this model is clearly on becoming aware of and mastering the inquiry process, not on the content of any particular problem situation. Although the model should also be enormously appealing and effective as a mode of acquiring and using information, the teacher cannot be too concerned with subject-matter coverage or "getting the right answer." In fact, this would violate the whole spirit of scientific inquiry, which envisions a community of scholars searching together for more accurate and powerful explanations for everyday phenomena.

THE MODEL OF TEACHING

SYNTAX

Inquiry training has five phases (see Table 10–1). The first phase is the student's *confrontation* with the puzzling situation. Phases two and three are the *data-gathering* operations of *verification* and *experimentation*. In these two phases, students ask a series of questions to which the teacher

TABLE 10–1   SYNTAX OF THE INQUIRY TRAINING MODEL

Phase One: Confrontation with the Problem	Phase Two: Data Gathering—Verification
Explain inquiry procedures. Present discrepant event.	Verify the nature of objects and conditions. Verify the occurrence of the problem situation.

Phase Three: Data Gathering— Experimentation	Phase Four: Organizing, Formulating an Explanation
Isolate relevant variables. Hypothesize (and test) causal relationships.	Formulate rules or explanations.

Phase Five: Analysis of the Inquiry Process
Analyze inquiry strategy and develop more effective ones.

replies yes or no, and they conduct a series of experiments on the environment of the problem situation. In the fourth phase, students *organize* the information they obtained during the data gathering and try to *explain* the discrepancy. Finally, in phase five, students *analyze* the problem-solving strategies they used during the inquiry.

Phase one requires that the teacher present the problem situation and explain the inquiry procedures to the students (the objectives and the procedure of the yes/no question). The formulation of a discrepant event such as the bimetallic strip problem requires some thought, although the strategy can be based on relatively simple problems—a puzzle, riddle, or magic trick—that do not require much background knowledge. Of course, the ultimate goal is to have students, especially older students, experience the creation of new knowledge, much as scholars do. However, beginning inquiries can be based on very simple ideas.

The distinguishing feature of the discrepancy is that it involves events that conflict with our notions of reality. In this sense, not every puzzling situation is a discrepant event. It may be puzzling because we do not know the answer, but we do not need new concepts to understand it, and therefore we do not need to conduct an inquiry. We mention this because occasionally teachers do not pick problems that are truly puzzling to the student. In these cases, the learning activity does not progress beyond a "20-questions" format. Even though the questioning activity has value for its own sake, it should not be confused with the notion of scientific inquiry.

Phase two, verification, is the process whereby students gather information about an event they see or experience. In experimentation, phase three, students introduce new elements into the situation to see if the event happens differently. Although verification and experimentation are described as separate phases of the model, the students' thinking and the types of questions they generate usually alternate between these two aspects of data gathering.

Experiments serve two functions: *exploration* and *direct testing*. Exploration—changing things to see what will happen—is not necessarily guided by a theory or hypothesis, but it may suggest ideas for a theory. Direct testing occurs when students try out a theory or hypothesis. The process of converting a hypothesis into an experiment is not easy and takes practice. Many verification and experimentation questions are required just to investigate one theory. We have found that even sophisticated adults find it easier to say, "I think it has something to do with . . ." than to think of a series of questions that will test the theory. Also, few theories can be discarded on the basis of one experiment. Although it is tempting to "throw away" a variable if the first experiment does not support it, it can be very misleading to do so. One of the teacher's roles is to restrain students whenever they assume that a variable has been disproven when it has not.

A second function of the teacher is to broaden the students' inquiry by expanding the type of information they obtain. During verification they may ask questions about objects, properties, conditions, and events. *Object* questions are intended to determine the nature or identity of objects. (Is the knife made of steel? Is the liquid water?) *Event* questions attempt to verify the occurrence or nature of an action. (Did the knife bend upward the second time?) *Condition* questions relate to the state of objects or systems at a particular time. (Was the blade hotter than room temperature when he held it up and showed that it was bent? Did the color change when the liquid was added?) *Property* questions aim to verify the behavior of objects under certain conditions as a way of gaining new information to help build a theory. (Does copper always bend when it is heated?) Because students tend not to verify all aspects of the problem, teachers can be aware of the type of information needed and work to change the questioning pattern.

In phase four, the teacher calls on the students to organize the data and to formulate an explanation. Some students have difficulty making the intellectual leap between comprehending the information they have gathered and constructing a clear explanation of it. They may give inadequate explanations, omitting essential details. Sometimes several theories or explanations are possible based on the same data. In such cases, it is often useful to ask students to state their explanations so that the range of possible hypotheses becomes obvious. Together the group can shape the explanation that fully responds to the problem situation. Finally, in phase five, the students are asked to analyze their pattern of inquiry. They may determine the questions that were most effective, the lines of questioning that were productive and those that were not, or the type of information they needed and did not obtain. This phase is essential if we are to make the inquiry process a conscious one and systematically try to improve it.

SOCIAL SYSTEM

Suchman's intention is that the social system be cooperative and rigorous. Although the inquiry training model can be quite highly structured, with the social system controlled largely by the teacher, the intellectual environment is open to all relevant ideas; teachers and students participate as equals where ideas are concerned. Moreover, the teacher should encourage students to initiate inquiry as much as possible. As the students learn the principles of inquiry, the structure can expand to include the use of resource material, dialogue with other students, experimentation, and discussion with the teacher.

After a period of practice in teacher-structured inquiry sessions, students can undertake inquiry in more student-controlled settings. A stimulating event can be set up in the room, and students can inquire on their own or in informal groups, alternating between open-ended inquiry sessions and data gathering with the aid of resource materials. In this way, the students can move back and forth between inquiry sessions and independent study. This utilization of the inquiry training model is especially suited to the open-classroom setting, where the teacher's role is that of instructional manager and monitor.

In the initial stages of inquiry the teacher's role is to select (or construct) the problem situation, to referee the inquiry according to inquiry procedures, to respond to students' inquiry probes with the necessary information, to help beginning inquirers establish a focus in their inquiry, and to facilitate discussion of the problem situation among the students.

PRINCIPLES OF REACTION

The most important reactions of the teacher take place during the second and third phases. During the second phase the teachers' task is to help the students to inquire but not to do the inquiry for them. If the teacher is asked questions that cannot be answered by a *yes* or *no*, he or she must ask the students to rephrase the questions so as to further their own attempts to collect data and relate them to the problem situation. The teacher can, if necessary, keep the inquiry moving by making new information available to the group and by focusing on particular problem events or by raising questions. During the last phase, the teacher's task is to keep the inquiry directed toward the process of investigation itself.

SUPPORT SYSTEM

The optimal support is a set of confronting materials, a teacher who understands the intellectual processes and strategies of inquiry, and resource materials bearing on the problem.

APPLICATION

Although inquiry training was originally developed for the natural sciences, its procedures are usable in all subject areas; any topic that can be formulated as a puzzling situation is a candidate for inquiry training. In literature, murder mysteries and science fiction stories or plots make excellent puzzling situations. Newspaper articles about bizarre or improbable situations may be used to construct stimulus events. One of the authors was at a Chinese restaurant not too long ago and puzzled over the question, "How is the fortune put into the fortune cookie, since it does not appear burned or cooked in any way?" It occurred to us that this would make an excellent inquiry-training topic for young children. The social sciences also offer numerous possibilities for inquiry training.

The construction of puzzling situations is the critical task, because it transforms curriculum content into problems to be explored. When objects and other materials are not available or appropriate to the problem situation, we recommend that teachers make up a *problem statement* for students and a *fact sheet* for themselves. The problem statement describes the discrepant event and provides the information that is shared initially with the students. The fact sheet gives the teacher further information about the problem, and the teacher draws on it to respond to the students' questions. Two examples of this process follow.

EXAMPLE ONE

In anthropology, students have the problem of reconstructing cultural events. For a social studies class, an instructor composed a problem statement and a student fact sheet based on an anthropological issue. The teacher passed the following statement out to his students:

PROBLEM STATEMENT

This map shows an island in the middle of a lake. The island is connected to the shore by a causeway made of stones piled on the bottom of the lake until the pile reached the surface. Then smoothed stones were laid down to make a road. The lake is surrounded by mountains, and the only flat land is near the lake. The island is covered with buildings whose walls are still standing, although the roofs are now gone. It is completely uninhabited.

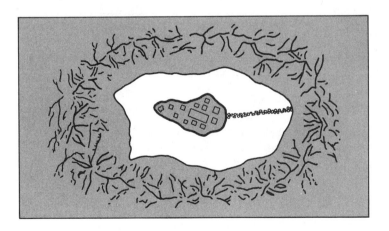

Your task is to discover what happened to the people who lived there. What caused the place to be empty of human beings?

As the students conducted their inquiry, the instructor drew on the following fact sheet for his responses:

INSTRUCTOR FACT SHEET

1. The lake is 500 feet deep, 600 feet across.
2. The lake is 6,500 feet above sea level. The mountains rise to 11,000 feet.

3. The causeway is made of dumped rocks.

4. The houses are close together. Each one is about 20 by 25 feet and has more than one room. They are made of limestone blocks.

5. Some broken tools and pottery have been found in the homes.

6. The edifice in the center is made of marble and has three levels. At the bottom it is six times larger than the houses. At the top level of the edifice, you can sight the planets and stars through a hole slit in a stone. You can sight Venus at its lowest rise, which occurs on December 21.

7. There is evidence that the islanders fished with traps. They also had livestock such as sheep, cows, and chickens.

8. Apparently, there was no art, but evidence of graphic writing has been found.

9. Cisterns have been found under limestone streets.

10. There is no habitation within 80 miles.

11. The island has been uninhabited for about 300 years.

12. The area was discovered in 1900.

13. It is located in a subtropical area of South America where there is plenty of drinking water and where every available area was farmed. There is evidence of irrigation but no evidence of crop rotation. In general, the land is marginal for farming.

14. There is a thin layer of topsoil over a limestone shelf.

15. About 1,000 to 1,500 people lived on the island.

16. The mountains around the island can be crossed, but with difficulty.

17. There is a stone quarry in nearby mountains and a burial ground across the lake.

18. Dead bodies with hands folded have been found.

19. There is no evidence of plague, disease, or war.

EXAMPLE TWO

An English teacher using inquiry training based a discrepant event on Chapter 6 of Kurt Vonnegut's *Venus on the Half Shell* (published under the pen name of Kilgore Trout). She formulated the following problem situation and then read a short excerpt from the book:

Simon, a space traveler from Earth, visited the planet Shaltoon. He was disconcerted to find that the Shaltoonians had different voices and personalities every day. Apparently they were different people every day, except for their physical appearance, which remained unchanged.

The students were asked to explain the principle behind the unusual phenomenon.

AGE-LEVEL ADAPTATION

Inquiry training can be used with children of all ages, but each age group requires adaptation. We have seen the method be successful with kindergarten children but encounter difficulty with third-graders. As with many other aspects of teaching, each group and each student are unique. However, there are several ways to simplify the model until students are able to engage in all phases.

For very young children, it is best to keep the content of the problem simple—perhaps with more emphasis on discovery than on a principle of causation. Problem situations like "What is in this box?" or "What is this unusual thing?" or "Why does one egg roll differently from the other?" are appropriate. One teacher we know showed her students a picture of a flying squirrel from a magazine for science teachers. Since most of us believe mammals do not fly, this was truly a discrepant event. She asked the students to come up with an explanation for this phenomenon using inquiry procedures.

Numerous children's science books are filled with simple science experiments, many of them suitable for primary grades. Mystery stories and riddles work well as stimuli for young children. Another way to adapt inquiry training to young children is to use visual material—props giving clues—which simplifies the stimuli and lessens the requirements for memory. It is useful to aim for only one or two specific objectives in a single inquiry training session. Initially (with students of all ages) it is good to start off with a simple game that requires yes/no questions. This game will give students confidence that they can formulate questions and avoid direct theory questions. Some teachers we know use the mystery bag; others play "I'm thinking of something I'm wearing. Guess what it is." Simple guessing games like this also give the students practice in distinguishing theory questions ("Is it your shirt?") from attribute questions ("Is it made of cotton?"). We recommend that teachers introduce and stress each element of inquiry separately. At first the teacher could pose all yes/no questions. Then they can ask students to convert their theory questions to experiments. One by one the teachers can tighten the constraints of the inquiry as they teach the students each of the elements. Trying to explain and enforce all of the elements at once will only frustrate both students and teachers.

Older students are better able to handle the inquiry process itself, and their subject matter—especially science—more readily lends itself to inquiry training. On the other hand, age and sex may be inhibiting factors in the process. Although there are more suitable discrepant events in the upper elementary and secondary curricula, it is usually necessary for the teacher to convert available materials from an expository mode into the inquiry mode—that is, to create a discrepant event.

LEARNING ENVIRONMENT ADAPTATIONS

Like many other models, especially information processing models, inquiry training can be taught in a teacher-directed setting or incorporated into more self-directed, learning-center environments. Discrepant events can be developed through print, film, or audio means, and task cards directing students to respond according to the model can be developed. The inquiry can be conducted over a period of several days, and the results of other students' inquiries can be shared. Students should have access to appropriate resources, and they may work together in groups. Students may also develop discrepant events and conduct inquiry sessions for peers.

INSTRUCTIONAL AND NURTURANT EFFECTS

The model promotes strategies of inquiry and the values and attitudes that are essential to an inquiring mind, including:

> Process skills (observing, collecting, and organizing data; identifying and controlling variables; formulating and testing hypotheses and explanations; inferring)
> Active, autonomous learning
> Verbal expressiveness
> Tolerance of ambiguity, persistence
> Logical thinking
> Attitude that all knowledge is tentative

The chief learning outcomes of inquiry training are the processes involved—observing, collecting and organizing data, identifying and controlling variables, making and testing hypotheses, formulating explana-

FIGURE 10–1   Instructional and nurturant effects: inquiry training model.

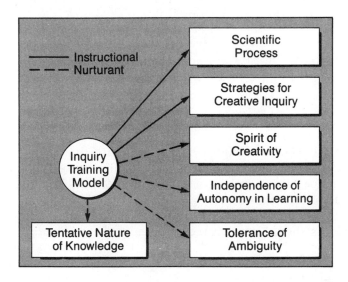

tions, and drawing inferences (see Figure 10–1). The model splendidly integrates these several process skills into a single, meaningful unit of experience.

The format of the model promotes active, autonomous learning as the students formulate questions and test ideas. It take courage to ask questions, but it is hoped that this type of risk will become second nature to the students. They will also become more proficient in verbal expression as well as in listening to others and remembering what has been said.

Although its emphasis is on process, inquiry training also results in the learning of content in any curriculum area from which problems are selected. For example, Suchman developed entire curricula in economics and geology. In our opinion, it is adaptable to all elementary and secondary curriculum areas.

SUMMARY CHART ▶ INQUIRY TRAINING MODEL

Syntax

Phase One: Confrontation with the Problem
    Explain inquiry procedures.
    Present discrepant event.

Phase Two: Data Gathering—Verification
    Verify the nature of objects and conditions.
    Verify the occurrence of the problem situation.

Phase Three: Data Gathering—Experimentation
    Isolate relevant variables.
    Hypothesize (and test) causal relationships.

Phase Four: Organizing, Formulating an Explanation
    Formulate rules or explanations.

Phase Five: Analysis of the Inquiry Process
    Analyze inquiry strategy and develop more effective ones.

Social System

The inquiry training model can be highly structured, with the teacher controlling the interaction and prescribing the inquiry procedures. However, the norms of inquiry are those of cooperation, intellectual freedom, and equality. Interaction among students should be encouraged. The intellectual environment is open to all relevant ideas, and teachers and students should participate as equals where ideas are concerned.

Principles of Reaction

1. Ensure that questions are phrased so they can be answered with yeses or nos, and that their substance does not require the teacher to do the inquiry.
2. Ask students to rephrase invalid questions.
3. Point out unvalidated points—for example, "We have not established that this is liquid."
4. Use the language of the inquiry process—for instance, identify student questions as theories and invite testing (experimenting).
5. Try to provide a free intellectual environment by not evaluating student theories.
6. Press students to make clearer statements of theories and provide support for their generalization.
7. Encourage interaction among students.

Support System

The optimal support is a set of confronting materials, a teacher who understands the intellectual processes and strategies of inquiry, and resource materials bearing on the problem.

CHAPTER 11

SYNECTICS
Enhancing Creative Thought

A junior high school class is creating a book of short stories and poems. Their English teacher, Martin Abramowitz, has gradually become aware that some stories and many of the poems are hackneyed and ordinary. He has been helping individuals rewrite their poems and stories, and some of them have been improved, but on the whole he is disappointed with the work.

Then Abramowitz runs across the work of William Gordon of Cambridge, Massachusetts, who believes that creativity can be enhanced by a series of group exercises. These exercises are designed to help us understand the process of creativity more completely and to use new metaphors and analogies, to "break set" and generate new alternatives. Abramowitz decides to try Gordon's methods. One morning, he has each of his students read a poem and a short story. He then says, "Today we're going to try something new that I hope will help us see our stories and poems in a different light. For the next 15 or 20 minutes I want us to play with ideas and then have you go back to your work and see what you can do to improve it. At the end of this exercise, I'm going to ask you to rewrite part or all of your poems and stories." He begins by asking what a poem is. The children give a variety of answers, from which Abramowitz selects key words and writes them on the board.

"It doesn't have to rhyme."
"It lets your feelings come out."
"It uses different kinds of words."

He then asks, "How is a poem like an automobile?" The children are puzzled. Then one ventures, "It takes you on a trip. It's a word trip, and you have to have the road in your imagination."

Someone else observes, "It is self-propelled—you just get in it and it goes."

Another student comments, "When you're writing one, sometimes you have trouble getting the motor started."

After a time, Abramowitz says, "Pick an animal—any animal." "How about a giraffe?" someone suggests. "OK," the teacher asks, "how is a poem like a giraffe?"

"It has a lot of parts fastened together in funny ways," one student laughs.

"It kind of stands above everything else and looks at things in a different way," another adds.

The exercise goes on. After a time, Abramowitz asks the students to select one of the words that they have dealt with in discussing a poem. They select the word *above.*

"How does it feel," he asks, "to be above?"

"You feel different," replies one. "You can see things you don't ordinarily even notice," says another.

"You'll start feeling superior if you don't watch out," says a third student.

And so it goes. Finally, Abramowitz asks the students to make lists of words they have been dealing with that seem to be opposite in some fashion—words that apply tension to each other. The students pick *giraffe* and *snail,* for they feel that both are animals but that they are very different in the way they live and move.

"Well," Abramowitz says, "let's come back to your poems and short stories. Think of them as giraffes and snails together; write your poems or stories as if they were a giraffe and a snail holding hands, going through the woods together."

Here are two products of that exercise.

THE MOTORCYCLE

It sounds like an enraged mountain lion.
It looks like a steel horse.
It shifts gears and changes notes.
It goes very fast.
The sound of the motorcycle
    breaks the stillness
        of the night.

THE ADVENTURES OF SAMUAL O'BRIAN, SECRET SPY

It all happened when Samual Watkins O'Brian, an average blonde-haired 35-year-old chemist, was working in Laboratory 200, Hartford, Connecticut, for the government. While mixing chemicals in a beaker, the substance started glowing strangely. It also became very hot. At that moment he dropped it to the floor. He turned to run, but before he had time to take a step it crashed to the floor, followed by a blinding explosion! As he started to run, he felt his skin shrinking. As he ran he shrank to a height of 5.5 inches, one-tenth his normal height!

His superior ran in with a fire extinguisher yelling, "What happened in here, Sam?"

While jumping up and down, Sam yelled, "I've shrunk! I've shrunk!" His superior made no reply. He again yelled out his cry for help. Then Sam, realizing that his yelling was useless over the roar of the fire that had now started, tugged at his superior's giant shoelace. His superior bent down to see what was happening with his shoelace, and he saw a very small and scared Samual O'Brian.

Samual yelled, "Hey Jack, pick me up *carefully!*"

His superior's reply was *"Cripes!* What happened to you?" Sam explained the story in Jack's ear while Jack ran swiftly with Sam in the palm of his hand to the guard on the second floor.

Jack said (when they got there), "Seal off the building! I have Top Secret government personnel and *speed it up*!!!" Because of the excitement, Sam fainted.

The next thing he knew he was in the Central Security President's office lying in a marble ashtray, filled with warm water (and plenty of bubbles, of course). He found himself staring into the face of David Shields, President of C.S.

Sam stated that he was so sorry to clutter up the President's desk but.... Then David broke in "Oh, it's nothing, people shrink every day around here, but I guess you wouldn't know because you can't see the rings around the bathtub ... er, uh, ashtray."

David presented Sam with a small box of cigars and a custom-fitted suit, James Bond style (if you know what I mean). Sam got dressed and David said, "We'd like you to work for us, Sam."

Martin Abramowitz has induced metaphoric thinking, a type of creativity, in his students. Synectics is an interesting approach to the development of creativity designed by William J. J. Gordon and his associates (1961). Gordon's initial work with synectics procedures was to develop "creativity groups" within industrial organizations—that is, groups of persons trained to work together to function as problem solvers or product developers. In recent years, Gordon has adapted synectics for use with school children, and materials containing many of the synectics activities are now being published. (For a complete list of synectics materials write to Synectics Education Systems, 121 Brattle Street, Cambridge, MA 02138.) The chief element in synectics is the use of analogies. In synectics exercises, students "play" with analogies until they relax and begin to enjoy making more and more metaphoric comparisons, as did Abramowitz's students. Then they use analogies to attack problems or ideas.

Ordinarily, when we are confronted with a task—say a problem to be solved or a piece of writing to be produced—we consciously become logical. We prepare to write by making an outline of the points to be made. We analyze the elements of a problem and try to think it through. We use our existing storehouse of words and phrases to set down our ideas; we use our storehouse of learned solutions to face a problem.

For most problems and tasks of expressing ourselves our logic works well enough. What do we do when our old solutions or ways of expressing ourselves are not sufficient to do the job? That is when we use synectics. It is designed to lead us into a slightly illogical world—to give us the opportunity to invent new ways of seeing things, expressing ourselves, and approaching problems.

For example, school officials struggle with the problem of how to deal with absenteeism. When a student repeatedly fails to come to school, what do they do? Frequently, they turn to punishment. And what punishment is available? Frequently, suspension. That is logical, isn't it? To choose a severe punishment to match what is regarded as a severe infraction? The trouble with the solution is that it imposes on the student as a penalty exactly the same condition that the student had chosen in lieu of school. Synectics is used to help us develop fresh ways of thinking about the student, the student's motives, the nature of penalties, our goals, and the nature of the problem. We have to develop empathy with someone who is in conflict with us. We have to deliberately avoid what appears to be logical thought because it leads us to an inadequate conception of the problem and, thus, an absurd (if logical) solution.

Through analogies we might conceive of our absentee as an "unhappy lark," as on a "destructive vacation," and the problem as one of ending an "empty feast." Our own needed behaviors may be ones of "seductive strictness," "strong lovingness," and "dangerous peacemaking."

If we can relax the premises that have blocked us, we can begin to generate new solutions. We can consider that we have been taking responsibility for the students in areas where they may need to be responsible for themselves. We can wonder whether the solution lies as much in our administration of the rules as it does in how we teach. We may wonder whether communities of peers might not create the energy and sense of belongingness that would attack the problem from a different perspective.

The social and scientific world in which we live abounds with problems for which new solutions are needed. Problems of poverty, international law, crime, just taxation, and war and peace would not exist if our logic did not fail us.

Striving for appropriate self-expression—trying to learn how to write and speak lucidly and compellingly—bedevils all of us. Two problems are persistent: grasping the subject clearly and comprehensively and generating appropriate forms of expression.

Let us consider another example from Martin Abramowitz's classroom in New York City:

Now, Martin Abramowitz's 7th-grade class, which we met earlier, is preparing a campaign in opposition to a change in Forest Service regulations that would permit a large grove of redwood trees to be cut down as part of a lumbering operation. They have made posters that they intend to display around their community and send to the members of the stage legislature. They have the rough sketches for the posters and their captions, and they are examining them . . .

"Well, what do you think?" asks Priscilla.

"Well, they're OK," says Tommy. "They sure say where we stand. Actually, though, I think they're a little dull."

"So do I," adds Maryann. "A couple of them are OK, but the others are real preachy and stiff."

"There's nothing really wrong with them," chimes in another, "they're just not very zingy."

After some discussion, it is obvious that nearly everybody feels the same way. They decide that two or three of the posters are well designed and convey their message, but they need some others that would be more poignant.

"Let's try synectics," suggests one of the children.

"With pictures and captions?" asks one of the other children. "I thought we could only use synectics with poetry. Can we use synectics with stuff like this?"

"Why sure we can," says Priscilla. "I don't know why I didn't think of it. We've been doing it with poetry all year long."

"Well we sure have nothing to lose," adds Tommy. "How would it work?"

"Well," says Priscilla, "we could see these posters we've done as the beginning point and then go through a synectics training exercise and see if it gives us some ideas for pictures and captions. We could think of redwood trees in terms of various personal and direct analogies and compressed conflicts."

"Well let's try it," chimes in George.

"Let's start right now," says Sally. "We could go through our exercises and then have lunch time to think about the posters."

"Can I be the leader?" asks Marsha. "I've got some super ideas for some stretching exercises."

"Is that OK?" says Priscilla.

The children agree and Marsha begins.

"How is a redwood tree like a toothpick?" she asks.

"You use the tree to pick the teeth of the gods," laughs George. Everyone joins in the laughter and they are off.

It's clear that Mr. Abramowitz has spent enough time using synectics that the students internalized the process and purpose. They can proceed on their own, drawing on the model when they find it helpful.

One of the present authors struggled for a month to write a single page that would introduce a book on school improvement. The introduction has to express the complexity of the situation the school occupies in society and to convey that it needs improvement, but it had to do so in an upbeat and not discouraging fashion. Finally, after an afternoon of synectics, he produced the following passages:

> Richly connected to its social milieu, tightly clasped by tradition and yet the medium of modern ideas and artifacts, the school floats paradoxically in its ocean of social forces. It is a cradle of social stability and the harbinger of cultural change. Throughout history its critics have found it both too backward and too advanced. It falls behind the times and fails to keep us in simultaneous cadence.
>
> Its missions are elusive. Basic education is prized but so are creativity, problem solving, academic excellence, and vocational skills, sometimes by the same people, sometimes not. Liberals and conservatives alike seek to make the school the instrument of social policy. It is the sword of the militant and the warm bosom of the humanist. Its students are varied. Talents and handicaps mingle, sometimes in the same minds and bodies.
>
> The inner city and rural hinterland make their claims on creaky old schoolhouses while shiny suburban schools grope for a coherent mission. Powerful self-concepts march through the front door of the school while timid souls slip in by the back stairs. Cultural differences are mixed together, with problems of identity and adaptation surfacing chaotically to be dealt with.
>
> Technologies strengthen the school's potential and threaten to replace it. Its personnel receive very little training but are asked to manage one of the most complex professional tasks in our society. They have little status but awesome responsibility both for individual children and for the health of the society as a whole.
>
> Because education exerts great influence on the young, society places great constraints on its schools so that they will reflect the prevailing social attitudes and will fit current views about how its children should be trained. Its very size draws attention. (In the United States there are more than 2,000,000 education professionals and about 8 percent of the gross national product is directly or indirectly consumed by the enterprises of education.) The public watches its investment carefully, scrutinizing educational practices, both traditional and innovative. (Joyce & Morine, 1976)
>
> Efficiency is highly prized, but innovations are watched with apprehension. Our societal patterns of schooling, established in the early 1800s, have become familiar and comfortable, and we want our children to have an education that has continuity with our own. Thus most citizens are cautious about educational innovation. People like the familiar old schoolhouse as much as they criticize it. They tend to believe that current problems in education are caused

by changes (perceived as a "lowering of standards") rather than because the old comfortable model of the school may be a little rusty and out-of-date. In fact, our society has changed a great deal since the days when the familiar and comfortable patterns of education were established, and many schools have become badly out of phase with the needs of children in today's world (Joyce, Hersh, and McKibbin, 1983, pp. 3–4).

This passage is by no means perfect, but it is much better than the prosaic passages that were its early drafts (e.g., "The public is somewhat ambivalent about the schools. In some ways they want a forward-looking education for their children and in others they want a familiar, stable education.").

ORIENTATION TO THE MODEL

GOALS AND ASSUMPTIONS

Gordon grounds synectics in four ideas that challenge conventional views about creativity. First, creativity is important in everyday activities. Most of us associate the creative process with the development of great works of art or music, or perhaps with a clever new invention. Gordon emphasizes creativity as a part of our daily work and leisure lives. His model is designed to increase problem-solving capacity, creative expression, empathy, and insight into social relations. He also stresses that the meanings of ideas can be enhanced through creative activity by helping us see things more richly.

Second, the creative process is not at all mysterious. It can be described, and it is possible to train persons directly to increase their creativity. Traditionally, creativity is viewed as a mysterious, innate, and personal capacity that can be destroyed if its processes are probed too deeply. In contrast, Gordon believes that if individuals understand the basis of the creative process, they can learn to use that understanding to increase the creativity with which they live and work, independently and as members of groups. Gordon's view that creativity is enhanced by conscious analysis led him to describe it and create training procedures that can be applied in schools and other settings.

Third, creative invention is similar in all fields—the arts, the sciences, engineering—and is characterized by the same underlying intellectual processes. This idea is contrary to common belief. In fact, to many people, creativity is confined to the arts. In engineering and the sciences, however, it is simply called by another name: *invention*. Gordon maintains that the link between generative thinking in the arts and that in the sciences is quite strong.

Gordon's fourth assumption is that individual and group invention (creative thinking) are very similar. Individuals and groups generate ideas and products in much the same fashion. Again, this is very different from the stance that creativity is an intensely personal experience, not to be shared.

THE CREATIVE STATE AND THE SYNECTICS PROCESS

The specific processes of synectics are developed from a set of assumptions about the psychology of creativity. First, by bringing the creative process to consciousness and by developing explicit aids to creativity, we can directly increase the creative capacity of both individuals and groups.

A second assumption is that the "emotional component is more important than the intellectual, the irrational more important than the rational" (Gordon, 1961, p. 6). Creativity is the development of new mental patterns. Nonrational interplay leaves room for open-ended thoughts that can lead to a mental state in which new ideas are possible. The basis for decisions, however, is always the rational; the irrational state is the best mental environment for exploring and expanding ideas, but it is not a decision-making stage. Gordon does not undervalue the intellect; he assumes that a logic is used in decision making and that technical competence is necessary to the formation of ideas in many areas. But he believes that creativity is essentially an *emotional* process, one that requires elements of irrationality and emotion to enhance intellectual processes. Much problem solving is rational and intellectual, but by adding the irrational we increase the likelihood that we will generate fresh ideas.

The third assumption is that the "emotional, irrational elements must be understood in order to increase the probability of success in a problem solving situation" (Gordon, 1961, p. 1). In other words, the analysis of certain irrational and emotional processes can help the individual and the group to increase their creativity by using irrationality constructively. Aspects of the irrational can be understood and consciously controlled. Achievement of this control, through the deliberate use of metaphor and analogy, is the object of synectics.

METAPHORIC ACTIVITY

Through the metaphoric activity of the synectics model, creativity becomes a conscious process. Metaphors establish a relationship of likeness, the comparison of one object or idea with another object or idea by using one in place of the other. Through these substitutions the creative process occurs, connecting the familiar with the unfamiliar or creating a new idea from familiar ideas.

Metaphor introduces conceptual distance between the student and the object or subject matter and prompts original thoughts. For example, by asking students to think of their textbook as an old shoe or as a river, we provide a structure, a metaphor, with which the students can think about something familiar in a new way. Conversely, we can ask students to think about a new topic, say the human body, in an old way by asking them to compare it to the transportation system. Metaphoric activity thus depends on and draws from the students' knowledge, helping them connect ideas from familiar content to those from new content, or view familiar content from a new perspective. Synectics strategies using metaphoric activity are designed, then, to provide a structure through which persons can free themselves to develop imagination and insight into everyday activities. Three types of analogies are used as the basis of synectics exercises: personal analogy, direct analogy, and compressed conflict.

PERSONAL ANALOGY

To make personal analogies requires students to empathize with the ideas or objects to be compared. Students must feel they have become part of the physical elements of the problem. The identification may be with a person, plant, animal, or nonliving thing. For example, students may be instructed, "Be an automobile engine. What do you feel like? Describe how you feel when you are started in the morning; when your battery goes dead; when you come to a stop light."

The emphasis in personal analogy is on empathetic involvement. Gordon gives the example of a problem situation in which the chemist personally identifies with the molecules in action. He might ask, "How would I feel if I were a molecule?" and then feel himself being part of the "stream of dancing molecules."

Personal analogy requires loss of self as one transports oneself into another space or object. The greater the conceptual distance created by loss of self, the more likely it is that the analogy is new and that the students have created or innovated. Gordon identifies four levels of involvement in personal analogy:

1. *First-person description of facts.* The person recites a list of well-known facts but presents no new way of viewing the object or animal and shows no empathetic involvement. In terms of the car engine, the person might say, "I feel greasy" or "I feel hot."
2. *First-person identification with emotion.* The person recites common emotions but does not present new insights. "I feel powerful" (as the car engine).
3. *Empathetic identification with a living thing.* The student identifies emotionally and kinesthetically with the subject of the analogy.
4. *Empathetic identification with a nonliving object.* This level requires the most commitment. The person sees himself or herself as an inorganic object and tries to explore the problem from a sympathetic point of view. "I feel exploited. I cannot determine when I start and stop. Someone does that for me" (as the car engine).

The purpose of introducing these levels of personal analogy is not to identify forms of metaphoric activity but to provide guidelines for how well conceptual distance has been established. Gordon believes that the usefulness of analogies is directly proportional to the distance created. The greater the distance, the more likely the student is to come up with new ideas.

DIRECT ANALOGY

Direct analogy is a simple comparison of two objects or concepts. The comparison does not have to be identical in all respects. Its function is simply to transpose the conditions of the real topic or problem situation to another situation in order to present a new view of an idea or problem. This involves identification with a person, plant, animal, or nonliving thing. Gordon cites the experience of the engineer watching a shipworm tunneling into a timber. As the worm ate its way into the timber by constructing a tube for itself and moving forward, the engineer, Sir March Isumbard Brunel, got the notion of using caissons to construct underwater tunnels (Gordon, 1961, pp. 40–41). Another example of direct analogy occurred when a group was attempting to devise a can with a top that could be used to cover the can once it had been opened. In this instance, the analogy of the pea pod gradually emerged, which produced the idea of a seam placed a distance below the top of the can, thus permitting a removable lid.

COMPRESSED CONFLICT

The third metaphorical form is compressed conflict, generally a two-word description of an object in which the words seem to be opposites or to contradict each other. *Tiredly aggressive* and *friendly foe* are two examples. Gordon's examples are *life-saving destroyer* and *nourishing flame*. He also cites Pasteur's expression, *safe attack*. Compressed conflicts, according to Gordon, provide the broadest insight into a new subject. They reflect the student's ability to incorporate two frames of reference with respect to a single object. The greater the distance between frames of reference, the greater the mental flexibility.

STRETCHING EXERCISES: USING METAPHORS

These three types of metaphors form the basis of the sequence of activities in this model of teaching. They can also be used separately with groups, as a warm-up to the creative process—that is, to problem solving; we refer to this use as *stretching exercises*.

Stretching exercises provide experience with the three types of metaphoric activity, but they are not related to any particular problem situation nor do they follow a sequence of phases. They teach students the process of metaphoric thinking before asking them to use it to solve a problem, create a design, or explore a concept. They are simply asked to respond to ideas such as the following:

DIRECT ANALOGIES

An orange is like what living thing?
How is a school like a salad?
How are polar bears like frozen yogurt?
Which is softer—a whisper or a kitten's fur?

PERSONAL ANALOGIES

Be a cloud. Where are you? What are you doing?
How do you feel when the sun comes out and dries you up?
Pretend you are your favorite book. Describe yourself.
What are your three wishes?

COMPRESSED CONFLICTS

How is a computer shy and aggressive?
What machine is like a smile and a frown?

THE MODEL OF TEACHING

SYNTAX

There are actually two strategies or models of teaching based on synectics procedures. One of these (*creating something new*) is designed to make the familiar strange, to help students see old problems, ideas, or products in a new, more creative light. The other strategy (*making the strange familiar*) is designed to make new, unfamiliar ideas more meaningful. Although both strategies employ the three types of analogy, their objectives, syntax, and principles of reaction are different. We refer to creating something new as strategy one, and making the strange familiar as strategy two.

Strategy one helps students see familiar things in unfamiliar ways by using analogies to create conceptual distance. Except for the final step, in which the students return to the original problem, they do not make simple comparisons. The objective of this strategy may be to develop a new understanding; to empathize with a show-off or bully; to design a new doorway or city; to solve social or interpersonal problems, such as a garbage strike or two students fighting with each other; or to solve personal problems, such as how to concentrate better when reading. The role of the teacher is to guard against premature analyses and closure. The syntax of strategy one appears in Table 11–1.

The following transcript of a synectics session shows a teacher helping students to see a familiar concept in fresh ways. At the beginning, the students pick the concept of "The Hood," to be described later in a writing

TABLE 11–1   SYNTAX FOR CREATING SOMETHING NEW, STRATEGY ONE

Phase One: Description of Present Condition	Phase Two: Direct Analogy
Teacher has students describe situation or situation as they see it now.	Students suggest direct analogies, select one, and explore (describe) it further.

Phase Three: Personal Analogy	Phase Four: Compressed Conflict
Students "become" the analogy they selected in phase two.	Students take their descriptions from phases two and three, suggest several compressed conflicts, and choose one.

Phase Five: Direct Analogy	Phase Six: Reexamination of the Original Task
Students generate and select another direct analogy, based on the compressed conflict.	Teacher has students move back to original task or problem and use the last analogy and/or the entire synectics experience.

composition. The lesson illustrates the six phases of the model (Gordon, 1971, pp. 7–11):

1. **TEACHER:** Now the problem is how to present this hood so that he's the hoodiest of hoods, but also a special, individualized person.
STUDENT: He robs the Rabbinical School.
STUDENT: Let's name him.
STUDENT:: Trog.
STUDENT: Al.
STUDENT: Slash.
STUDENT: Eric.
TEACHER: His names don't matter all that much. Let's call him Eric. What can we say about Eric?
STUDENT: Black, greasy hair. They all have black, greasy hair.

1. *Phase One: Describing the Problem or Present Condition.* Teacher asks students to discuss the familiar idea.

STUDENT: Long, blonde hair—bleached—peroxided—with baby-blues. Eyes, I mean.

STUDENT: Bitten fingernails.

STUDENT: He's short and muscular.

STUDENT: Maybe he should be scrawny.

STUDENT: Bow-legged and yellow teeth and white, tight Levis.

2. TEACHER: Is there anything here that's original? If you wrote that and backed off and read it, what would you think?

CLASS: No! Stereotyped! Standard! No personality! Very general! Same old stuff!

TEACHER: I agree. Eric, so far, is like every other hood. Now we have a problem to attack!

TEACHER: We must define a personality for this hood, for Eric.

STUDENT: He's got to be individualized.

STUDENT: He has to have a way of getting money.

3. TEACHER: That's still an over-general idea of Eric. Let's put some strain into this idea. Hold it. Suppose I ask you to give me a Direct Analogy, something like Eric, but it's a machine. Tell me about a machine that has Eric's qualities as you see him. Not a human being, a machine.

STUDENT: He's a washing machine. A dishwasher.

STUDENT: An old beat-up car.

STUDENT: I want him to be a rich hood.

STUDENT: A beer factory.

STUDENT: A pinball machine in a dive.

STUDENT: Roulette.

4. TEACHER: You're focusing on the kinds of machines that Eric plays with. What is the thing that has his qualities in it?

2. Teacher has students state the problem . . .

and define the task.

3. *Phase Two: Direct Analogy.* Teacher moves the students into analogies. He asks for a direct analogy. He also specifies the nature of the analogy—that is, a machine—in order to assure getting one of some distance (organic-inorganic comparison).

4. Teacher reflects to students what they are doing so that they can be pushed to more creative analogies.

STUDENT: An electric can opener.
STUDENT: A vacuum cleaner.
STUDENT: A neon sign.
STUDENT: A jello mold.

5. TEACHER: What is the machine that would make the strangest comparison between it and Eric? Go ahead and vote. (The class voted for the dishwasher.)

5. Teacher lets students select the analogy to develop, but he provides the criterion for selection: "strangest comparison."

6. TEACHER: First of all, how does a dishwasher work?

6. Teacher moves students simply to *explore* (describe) the machine they selected before making comparisons to their original source.

STUDENT: People put in the dirty dishes and the water goes around and around and the dishes come out clean.
STUDENT: There's a blower in the one that's in the common room.
STUDENT: It's all steam inside. Hot!
STUDENT: I was thinking that if you want to make an analogy between the washer and the joy . . .

7. TEACHER: Hold it. Just stay with me. Don't look backward and make an analogical comparison too soon . . . and now is probably too soon.

7. Teacher controls responses to keep students from pushing to a comparison too soon. No comparisons to original source are made before moving on to another analogy.

8. TEACHER: OK. Now, try being the dishwasher. What does it feel like to be a dishwasher? Tell us. Make yourself the dishwasher.
STUDENT: Well, all these things are given to me. Dishes are dirty. I want to get them clean. I'm trying. I throw off some steam and finally I get them clean. That's my duty.

8. *Phase Three: Personal Analogy.* Teacher asks for personal analogy.

9. TEACHER: Come on now people! You've got to put yourselves into the dishwasher and be it. All Lee's told us is what we already know about a dishwasher. There's none of *Lee* in it. It's hard, but try to *be* the dishwasher.
STUDENT: It's very discouraging. You're washing all day long. I never get to know anybody. They keep

9. Teacher reflects to students the fact that they are describing the dishwasher, not what it *feels* like to be a dishwasher.

throwing these dishes at me, and I just throw the steam at them. I see the same type of dishes.

STUDENT: I get mad and get the dishes extra hot, and I burn people's fingers.

STUDENT: I feel very repressed. They keep feeding me dishes. All I can do is shut myself off.

STUDENT: I get so mad at everybody maybe I won't clean the dishes and then everybody will get sick.

STUDENT: I just love garbage. I want more and more. The stuff that falls off the dishes is soft and mushy and good to eat.

10. TEACHER: Let's look at the notes I've been making about your responses. Can you pick two words that argue with each other?

STUDENT: "Used" vs. "clean."

STUDENT: "Duty" vs. "what you want to do."

TEACHER: How can we put that more poetically?

STUDENT: "Duty" vs. "inclination."

STUDENT: "Duty" vs. "whim."

STUDENT: "Discouraging fun."

STUDENT: "Angry game."

11. TEACHER: All right. What one do you like best? Which one has the truest ring of conflict?

CLASS: "Angry game."

12. TEACHER: All right. Can you think of a direct analogy, an example from the animal world, of "angry game?"

STUDENT: A lion in the cage at the circus.

STUDENT: Rattlesnake.

10. *Phase Four: Compressed Conflict.* Teacher asks for compressed conflict as outgrowth of the personal analogy: "Can you pick two words that argue with each other?

11. Teacher ends enumeration of possible compressed conflicts and asks them to select one. The teacher furnishes the criterion: "Which has the truest ring of conflict?"

12. *Phase Five: Direct Analogy.* Recycling the analogies; compressed conflict is not explored but serves as the basis of the next direct analogy, an example from the animal world of "angry game." There is no mention of the original.

STUDENT: A pig ready for slaughter.
STUDENT: A bear when it's attacking.
STUDENT: Bullfrog.
STUDENT: A bird protecting its young.
STUDENT: Bullfight.
STUDENT: A fish being caught.
STUDENT: A skunk.
STUDENT: A horse.
STUDENT: A charging elephant.
STUDENT: A fox hunt on horseback.
STUDENT: Rodeo.
STUDENT: Porcupine.
TEACHER: Does anyone know where we are?
STUDENT: We're trying to put personality into Eric, trying to make him more original.

13. TEACHER: All right. Which of all the things you just thought of do you think would make the most exciting direct analogy?
(Class chooses the bullfight.)

TEACHER: Now we go back to Eric. How can we get the bullfight to describe Eric for us. Does anyone know what I mean by that?
14. (Class doesn't respond.)

15. TEACHER: All right. What do we know about a bullfight?

STUDENT: He'll have to be the bull or the matador. I say he's the bull.
STUDENT: Bull runs into the ring and he's surrounded by strangeness.
STUDENT: They stick things into him and goad him . . .
STUDENT: . . . from horses and from the ground.
STUDENT: But sometimes he doesn't get killed.
STUDENT: And everytime the bull is downgraded the crowd yells.

13. Teacher ends the enumeration of direct analogies. Again, he has the students select one but he gives the criterion: "Which of all the things you just thought of do you think would make the most *exciting* direct analogy?"

14. Students are not into the analogy of the bullfight yet.
15. Teacher gets students to explore the characteristics of the bullfight, the analogy.

16. TEACHER: What happens at the end?
STUDENT: They drag him off with horses.
STUDENT: How do they finish him off?
STUDENT: A short sword.
17. TEACHER: How can we use this information to tell us something about Eric? How will you talk about Eric in terms of the material we've developed about a bullfight?
STUDENT: He's the bull.
STUDENT: He's the matador.
STUDENT: If he's the bull, then the matador is society.
TEACHER: Why don't you write something about Eric in terms of the bullfight? Talk about his personality and the outward signs of it. The reader opens your story about Eric, and he reads. It is your reader's first introduction to Eric. (A pause while the students write.)
TEACHER: All finished? All right, let's read your stuff, from left to right.

16. Teacher tries to obtain more information about the analogy.

17. *Phase Six: Reexamination of the Task.* Getting students to make comparisons; return to the original problem or task.

Here are a few examples of the students' writing.

In rage, running against a red neon flag and blinded by its shadow, Eric threw himself down on the ground. As if they were going to fall off, blood throbbed in his ears. No use fighting anymore. The knife wound in his side; the metallic jeers that hurt worse than the knife; the flash of uniforms and the flushed faces of the crowd made him want to vomit all over their clean robes.

He stood there in the middle of the street staring defiantly at the crowd. Faces leered back at him. Scornful eyes, huge red mouths, twisted laughs; Eric looked back as the crowd approached and drew his hand up sharply as one man began to speak. "Pipe down kid. We don't want any of your nonsense."

He was enclosed in a ring. People cheering all around for his enemy. He has been trained all his life to go out and take what he wanted and now there was an obstacle in his course. Society was bearing down and telling him he was all wrong. He must go to them and he was becoming confused. People should cheer at the matador.

The matador hunts his prey. His claim to glory is raised by the approaching approval of the crowd. For although they brought all their holiday finery, the bull is goaded, and the matador smiles complacently. You are but my instrument and I hold the sword. (Gordon, 1970, pp. 7–11)

The synectics model has stimulated the students to see and feel the original idea (a gangster or hood, described in stereotypic terms) in a variety of fresh ways. If they had been solving a problem, we would expect that they would see it more richly and increase the solutions they could explore.

By contrast, strategy two, making the strange familiar, seeks to increase the students' understanding and internalization of substantially new or difficult material. In this analogy, metaphor is used for *analyzing*, not for creating conceptual distance as in strategy one. For instance, the teacher might present the concept of culture to her class. Using familiar analogies (such as a stove or a house), the students begin to define the characteristics that are present and those that are lacking in the concept. The strategy is both analytical, and convergent: Students constantly alternate between defining the characteristics of the more familiar subject and comparing these to the characteristics of the unfamiliar topic.

In phase one of this strategy, explaining the new topic, the students are provided with information. In phase two the teacher, or the students, suggest a direct analogy. Phase three involves "being the familiar" (personalizing the direct analogy). In phase four, students identify and explain the points of similarity between the analogy and the substantive material. In phase five, students explain the differences between analogies. As a measure of their acquisition of the new information, students can suggest and analyze their own familiar analogies in phases six and seven. The syntax of strategy two appears in Table 11–2.

The following is an illustration of strategy two as it has been used in a programmed workbook. The students are asked to make a comparison between democracy (new topic) and the body (familiar topic). The sample presented here does not include the personal analogy (phase three), which we recommend as part of the strategy. We feel that asking the students to "be the thing" before asking them to make intellectual connections will increase the richness of their thinking. In this example, the student is first presented with a short, substantive paragraph:

Democracy is a form of government that is based on the highest possible respect for the individual. All individuals have equal rights, protected by law. Since each person has a vote, when the people so desire they can change the law to further protect themselves. The role of education in a democracy is critically important because the right to vote carries with it the responsibility to understand issues. An uneducated voting public could be led by a power-hungry political group into voting away their right to freedom. Thus democracy puts all its faith in the individual, in all the people . . . democracy's respect for the individual is expressed in the right of individuals to own property such as industries whose purpose is to make profit in competition with others.

TABLE 11—2   SYNTAX FOR MAKING THE STRANGE FAMILIAR,
              STRATEGY TWO

Phase One: Substantive Input	Phase Two: Direct Analogy
Teacher provides information on new topic.	Teacher suggests direct analogy and asks students to describe the analogy.

Phase Three: Personal Analogy	Phase Four: Comparing Analogies
Teacher has students "become" the direct analogy.	Students identify and explain the points of similarity between the new material and the direct analogy.

Phase Five: Explaining Differences	Phase Six: Exploration
Students explain where the analogy does not fit.	Students reexplore the original topic on its own terms.

Phase Seven: Generating Analogy
Students provide their own direct analogy and explore the similarities and differences.

Next the student is told:

List the connections you see between the description of democracy and the human body. Certain elements of the human body are written in the left-hand column. In the right-hand column jot down the elements in the paragraph on democracy that you think are parallel.

Body

each cell
muscles
brain
body as whole
disease

Democracy

each individual
education
law
democratic country
loss of freedom

After the student has filled in his connection list he is asked to "Write a short paragraph showing your analogical connections. Be sure to point out where you think the body analogue fits and where it doesn't."

A sample response:

Each body cell is an individual. It may not look like it to the naked eye, but that's how it looks under a microscope. The muscles are education because they must be taught (except for automatic things such as blinking and digestion, and there may be teaching here that we don't know about) to do certain acts—walking, games, knitting, etc. The brain is the law. If I do something wrong, my mind tells me and my brain is in my mind. The body as a whole is democratic because it depends on the health of all the cells. When there is disease the body loses freedom and a power-hungry disease takes over. The body dies when the disease takes over all the cells.

Non-fit. In democracy the people control the government by voting, and then they can always repair bad laws. You can't always repair a body that is growing older . . . it will finally die.

So far in this sample exercise the student has been held by the hand. An analogue was presented to him, and all he had to do was make the connections as he saw them. The final skill taught in this exercise is *application*. The student's program tells him:

Now think up your own analogue for democracy. Draw on the non-living world to make sure that your analogue is not like the body analogue. Write your choice of analogue on the line below. If your analogue doesn't fit, pick a new one. REMEMBER that analogues never fit exactly, they are just a way of thinking.

Use this list form to get you going. Fill in the elements of your analogue and add more elements about democracy if you want.

Your Analogue	Democracy
automobile	democracy
each part	each individual
education	design of parts
car itself	democracy
no gas	loss of freedom

In the final phase of the programmed exercise he is told:

Now write your connections in the best prose you can. First get your connective thoughts down; then go back and worry about grammar. Don't let grammar get in your way while you are trying to say what you mean. Grammar is a skill that makes it easier for your reader; so do it later. Try *not* to write more than the following lines allow. *Quality not quantity*. Remember, show the fits and non-fits.

The student writes:

> All parts of a car are like the individuals in a democracy. When they are all in good shape, they are free and the car runs well. The way each part was made was its education. God gave men the right to be free, and God gave the car's engine the right to run—how the gases explode in the engine is God's gift. If democracy is neglected, then no freedom. If the car runs out of gas, then no freedom.

One further small phase is necessary to make sure the students realize that analogues are not exact parallels.... The student is told: "On the lines below, explain where your analogue doesn't fit."

A sample response follows:

> In a democracy, all the people must not neglect the country. In a car, it is the owner who neglects when he forgets to fill her up. Also I tried to find "profit" in a car—and couldn't. Any competition is a race in a car—not like competition in a democracy. Also, there are so many freedom laws in a democracy, and the only law I can think of for a car is the science law that makes the engine run.

The major difference between the two strategies lies in their use of analogy. In strategy one, students move through a series of analogies without logical constraints; conceptual distance is increased, and imagination is free to wander. In strategy two, students try to connect two ideas and to identify the connections as they move through the analogies. The strategy the teacher selects depends on whether he or she is trying to help students create something new or to explore the unfamiliar.

SOCIAL SYSTEM

The model is moderately structured, with the teacher initiating the sequence and guiding the use of the operational mechanisms. The teacher also helps the students intellectualize their mental processes. The students, however, have freedom in their open-ended discussions as they engage in metaphorical problem solving. Norms of cooperation, "play of fancy," and intellectual and emotional equality are essential to establishing the setting for creative problem solving. The rewards are internal, coming from students' satisfaction and pleasure with the learning activity.

PRINCIPLES OF REACTION

The instructor notes the extent to which individuals seem to be tied to regularized patterns of thinking, and he or she tries to induce psychological states likely to generate a creative response. In addition, the teacher himself or herself must use the nonrational to encourage the reluctant student to indulge in irrelevance, fantasy, symbolism, and other devices necessary to break out of set channels of thinking. Because the teacher as model is probably an essential of the method, he or she has to learn to accept the bizarre and the unusual. The instructor must accept all student responses to ensure that students feel no external judgments on their creative expressions. The more difficult the problem is, or seems to be, to solve, the more it is necessary for the teacher to accept far-fetched analogies so that individuals develop fresh perspectives on problems.

In strategy two the teacher should guard against premature analyses. He or she also clarifies and summarizes the progress of the learning activity and, hence, the students' problem-solving behavior.

SUPPORT SYSTEM

The group most of all needs facilitation by a leader competent in synectics procedures. It also needs, in the case of scientific problems, a laboratory in which it can build models and other devices to make problems concrete and to permit practical invention to take place. The class requires a work space of its own and an environment in which creativity will be prized and utilized. A typical classroom can probably provide these necessities, but a classroom-sized group may be too large for many synectics activities, and smaller groups would need to be created.

APPLICATION

USING SYNECTICS IN THE CURRICULUM

Synectics is designed to increase the creativity of individuals and groups. Sharing the synectics experience can build a feeling of community among students. Students learn about their fellow classmates as they watch them react to an idea or problem. Thoughts are valued for their potential contribution to the group process. Synectics procedures help create a community of equals in which simply having a thought is the sole basis for status. This norm and that of playfulness quickly give support to even the most timid participant.

Synectics procedures may be used with students in all areas of the curriculum, the sciences as well as the arts. They can be applied to both teacher-student discussion in the classroom and to teacher-made materials for the students. The products or vehicles of synectics activity need not always be written: They can be oral, or they can take the form of role plays, paintings and graphics, or simply changes in behavior. When using synectics to look at social or behavioral problems, you may wish to notice situational behavior before and after synectics activity and observe changes. It is also interesting to select modes of expression that contrast with the original topic, such as having students paint a picture of prejudice or discrimination. The concept is abstract, but the mode of expression is concrete.

Some possible uses of the creative process and its accompanying emotional states are discussed in the following paragraphs.

CREATIVE WRITING

Strategy one of the synectics model is an excellent instructional strategy for developing creative-writing abilities. Writing, either expository writing about a particular concept (such as friendship) or more personalized writing (regarding an emotion or an experience), is an area of the language arts program where synectics can help students develop highly creative styles of expression. The metaphoric activity stimulates students' imaginations and helps them record their thoughts and feelings.

EXPLORING SOCIAL PROBLEMS

Strategy one is excellent for exploring social and disciplinary problems. The metaphor creates distance, so the confrontation does not threaten the learner, and discussion and self-examination are possible. The personal analogy phase is critical for developing insight.

PROBLEM SOLVING

Problem solving concerned with social issues, interpersonal relations, or personal problems is amenable to synectics. The objective of strategy two is to break set and conceptualize the problem in a new way in order to suggest fresh approaches to it. An example of a social issue would be how to improve relations between the police and the community. Reducing family spending is an example of an interpersonal-relations problem. Personal problems might include how to stop fighting with a friend, how to do math lessons, how to feel better about wearing glasses, or how to stop making fun of people.

CREATING A DESIGN OR PRODUCT

Synectics can also be used to create a product or design. A product is something tangible, such as a painting, a building, or a bookshelf, whereas a design is a plan, such as an idea for a party or a new means of transportation. Eventually, designs or plans become real, but for the purposes of this model they remain as sketches or outlines.

BROADENING OUR PERSPECTIVE OF A CONCEPT

Abstract ideas such as culture, prejudice, and economy are difficult to internalize because we cannot see them in the same way we can see a table or building, yet we frequently use them in our language. Synectics is a good way to make a familiar idea "strange" and thereby obtain another perspective on it.

We have found that synectics can be used with all ages, though with very young children it is best to stick to stretching exercises. Beyond this, adjustments are the same as for any other approach to teaching—care to work within their experience, rich use of concrete materials, attentive pacing, and explicit outlining of procedures.

The model often works effectively with students who withdraw from more "academic" learning activities because they are not willing to risk being wrong. Conversely, high-achieving students who are only comfortable giving a response they are sure is "right" often feel reluctant to participate. We believe that for these reasons alone, synectics is valuable to everyone.

Synectics combines easily with other models. It can stretch concepts being explored with the information-processing family; open up dimensions of social issues explored through role playing, group investigation, or jurisprudential thinking; and expand the richness of problems and feelings opened up by other models in the personal family.

The most effective use of synectics develops over time. It has short-term results in stretching views of concepts and problems, but when students are exposed to it repeatedly, they can learn how to use it with increasing skill—and they learn to enter a metaphoric mode with increasing ease and completeness.

Gordon, Poze, and their associates have developed a wide assortment of materials for use in schools, especially in the language development areas (Gordon and Poze, n.d.). The strategy is universally attractive, and its fortunate combination of enhancing productive thinking and nurturing empathy and interpersonal closeness finds it many uses with all ages and most curriculum areas.

Instructional and Nurturant Effects

As shown in Figure 11–1, the synectics model contains strong elements of both instructional and nurturant values. Through his belief that the creative process can be communicated and that it can be improved through direct training, Gordon has developed specific instructional techniques. Synectics is applied, however, not only to the development of general creative power but also to the development of creative responses over a variety of subject-matter domains. Gordon clearly believes that the creative energy will enhance learning in these areas. To this end, he emphasizes a social environment that encourages creativity and uses group cohesion to generate energy that enables the participants to function interdependently in a metaphoric world.

The method of synectics has been explicitly designed to improve the creativity of individuals and of groups. However, the implicit learning from this model is equally vivid. Participation in a synectics group invariably creates a unique shared experience that fosters interpersonal understanding and a sense of community. Members learn about one another as each person reacts to the common event in his or her unique way. Individ-

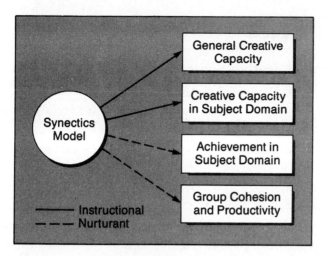

FIGURE 11–1   Instructional and nurturant effects: synectics model.

uals become acutely aware of their dependence on the various perceptions of other group members. Each thought, no matter how prosaic, is valued for its potential catalytic effect on one's own thoughts. Simply having a thought is the sole basis for status in this community, and the playfulness of synectics activities encourages even the most timid participant.

Another approach to the stimulation of creativity through metaphoric activity is presented by Judith and Donald Sanders (1984). Their book is particularly useful for the range of explicit applications that are included. We have noticed that many educators are not automatically aware of the spectrum of useful applications for models designed to induce divergent thinking. For some reason, many people think of "creativity" as an aptitude that defines talent in the arts, especially writing, painting, and sculpture; whereas the creators of these models believe that this aptitude can be improved and that it has applications in nearly every human endeavor and, thus, in every curriculum area. By providing illustrations in the setting of goals, the development of empathy, the study of values, a variety of areas of problem solving, and the increase of perspectives for viewing topics, the Sanders make a clear and convincing case for the power of these models.

SUMMARY CHART ▶ SYNECTICS

Syntax of Strategy One: Creating Something New

Phase One: Description of the Present Condition
Teacher has students describe situation or topic as they see it now.

Phase Two: Direct Analogy
Students suggest direct analogies, select one, and explore (describe) it further.

Phase Three: Personal Analogy
Students "become" the analogy they selected in phase two.

Phase Four: Compressed Conflict
Students take their descriptions from phase two and three, suggest several compressed conflicts, and choose one.

Phase Five: Direct Analogy
Students generate and select another direct analogy, based on the compressed conflict.

Phase Six: Reexamination of the Original Task
Teacher has students move back to original task or problem and use the last analogy and/or the entire synectics experience.

Social System

The model is moderately structured. Teacher initiates phases, but students' responses are quite open. Norms of creativity and "play-of-fancy" are encouraged. Rewards are internal.

Principles of Reaction

Encourages openness, nonrational, creative expression. Model, if necessary.
Accept all student responses.
Select analogies that help students stretch their thinking.

Support System

No special support system.

Syntax of Strategy Two: Making the Strange Familiar

Phase One: Substantive Input
  Teacher provides information on new topic.

Phase Two: Direct Analogy
  Teacher suggests direct analogy and asks students to describe the analogy.

Phase Three: Personal Analogy
  Teacher has students "become" the direct analogy.

Phase Four: Comparing Analogies
  Students identify and explain the points of similarity between the new material and the direct analogy.

Phase Five: Explaining Differences
  Students explain where the analogy does not fit.

Phase Six: Exploration
  Students reexplore the original topic on its own terms.

Phase Seven: Generating Analogy
  Students provide their own direct analogy and explore the similarities and differences.

CHAPTER 12

THE DEVELOPING INTELLECT
Adjusting Models to Cognitive Development

S C E N A R I O

A high school in Seattle, Washington, has arranged a minicourse to help junior students identify the higher-education options available and learn how to apply to junior colleges, business schools, colleges, and universities.

The minicourse has included discussions with college admissions officers and the reading of *Barrons Guide to Colleges*. In addition, representatives of local business and trade schools have spoken to the group.

In the course of their exploration, the students have discovered that some colleges give preferential treatment to minority persons to increase the racial and ethnic balances at their schools. One of the students, however, has brought in a newspaper clipping about deliberations in the Bakke case in which an applicant to law school has challenged whether a school has the right to admit students who belong to racial and ethnic minorities while denying admission to Caucasian students whose credentials may exceed those of the admitted students.

This precipitates a discussion about the problems entailed in differential admissions policies. Some students feel that the issue should be decided strictly on the basis of achievement in high school and test scores.

"That's the only way," says one. "Anything else is unfair. What the heck are we working for anyway?"

Some students feel that the only way to bring about a better balance in the professions is to have admissions quotas. Others feel that the problem is one of economic opportunity and that there would be plenty of qualified minority students if there were enough scholarships to go around.

Mr. Jones, the guidance counselor, concludes that although many students are arguing from a "right-and-wrong" orientation, a few students seem to have the attitude that if the system works for them they are not going to worry about the issues involved. Some students feel that prior achievement ought to be enough for admission regardless of the social consequences, while others feel that equality must be achieved regardless of the feelings of individuals who believe they are victims of "reverse discrimination."

Since he has responsibility for a weekly seminar on general issues of adjustment and personal development, Mr. Jones decides to use this opportunity to help students develop a more complex view of the moral issues involved. He comments, "I'd like to see if each of you can think this problem out in terms of principles you're willing to live with for a long time to come. Let's suppose that you are responsible for the admission of students to colleges. As a group, let's decide on the issues. Then each of you, as an admissions officer, will prepare an argument about the issues— you will decide where you stand on the issues, and you will develop admissions principles with which you think you can live."

Mr. Jones has used the framework developed by Lawrence Kohlberg to analyze the stages of students' moral development. He is applying the model to help students rise toward the next, more complex, level of development.

How do we adjust teaching to the intellectual development of our students?

One of the most important areas of psychology is devoted to the study of how humans learn to think. It focuses on the question of development— that is, on what kinds of thinking characterize us as infants and on what changes occur as we mature. Especially important for teachers is the study of how we can influence the development of thinking and how we can match instruction to the developmental levels of our students.

In this chapter we concentrate on the work of Swiss psychologist Jean Piaget (Piaget, 1952) who published his first studies in the mid-1920s and whose active work spanned 50 years. Recently, Piaget's philosophy of development has gained increasing popularity with educators. Currently, the most widespread applications of Piaget are in the areas of curriculum for young children and in the organization of educational environment for students of all ages. Two strategies are used to apply developmental psychology to teaching. One strategy matches the curriculum to the student's level of development, which necessarily involves accurately assessing the student's stage of growth. Another calls for instruction that accelerates intellectual development, making it occur more rapidly than if teaching did not take place. The framework presented here adjusts instruction to the learner's stage of development.

In our discussion about Piaget we draw heavily on the work of those who have summarized Piaget's theory and have explained its application, especially Flavell (1963), Hunt (1961), Furth (1969), Sigel and Hooper (1968), and Wadsworth (1978).

Theory of Development: Intellectual Stages

Piaget believes that human beings develop increasingly more complex levels of thinking in definite stages. Each stage is characterized by the possession of certain concepts or intellectual structures, which he refers to as *schemas*. Schemas organize the world in some way (the early schemas, for example, are very egocentric and place the student at the center of the universe); schemas are programs or strategies that the individual uses as he or she interacts with the environment.

In the course of life, students acquire experience. They assimilate this experience into their present patterns of behavior. After awhile, however, their present patterns become inadequate to explain their new experiences, and then they develop new schemas by accommodating to the new information. The process of *assimilation* is the incorporation of new experience. *Accommodation* is changing one's structure to fit the new experiences that occur.

The schemas mediate between the child and his or her environment. Furth uses the example of a baby who has acquired the ability to grasp objects. The baby moves about the environment relating to many things by grasping them—that is, by reaching out a hand and closing it over them. Thus, much experience that the baby receives during a certain period is in terms of grasping behavior, which is his or her schema, or strategy, for relating to his or her surroundings. The child's intellectual capacities grow through the development of more complex schemas for assimilating the environment. The major mechanism by which this occurs is accommodation.

Experience slowly supplies the child with information that cannot be handled adequately through the existing structures; the schemas gradually accommodate, and new ones develop. For example, children shopping with their mothers in the supermarket gradually learn that there is an order to the aisles in which the goods are stacked. Encountering this order again and again, and learning that certain objects are always in the same places are likely, together with other experiences, to result in an understanding of order. Prior to acquiring such an appreciation, the child sees any collection of objects as unordered. After that, he or she is able to perceive their order. The child is now intellectually able to assimilate new information, such as that baseball players run to first base first, whereas before that the schema to assimilate that information was lacking.

At each stage of development the human organism is, for a while, in a state of equilibrium—that is, the experiences that are assimilated are compatible with the schemas in operation. After a certain period the child has assimilated new experiences that cannot be handled by the existing schema, and this sets up an imbalance between the data being assimilated from the environment and the existing cognitive structure. When this point is reached a cognitive reorganization is necessary. In a sense, pressure has built up, and intellectual movement must take place: a new shape of development is entered.

Piaget's stance is that the development of the schemas or structures occurs in the same order in all of us and at a relatively predetermined rate—a rate governed by our physiological maturation. Until the requisite neurological structures are developed, these schemas cannot appear.

Piaget thus classifies intellectual development in terms of stages that are characterized by the way the schemas permit the organism to relate to the world. At any given stage, one is able to perform certain kinds of thinking and not others. The earlier stages, however, lay the basis for future development. The stages are:

1. Sensorimotor stage (0 to 2 years)
2. Preoperational stage (2 to 7 years)
   a. Preconceptual thought (2 to 4 years)
   b. Intuitive thought (4 to 7 years)
3. Operational stage (7 to 16 years)
   a. Concrete operational thought (7 to 11 years)
   b. Formal operational thought (11 to 16 years)

According to Edmund Sullivan:

Sensorimotor thought (birth to about 2 years) refers to those behaviors which are preverbal and are not mediated by signs or symbols. At birth the child mediates with the world with inborn reflex schemas and has no conception of object permanence. During this period the child is concerned with objects as objects. Thus, when a toy is hidden from his view, he shows no searching movements, since he has no internal representation of the objective world (i.e., object schemas) when not perceiving it. Gradually object permanence develops through repeated experiences with the world. As the child constructs object permanence through experience, primitive concepts of space, time, causality, and intentionality, which were not present at birth, develop and are incorporated into present patterns of behavior.

The second stage involves preoperational thought (about age 2 to 7 years). This stage is further divided into two substages: preconceptual thought (transductive), which extends from age 2 to about 4, and intuitive thought, which extends from about age 4 to 7.

(a) The substage of preconceptual thought marks the beginning of what Piaget (1960) calls conceptual intelligence. In contrast to sensorimotor intelligence, adaptations are now beginning to be mediated by signs and symbols, particularly words and images. During this period, the child develops what Piaget calls the "symbolic function," or imagery. The main concern during this period will be with such activities as imitation, play, and the preconcepts shown in language behavior.

(b) The substage of intuitive thought appears at approxiamtely age 4 and marks the halfway house between preconceptual thought and the more advanced stage of concrete operations. The thought exemplified in this stage is illustrated in the following problem. The child is presented with two small glasses, A1 and A2, which are identically the same in height and dimensions. The child places one bead in each glass alternatively until both are filled. Glass A2 is emptied into a taller but thinner glass B. The child in the preconceptual stage thinks that the amount of beads has changed in the process, even though he says no beads were removed or added. The child says that there are more beads in B, since it is taller than A, or that there are more beads in A1, since it is wider than B. The child is centered on one aspect of the situation, "height" or "width." Because the child cannot hold the centering simultaneously, he is unable to solve the conservation problem. The child in the intuitive stage still remains prelogical, but decenterings occur where previous centerings led to absurd conclusions. Thus the child who estimated that there are more beads in the taller glass because the level has been raised centers his attention on height and ignores width. If the experimenter continues to empty the beads into the thinner and taller glass, there will be a time when the child replies that there are fewer beads in the taller glass, since it is too narrow.

The stage of operational thought marks the advent of rational activity in the child. Up to this time the child demonstrates a logic (transductive) which is quite different from that of the adult members of his species (i.e., inductive and deductive).

(a) Concrete operational thought. The first substage of operational thought is labelled "concrete operations." Piaget (1960) defines an operation as an internalized action which can return to its starting point, and which can be integrated with other actions also possessing this feature of reversibility. Operations are "mental acts" which were formerly actions with reversible properties. Piaget calls the operational structures between the ages of 7 and 11 years "concrete" because their starting point is always some real system of objects and relations that the child perceives; that is, the operations are carried out on concrete objects. The emergence of concrete operations is often a sudden phenomenon in development. Piaget (1960) attributes their emergence to a sudden thawing of intuitive structures which were up to now more rigid, despite their progressive articulation.

(b) Formal operational thought. The substage of formal operations (11 to 16 years) marks the emergence of *vertical decalages*, that is, the ability to make vertical separations by solving problems at a level which transcends concrete experience (the area of *horizontal decalages*). Formal thinking marks the completion of the child's emancipation from reliance on direct perception and action. In contrast to the concrete action-oriented thought of the child, the adolescent thinker goes beyond the present and forms theories about everything. This thought is considered "reflective" since the adolescent reasons on the basis of purely formal assumptions. He can consider hypothesis as either true or false and work out inferences which would follow if the hypotheses were true (Sullivan, 1967, pp. 4–9).

To summarize the major points covered so far: (1) Intelligence is defined as operations for transforming data from the environment. These operations change with age and are described as logical structures (or schemas) for processing information. (2) Development is associated with passage from one stage of operation to another. (3) Development is a function of experience and maturation.

ADJUSTING LEARNING ACTIVITIES TO COGNITIVE DEVELOPMENT

Whereas Piaget concentrated his work on describing the stages of intelligence, American educators have been interested in the factors that might affect development. Barry Wadsworth has provided a summary of their ideas on teaching and learning, which affect how we review Piaget's framework.

The first notion is that *teaching is the creation of environments* in which students' cognitive structures can emerge and change. The goal is to provide learning experiences that give the student practice with particular operations. Piaget believes that cognitive structures will grow only when students initiate their own learning experiences; learning must be *spontaneous*. The assumption is that students will initiate learning experiences that optimally match their cognitive structures, provided the opportunity exists in the environment, because students intuitively know what activities they need. Piaget believes that if we teach too far above the students, learning is not possible. Each person must construct his or her own knowledge, which cannot be absorbed ready-made from adults. He feels that we may alter students' verbal responses and behaviors as a result of direct teaching and reinforcement, but he does not consider verbal fluency to be "real knowledge" that can occur only as a result of development—that is, when the task is useful to the student, and when he or she is psychologically ready.

The student's role in the learning experience must be an active, self-discovering one, and the experiences themselves must be inductive. In learning new operations children must be given extensive opportunity to manipulate the environment. For young children the materials we use should be concrete instead of symbolic representations (for example, blocks or bottle caps instead of numbers). The environment should be rich in sensory experiences. Piaget sees important symbolic meaning in the manipulation, play, and aesthetic behaviors of children, activities that have much to tell us about children's intellectual development. The teacher's function is to arrange for learning experiences that facilitate stage-relevant thinking and to organize instruction so that students can initiate the activity and discover for themselves the logical connections between objects or events (for example, three marbles plus two marbles equals two marbles plus three marbles).

The second principle is based on Piaget's distinction among three types of knowledge: physical, social, and logical. The demands of the learning situation are different for the three types of knowledge. Physical knowledge refers to learning about the nature of matter (for example, cotton is soft, metal is hard and often unbendable, balls drop to the ground when you release them). Social knowledge is obtained through feedback from other people. It provides a framework for determining the effects of social actions and social connections (for example, most people say hello when they first see each other, and celebrate their birthdays each year). Social knowledge must come through free interaction with other people in the environment. We need to hear other people's views, have different role models available, and make choices for ourselves. Logical knowledge is concerned with mathematics and logic. It is constructed by processes of reflection and abstraction. The teacher's role in physical and logical knowledge is to provide a setting in which students construct this knowledge for themselves through questioning and experimenting. Teachers should refrain from giving answers directly but may use prompting questions that encourage further thought and exploration. For example, suppose a child is playing with two eggs—one hard-boiled—near a bowl of water. The teacher might ask, "What happens if you put the eggs in the water?" Or the teacher might be serving juice to the students and ask "How many juices do we need?" It is important to establish a climate in which wrong answers are perfectly acceptable, even valued, because they reveal what we know and how we think.

With respect to moral development, Piaget describes children as moving in a general direction away from egocentric and individualized ways of thinking to more socially centered, publicly validated ways of thinking. In the egocentric stages, the children tend to judge actions solely by their consequences. For example, if someone bumps into them, they usually judge the act by whether they are hurt. An intentional "hurt" is judged to be "bad." As people move toward a more sociocentric organization, they begin to judge acts by intentions, and become concerned not only with whether injury was justified but also with whether perhaps anyone intended to hurt them. Participation with others is more on a basis of equality and mutual respect. The opportunity to exchange viewpoints and share personal experiences produces the cognitive conflict that is fundamental to intellectual development. Teachers can foster social knowledge by providing many opportunities for students to interact with each other, especially by sharing their views and cooperating on tasks. In addition, teachers themselves must provide structured social feedback (for example, "John, we can only have one person sharing at a time. Can you wait until Kevin is finished?") so that social conventions are conveyed.

The last principle of teaching and learning has to do with the role of the social environment. Piaget maintains that especially logical and social knowledge are best learned from other children. They provide a source of motivation and information in a linguistic form that matches each other's cognitive structures. The peer group is also a reliable source of disequilibrium.

Given these principles, Wadsworth (1978) outlines three roles for teachers who operate from a Piagetian orientation: (1) organizer of the learning environment; (2) assessor of children's thinking; and (3) initiator of group activities, especially play, games, and discussions.

During the past 10 years, three Piaget-derived educational models have become prominent, particularly among early childhood educators. Each places a different amount of emphasis on each of the three roles identified by Wadsworth. Each model emphasizes ways of adjusting instruction to the cognitive development of the students.

The first model was developed by Celia Lavatelle and is referred to as a packaged Piaget-based curriculum for children 4 to 7 years old (Lavatelle, 1970). It consists of 100 activities occurring over a 30-week period. Lavatelle recommends that the activities be completed in 10-to 15-minute periods with small groups of five to six children. She also outlines other activities, especially with self-directed play. The objective of Lavatelle's curriculum is to develop children's intellectual processes through self-directed activity. The topics include classification; number, measurement, and space operations; and seriation operations. A typical early activity might have the children identify all squares that are blue (object matching on basis of two or more properties).

While Lavatelle accents the curriculum, in his program *Project Follow-through: The Cognitively Oriented Curriculum*, David Weikart (1971) includes the entire learning environment. The curriculum is similar to Lavatelle's, with the core areas being classification (grouping), seriation (ordering), spatial relations, and temporal relations. Weikart's activities stress experiencing concepts first on a motoric (physical manipulation) level and then gradually adding the verbal level—first the sign (objects from pictures) and then the symbol (words alone). Each goal is implemented along all three levels.

The third educational model is that of Kamii and DeVries (1974). Their current model represents a shift away from specific objectives and a sequenced curriculum. The new program is based on Piaget's ideas about the nature of knowledge and teachers' special role in relationship to each type of knowledge.

In Kamii and DeVries's program, the long-term objectives are general ones: intellectual inventiveness, critical thinking, and autonomous judgment. The focus is on both cognitive and socioemotional development, because they are interdependent in the learning process. Content serves as a motivator, capturing children's interest enough to act upon it as they discover the three basic kinds of knowledge. The program developers identify this knowledge in general terms. *Physical knowledge* refers to knowledge about such attributes of everyday objects, as weight, texture, and size, and knowledge about a repertoire of actions, such as folding, cutting, squeezing. *Social knowledge* refers to knowledge of social information—for example, about occupational roles—and to knowledge of norms for social conduct and social regularities. *Logico-mathematical knowledge* includes knowledge of classification, seriation, number, space, and time concepts. Kamii and DeVries believe strongly that the child must construct his or her own knowledge but that the teacher can, through appropriate questions or comments, facilitate this process. Finally, Kamii and DeVries stress the importance of children's play as a learning medium and include a set of games.

Despite clear differences among these Piagetian model-builders, they generally agree about the value of concrete experiences, of play, and of problem solving. They also all de-emphasize didactic instruction. Although they disagree about how, specifically, learning experiences should be designed, they do not dispute the need for active, inquiry-oriented experiences.

David Olson (1970) has identified three modes of instruction that can be built around Piaget's model. The first is to develop situations that pull the students toward a more complex level of thinking. The second is a language-oriented teaching style in which the student is presented with rules that require a more complex level of thinking. In a sense, the teacher provides the next step of thinking to the child with the assumption that if the child can grasp what is being said, he or she will take on the more complex way of operating. The third strategy can be described as modeling. Essentially one demonstrates the performance of the operation for the student either in person, or through a film or television. For example, to teach the concept of reversibility as it is represented in the commutative property of multiplication ($a \times b = b \times a$), a teacher might set up a three-by-four matrix and count off concrete aids such as checkers. Then the teacher could count the material first by threes and then by fours, thus modeling the proposition that the product is the same regardless of whether the three or the four takes the first position.

Psychologist Irving Sigel has developed and studied the use of a model resembling the first of Olson's alternatives. That is, the student is set up with a situation that does not make sense at his or her level of thinking. The idea is that, confronted with clear evidence that his or her thinking is not adequate, the student will reach toward another level of development. For Sigel, teaching involves providing experiences which will produce a deep disequilibrium, so that the child will have to develop a new kind of logic to deal with the experiences he or she is having. In other words, the teacher must set up confrontations that are well matched to the child's stage of development (Sigel, 1969, p. 473). According to Sigel, the form of the confrontation as well as its nature depend on the developmental level of the child. "Verbal and/or nonverbal techniques ranging from questions, demonstrations, and/or environmental manipulations can be employed in the service of confrontation" (Sigel, 1969, p. 173). Thus, like Olson, Sigel acknowledges alternative instructional approaches for setting up situations that require of students slightly higher levels of thinking.

For moral development, Lawrence Kohlberg stresses the importance of an atmosphere in which open and searching discussion is the norm. In addition, he recommends that the classroom and, whenever possible, the school model a just society in which the value of moral inquiry is strongly nurtured. His research, in the United States and abroad, indicates that home and school atmosphere are critically important to moral development.

The developmental framework is applicable to both cognitive and social development. It cuts across all areas in which illogic or problems in thinking arise, and it can be used for diagnosis and evaluation as well as for instructional purposes. The model, inherently interwoven with developmental considerations, can be employed to ensure that a child can operate smoothly in his or her environment or to specify activities that will accelerate the child's cognitive growth.

MORAL DEVELOPMENT

Kohlberg's work on moral development is especially descriptive of older students. He identifies three major levels of moral development: preconventional, conventional, and postconventional (principled or autonomous). Each level has two stages. These are described here:

A. *Preconventional level.* At this level, the child is responsive to cultural rules and labels of good and bad, right and wrong, but interprets these labels in terms of either the physical or the hedonistic consequences of action (punishment, reward, exchange of favors) or in terms of the physical power of those who enunciate the rules and labels. The level is divided into the following two stages:
1. *The punishment and obedience orientation.* The physical consequences of action determine its goodness or badness regardless of the human meaning or value of these consequences. Avoidance of punishment and unquestioning deference to power are valued in their own right, not in terms of respect for an underlying moral order supported by punishment and authority (the latter being stage four).
2. *The instrumental relativist orientation.* Right action consists of that which instrumentally satisfies one's own needs and occasionally the needs of others. Human relations are viewed in the terms of the marketplace. Elements of fairness, of reciprocity, and of equal sharing are present, but they are always interpreted in a physical, pragmatic way. Reciprocity is a matter of "you scratch my back and I'll scratch yours," not of loyalty or justice.
B. *Conventional level.* At this level, maintaining the expectations of the individual's family, group, or nation is perceived as valuable in its own right, regardless of immediate and obvious consequences. The attitude is not only one of *conformity* to personal expectations and social order, but of loyalty to it—of actively maintaining, supporting, and justifying the order and of identifying with the persons or group involved in it. At this level, there are the following two stages:
1. *The interpersonal concordance or "good boy-nice girl" orientation.* Good behavior is that which pleases or helps others and is approved by them.

There is much conformity to stereotypical images of what is majority or "natural" behavior. Behavior is frequently judged by intention—"he means well" becomes important for the first time. One earns approval by being "nice."

2. *The "law and order" orientation.* Orientation at this stage is toward authority, fixed rules, and the maintenance of the social order. Right behavior consists of doing one's duty, showing respect for authority, and maintaining the given social order for its own sake.

C. *Postconventional, autonomous, or principled level.* At this level, there is a clear effort to define moral values and principles that have validity and application apart from the authority of the groups or persons holding these principles and apart from the individual's own identification with these groups. This level again has two stages.

1. *The social-contract, legalistic orientation.* Generally this stage has utilitarian overtones. Right action tends to be defined in terms of general individual rights and in terms of standards that have been critically examined and agreed on by the whole society. There is a clear awareness of the relativism of personal values and opinions and a corresponding emphasis on procedural rules for reaching consensus. Aside from what is constitutionally and democratically agreed on, the right is a matter of personal values and opinion. The result is an emphasis on the "legal point of view," but with the possibility of changing law in terms of rational considerations of social utility (rather than freezing it in terms of stage 4 "law and order"). Outside the legal realm, free agreement and contract are the binding elements of obligation. This is the "official" morality of the American government and Constitution.

2. *The universal ethical principle orientation.* Right is defined by the decision of conscience in accord with self-chosen *ethical principles* appealing to logical comprehensiveness, universality, and consistency. These principles are abstract and ethical (the Golden Rule, or a categorical imperative); they are not concrete moral rules like the Ten Commandments. At heart, these are universal principles of *justice*, or of the *reciprocity* and *equality* of human *rights*, and of respect for the dignity of human beings as *individual persons.* (Kohlberg, 1976, pp. 215–216)

Kohlberg believes it is possible to influence a student's level of thinking and that it is essential to organize instruction with development as a guiding principle. The important conditions appear to be: (1) exposure to the next higher stage of reasoning; (2) exposure to situations posing problems and contradictions for the child's current structure, leading to dissatisfaction with his or her current level; and (3) an atmosphere of interchange and dialogue combining the first two conditions, in which conflicting moral views are compared in an open manner (Kohlberg, 1976, p. 190). For example, suppose the student is involved in an argument and cannot make judgments based on general moral grounds. The teacher would try to confront him or her with the need to operate on a more general level. If the student reacted to city council action only in terms of "I like that" or "I don't like that," the task would be to help him or her try to find whether general principles underlie his or her judgment and to move toward a more general basis of judgment. Teachers need to be familiar with the development hierarchy and have probing questions and counter-suggestions ready.

Kohlberg stresses that matching teaching to moral levels is not a minor point. To provide a stage-one child with stage-five tasks would be unproductive. Teaching should aim about one level above the student's level of functioning. The optimal grouping pattern is probably one that spans two, perhaps three stages.

In terms of specific educational practice the first task, of course, is to learn about the children's level of moral judgment. This can be done through the use of carefully selected tasks or more informally through observing students' behavior in conflict situations. For example, if students learning about the patterns of bills passed by a legislature find that pressure groups have been getting their own way by lobbying, we can expect that the students' responses will vary substantially in terms of moral judgment. Some may be reluctant to believe that council members are anything but wise and just (probably an indication of stage-four orientation: authority and maintaining social order). Others may be quick to condemn, especially if the majority leans that way (orientation to pleasing). In these cases the teacher can introduce them to a more complex analysis by getting them to look at the general implications of their position. ("Should we say a pressure group should *never* have access to lawmakers—what are the pros and cons?" "What are the positions of other groups in the community who have not been able to lobby successfully?") Teachers should not preach a set of principles for the behavior of lawmakers, however. This both denies the students the new elements they need for development *and* is ineffective as a method.

Much research describes the stages of moral development, and the findings are relatively consistent in confirming the progression through the stages and the movement from the relatively egocentric toward the less self-centered views of moral development. However, it should not be assumed that all persons progress naturally through the higher stages of development. Many persons appear to be arrested in their development before or at the stage of the "good boy" orientation. Thus, the attempt to increase moral development is relatively critical.

EVALUATION OF DEVELOPMENTAL MODELS

Over the last 20 years there has been a considerable amount of research to determine the effectiveness of the various models built on developmental psychology, and there are a number of excellent summaries of this work. The reader is referred to: (1) Myron Rosskopf and others, *Piagetian Cognitive Development Research in Mathematical Education* (Washington, D.C.: National Council of Teachers of Mathematics, 1971); (2) a review by Herbert J. Klausmeier and Frank H. Hooper, "Conceptual Development on Instruction," chapter 1, *Review of Research in Education*, ed. Fred N. Kerlinger and John B. Carroll (Itasca, Ill.: F.E. Peacock Publisher, Inc., 1974), pp. 3–54; (3) a very thorough review by F.H. Hooper, "An Evaluation of Logical Operations in Instruction in the Preschool," in *The Preschool in Action: Exploring Early Childhood Education Programs*, rev. ed., ed. R.K. Parker (Boston: Allyn & Bacon, 1974), pp. 134–86; and (4) *Recent Research in Moral Development*, ed. Lawrence Kohlberg (New York: Holt, Rinehart & Winston, 1977). Taken together these sources provide a very thorough analysis.

The results of short-term studies are generally positive. That is, directly targeted instruction such as that advocated by Sigel, Olson, and Kohlberg results in the particular types of learning desired. Interestingly enough, some of the more general approaches—putting the student in a rich environment (Kamii and DeVries; Weikart) and modeling generally more complex logical operations—appear to have much the same result as the more narrowly focused models. We are just beginning to see the results of the first long-term studies, which should indicate whether teaching during the early years results in lasting increments in logical operations. (Research from the Weikart program discussed earlier in the chapter indicates that students now in high school show high achievement and low deviancy rates.)

DEVELOPMENTAL PSYCHOLOGY AND OTHER MODELS OF TEACHING

One of the important uses of developmental psychology is a guide for adjusting instruction to the developmental level of the students. We can seek to frame instruction to the present stage of development, or we can seek the "optimal mismatch" by pitching instruction slightly above the current operating level of the students.

Nearly all current research is with relatively young children. Improving the cognitive development model of older children has not been explored fully, but we feel the probability is that the older, generally more able, learner will profit even more than the younger child from developmentally appropriate teaching.

The essence of the idea for adjusting instruction to the developmental stages of the learner is captured in the idea of the "optimal mismatch." We observe the learners as they react to the cognitive task demands of instruction as, for example, a classification task. We attempt to determine the level of development indicated by the responses of the students. Then, we gently nudge the student toward the next more complex level by modulating the task demands. Over a period of weeks we should begin to see the students push their way toward the next stages.

THE INFORMATION-PROCESSING FAMILY: AN ADDITIONAL NOTE ON EXPECTED EFFECTS

These models cover a broad range of educational objectives. For some, we simply ask whether they achieve their specific purposes, as "Can inquiry-oriented science programs teach students to use the models of inquiry of the academic disciplines?" (the answer is that they can). Or ask whether students can learn metaphoric thinking through synectics (they can). Or ask whether students can learn concepts through the concept-attainment process (they can).

In other cases, the research underlying the information-processing family has involved comparisons with approaches dominated by the textbook and the lecture-recitation and asks what are the comparative effects on lower-order and higher-order academic learning.

Because concept-formation is such a basic higher-order thinking process, there has been a good deal of attention paid to it, especially in comparison with courses involving the delivery of information to children. There is not much question that students can learn to form concepts and little point in comparing concept-formation through inductive methods with courses that do not provide the opportunity to form concepts. Also, students like inductive activity and become more positive toward scientific methods when given an opportunity to practice induction.

Because of concern that students might "lose" basic information, there have been a number of studies comparing information gleaned from inductive approaches and from textbook-oriented approaches to the teaching of courses. For many years the results vexed advocates of both approaches because the differences were relatively small. One might ask whether, given such small differences, one might as well choose inductive approaches given the advantage in the teaching of concepts and skills in thinking, the pleasurability of the activity, and positive attitudes toward scholarly activity.

However, tradition dies hard, and evidence on those terms has convinced few who hold tightly to the textbook. However, recent analyses have provided some interesting results. First was Worthen's finding that

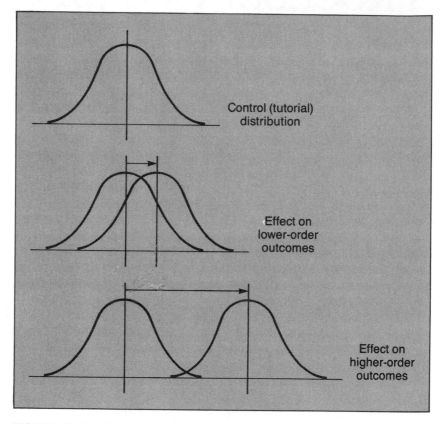

FIGURE 12–1   Sample effect size from Baveja, Showers, and Joyce study.

retention of information was facilitated by concept formation. Then came Bredderman's analysis indicating that ability to learn was facilitated by inductive curriculums.

Now, current experiments are combining cooperative and inductive activity with concept attainment. The results of one such study are depicted in Figure 12–1.

In this study, conducted by Baveja, Showers, and Joyce, the control group was provided with classroom instruction and a tutorial in a unit in a botany course. The experimental group used the combination of models. With respect to lower-order outcomes the effect size (ES) was 1.0, which increased even more when a delayed posttest was administered ten months later. With respect to higher-order outcomes the distributions did not overlap (the highest scorer in the control group was exceeded by the lowest scorer in the experimental group). The latter was no doubt due to the much greater emphasis on concepts in the experimental group. We theorize that the difference in information gained and retained (the lower-order outcomes) was due to the greater attention to concepts.

Research underlying advance organizers has been given new life in recent years after many years of relatively small effects. This research suggests that didactic courses can be improved substantially by the use of advance organizers. Carefully constructed organizers have improved outcomes as much as ES .5 or even more, suggesting that didactic courses can have more positive effects and suggesting that Ausubel's contention that organizers improve active learning has practical as well as theoretical value.

Research on all these models continues to demonstrate that the information-processing models are effective for their purposes and can be improved by continued research and development.

PART III

THE PERSONAL FAMILY

Focus on the Person

The rich texture of human life lies in the individual consciousness we all have. Our personal qualities act on the world, substantially affecting the environments in which we live. Reciprocally, we are acted on by the world. Our social environment gives us our language and the other facets of our culture. It teaches us how to behave and affects how we feel. Our personalities have remarkable continuity from early in life (White, 1980), and yet we have great capacity to change. We can adapt to a wide range of climates and physical environments but, paradoxically, we also have the capacities to pursue unadaptive behaviors—as if to force the world to yield and make our incompetencies productive.

Personal models of teaching refer to approaches that share one or more of the following purposes: One is to lead the student toward greater and greater mental and emotional health by improving the concept of self, increasing realism, creating self-confidence, and extending sympathetic and empathetic reactions to others. A second is to increase the proportion of education that emanates from the needs and aspirations of the students themselves, taking each student as a partner in determining what he or she will learn and how he or she will learn it. In other words, students are taught to take charge of their own educations. A third is to develop specific kinds of qualitative thinking, such as creativity and personal expression.

These models can be used in several ways. First, they can be used to moderate the entire learning environment. For example, we can "carry around with us" concern for the students' self-concepts, and we can think carefully about how to shape everything we do to maximize their positive feelings about self and to minimize the likelihood that our teaching will diminish them as people. In other words, we can use these models to attend to the personal qualities and feelings of our students and to look for opportunities to make them partners with us and to communicate affirmatively with them.

Second, we use these models when we wish to achieve specific goals for which they are uniquely designed. We use nondirective techniques when we are counseling students and growth-state related activities when we wish to help students learn to reach out to the world more fully and positively.

Finally, some of the personal models can be used as general models of teaching. Some schools have adopted a nondirective philosophy as the core of their approaches to education (e.g., Aspy and Roebuck, 1973; Neill, 1960) or as a major component (Chamberlin and Chamberlin, 1943). In addition, certain approaches to teaching academic subjects have been developed around personal models. The "experience" methods for teaching reading, for example, use student-dictated stories as the initial reading materials and student-selected literature as the chief materials once initial competence has been established.

In addition to the belief that enhancing the learner as a person is a worthwhile educational goal in its own right, a major thesis of this family of models is that better-developed, more affirmative, self-actualizing learners have increased learning capabilities. Thus, personal models will increase academic achievement by tending the learners. This thesis is supported by a number of studies (Roebuck, Buhler, and Aspy, 1976) that indicate that the students of teachers who incorporate personal models into their repertoires increase their achievement.

From the range of personal models, we have selected several to illustrate the genre. The chapter on Carl Rogers's nondirective teaching model illustrates the philosophy and techniques of the major spokesperson for the family, and the chapter on states of growth deals with the organization of the classroom as a self-disciplining community of learners.

CHAPTER 13

NONDIRECTIVE TEACHING
The Learner at the Center

S C E N A R I O

John Denbro, a 26-year-old high school English teacher in suburban Chicago, is very concerned about Mary Ann Fortnay, one of his students. Mary Ann is a compulsive worker who does an excellent job with literature assignments and writes excellent short stories. She is, however, reluctant to share those stories with other members of the class and declines to participate in any activities in the performing arts.

Mr. Denbro recognizes that the issue cannot be forced, but he wants Mary Ann to understand why she is reluctant to allow any public display of her talents. She will make her own decisions about participation that involves sharing her ideas.

One afternoon she asks him to read some of her pieces and give her his opinion.

Mary Ann Mr. Denbro, could you take a look at these for me?

Denbro Why sure, Mary Ann. Another short story?

Mary Ann No, some poems I've been working on. I don't think they're very good, but I'd like you to tell me what you think.

Denbro When did you write them?

Mary Ann One Sunday afternoon a couple of weeks ago.

Denbro Do you remember what started you thinking that you wanted to write a poem?

Mary Ann I was feeling kind of sad and I remembered last month when we tried to read "The Waste Land," and it seemed to be trying to say a lot of things that we couldn't say in the usual way. I liked the beginning lines, "April is the cruelest month, breeding lilacs out of the dead land." (T.S. Eliot, "The Waste Land")

Denbro And this is what you wrote down?

Mary Ann   Yes. It's the first time I've ever tried writing anything like this.

Denbro   (reads for a few minutes and then looks up) Mary Ann, these are really good.

Mary Ann   What makes a poem good, Mr. Denbro?

Denbro   Well, there are a variety of ways to judge poetry. Some methods are technical and have to do with the quality of expression and the way one uses metaphors and analogies and other literary devices. Others are subjective and involve the quality of expression, the real beauty of the words themselves.

Mary Ann   I felt very good when I was writing them, but when I read them over, they sound a little dumb to me.

Denbro   What do you mean?

Mary Ann   Oh, I don't know. I guess the main thing is that I feel ashamed if anybody else sees them.

Denbro   Ashamed?

Mary Ann   I really don't know. I just know that if these were to be read aloud, say to my class, I would die of mortification.

Denbro   You really feel that the class would laugh at these?

Mary Ann   Oh sure, they wouldn't understand.

Denbro   How about your short stories? How do you feel about them?

Mary Ann   You know I don't want *anybody* to see what I write.

Denbro   You really feel that you want to put them away somewhere so nobody can see them?

Mary Ann   Yes, I really think so. I don't know exactly why, but I'm pretty sure that no one in my class would understand them.

Denbro   Can you think of anybody else that might understand them?

Mary Ann   I don't know. I kind of think there are people out there who might, but nobody around here, probably.

Denbro   How about your parents?

Mary Ann   Oh, they like everything I write.

Denbro   Well, that makes three of us. Can you think of anybody else?

Mary Ann   I guess I think adults would, but I'm not really so sure about other kids.

Denbro   Kids are somehow different from adults in this respect?

Mary Ann   Well, kids just don't seem to be interested in these kinds of things. I feel they put down anybody who tries to write anything.

Denbro   Do you think they feel this way about the authors we read in class?

Mary Ann   Well, sometimes they do, but I guess a lot of the time they really enjoy the stories.

Denbro   Well then, why do you think they wouldn't like what you write?

Mary Ann   I guess I really don't know, Mr. Denbro. I guess I'm really afraid, but I can't put my finger on it.

Denbro Something holds you back.

Mary Ann In a lot of ways, I really would like to find out whether anybody would appreciate what I write. I just don't know how to go about it.

Denbro How would you feel if I were to read one of your short stories but not tell them who wrote it?

Mary Ann Would you promise?

Denbro Of course I would. Then we could talk about how everybody reacted. You would know that they didn't know who had written it.

Mary Ann I don't know, but it sounds interesting.

Denbro Depending on what happened, we could cook up some kind of strategy about what to do next.

Mary Ann Well, I guess you've got me right where I don't have anything to lose.

Denbro I hope we're always where you don't have anything to lose, Mary Ann; but there's always a risk in telling about ourselves.

Mary Ann What do you mean, telling about ourselves?

Denbro I think I should go now—but let me pick one of your stories and read it next week, and then let's get together on Wednesday and talk about what happened.

Mary Ann OK, and you promise not to tell?

Denbro I promise. I'll see you next Wednesday after school.

Mary Ann OK. Thanks a lot, Mr. Denbro. Have a good weekend.

The nondirective teaching model is based on the work of Carl Rogers (1951, 1983) and other advocates of nondirective counseling. Rogers extended to education his view of therapy as a mode of learning. He believed that positive human relationships enable people to grow; and, therefore, instruction should be based on concepts of human relations in contrast to concepts of subject matter or thought processes. The teacher's role in nondirective teaching is that of a facilitator who has a personal relationship with students and who guides their growth and development. In this role, the teacher helps students explore new ideas about their lives, their schoolwork, and their relations with others. The model assumes that students are willing to be responsible for their own learning, and its success depends on the willingness of student and teacher to share ideas openly and to communicate honestly with one another.

In general, the personal family models of teaching describe learning environments that hope to nurture students rather than to control the sequence of learning. These models are more concerned with long-term learning styles and with developing individual personalities than they are with short-term instructional or content objectives. The nondirective teacher is patient and does not sacrifice the long view by forcing immediate results.

ORIENTATION TO THE MODEL

GOALS AND ASSUMPTIONS

The nondirective teaching model focuses on *facilitating* learning. The primary goal of nondirective teaching is to assist students in attaining greater personal integration, effectiveness, and realistic self-appraisal. A related goal is to create a learning environment conducive to the process of stimulating, examining, and evaluating new perceptions. A reexamination of needs and values—their sources and outcomes—is crucial to personal integration. Students do not necessarily need to change, but the teacher's goal is to help them understand their own needs and values so that they can effectively direct their own educational decisions.

The model draws on Rogers's stance toward nondirective counseling, in which the client's capacity to deal constructively with his or her own life is respected. Thus, in nondirective teaching, the teacher respects the students' ability to identify their own problems and to formulate solutions.

When operating nondirectively, the teacher attempts to see the world as the student sees it. This creates an atmosphere of empathetic communication in which the student's self-direction can be nurtured and developed. The primary means used is the nondirective interview strategy, a mode in which the teacher mirrors students' thoughts and feelings. By using reflective comments, the teacher raises the students' consciousness of their own perceptions and feelings, thus helping them clarify their ideas. The facilitative counseling style results in the strengthened understanding and knowledge of oneself and others that develops within the security of an empathetic relationship.

The teacher also serves as a benevolent alter ego, one who accepts all feelings and thoughts, even those the students may be afraid of or may view as wrong, or perhaps even punishable. In being accepting and nonpunitive, the teacher indirectly communicates to the students that all thoughts and feelings are acceptable. In fact, recognition of both positive and negative feelings is essential to emotional development and positive solutions.

A teacher using the nondirective interview strategy can counsel students about class assignment progress, evaluate the progress of individual students in their work, and help students explore new topics that may be of interest to them. Although the nondirective strategy is appropriate for dealing with students who are having personal or academic problems, it is equally appropriate to use the technique with successful, happy students. In general, nondirective interview techniques help students strengthen their self-perceptions and evaluate their own progress and development.

The teacher gives up the traditional decision-making role, choosing instead the role of a facilitator who focuses on student feelings. The relationship between student and teacher in a nondirective interview is best described as a partnership. Thus, if the student complains of poor grades and an inability to study, the teacher does not attempt to resolve the problem simply by explaining the art of good study habits. Instead, the teacher encourages the student to express the feelings that may surround his or her inability to concentrate, as feelings about self and others. When these feelings are fully explored and perceptions are clarified, the student himself or herself tries to identify appropriate changes and bring them about.

The nondirective atmosphere has four qualities. First, the teacher shows warmth and responsiveness, expressing genuine interest in the student and accepting him or her as a person. Second, it is characterized by permissiveness in regard to the expression of feeling; the teacher does not judge or moralize. Because of the importance of emotions, much content is discussed that would normally be guarded against in more customary student relationships with teachers or advisors. Third, the student is free to express feelings symbolically but is not free to control the teacher or to carry impulses into action. Fourth, the counseling relationship is free from any type of pressure or coercion. The teacher avoids showing personal bias or reacting in a personally critical manner to the student.

Generally, understanding feelings takes place in: (1) releasing the feelings, (2) developing insight followed by (3) action; and (4) integration that leads to a new orientation (see Figure 13-1).

FIGURE 13–1 Phases of personal growth in the nondirective interview process.

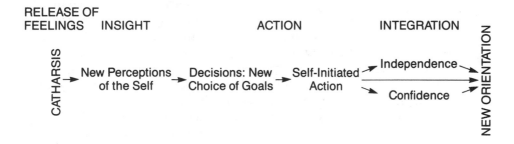

The release of feelings involves breaking down the emotional barriers that often impair a person's ability to solve dilemmas. By discharging the emotions surrounding a problem, a person paves the way for developing a new perspective or insight into the problem.

According to Rogers, responding on a purely intellectual basis to students' problems inhibits the expression of the feelings, which are at the root of the problems. For example, if a student is struggling with writing, an intellectual response would be, "Start by making an outline." An empathetic response would be, "When I get stuck I often feel panicky. How do you feel?" Without the release and exploration of these feelings, students will reject suggestions and be unable to sustain real behavior changes.

Typically, the problem-solving process proceeds as follows: At first, the students have pent-up feelings. They are tense, defensive, and as a result, unable to see the problem and themselves clearly. The student-centered counseling situation presents an opportunity for free personal expression. The students become less tense by experiencing the release that comes with the expression of pent-up feelings. Free of these feelings, the students become more comfortable and explore more aspects of themselves. Gradually, they become aware of and accept more sides of themselves—strengths as well as weaknesses.

Insight is the short-term goal of the process. By expressing feelings the student becomes able to look at the problem—in the case of the scenario, the problem of allowing others to experience one's writing. Indications of insight come from statements by the students that describe behavior in terms of cause and effect or in terms of personal meaning. In the scenario, the student comes to realize that the problem lies in her own fear, rather than the objective possibility of judgments by others. As they begin to understand the reasons for their behaviors, they begin to see other more functional ways of satisfying their needs. Through the release of emotions, the students can perceive options more clearly. New insights enable the students to select delayed goals that are more satisfying than goals that give immediate but only temporary satisfaction.

Ultimately, the test of personal insight is the presence of actions that motivate the students toward new goals. At first, these positive actions may concern minor issues, but they create a sense of confidence and independence in the student. The teacher in the scenario is trying to create "safe space" for the action of sharing the writing. Gradually, the students' positive actions lead to a new, more comprehensive orientation. This is the integration phase. Again referring to the scenario, the long-term goal is a mature ability to share writing derived from a better understanding of the social dynamics of sharing. In other words, the student will gradually find that the action of sharing has more good consequences than bad ones and that satisfaction can come from the integrated understanding of the problem of sharing.

The nondirective approach maintains that the most effective means of uncovering the emotions underlying a problem is to follow the pattern of the students' feelings as they are freely expressed. Instead of asking direct questions for the purpose of eliciting feelings, the teacher lets the students direct the flow of thoughts and feelings. If the students express themselves freely, the problems and their underlying emotions will emerge. This process is facilitated by reflecting the students' feelings, thereby bringing them into awareness and sharper focus.

This is a difficult skill for most of us because we are more attuned to the content of what people are saying than to their emotional attitudes.

Unlike other kinds of teacher-student relationships, nondirective counseling focuses on the emotional element of the students' behavior. The nondirective strategy usually looks to three sources of student problems: (1) present feelings; (2) distorted perceptions; and (3) alternatives that have been unexplored because of an emotional reaction to them. Elimination of these difficulties is brought about, not by direct solutions (deciding what to do), but by getting rid of negative feelings and distorted perceptions and beginning to experiment with new behavior, thus gaining new experience—leading, hopefully, to insight and a new integrated perception of the problem area.

TEACHER RESPONSES IN NONDIRECTIVE TEACHING

The student and teacher share the responsibility for the discussion; however, at times the teacher must make "lead-taking" responses to direct or maintain the conversation (see Table 13-1). Appropriate nondirective lead-taking responses are statements by the teacher that help start the discussion, establish the direction in an open manner, or that give the student some indication as to what he or she should discuss, either specifically or generally.

TABLE 13-1   NONDIRECTIVE RESPONSES IN INTERVIEW

A. Nondirective Responses to Feelings	B. Nondirective Lead-Taking Responses
1. Simple acceptance	1. Structuring
2. Reflection of feelings	2. Directive questioning
3. Paraphrasing of content	3. Forcing student to choose and develop a topic
	4. Nondirective leads and open questions
	5. Minimal encouragements to talk

The essential skill to lead without taking responsibility from the students. Nondirective lead-taking remarks are stated directly in a pleasant, positive, and amiable manner. Some examples are:

"What do you think of that?"
"Can you say more about that?"
"How do you react when that happens?"

Nondirective responses to feelings are attempts to respond either to the feelings the student expresses or to the content of the expressions. In making these comments, the teacher does not interpret, evaluate, or offer advice, but reflects, clarifies, accepts, and demonstrates understanding. The purpose of these comments is to create an atmosphere in which the student is willing to expand the ideas he or she is expressing. Usually, the responses are short statements that are supportive and enable the student to continue the discussion. Some examples are:

"I see."
"It's especially hard to be alone."
"Sort of like it doesn't matter what you do, it will go on the same way."

There are two types of semidirective responses: *interpretation* and *approval*. Both are used sparingly because they intrude on the nondirective style, but occasionally they are useful in moving the interview forward.

An interpretation by the teacher can often promote further discussion by a student who is unable to offer any explanation for his or her behavior. Interpretative responses are attempts to suggest to the student his or her reasons for being unable to continue the discussion. But interpretation is given only to those feelings that can definitely be accepted by the student. The decision to use interpretation is made cautiously by the teacher and is used only in situations in which the teacher feels confident that interpretation will advance rather than close a dialogue. Some examples of interpretative openers are:

"You do this because . . ."
"Perhaps you feel you won't succeed."
"It sounds like your reasons for your actions this week are . . ."
"You are saying to me that the problem is . . ."

Approval is usually given only when genuine progress has been achieved. It must be used sparingly, or the nondirective relationship is likely to drift rapidly into the traditional teacher-student relationship. Approval as a closure technique must be used carefully, or it may become a signal to the student that the interview is over. Other techniques, such as summarizing or recapping the session using the student's own words, are more appropriate to the nondirective strategy. In making approval statements, the teacher might say:

"That's right."
"That's a very interesting comment and may well be worth considering again."
"That last idea was particularly strong. Could you elaborate on it some more?"
"I think we are really making progress together."

Directive counseling moves imply a relationship in which the teacher attempts to change the ideas of the student or influence his or her attitudes. The teacher does this by giving support, expressing disapproval and criticism, giving information or explanations, proposing a solution, or attempting to convince the student. For example, "Don't you think it would be better if . . ." directly suggests a choice to the student. Attempts to support the student directly are usually made to reduce apparent anxiety, but they do not contribute to the nondirective problem-solving technique. Directive counseling moves should be used sparingly; otherwise they can defeat the nondirective interview strategy. When using directive counseling moves, the teacher maintains a more traditional role and does not help the student as an equal. The relationship remains traditional, and the teacher can easily become an authority figure rather than a partner.

THE MODEL OF TEACHING

The nondirective stance presents some interesting problems. First, the responsibility is shared. In most models of teaching, the teacher actively shapes events and can picture the pattern of activities that lies ahead; but in most nondirective situations, events emerge and the pattern of activities is more fluid. Second, from the teacher's point of view, counseling is made up of a series of responses that occur in an unpredictable sequence. Thus, to master nondirective teaching, teachers learn general principles, work to increase their sensitivity to others, master the nondirective skills, and then practice making contact with students and responding to them, using skills drawn from a repertoire of nondirective counseling techniques.

SYNTAX

Despite the fluidity and unpredictability of the nondirective strategy, Rogers points out that the nondirective interview has a sequence. We have divided this sequence into five phases of activity, as shown in Table 13-2 on the following page.

In phase one, the helping situation is defined. This includes structuring remarks by the counselor that define the student's freedom to express feelings, an agreement on the general focus of the interview, an initial problem statement, some discussion of the relationship if it is to be ongoing, and the establishment of procedures for meeting. Phase one generally occurs during the initial session on a problem. However, some structuring or definition by the teacher may be necessary for some time, even if this consists only of occasional summarizing moves that redefine the problem and reflect progress. Naturally, these structuring and definitional comments vary considerably with the type of interview, the specific problem, and the student. Negotiating academic contracts will likely differ from working with behavioral problem situations.

In phase two, the student is encouraged by the teacher's acceptance and clarification to express negative and positive feelings, to state and explore the problem.

TABLE 13–2   SEQUENCE OF THE NONDIRECTIVE EPISODE

Phase One: Defining the Helping Situation	Phase Two: Exploring the Problem
Teacher encourages free expression of feelings.	Student is encouraged to define problem. Teacher accepts and clarifies feelings.

Phase Three: Developing Insight	Phase Four: Planning and Decision Making
Student discusses problem. Teacher supports student.	Student plans initial decision making. Teacher clarifies possible decisions.

Phase Five: Integration	Action Outside the Interview
Student gains further insight and develops more positive actions. Teacher is supportive.	Student initiates positive actions.

In phase three, the student gradually develops insight: He or she perceives new meaning in his or her experiences, sees new relationships of cause and effect, and understands the meaning of his or her previous behavior. In most situations, the student seems to alternate between exploring the problem itself and developing new insight into his or her feelings. Both activities are necessary for progress. Discussion of the problem without exploration of feelings would indicate that the student him- or herself was being avoided.

In phase four, the student moves toward planning and decision making with respect to the problem. The role of the teacher is to clarify the alternatives.

In phase five, the student reports the actions he or she has taken, develops further insight, and plans increasingly more integrated and positive actions.

The syntax presented here could occur in one session or, more likely, over a series. In the latter case, phases one and two could occur in the first few interviews, phases three and four in the next, and phase five in the last interview. Or, if the interview consists of a voluntary meeting with a student who has an immediate problem, phases one through four could occur in only one meeting, with the student returning briefly to report his or her actions and insights. On the other hand, the sessions involved in negotiating academic contracts are sustained for a period of time, and the context of each meeting generally involves some kind of planning and decision making, although several sessions devoted entirely to exploring a problem might occur.

SOCIAL SYSTEM

The social system of the nondirective strategy requires the teacher to assume the roles of facilitator and reflector. The student is primarily responsible for the initiation and maintenance of the interaction process (control); authority is shared between student and teacher. The norms are those of open expression of feelings and autonomy of thought and behavior. Rewards, in the usual sense of approval of specific behavior—and particularly punishment—do not apply in this strategy. The rewards in a nondirective interview are more subtle and intrinsic—acceptance, understanding, and empathy from the teacher. The knowledge of oneself and the psychological rewards gained from self-reliance are generated by the student himself or herself.

PRINCIPLES OF REACTION

The principles of reaction for the teacher are based on nondirective responses. The teacher reaches out to the students, empathizes with their personalities and problems, and reacts in such a way as to help them define their problems and feelings, take responsibility for their actions, and plan objectives and how to achieve them.

SUPPORT SYSTEM

The support system for this strategy varies with the function of the interview. If a session is to negotiate academic contracts, then the necessary resources for self-directed learning must be made available. If the interview consists of counseling for a behavioral problem, no resources beyond the skills of the teacher are necessary. In both cases, the one-to-one situation requires spatial arrangements that allow for privacy, removal from other classroom forces and activities, and time to explore a problem adequately and in an unhurried fashion. For academic curriculum areas—reading, writing, literature, science, and social science—rich arrays of materials are necessary.

APPLICATION

The nondirective teaching model may be used for several types of problem situations: personal, social, and academic. In the case of personal problems, the individuals explore feelings about self. In social problems, students explore their feelings about relationships with others and investigate how feelings about self may influence these relationships. In academic problems, students explore their feelings about their competence and interests. In each case, however, the interview content is always personal rather than external; it centers on each individual's own feelings, experiences, insights, and solutions.

To use the nondirective teaching model effectively, a teacher must be willing to accept that a student can understand and cope with his or her own life. Belief in the student's capacity to direct himself or herself is communicated through the teacher's attitude and verbal behavior. The teacher does not attempt to judge the student. Such a stance indicates limited confidence in the student's capabilities. The teacher does not attempt to diagnose problems. Instead, the teacher attempts to perceive the student's world as he or she sees it and feels it. And, at the moment of the student's self-perception, the teacher reflects the new understanding to him or her. In this model, the teacher temporarily sets aside personal thoughts and feelings and reflects the student's thoughts and feelings. By doing this, the teacher conveys understanding and acceptance of the feelings.

The theory behind the teacher's role in the nondirective interview is that people deny feelings they perceive as incongruous or incompatible with their views of themselves. If we perceive ourselves as kind, sympathetic individuals, we usually repress feelings of anger and hostility, for these contradict our views of ourselves. Yet when we do this, the problems surrounding these feelings fail to be resolved and we continue to occupy less effective states of being. What we need, the theory holds, is an alter ego who can bring these feelings into our awareness in an atmosphere of safety and acceptance.

To function in an alter-ego role, the teacher needs to develop an *internal* frame of reference—the ability to perceive as the student perceives. Expressing the student's feelings in terms of "you" rather than "he" or "I" demonstrates the use of an internal frame of reference. Rogers points out that some situations are genuinely difficult to perceive from the student's perspective, especially if the student is confused. At times all teachers will experience evaluative and diagnostic thoughts, but teachers beginning to use the nondirective interview are often concerned with themselves and concentrate on thinking about what they should do. They do not listen to the student. The strategy works only if the teacher enters the perceptual world of the student and leaves behind the more traditional external frame of reference. Developing an internal frame of reference is not easy to do at first, but it is essential if the teacher is to understand *with* the student, not merely *about* the student.

Nondirective counseling stresses the emotional elements of the situation more than the intellectual. That is, nondirective counseling strives for reorganization through the realm of feeling rather than through purely intellectual approaches. Often this view leads teachers who are considering adopting the nondirective stance to question the possibility of conflicting roles. How (*they* reason) can I be a disciplinarian, a referee, an instructor, and also be a counselor implementing nondirective principles?

In elementary schools the establishment of "open" classrooms reflects the adoption of nondirective principles. An open classroom typically has the following characteristics: First, its *objectives* include affective development, growth of student self-concept, and student determination of learning needs. Second, its *methods* of instruction are directed toward student flexibility in learning. Group work that concentrates on creativity and self-knowledge is the main instructional technique. Third, the *teacher's role* is that of facilitator, resource person, guide, and advisor. Fourth, *the students determine what is important to learn.* They are free to set their own educational objectives and to select the method(s) for attaining their goals. Fifth, the *evaluation* of progress in the classroom consists more of student self-evaluation than of teacher evaluation. Progress is measured qualitatively rather than quantitatively.

One of the important uses of nondirective teaching occurs when a class becomes "stale" and the teacher finds himself or herself just "pushing" the students through exercises and subject matter. One sixth-grade teacher, exhausted by the failure of more traditional attempts to cope with the discipline problems and the lack of interest on the part of her class, decided to experiment with student-centered teaching. She turned to nondirective approaches to help her students take more responsibility for their learning and to ensure that the subject matter would be related to their needs and learning styles. She has provided an account of that experience, from which excerpts are presented here:

MARCH 5, WE BEGIN

A week ago I decided to initiate a new program in my sixth grade classroom, based on student-centered teaching—an unstructured or non-directive approach.

I began by telling the class that we were going to try an "experiment." I explained that for one day I would let them do anything they wanted to do—they did not have to do anything if they did not want to.

Many started with art projects; some drew or painted for most of the day. Others read or did work in math and other subjects. There was an air of excitement all day. Many were so interested in what they were doing that they did not want to go out at recess or noon!

At the end of the day I asked the class to evaluate the experiment. The comments were most interesting. Some were "confused," distressed without the teacher telling them what to do, without specific assignments to complete.

The majority of the class thought the day was "great," but some expressed concern over the noise level and the fact that a few "goofed off" all day. Most felt that they had accomplished as much work as we usually do, and they enjoyed being able to work at a task until it was completed, without the pressure of a time limit. They liked doing things without being "forced" to do them and liked deciding what to do.

They begged to continue the "experiment" so it was decided to do so, for two more days. We could then re-evaluate the plan.

The next morning I implemented the idea of a "work contract." I gave them ditto sheets listing all our subjects with suggestions under each. There was a space provided for their "plans" in each area and for checking upon completion.

Each child was to write his or her contract for the day—choosing the areas in which to work and planning specifically what to do. Upon completion of any exercise, drill, review, etc., the student was to check and correct his or her own work, using the teacher's manual. The work was to be kept in a folder with the contract.

I met with each child to discuss his or her plans. Some completed theirs in a very short time; we discussed as a group what this might mean, and what to do about it. It was suggested that the plan might not be challenging enough, that an adjustment should be made—perhaps going on or adding another idea to the day's plan.

Resource materials were provided, suggestions made, and drill materials made available to use when needed.

I found I had much more time, so I worked, talked, and spent the time with individuals and groups. At the end of the third day I evaluated the work folder with each child. To solve the problem of grades, I had each child tell me what he or she had learned.

March 12, PROGRESS REPORT

Our "experiment" has, in fact, become our program—with some adjustments.

Some children continued to be frustrated and felt insecure without teacher direction. Discipline also continued to be a problem with some; and I began to realize that, although some of the children may need the program more than others, I was expecting too much from them too soon—they were not ready to assume self-direction yet. Perhaps a gradual weaning from the spoon-fed procedures was necessary.

I regrouped the class—creating two groups. The largest group is the nondirected. The smallest is teacher-directed, made up of children who wanted to return to the former teacher-directed method, and those who, for varied reasons, were unable to function in the self-directed situation. I would have waited longer to see what would happen, but the situation for some disintegrated a little more each day—penalizing the whole class. The disrupting factor kept everyone upset and limited those who wanted to study and work. So it seemed to me best for the group as a whole as well as the program to modify the plan.

Those who continued the "experiment" have forged ahead. I showed them how to program their work, using their texts as a basic guide. They have learned that they can teach themselves (and each other), and that I am available when a step is not clear or advice is needed.

At the end of the week they evaluate themselves in each area—in terms of work accomplished, accuracy, etc. We have learned that the number of errors is not a criterion of failure or success. Errors can and should be part of the learning process; we learn through our own mistakes. We also discussed the fact that consistently perfect scores may mean that the work is not challenging enough and perhaps we should move on.

After self-evaluation, each child brings the evaluation sheet and work folder to discuss with me.

Some of the members of the group working with me are most anxious to become "independent" students. We will evaluate together each week their progress toward that goal.

I have only experienced one parental objection so far. A parent felt that her child was not able to function without direction.

Some students (there were two or three) who originally wanted to return to the teacher-directed program are now anticipating going back into the self-directed program. (I sense that it has been difficult for them to readjust to the old program as it would be for me to do so.)

INSTRUCTIONAL AND NURTURANT EFFECTS

Since the activities are not prescribed but are determined by the learner as he or she interacts with the teacher and other students, the nondirective environment depends largely on its nurturant effects, with the instructional effects dependent on its success in nurturing more effective self-development (Figure 13-2). The model thus can be thought of as entirely nurturant in character, dependent for effects on experiencing the nondirective environment rather than carrying content and skills through specifically designed activity.

In the introduction to Part II, we stated that there are three ways that the personal models are used: first, as a general moderating influence on our teaching; second, in intensive applications for specific purposes; third, as a general model of teaching. When we add nondirective teaching to our repertoire, all three applications are possible.

As a moderating influence, elements of the approach can be used to help us keep contact with the students' self-concepts and feelings. For example, when students are struggling with a learning task, we can remember that frustration often accompanies struggle. We can be understanding and accepting of the frustration, legitimize the students' expression of their feelings, and help them recognize the frustration and find ways to deal with it.

With respect to the second use, we can employ the model intensively for those activities for which partnership and initiative are essential. For example, when we are guiding independent study projects, we can help the students identify their goals and decide how to achieve them. When teaching writing, we can help the students analyze their feelings and learn to put them into written form. When working with failure, we can help the students define reasonable goals and support them as they work their way toward success.

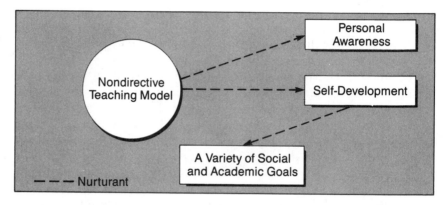

FIGURE 13–2   Instructional and nurturant effects: nondirective teaching model.

Finally, when this model is used as the dominant one, we can organize the classroom or learning center so that the students take a major share in determining their activities. In one of the preceding examples we described teachers who teach reading through literature, helping students to select books and to analyze their own progress.

S U M M A R Y
C H A R T ▶ **NONDIRECTIVE TEACHING MODEL**

Syntax

Phase One: Defining the Helping Situation
    Teacher encourages free expression of feelings.

Phase Two: Exploring the Problem
    Student is encouraged to define problem.
    Teacher accepts and clarifies feelings.

Phase Three: Developing Insight
    Student discusses problem.
    Teacher supports student.

Phase Four: Planning and Decision Making
    Student plans initial decision making.
    Teacher clarifies possible decisions.

Phase Five: Integration
    Student gains further insight and develops more positive actions.
    Teacher is supportive.

Social System

The model has little external structure: teacher facilitates; student initiates; and the discussion is problem-centered. Rewards, in the usual sense of approval of specific behavior, and punishment do not apply in this strategy. The rewards are intrinsic and include acceptance, empathy, and understanding from the teacher.

Principles of Reaction

Teacher reaches out to students, empathizes, reacts to help students define problems and take action to achieve solutions.

Support System

Teacher needs quiet, private place for one-to-one contacts, resource center for conferences on academic contracts.

CHAPTER 14

CONCEPTS OF SELF
Modeling Rich States
of Growth

Although people and their growth are the important substance of this book, this is the first chapter that attempts to deal conceptually with the most important underlying element in general education—the states of growth that result from schooling.

We have made a number of statements about people, however, and as we directly approach the subject it is worthwhile to summarize some of them.

First, the research on the spectrum of models of teaching supports the proposition that all students can learn how to learn and they can respond to a great variety of teaching/learning environments. Students can accelerate their ability to learn in a great number of ways if we provide them with the opportunity.

Second, the more skills students develop and the more they widen their repertoire, the greater their ability to master an even greater range of skills and strategies. (This is true of teachers as well. The better we get, the better we *can* get!)

Third, the learning community developed in the school and the classroom has great influence on how students feel about themselves, how they interact, and how they learn. The social climate, in other words, is part of the substance of schooling. It provides a "curriculum" that greatly affects the results of the academic curriculum.

The important message is that students can learn, not only academic content and social skills, but how to become integrated selves that reach out into the world and reciprocally contribute to and profit from their transactions with it.

Now we turn to modeling active states of growth for our students. We will examine a framework for looking at the ways children and adults interact with the world—from states of actively seeking growth to more passive interaction to states of pushing experience away. In many ways students become what we model for them, and part of our influence on them depends on our own states of growth—our own self-concepts—and how we communicate them to children.

INDIVIDUAL DIFFERENCES

We begin with a frame of reference that will enable us to think about individual differences in growth and particularly in the readiness to grow.

There are a number of ways of thinking about individual differences that are candidates for our use at the present time. Some of these have been developed to help us think about the learning styles of children (Dunn and Dunn, 1975; Gregorc, 1982; McCarthy, 1981) and can be applied to adults as well. Some are developed to distinguish various styles of thinking (e.g., Myers, 1962) and examine how those styles affect problem-solving. There is at least one current theory that attempts to describe differences between children and adults as learners (Knowles, 1978).

A number of broad conceptualizations of personality can be applied to the behavior of teachers as instructors and as learners (Erikson, 1950; Harvey, Hunt, and Schroder, 1961; Maslow, 1962). Especially conceptual systems theory (Hunt, 1971) has been heavily studied and has been a useful predictor of teacher-student interaction (See Chapter 5), the breadth of styles employed by teachers, sensitivity to students and responsiveness to them, and (most pertinent here) aptitude to acquire the competence to use teaching skills and strategies (see Joyce, Peck, and Brown, 1981).

In this chapter we will discuss a framework that was developed from the study of the professional and personal lives of teachers in the California Staff Development Study (Joyce, Bush, and McKibbin, 1983). The framework was developed to guide practice in the organization of human resource development programs and school improvement efforts (McKibbin and Joyce, 1980; Joyce, Hersh, and McKibbin, 1983). Although it was developed from a strictly practical orientation, the findings are correlated with the theories of personality growth and takes conceptual development, self-concept, and psychological maturity into account. It owes a particular debt to the work of Abraham Maslow (1962).

THE CONCEPT OF STATE OF GROWTH

As we indicated earlier, the framework was developed during a large-scale longitudinal study of staff development and school improvement practices in California. The objective was to obtain a detailed picture of the opportunities for growth experienced by teachers from their school setting, the district, universities, intermediate agencies (county offices of education and professional development centers), and other institutions. Case studies were made of more than 300 teachers from 21 districts in seven counties, and more than 2,000 others were surveyed through questionnaires. In addition to information about participation in the formal systems of support (courses, workshops, and the services of administrators and supervisors), interaction with peers was examined, as were those aspects of personal lives that might have implications for professional growth. Thus, data were collected on what came to be termed the "formal," the "peer-generated," and the "personal" domains, depending on the origins of the activities that people engaged in.

The focus was the dynamic of individual interaction with the environment. The thesis was that within any given environment (say, a school in the San Francisco Bay area), the opportunities for productive interaction leading to growth theoretically would be about equal. That is, formal staff development systems, colleagues, and opportunities to read, attend films and events in the performing arts, engage in athletic activity, etc., would be available to all personnel in profusion. *Thus, differences in activity would be a function of the individual's disposition to interact productively with the environment.* If we discovered differences, we could proceed to try to understand their origins and develop ideas for capitalizing on them.

THE FORMAL, PEER-GENERATED, AND PERSONAL DOMAINS

The amount of interaction in all three domains varied greatly. The differences were vast in both urban and rural areas and among elementary and secondary teachers. They are easily illustrated in regions like the Bay Area and the Los Angeles Basin where literally thousands of courses and workshops are available, most principals and supervisors have been trained to provide active clinical support, many professional development centers in county offices and other agencies involve teachers in the selection of staff development opportunities, and there are active organizations of teachers of writing, science, and other curriculum areas. In addition, the opportunities for personal activity of all sorts abound in these great metropolitan areas, which also are close to mountain ranges, waterways, and oceans. The nature of the differences in each domain is interesting.

FORMAL STAFF-DEVELOPMENT OPPORTUNITIES

Participation ranged from persons who experienced only the activities sponsored and required by the district (possibly only one or two workshops or presentations and one or two visits by supervisors or consultants) *and who were aware of very few options,* to very active, aware persons with definite plans for professional enhancement. A small number effectively exploited the opportunities in universities and the larger teacher centers.

PEER-GENERATED OPPORTUNITIES FOR GROWTH

The range here was from persons who had virtually no professional discussions with any other teachers, to persons who had close and frequent interaction, who experienced mentoring relationships (on the giving or re-

ceiving end or both), and who gathered with others to instigate the introduction of innovations or initiatives for the improvement of the school.

THE PERSONAL DOMAIN

In their personal lives some teachers were extremely active, with one
or two well-developed areas of participation, and some others made virtually no use of the rich environments in which they lived. We found some
very active readers and others who barely skim the headlines of the daily
paper, some Sierra Club activists and others who had never visited Yosem-
ite, some members of performing arts groups and others who have not
seen a film or a live performance in 10 or more years.

STATES OF GROWTH

Somewhat to our surprise, the levels of activity were correlated across
domains. That is, those who were more active professionally were also
more active personally. Looking for reasons, we concluded that the differences in levels of activity were produced by the individuals' orientations
toward their environments, moderated by social influence.

ORIENTATIONS TOWARD THE ENVIRONMENT

The essence of the concept is the degree to which the environment is
viewed as an opportunity for satisfying growth. Thus the more active people view the environment as a set of possibilities for satisfying interaction.
They initiate contact and exploit the possibilities. Less active persons are
less aware of the possibilities or more indifferent to them. The least active
persons expend energy protecting themselves from what they see as a
threatening or unpleasant environment, avoiding contact and fending off
the initiatives of others. Also, the persons who are more active and more
initiating are also more *proactive.* That is, they *draw* more attention from
the environment, bringing more possibilities within their reach. This phenomenon multiplies the opportunities for many people. It was not unusual
for us to discover that certain schools that were characterized by a cluster
of active people (and generally by an active principal) were regularly approached by central-office personnel, teacher centers, and universities to
be the "trial" sites for everything from computer technology to community
involvement programs. Those people and their schools receive more resources and training, while some schools—characterized by a cluster of
resistant persons—were approached last, and many initiatives passed
them by.

SOCIAL INFLUENCE

Close friends and colleagues, and the social climate of the workplace
and the neighborhood, moderate the general dispositions toward growth.

Affirmative and active friends and colleagues and positive social climates induce persons to engage in greater activity than they would if left to themselves. This finding provides another dimension to the general theme of Chapter 2. The synergistic environment is not only essential for collective action but to generate the kind of colleagueship that will be productive for the states of growth of individuals.

Also, as we will emphasize later, a major goal of a human resource development system is to increase the states of growth of the personnel in the system, potentially benefiting the individuals as well as the organization and ensuring that the children are in contact with active, seeking personalities.

Levels of Activity

Although the orientations toward growth are best represented on a continuum, people gradually, over time, develop patterns that have more clearly discernible edges, and it is not unreasonable to categorize them—provided we recognize that the categories blend into one another. With that caveat, the following prototypes are presented because they can be useful in explaining behavior and in planning staff development programs and organizing faculties to exploit them vigorously.

A GOURMET OMNIVORE

Our prototypes here are mature, high-activity people who have learned to canvass the environment and exploit it successfully. In the formal domain they keep aware of the possibilities for growth, identify high-probability events, and work hard at squeezing them for their growth potential.

They constitute the hard-core clientele for teacher centers and district and intermediate-agency offerings for volunteers. They initiate ideas for programs and find ways of influencing the policy makers. However, they are not negative toward system initiatives. They have the complexity to balance their personal interests with the awareness that they belong to an organization.

Our prototype omnivores find kindred souls with whom to interact professionally. They learn from informal interaction with their peers. A group of omnivores may work together and generate initiatives or attend workshops or courses together. When computers appeared on the educational scene, it was often groups of omnivores who learned to use them and developed the computer centers in their schools.

It is in their personal lives that our prototype omnivores become most clearly defined. They are characterized by a general high level of awareness, but the distinguishing feature is one or two areas in which they are enthusiastically involved. These areas vary quite a bit from person to person. One may be an omnivorous reader; another, a theater-goer; a third, an avid backpacker or skier; a fourth, a maker of ceramics. Some run businesses. In close consort with others, they generate activities. The spouses of omnivore tennis players are likely to find themselves with rackets in their hands, and the close friends of moviegoers will be importuned to share films. Because of their proactivity, our mature omnivores have learned to fend off opportunities and protect time for their chosen avocations.

What is striking is their habit of both exploiting and enriching whatever environment they find themselves in. In the workplace, they strive to learn all they can about their craft and give and take energy from their peers. In their private lives they find opportunities for development.

They are also distinguished by their persistence. In McKibbin and Joyce's (1980) study, they sought training that would have a high likelihood for transfer and, once back in the workplace, they practiced and created the conditions of peer support that enabled them to implement a remarkably high proportion of the skills to which they were exposed. They are also more likely than others to bring the ideas they gain in their personal lives into the workplace and use them in their teaching.

A PASSIVE CONSUMER

About 10 percent of the persons we studied fit the profile of our "gourmet omnivores," and another 10 percent we call active consumers, also quite engaged with aspects of their environment. By far the largest number, however, (about 70 percent) resembled the prototype we term the "passive consumer."

The distinguishing characteristics of our passive consumers are a more or less amiable conformity to the environment and a high degree of dependence on the immediate social context. In other words their degree of activity depends greatly on who they are with. In the company of other passive consumers, our prototype is relatively inactive. We studied one school in which all of the personnel in one "wing" of the building were passive, and their interchange with others was amiable but involved few serious discussions about teaching and learning. They visited one another's classrooms rarely. None attended staff development activities that were not required by the administration. They had no objections to being required to attend those workshops, one day in the fall and one in the spring, and they enjoyed them but did nothing with the content.

In another wing of the school, two passive consumers found themselves in the company of two omnivores and an active consumer and were drawn into many of the activities generated by their more enterprising colleagues. They found themselves helping to set up computer workstations for the students, cooperating in scheduling and the selection of software, learning word processing and how to teach their students to use self-instructional programs. They attended workshops on the teaching of writing with the study group instigated by the omnivores and began re-vamping their writing programs.

In personal life our prototype passive consumer is also dependent on consort. If they have relatively inactive spouses and extended families, they will be relatively inactive. If they are with relatives, friends, and neighbors who initiate activity, their levels of activity will increase.

A RETICENT CONSUMER

Whereas our passive consumer has a relatively amiable, if rather unenterprising, view of the world, about 10 percent of the persons we studied expend energy actually pushing away opportunities for growth. We speak of these persons as "reticent" because they have developed an orientation of reluctance to interact positively with their cultural environment. We can observe this dynamic in both professional and domestic settings.

Our prototype reticent attends only the staff development that is re-quired and is often angry about having to be there, deprecates the content, whatever it is, and tries to avoid follow-up activities. Our reticent treats administrative initiatives and those from peers with equal suspicion and tends to believe that negative attitudes are justified because "the system" is inherently oppressive and unfeeling. Thus even peers who make initia-tives are deprecated "because they are naive" if they believe that they will gain administrative support for their "idealistic" notions. Hence our reti-cent tends to view our omnivores as negatively as they do the hated administration. The hard-core reticent even rejects opportunities for in-volvement in decision making, regarding them as co-opting moves by ba-sically malign forces.

In discussions about personal lives, the structure of attitudes was sim-ilar. Our reticents tend to emphasize what they see as defects in people, institutions, services, and opportunities in a range of fields. Film, theater, athletic activity, state and national parks, books and newspapers—all are suffering rapid decay. ("Only trash gets published these days. . . . Movies are full of sex and violence.") In the richness of an urban environment, they tend to emphasize crowding as an obstacle to participation in events ("If I could get tickets. . . . If you didn't have to wait for a court. . . . You can never get in to the good movies. . . ."). In the rural environments, it is lack of facilities that gets the blame.

Even so, our reticent is not unaffected by the immediate social context. In affirmative school climates they do not "act out" their negative views as much. In the company of omnivores they can be carried along in school-improvement efforts. Affirmative spouses who tolerate their jaundiced opinions good-naturedly, involve them in a surprising number of activi-ties. In the right circumstances they learn to take advantage of the oppor-tunities in their lives.

CONCEPTUAL STRUCTURE, SELF CONCEPT, AND STATES OF GROWTH

In an attempt to seek reasons for the differences in states of growth manifested by the teachers we were studying, we turned to a number of developmental theories. Two of them are of particular interest to us here because their descriptions of development appear to correlate with the states of growth we found (Joyce, McKibbin, and Bush, 1983). One is conceptual systems theory (Harvey, Hunt, and Schroder, 1961; Hunt, 1971), and the other is self-concept theory (Maslow, 1962).

CONCEPTUAL DEVELOPMENT

Conceptual systems theory describes persons in terms of the structure of concepts they use to organize information about the world. In the lowest developmental stages, persons use relatively few concepts for organizing their world, tend to have dichotomous views with few "shades of gray," and much emotion is attached to their views. They tend to reject information that does not fit into their concepts or to distort it to make it fit. Thus people and events are viewed as "right" or "wrong." Existing concepts are preserved.

At higher stages of development, people develop greater ability to integrate new information, are more decentered and can tolerate alternative views better, and their conceptual structure is modified as old concepts become obsolete and new ones are developed. New experiences are tolerated and bring new information and ideas, rather than being rejected or distorted to preserve the existing state.

For an example, let us consider persons at the lower and higher developmental stages on a first visit to a foreign culture. Persons characterized by the lower conceptual levels are suspicious of the "different" and tend to find fault with it. ("You can't *believe* what they eat there.") They peer through the windows of the tour buses with increasing gratitude that they will soon be returning to America. They speak loudly to the "stupid" hotel personnel who don't speak English. They clutch their wallets to keep them away from the conniving, dishonest natives and their unclean hands.

Their higher-conceptual-level companions are fascinated by the new sights, sounds, and smells. Gingerly they order the local dishes, comparing them with the familiar, finding some new and pleasing tastes, and bargaining for a recipe. They prefer to walk, avoiding the bus unless time forbids. They ask shopkeepers to pronounce the names of things. They brush off the grime to get a better look at the interesting vase in the corner. They speak quietly and wait for the hotel personnel to indicate the local custom.

There is a substantial correlation between conceptual development and the states of growth of the teachers and administrators we studied.

The omnivores are in a continual search for more productive ways of organizing information and have more complex conceptual structures as a result. Their openness to new experience requires an affirmative view of the world and the conceptual sophistication to deal with the new ideas they encounter. Our passive consumers have more limited structures and less ability to figure out how to reach for new experience and deal with it. Our reticents are busy protecting their present concepts and act offended by the presence of the unfamiliar. They can be as negative toward children they do not understand as they are toward the facilitators who try to bring new ideas and techniques into their orbit. Conceptual development is correlated with variety and flexibility in teaching styles (Hunt, 1971), with ease in learning new approaches to teaching, and with ability to understand students and modulate to them (Joyce, Peck, and Brown, eds., 1981).

A change to a more productive orientation involves a structural change—a more complex structure capable of analyzing people and events from multiple points of view and the ability to assimilate new information and accommodate to it.

SELF CONCEPT

More than 35 years ago, Abraham Maslow (1962) and Carl Rogers (1951) developed formulations of personal growth and functioning that have guided attempts since then to understand and deal with individual differences in response to the physical and social environment. Rather than concentrating on intellectual aptitude and development, their theories focused on individuals' views of self or self concepts. They took the position that our competence to relate to the environment is greatly affected by the stances we take toward ourselves.

Strong self-concepts are accompanied by "self-actualizing" behavior, a reaching out toward the environment with confidence that the interaction will be productive. The self-actualizing person interacts richly with the milieu, finding opportunities for growth and enhancement and, inevitably, contributing to the development of others.

Somewhat less-developed persons feel competent to deal with the environment but accept it for what it is and are less likely to develop growth-producing relationships from their own initiatives. They work within the environment and what it brings to them rather than generating opportunities from and with it.

The least developed persons bear a more precarious relationship with their surroundings. They are less sure of their ability to cope. Much of their energy is spent in efforts to ensure that they survive in a less-than-generous world.

It is not surprising that we found a relationship between the states of growth of the people we studied and their concepts of self. Our omnivores are self-actualizing. They feel good about themselves and their surroundings. Our passive consumers feel competent but are dependent on the environment for growth-producing opportunities. Our reticents feel that they live in a precarious and threatening world. The faults that they find in their surroundings are products not of being well-developed and able to discern problems the rest of us cannot see, but of an attempt to rationalize their need to protect themselves from a world of which they are afraid.

UNDERSTANDING GROWTH AND THE POTENTIAL FOR GROWTH

The theories of conceptual growth and self-concept both help us understand ourselves as growth-oriented programs are planned and carried out. They help us understand why people respond as they do and provide us with a basis for creating environments that are likely to be productive both in terms of the content of the programs and the people for whom they are intended.

David Hopkins (1990) and his colleagues recently reported a study conducted in England in which they studied the implementation by a group of teachers of a new curriculum in the arts for which they had volunteered to be the forerunners. They were to master the curriculum in their classrooms and then become the disseminators to other teachers. Hopkins studied the states of growth and self-concepts of the teachers and the organizational climates of the schools in which they worked. All were influential, but the states of growth alone were predictors of the teachers' uses of the arts curricula. Essentially, the reticent and passive consumers were unable to achieve implementation in any organizational climate, while climate facilitated the work of the active consumers and gourmet omnivores.

Not only were the teachers at the lower states of growth unable to profit from the training they received, but their students were deprived of the opportunities to learn presented by the new curriculum!

DEVELOPING RICHER STATES OF GROWTH

We want to grow as people and also to help our students develop richer orientations for growth. These are closely connected, for our primary influence on our students is what we model as people. If we model passivity, we encourage it. If we model activity and reaching out toward the world, we encourage active states.

The good news is that we are far more likely to develop an upward progression than a downward one. Also, we develop by practicing reaching out—we simply "do it!"

Thus, the message is that we need to reach out by developing a couple of lines of activity in which we push ourselves for richness and excellence.

These areas need to be balanced. Reading or the cinema needs to be balanced by a social or athletic pursuit. We can have confidence that modeling omnivorous reading will not only breed active readers but also will pull students toward different pursuits.

The models of teaching described in this book are also strong tools. A cooperative learning community—tooled up with the active models for gathering and interpreting information, examining social issues, and seeking ways of learning more—will have its effect on the students. A rich and active social climate will have its effect.

We are what we eat, not just biologically but socially and emotionally. Rich substance, well organized, in positive circumstance makes us richer, more outreaching, and more productive. And, in our professional work, it gives us the tools for developing self-actualizing students.

THE PERSONAL FAMILY: AN ADDITIONAL NOTE ON EXPECTED EFFECTS

As with all models, making estimates of expected effects on student learning is a complicated but important process. The personal models employ gentle, indirect means to nurture the students and help them gradually reach out to the world rather than providing them quickly with relatively high-impact tools for learning. Unquestionably, they build the nurturant environment that provides a solid social context for the students to try to find self-definition and reach toward self-actualization, and the broad research in the field of therapy provides them with ample theoretical and empirical justification.

Assessing the personal models by asking whether they increase student learning in schools is a difficult and somewhat unfair question. Certainly short-term experiments are not a good test when one type of approach rushes to help the student build specific capacity and the other uses indirect methods. Also, indirect methods encourage students to reach out in their own directions, and it is hard to anticipate where academic growth may first appear for any given student and to design a broad enough battery of measures to "catch" many of the effects, so to speak. One can, of course, look at the very long-term, as did the Eight Year Study (Chamberlin and Chamberlin, 1943) that found that cooperative, inquiry-oriented schools that cherished individual differences advantaged their students once they reached college.

A relatively large-scale study (Aspy, Roebuck, et al., 1974) examined not only the directly intended effects of employing nondirective teaching methods but also the effects on traditional academic achievement and discovered a modest but consistent effect-size of about .15 on reading and mathematics, placing the average student at about the 55th percentile of comparison groups. The effects on self-esteem and interaction patterns were much larger. The study was done with elementary students having patterns of learning difficulty.

That the two studies support the use of mental-health oriented education, one with the college-bound and the other with struggling elementary school students, is really not surprising. The findings parallel those that have found that cooperative classrooms benefit the students with all levels of learning history. Essentially, mental health is incredibly important to quality of life and, therefore, the models that enhance it will surely enhance quality of learning as well.

A blend of models is what we advocate. The message from this family is that teaching can be carried on in a gentle, nurturant fashion whose leaven will enhance the other models.

PART IV

THE BEHAVIORAL SYSTEMS FAMILY

Behavior Theory

Behavioral models of learning and instruction have their origins in the classical conditioning experiments of Pavlov (1927), the work of Thorndike on reward learning (1911, 1913), and the studies of Watson and Rayner (1921), who applied Pavlovian principles to the psychological disorders of human beings. In the past 20 years, behavior (learning) theory, systematically applied in school settings, has been greatly influenced by B. F. Skinner's *Science and Human Behavior* (1953) and J. Wolpe's *Psychotherapy by Reciprocal Inhibition* (1958). Wolpe's influence also stems from his descriptions of specific therapeutic procedures for dealing with human problems (for example, in systematic desensitization and assertiveness training).

In the late 1950s educators began to employ behavioral techniques, particularly forms of contingency management and programmed learning materials, in school settings. For some types of learners these have had great success. For example, some youngsters who previously had made no progress in language development and social learning are now trainable and often able to mix with normal individuals. Milder forms of learning problems have responded to behavior models as well (Becker, 1977; Becker & Carnine, 1980; Becker, Englemann, Carnine, & Rhine, 1981).

During the past 10 years, there has been an impressive amount of research demonstrating the effectiveness of behavioral techniques with a wide range of problems, from snake phobias to social-skill deficits, behavioral problems, and test anxiety. The research also indicates that these procedures can be used effectively in group settings and by laypeople. We believe that behavior theory presently offers an array of procedures that are extremely useful to teachers and curriculum planners. Many of them are not widely known or used in school settings; others are frequently used by some practitioners but too often dismissed by others, perhaps for lack of genuine understanding.

The models we have developed or borrowed from behavior theory include one for mastery learning and direct instruction, another for learning from simulations, and another for assertiveness training.

These models are drawn from the body of knowledge we call *behavior theory*. Other terms such as *learning theory, social learning theory, behavior modification*, and *behavior therapy* have been used by various leaders in this field to refer to the models we discuss here (Bandura, 1969; Lazarus, 1971; Salter, Wolpe, and Reyna, 1964; Wolpe, 1969; see also Estes, 1975). Because each term is generally associated with one particular form of the basic theory, we prefer to use the more neutral term *behavior theory* to cover those procedures emanating from both operant and countercondi-tioning principles, which have been useful in educational and psycholog-ical settings. Although there have been many school applications of models based on operant principles, we find less use of the countercondi-tioning models that are discussed in many psychotherapy references, es-pecially relaxation, desensitization, and assertiveness training. We believe that these models, too, are valuable for educational purposes, are appli-cable in school settings, and can easily be transferred to them.

ASSUMPTIONS OF MODERN BEHAVIORAL THEORY

BEHAVIOR IS LAWFUL AND SUBJECT TO VARIABLES IN THE ENVIRONMENT

People respond to variables in their environment. These external forces stimulate individuals to act in certain ways: either to exhibit or avoid behaviors. According to the principle of operant conditioning, once a behavior has been manifested, the probability that it will occur again can be strengthened or decreased by responses from the environment. Thus, if a two-year-old sees a table in the room (stimulus), points to it, and verbalizes the word *table* (response behavior), he or she is responding to external forces. If, after the child says the word *table*, the child's mother picks him or her up, gives him or her a big hug, and repeats, "*Table*, that's right" (reinforcing stimuli), the child is likely to say the word again (re-sponse behavior). On the other hand, suppose the child sees a rattlesnake curled nearby (stimulus) and experiences a sudden surge of anxiety and fear (response behaviors). If the child runs away (another response behavior) and thereby avoids the snake, the act reduces his or her anxiety (reinforcing stimulus). The reinforcement increases the likelihood that the child will try to avoid snakes. Both of these examples illustrate the basic behavioral notion that behavior is acquired or enacted through external variables that serve either as the original stimulus or as the reinforcing stimulus. In one case we are learning to do something; in the other case, to avoid something.

Counterconditioning is related, but slightly different. In counterconditioning, a new behavior that is incompatible with the old behavior is substituted, such as relaxation for anxiety. To cure a phobia toward snakes, the individual substitutes positive feelings for anxiety.

From this stance the task of the psychologist is to discover what kinds of environmental variables affect behavior in which ways. The educator ascertaining these relationships can apply the findings directly to his or her work—changing variables to change behavior. The leverage of external control can also be given to the individual. If the teacher can, by appropriate techniques, ascertain and control the external variables, so can the student. Thus, what appears at first to be a technique for controlling others can be used to free people by increasing *their* capabilities for self-control.

BEHAVIOR AS AN OBSERVABLE, IDENTIFIABLE PHENOMENON

Behavior theory concentrates on the behavior itself, and takes an optimistic view. Given the right conditions and enough time we can (and will) succeed.

$$\text{Original Stimulus} \rightarrow \text{Response Behavior} \rightarrow \text{Reinforcing Stimuli}$$

Behavior theorists believe that even internal responses (such as anxiety in the presence of snakes), which mediate our observable responses (such as running away), can be changed. For example, biofeedback represents a successful attempt to alter so-called internal states such as anxiety, tension, or stress (Rimm and Masters, 1974).

MALADAPTIVE BEHAVIORS ARE ACQUIRED THROUGH LEARNING AND CAN BE MONITORED THROUGH LEARNING PRINCIPLES

Many people have assumed, quite erroneously, that many children have "blocks to learning" (internal states that cannot be changed). Yet in recent years, we have seen numerous examples of growth through the systematic application of learning principles. Other more typical, but frustrating, behavioral problems of normal children have been handled successfully with behavioral techniques. Perhaps more than any other school of thought, behavior theorists have documented their effectiveness simply by manipulating the stimulus conditions in the environment (operant principles), or by substituting the behavioral response (counterconditioning). Maladaptive behavior can be changed, often producing changes in feelings and attitudes.

BEHAVIORAL GOALS ARE SPECIFIC, DISCRETE, AND INDIVIDUALIZED

It is assumed that all behavioral problems, however globally presented, can be described in specific, concrete terms, given enough probing or observation. Another assumption is that two externally similar responses do not necessarily proceed from the same original stimulus. Conversely, no two people will respond to the same stimulus in the same way. Consequently, the procedures for encouraging new behaviors involve setting specific, individualized behavioral goals. This does not mean that some group training (as in programmed instruction or assertiveness groups) is not possible. On the contrary, group training for assertiveness, reading instruction, and even the elimination of phobias has been quite effective. It does mean that the goals for each student may differ and that the training process will need to be individualized in terms of pacing or content.

BEHAVIORAL THEORY FOCUSES ON THE HERE-AND-NOW

The role of the past in shaping a person's behavior is de-emphasized. The conditions stimulating the behavior are ascertainable through observation or interviewing. What is crucial is determining (describing) the functional relationship currently operating in producing or maintaining the behavior. Once this is done, the best procedure for altering the behavior can be selected and implemented.

Behavioral practitioners have often reported that they have been able to alter maladaptive behaviors in a short time, even in the case of severe phobias or long-term withdrawal patterns. Many people have felt relaxed and socially effective in a short time, and students who had remained virtually illiterate have progressed quickly (Resnick, 1967).

OPERANT CONDITIONING AND COUNTERCONDITIONING

The procedures or models evolving from behavior theory fall into two general categories: those emphasizing the principle of operant conditioning (Skinner) and those using principles of counterconditioning (Wolpe). Operant principles stress the role of reinforcement (particularly reward and punishment); counterconditioning emphasizes procedures for substituting an adaptive for a maladaptive response—for example, substituting tapping on the table with one's fingers for nail biting. Programmed instruction and training (operant-based models) and desensitization (a counterconditioning model) all rely heavily on stimulus control.

In Chapter 15 we will deal with mastery learning, direct instruction, and social learning theory. In Chapter 16 we will examine a model that helps students use operant principles to control their own behavior. In Chapter 17 we will discuss training and how to organize it.

There is a vast amount of conceptual and empirical literature on behavior therapy, much of which is summarized in David C. Rimm and John C. Masters, *Behavior Therapy: Techniques and Empirical Findings* (1974). We draw heavily from their work, although we are concerned with teaching rather than therapy. Rimm and Masters encourage the use of behavioral procedures by laypeople and by teachers in the classroom—particularly the latter because they feel that many school-related problems could benefit from it. Many educators, too, believe that one purpose of schooling is to increase students' self-esteem and life skills. These models offer one way of addressing preventive mental health as well as basic intellectual knowledge and skills.

Major concepts

The key ideas in behavior theory are based on the stimulus-response-reinforcement paradigm in which human behavior is thought to be under the control of the external environment. A *stimulus* is "any condition, event, or change in the environment of an individual which produces a change in behavior" (Taber, Glaser, and Halmuth, 1967, p. 16). It may be verbal (oral or written) or physical. A response may be defined as a unit of behavior. It is the basic unit upon which complex performances or response repertoires are built. Responses may be covert, as anxiety or tension, or overt, as talking, hitting a ball, or marking a paper. Complex behaviors are made up of response repertoires consisting of many kinds of responses that are functionally related (as in the solution of a long-division problem).

The condition upon which reinforcement will occur depends on the standard set by the teacher. In skill development, what is acceptable for the beginner may be less than adequate for the advanced student. Thus, as practice increases, the teacher expects better performance and so will reward only more advanced responses. In mathematics the teacher may on one occasion accept the response *triangle* and later accept only *isosceles triangle* as a response to the same stimulus. Obviously, the behavior ultimately desired does not come forth in the first stages but is the result of a continuous *shaping* process executed by changing stimuli and conditions of reinforcement. A person's initial response must exist in some strength in his or her repertoire; the task of the instructor is to build more complex patterns of responses from this initial response by changing the demands and rewards in the environment. The essence of operant conditioning is to have reinforcement contingent only on emission of the desired behavior. This process is known as *contingency management*.

According to behavioral theorists, the most effective reinforcement immediately follows a response. Delayed reinforcement is much less powerful in modifying behavior. *Reinforcement* is at the heart of the behavioral model, for without it behavior (responses) cannot be brought under the control of particular environmental stimuli. A *reinforcer* always increases the frequency of a response on which it is contingent.

Reinforcers may be either *positive* or *negative*. *Positive reinforcers* are those events whose presentation increases response. Money, affection, approval, smiles, and attention are examples of positive reinforcers. When they appear, the contingent responses usually occur. Another positive reinforcer familiar to educators is *confirmation or knowledge of results*. Knowing that you have behaved correctly or adequately is highly reinforcing. Self-instructional programmed material is sequenced in such small steps as to virtually ensure correct responses. The reinforcement the learner derives from knowledge of his or her correctness both makes the achievement enduring and propels the learner toward new tasks. This is why highly sequenced programmed materials often work well with students who previously experienced little success.

Finally, students are also *reinforced by controlling their environments*. Such simple activities as turning a page after reading its contents stimulate continued activity. Part of the attraction of self-instructional computer programs is the reinforcement quality of mechanical manipulation. One can design a program to encourage many satisfying actions. Simulators often provide opportunities for similar pleasurable activities.

The range of naturally occurring positive reinforcers available to teachers is broad—for example, a smile, enthusiasm, show of interest, attention, physical contact, enjoyment, and casual conversation. Most often their use is not monitored carefully, and this increases students' maladaptive behaviors. How many times have teachers called on the student who interrupts others because he or she catches the teachers' eyes and ears first?

Negative reinforcement, on the other hand, removes something from the situation (possibly by adding something disagreeable). Punishment, such as threats that decrease response probability, is an example of a negative reinforcer (aversive stimulus). The management mode in many classrooms is based on aversive control; students are threatened with reprisals if they do not learn. Many years ago the birch rod was used; today the aversive stimuli are less physical (poor grades, disapproval). According to behavior theorists, punishment suffers from several drawbacks. First, its effects are temporary; punished behavior is likely to recur. Second, the aversive stimuli used in punishment may generate unwanted emotions, such as predispositions to escape or retaliate, and disabling anxieties (Skinner, 1956, p. 183). Wherever possible, positive rather than negative reinforcements should be used.

The effectiveness of reinforcement programs is determined not only by establishing a close temporal relation between reinforcement and behavior and by the type of reinforcement selected, but also by the scheduling or frequency of reinforcement (*reinforcement schedule*). In Skinner's opinion, reinforcement should be as continuous as possible, occurring after every response. Research on reinforcement schedules shows that although continuous reinforcement contributes to the most rapid acquisition of behavior, it does not bring about the strongest retention rate. A *variable* ratio schedule in which reinforcement is contingent on the number of responses and is administered irregularly creates the most durable response levels. One of the most difficult skills for teachers, or anyone, to master is to be consistent, immediate, and frequent in rewarding the desired responses when they occur. Often contingency management programs break down because the reinforcement is not consistent. If a response goes unreinforced it will become less and less frequent until it is extinguished.

In many classrooms the primary instructional objective is to bring the students' behavior under the control of subject-matter stimulus (stimulus control). The learner connects appropriate responses to various stimuli (as words for objects). *Stimulus discrimination* is particularly important in the learning situation. When we respond differently to different stimuli, we are distinguishing or discriminating between their properties. Most subject matter is brought under control through discrimination training. For example, suppose we have previously conditioned the response *ball* to the spherical object, ball, and *ring* for an enclosed circular band. To ensure that the new response *ring* is not called forth in the presence of a ball, we must present the ball and extinguish the response *ring* if it is made. In this manner, the control of the response *ring* to the appropriate stimulus is sharpened. Or a child may have learned to respond to the letter *d* and may then need to distinguish *d* from *b* and learn not to give the *d* response when *b* is the stimulus.

A related process is known as *stimulus generalization*, or extension of stimulus control. In this case, several stimuli possessing similar properties share the response control. The response *animal* is shared with many discriminative stimuli. The child learns to apply it to a few animals, then more, then all. In this way concepts are acquired that refer to classes of objects and events.

Desensitization procedures make use of stimulus control by gradually enlarging the range of stimuli to which individuals can respond without anxiety. Stress-reduction models depend on people's recognizing a range of cues indicating body tension or mental stress.

Training models using observation and practice illustrate the basic behavioral concepts. For example, when one goes to a hotel, the registration desk is a stimulus to the patterns of behavior one uses to obtain a room.

Seeing someone else ask for a room gives one a model to follow. Hearing the correct pronunciation of foreign words functions in the same way. Thus, an instructional pattern can take the form of:

1. Presenting a stimulus.
2. Observing or modeling a response (optional).
3. Providing practice in responding to the stimulus.
4. Reinforcing appropriate responses as immediately as possible.

Imagine a teacher whose objective is to help a class read a section of one of Shakespeare's plays in an appropriate way. He or she might:

1. Present the written passage.
2. Demonstrate some ways of reading it.
3. Induce the students to practice reading the passage.
4. Reinforce performance selectively. (For some, participation might be rewarded. For others, high standards of reading and performing would be applied.)

As we explore the models derived from the behavioral stance, we find each of these elements (stimulus control; generalization and discrimination; response repertoires and response substitution; reinforcers and reinforcement schedules; observation, modeling, and practice) present in various combinations and with different amounts of emphasis.

15

MASTERY LEARNING, DIRECT INSTRUCTION, AND SOCIAL LEARNING THEORY

In this chapter we begin with mastery learning, a framework for planning instructional sequences. We then present one form of what is currently called "direct instruction". We then explore aspects of social learning theory, a powerful framework for understanding how we learn (from a behavior systems perspective) and how we can shape learning environments from its perspective.

Mastery learning

In recent years much attention has been given to an approach for organizing instruction termed *mastery learning*, formulated by John B. Carroll (1971) and Benjamin Bloom (1971). Mastery learning provides a compact and interesting way of increasing the likelihood that more students will attain a satisfactory level of performance in school subjects. Many of its elements are not new. Both Bloom and Carroll cite practices developed by Carlton Washburn and Henry Morrison in the 1920s. But recent work has sharpened the idea, and contemporary instructional technology has made it more feasible. A strong body of research supports the application of the approach.

A CONCEPT OF APTITUDE

The core theoretical idea in mastery learning is based on John Carroll's interesting perspective on the meaning of aptitude. Traditionally, aptitude has been thought of as a characteristic that correlates with a student's achievement. (The more aptitude one has, the more he or she is likely to learn.) Carroll, however, views aptitude as the *amount of time* it takes someone to learn any given material, rather than his or her capacity to master it. By Carroll's view, students with very low aptitude with respect to a particular kind of learning simply take a much longer time to reach mastery than students with a higher aptitude.

This view is optimistic in the sense that it suggests that it is possible for nearly all students to master any given set of objectives, if sufficient time (the opportunity to learn) is provided along with appropriate materials and instruction. Thus viewed, aptitude becomes primarily a guide to how much time a learner will need. Aptitude also suggests *how* to instruct, because learners of different aptitudes will learn more efficiently if the style of instruction is suited to their configurations. (In *our* terms, some aptitudes are model-relevant—they help us choose and adapt models.) For any given objective, according to Carroll, the degree of learning achieved by any given student will be a function of time allowed, the perseverance of the student, the quality of instruction, the student's ability to understand instruction, and his or her aptitude. The problem in managing instruction is deciding how to organize the curriculum and the classroom so that students will have optimal time, benefit from good instruction, be induced to persevere, and receive assistance in understanding the learning tasks.

Bloom transformed Carroll's stance into a system with the following characteristics:

1. Mastery of any subject is defined in terms of sets of major objectives which represent the purposes of the course or unit.
2. The substance is then divided into a larger set of relatively small learning units, each one accompanied by its own objectives, which are parts of the larger ones or thought essential to their mastery.
3. Learning materials are then identified and the instructional strategy selected.
4. Each unit is accompanied by brief diagnostic tests which measure the student's developing progress (the formative evaluation) and identify the particular problems each student is having.
5. The data obtained from administering the tests is used to provide supplementary instruction to the student to help him overcome his problems (Bloom, 1971, pp. 47–63).

If instruction is managed in this way, Bloom believes, then time to learn can be adjusted to fit aptitude. Students of lesser aptitude can be given more time and more feedback while the progress of all is monitored with the assistance of the tests.

INDIVIDUALLY PRESCRIBED INSTRUCTION (IPI)

Bloom, Block, and the other advocates of mastery learning believe that it can be implemented simply by modifying traditional group instructional procedures to ensure that some students have more time and that they receive appropriate individual instruction according to the results of the formative evaluation (Carroll, 1971, pp. 37–41). We are not so sure that mastery learning can be easily and simply implemented in many classrooms without substantial amounts of technical support.

However, modern instructional technology, especially the development of self-administering multimedia units and the application of programmed learning procedures, has encouraged curriculum developers to invent comprehensive curricular systems and to reorganize schools to provide for a much greater degree of individualized instruction than is generally possible under conventional school organizations.

A prominent example of an application of systems planning to elementary and secondary school instruction is the Individually Prescribed Instructional Program (IPI), developed by the Learning Research and Development Center of the University of Pittsburgh, in collaboration with the Baldwin-Whitehall School District. The system, originally designed for the Oakleaf School in suburban Pittsburgh, now operates in more than 100 schools across the country and includes instructional materials in five curriculum areas: mathematics, reading, science, handwriting, and spelling. A student receiving IPI usually works independently on the materials prescribed daily (or every few days) for him or her, depending on his or her demonstrated level of competence, learning style, and particular learning needs.

STEPS IN THE PROGRAM

IPI illustrates a modular curriculum developed by applying systems analysis procedures to curriculum materials development. It is a particularly useful case study because it readily demonstrates the steps the IPI planners took in creating the system. As we examine these steps, we stop briefly to show how each reflects the inner workings of the performance model.

First, in conceptualizing a performance model the planners operate with a set of goals and assumptions about the learner, the learning process, and the learner vis-a-vis the system in which he or she will work. The goals with respect to the learner are:

1. To enable each pupil to work at his own rate through units of study in a learning sequence.
2. To develop in each pupil a demonstrable degree of mastery.
3. To develop self-initiation and self-direction of learning.
4. To foster the development of problem-solving through processes.
5. To encourage self-evaluation and motivation for learning (University of Pittsburgh, 1966, p. 5)

The assumptions regarding the learning process and the related learning environment are as follows:

1. One obvious way in which pupils differ is in the amount of time and practice that it takes to master given instructional objectives.

2. One important aspect of providing for individual differences is to arrange conditions so that each student can work through the sequence of instructional units at his or her own pace and with the amount of practice he or she needs.

3. If a school has the proper types of study materials, elementary school pupils, working in a tutorial environment that emphasizes self-learning, can with a minimum amount of direct teacher instruction, learn.

4. In working through a sequence of instructional units, no pupil should be permitted to start work on a new unit until he or she has acquired a specified minimum degree of mastery of the material in the units identified as prerequisites.

5. If pupils are to be permitted and encouraged to proceed at individual rates, it is important for both the individual pupil and the teacher that the program provide for frequent evaluations of pupil progress which can provide a basis for the development of individual instructional prescriptions.

6. Professionally trained teachers are employing themselves most productively when they are performing such tasks as instructing individual pupils or small groups, diagnosing pupil needs, and planning instructional programs rather than carrying out such clerical duties as keeping records, scoring tests, and so on. The efficiency and economy of a school program can be increased by employing clerical help to relieve teachers of many nonteaching duties.

7. Each pupil can assume more responsibility for planning and carrying out his own program of study than is permitted in most classrooms.

8. Learning can be enhanced, both for the tutor and the one being tutored, if pupils are permitted to help one another in certain ways (Lindvall and Bolvin, 1966, pp. 3–4).

The second step is to analyze the performance model into a set of sequentially organized behavioral objectives. IPI planners believe that such a listing is fundamental to other aspects of the program and must have the following characteristics:

a. Each objective should tell exactly what a pupil should be able to do to exhibit his mastery of the given content and skill. This should typically be something the average student can master in such a relatively short period as one class period. Objectives should involve such action verbs as *solve, state, explain, list, describe*, etc., rather than general terms such as *understand, appreciate, know*, and *comprehend*.

b. Objectives should be grouped in meaningful streams of content. For example, in arithmetic the objectives will be grouped (typically) into such areas as numeration, place value, addition, subtraction, etc. Such grouping aids in the meaningful development of instructional materials and in the diagnosis of pupil achievement. At the same time, this grouping does not preclude the possibility of having objectives that cut across areas.

c. Within each stream or area, the objectives should, to the extent possible, be sequenced in such an order that each one will build on those that precede it, and, in turn, be a prerequisite to those that follow. The goal here is to let the objectives constitute a "scale" of abilities.

d. Within the sequence of objectives in each area, the objectives should be grouped into meaningful subsequences or units. Such units can be designated as representing different levels in progress and can provide break points so that when a student finishes a unit in that area, he or she may either go on to the next unit in that area or may switch to a unit in another area. (For example, upon completing Level B addition, the pupil may either go on to Level C addition or move on to Level B subtraction.) (University of Pittsburgh, 1966, p. 3)

Over 400 specific behavioral objectives are included in the 13 topics of the mathematics curriculum. The following excerpt, one small series from the sequence, illustrates the minute detail of the plan:

LEVEL E

LEVEL F

ADDITION AND SUBTRACTION

1. Given any two whole numbers, the student adds or subtracts using the short algorithm.

1. Given any two numbers ≤ 9,999.99 and an operation of addition or subtraction, the student solves. LIMIT: Answers must be positive numbers.

2. Given an addition problem with ≤ 5 addends, the student solves using the short algorithm.

2. Given ≤ 5 addends which are mixed decimals with < 7 digits, the student adds. LIMIT: Decimals to millionths.

3. Given multiple-step word problems requiring addition and subtraction skills mastered to this point, the student solves them.

3. Given two mixed decimals, the student subtracts. LIMIT: ≤ 7 digits, decimals to millionths.

4. Solves multiple-step word problems: using addition and subtraction skills mastered to this point.

MULTIPLICATION

1. Given a two-digit number and a one-digit number, the student multiplies in horizontal form by using the distributive principle.

1. Given a two-digit number times a two-digit number, the student multiplies using the standard algorithm.

2. Given a problem with a three-digit multiplicand and a one-digit multiplier, the student solves using partial products.

3. Given a multiplication problem whose multipliers and multiplicands are whole numbers ≤ 10 times a multiple of 10, the student solves. LIMIT: Factors ≤ 9,000.

4. Given a multiplication problem whose multipliers are whole numbers < 10 times a power of 10, and whose multiplicand is three digits, the student solves. LIMIT: Multipliers ≤ 9,000.

5. Given a multiplication problem with a two-digit number times a two-digit number, the student solves using partial products.

2. Given a three-digit number times a two-digit number, the student multiplies using the standard algorithm.

3. Given a whole number and a mixed decimal to hundredths as factors, the student multiplies. LIMIT: Whole number part ≤ 100.

4. Given two pure decimals ≤ .99, the student multiplies and shows the equivalent problem in fractional form and converts product to decimal notation, compares answers for check.

5. Given a multiple-step word problem requiring multiplication skills mastered to this point, the student solves.

MULTIPLICATION

6. Given a two-digit number and a one-digit number, the student solves by using the multiplication algorithm.

7. Given a multiplication problem for skills to this point, the student checks the multiplication by commuting the factors and solving again.

8. Given a number ≤ 100, the student finds the complete factorization for the number. (University of Pittsburgh, 1968)

Each of the 13 areas of the mathematics curriculum has nine levels of difficulty, A through I. Within each level for a given topic area, several behavioral objectives are identified and sequentially organized. The breakdown of the 13 topics into levels creates certain options for the student and teacher. The student can cover one area in depth before moving to the next or can go from addition Level E to subtraction Level E. We can see that the content for the IPI math program is spelled out in great detail, ordered sequentially, and interrelated well in advance of the time the teachers and students come together.

The third step in the program is to develop the materials that the students use to achieve each objective. These are mostly self-study materials that a student can pursue by himself or herself with minimal assistance from the teacher: in the mathematics curriculum, worksheets, individual pages, or lesson groups of pages. In addition to the self-instruction, the program calls on the teacher to offer instruction to small or large groups and to individuals. For instance, if several students are having difficulty successfully completing a particular objective, the teacher may bring them together for small-group instruction. The mathematics program makes the additional assumption that not all students learn equally well by the same approach. Some students may need more practice in the use of the concept, while others learn the concept more effectively by being given examples in which they must decide what is and what is not an instance of the concept. Still others have difficulty transferring behavior from one situation to another and need experience with a variety of formats for using the concept. For example, students can add two-digit numbers using a number line, an abacus, or memorized addition tables with rulers for carrying! To accommodate these differences, the mathematics materials for a given behavioral objective include a variety of approaches and formats.

The fourth step for the system planner is to bring together the components of the system—student, teacher, materials—so that the behavioral objectives are achieved. One program devoted a portion of the school day at the beginning of the academic year to testing:

> It was essential to find out exactly what abilities each pupil had in each of the many areas in reading, arithmetic, and science. In arithmetic for example, sequenced materials had been developed for each topic, such as numeration, measurement, addition, and subtraction. Because so many topics were involved and because it was necessary to know where a pupil should start in each of them, several days had to be devoted to diagnosis of pupil abilities.
>
> On the basis of this diagnosis, a "prescription" was developed for each pupil in each subject. This prescription listed the materials that the pupil was to start with—which might be enough for one day, several days, or a week—depending on the ability of the student and the difficulty of the unit. Evaluation and feedback, then, were built into the ongoing curricular activities. This is in contrast to many educational programs which depend heavily on periods of examination and the like that are separated from other curricular activities.
>
> The faculty also developed a system for guiding the students as they worked. A student was to begin working on his prescribed materials usually by himself at a desk in a study area with eighty or ninety other pupils. In this room there were also two or three teachers to provide instructional assistance, and three or four clerks to distribute materials and grade papers. Most pupils were able to proceed through their study materials with a minimum of help from the teachers. If a teacher found a pupil who needed more help than she could give in this large-group situation, she directed him to a small side room where another teacher gave him more extensive individual help or involved him in small-group instruction. (Joyce and Harootunian, 1967, pp. 83–84)

Lastly comes the creation of a management system for monitoring the student's progress and adjusting prescriptions so that carefully tailored feedback, the heart of the cybernetic approach, can be given.

> The materials prescribed for a student at any given time typically would include as a final exercise, a "check test" or "curriculum embedded" test. This exercise, which the student viewed as just another worksheet, would play a large part in determining what the pupil did next. When a pupil completed his prescribed unit of work, he took it to a clerk for checking and then to the teacher who was developing the prescriptions. This teacher held a brief conference with the pupil, examined the work he had just completed, and then developed the next prescription. As we can see, the learner role variables are carefully defined and provision is made for developing them under this system. (Joyce and Harootunian, 1967, p. 84)

In this case the management system for tracking a pupil's progress and specifying the role of functionaries is embedded in the instructional system. As in business, the teacher-manager has the responsibility for bettering the system and adjusting it to the needs of the individual. The teacher's role in IPI is a crucial one. He or she serves as

> a diagnostician (analyzing the IPI diagnostic data about each student in order to tailor a program to meet the individual learning needs), a selector (drawing on the bank of both human and material resources available to the IPI instructional situation), and a tutor (building meaningful and appropriate learning experiences that lead a student to a more independent and responsible role in his IPI learning setting). (Scanlon and Brown, n.d., p. 1)

This represents an organizational approach to teaching quite different from that of the self-contained classroom teacher working with the groups of children he or she sees every day and for whose education he or she maintains total responsibility.

LANGUAGE LABORATORY

Another prominent example of an instructional system, one in which the machine components paved the way for an entirely different learning environment, is the *language laboratory*. Its development represents vivid application of the combined properties of systems analysis, task analysis, and cybernetic principles in the educational setting. Before the language laboratory became commonplace, the classroom teacher served as the model for foreign speech in a classroom of 25 to 35 students who were trying to reproduce sounds of speech. The individual in such a situation might have a maximum of one minute of speech practice per classroom session, hardly enough to produce fluency or accuracy.

Today in the typical classroom laboratory, learners use electrical equipment to hear, record, and play back spoken materials. The general physical equipment includes student stations and an instructor's central panel. Through this panel, the teacher can broadcast a variety of content materials, new and remedial programs, and instruction to individuals, selected groups, or the entire class. He or she can also monitor the students' performance. The students' stations are often a series of individual, acoustically treated carrels, usually equipped with headphones, a microphone, and a tape recorder. Each student listens through the headphones to live or recorded directions from the instructor to repeat, answer questions, or make other appropriate responses to the lesson. The instructor may also choose to use the chalkboard, textbook, or other visual stimuli to supplement audio inputs. Modern technology has made it possible for almost instantaneous situations in which students might:

1. Hear their own voices more clearly through earphones than they could otherwise.
2. Directly compare their speech with a model's.
3. Provide themselves with immediate feedback.
4. Isolate items for study.
5. Permit pacing for specific drill.
6. Permit more finely sequenced instructional content.

Learning a foreign language requires that the student hear vocabulary and speech pattern repeatedly. The exercises are carefully sequenced and are followed by new combinations of varying complexity. The ultimate goal is to have the student readily comprehend what he or she hears and make immediate and appropriate responses. From the student's viewpoint, the language laboratory serves as a base for tireless practicing of finely sequenced behavior, matching aural models, and developing speech fluency. From the instructor's viewpoint, it provides the facilities (hardware and software) for a more effective language-learning situation.

In systems analysis terminology, the language laboratory represents the development of a human-machine system based on the performance objectives and requirements of foreign language proficiency. Prior to the development of the language laboratory, it was possible to provide reasonably sequenced visual materials. But the critical elements of language training—individualized audial practice and dynamic feedback—far outran the human-management capacities and support facilities of the self-contained classroom teacher with 25 students. With electronic hardware and software support subsystems, the instructor can now divide his or her time more effectively between monitoring (management), diagnosis, and instruction. The student is provided immediate, direct sensory feedback so that he or she can compare his or her performance with the desired performance and make the necessary self-corrective adjustments.

Mastery learning has been investigated extensively. Slavin's (1990) re-analysis of the literature generally agrees with Kulik and Kulik's (1990) analysis that it usually increases learning modestly but consistently on curriculum-relevant tests. (The average student places about at the 65th percentile when compared with students in control groups studying the same material without the careful sequencing of objectives and modules of instruction.) Standardized tests, however, have been resistant to these gains, for reasons that are not well understood.

DIRECT INSTRUCTION

ORIGINS

Although empirically derived, direct instruction has its theoretical origins in the behavioral family, particularly in the thinking of training and behavioral psychologists. Training psychologists have focused on training people to perform complex behaviors that involve a high degree of precision and often coordination with others—for example, being a crew member on a submarine. Their main contributions to learning situations are task definition and task analysis. The instructional design principles they propose focus on conceptualizing learner performance into goals and tasks, breaking these tasks into smaller component tasks, developing training activities that ensure mastery of each subcomponent, and, finally, arranging the entire learning situation into sequences that ensure adequate transfer from one component to another and achievement of prerequisite learning before more advanced learning.

Whereas training psychologists have emphasized the design and planning of instruction, behavioral psychologists address the interaction between teachers and students. They speak of modeling, reinforcement, feedback, and successive approximation—concepts discussed earlier, in the introduction to the behavioral family of models. Behaviorists sometimes refer to their approach as "modeling with reinforced guided performance." In subsequent sections of this chapter, as we review the major findings regarding direct instruction, the similarity between the theoretical underpinnings of training and behavioral psychology and the empirical results from basic skills research become apparent.

GOALS AND ASSUMPTIONS

Direct instruction plays a limited but important role in a comprehensive educational program. Research on direct instruction indicates that this approach is effective in promoting student learning in reading and math, especially for students from lower socioeconomic backgrounds. In some studies the use of direct instruction also successfully improved students' self-concepts. Critics of direct instruction caution that this approach should not be used all the time, for all educational objectives, nor for all students. Indeed, later studies and reviews of research do point out that other teaching strategies may be more suitable for promoting such educational goals as abstract thinking, creativity, and problem solving (a conclusion entirely consistent with the point of view taken in this book!).

In addition, slight variations in implementing the teaching strategy appear to enhance the effect for students of different ability levels.

Despite the cautions and the caveats, this model of teaching stands out as one with a relatively solid empirical track record. Even though the effects may not be large, the research does suggest that students tend to perform better on math and reading achievement tests under direct-instruction conditions. For students of lower ability the difference may be even greater. The basic practice model is certainly one to consider when the goal is basic skills acquisition.

THE LEARNING ENVIRONMENT FOR DIRECT INSTRUCTION

Direct instruction, like all teaching strategies, occurs within the larger context of the classroom environment. Because the model is highly structured and teacher directed, it would not flourish in an environment that could not support a traditional educational approach. Fortunately, teacher-effectiveness research provides some guidelines as to the environmental variables that promote successful implementation of a direct-instruction teaching strategy. These are academic focus, teacher direction and control, high expectations for pupil progress, time, and neutral affect.

Academic focus means one places highest priority on the assignment and completion of academic tasks. During instruction academic activity is emphasized; the use of nonacademic materials—for example, toys, games, and puzzles—is de-emphasized or even discouraged, as is nonacademically oriented student-teacher interaction, such as questions about self or discussions of personal concern. Several studies have shown that a strong academic focus produces greater student engagement and, subsequently, achievement (Fisher et al., 1980; Madaus, Airasian, and Kellaghan, 1980; Rosenshine, 1970, 1971, 1985).

Teacher direction and control occur when the teacher selects and directs the learning tasks, determines grouping patterns, maintains a central role during instruction, keeps student choice and freedom at low levels, and minimizes the amount of nonacademic pupil talk. Teachers who have high expectations for their students and concern for academic progress demand academic excellence and behavior conducive to academic progress. They expect more of their students in terms of quantity and quality of work.

A major goal of direct instruction is the maximization of student learning time. Many teacher behaviors found to be associated with student achievement are in fact associated with student time on task and student rate of success, which in turn are associated with student achievement. Thus, the behaviors incorporated into direct instruction are designed to create a structured, academically oriented learning environment in which students are actively engaged (on task) during instruction and are experiencing a high rate of success (80 percent or better). Time spent by pupils in both these conditions is referred to as "academic learning time" (ALT). Since it appears to be highly related to pupil achievement, maximizing ALT is an important aspect of the strategy.

Finally, there is substantial evidence that negative affect inhibits student achievement (Rosenshine, 1971; Soar and Soar, 1979). Teachers who create an academic focus and avoid such negative practices as criticism of student behavior, screaming, sarcasm, scolding, and ridicule facilitate student learning. Research is less clear on the role of positive affect on student outcomes: Some students may benefit more from large amounts of praise than others; some types of praise are more effective than others (Brophy, 1981).

In summary, the direct-instruction environment is one in which there is a predominant focus on learning, and students are engaged in academic tasks a large percentage of time and achieve at a high rate of success. The social climate is positive and free of negative affect.

ORIENTATION TO THE MODEL

The term *direct instruction* has been used by researchers to refer to a pattern of teaching which consists of the teacher's explaining a new concept or skill to a large group of students, having them test their understanding by practicing under teacher direction (i.e., controlled practice), and encouraging them to continue to practice at their seats under teacher guidance (guided practice). More common terms for this pattern might be *recitation* and *seatwork*. As intuitive and familiar as this teaching pattern may seem, theory and research have done much to verify its effectiveness and to identify some fine points to better carry out this pattern; these are discussed next.

Before presenting and explaining new material, it is helpful to establish a framework for the lesson and orient the students to the new material. Structuring comments made at the beginning of a lesson are designed to clarify for the students the purposes, procedures, and actual content of the subsequent learning experience. Such comments are associated with improved student engagement during the learning activity and with overall achievement (Block, 1980; Medley, Coker, and Soar, 1984; Fisher, et al., 1980; Medley, 1977). These orienting comments can take various forms including: (1) introductory activities that elicit students' relevant existing knowledge structures (Anderson, et al., 1979), such as reviewing the previous day's work (Rosenshine, 1985); (2) discussing the objective of the lesson; (3) providing clear, explicit directions about work to be done; (4) telling the students about the materials they will use and the activities they will be engaged in during the lesson; and (5) providing an overview of the lesson.

Once the context for learning has been established, instruction can begin with the presentation of the new concept or skill. Students' success in learning the new material has much to do with the thoroughness and quality of the teacher's initial explanation. We know from research that effective teachers spend more time explaining and demonstrating new material than less-effective teachers (Rosenshine, 1985). Presentation practices that appear to facilitate learning include: (1) presenting material in small steps so that one point can be mastered at a time; (2) providing many, varied examples of the new skills or concepts; (3) modeling, or giving narrated demonstrations of the learning task; (4) avoiding digressions, staying on topic; and (5) reexplaining difficult points (Rosenshine, 1985). From research on concept learning we also know that when teaching a new concept it is important to clearly identify the characteristics (attributes) of the concept and to provide a rule or definition (or sequence of steps in skill learning). Finally, providing a visual representation of the concept or skill along with the verbal explanation assists students in following the explanation. Later, at other points in the learning process, the visual representation serves as a cue or prompt.

Following the explanation comes the recitation, in which the teacher checks for students' understanding of the new concept or skill. A common error is simply to ask students if they understand or have any questions and then to assume that if no one or only a few students respond everyone understands well enough to move on to seatwork. Effective teachers ask more questions that check for student understanding than less-effective teachers (Rosenshine, 1985). Such questions call for specific answers or ask for explanations of how answers were found. According to Rosenshine, effective teachers not only asked more questions, but they also spent more time on teacher-led practice and on repeating the new material they were teaching. Other aspects of effective questioning behavior for direct-instruction approaches are: (1) asking convergent, as opposed to divergent questions (Rosenshine, 1971, 1985); (2) ensuring that all students get a chance to respond—not just those who raise their hands or call out the loudest; this can be accomplished by calling on students in a patterned order, as in reading groups, calling the students' names first, before asking them questions, or calling for a choral response (Gage and Berliner, 1979; Rosenshine, 1985); (3) asking questions within students' "reach" a high percentage of the time (75 to 90 percent) (Rosenshine, 1985); (4) teacher initiating questions most of the time, not the students (Fisher, et al., 1980; Medley, 1977); and (5) avoiding nonacademic questions during direct instruction (Rosenshine, 1979; Soar, Soar, and Ragosta, 1971).

Once the teacher has initiated a question and a student has responded, the teacher needs to give the student feedback on his or her response. Research indicates that effective teachers do a better job of providing feedback than do noneffective ones (Rosenshine, 1971). They do not let errors go uncorrected, nor do they simply give the answers to students who have responded incorrectly. They use techniques for correcting responses or they reteach the material. In addition, effective teachers maintain a brisk pace during this recitation activity. When they provide corrective feedback or reteach, they do it efficiently so that many practice opportunities are provided and many students have the opportunity to respond. For example, when a correct answer has been given, the teacher simply asks a new question. In the early stages of learning, when answers may be correct but somewhat tentative, the teacher provides knowledge of results and quick-process feedback. ("Very good. You remembered that 'i' goes before 'e' when it comes after 'c.'") If the student has carelessly provided an incorrect answer, the teacher provides corrective feedback and moves on. If the incorrect response indicated lack of understanding, the teacher should provide hints or clues, such as referring back to the visual representation. It is important to probe for clarification and improved answers. Effective feedback is academically oriented, not behaviorally oriented (Fisher, et al., 1980). It is also substantive in that it tells students *what* they have done correctly. Feedback may be combined with praise; however, it is important that praise be deserved based on the quality of the response (Gage and Berliner, 1979). Students differ in the amount of praise they need; some students, particularly low-achieving students, need a lot, whereas others do not need as much. Even if a student's need for praise is great, he or she should not be praised for an incorrect response (Brophy, 1981).

To summarize, the kind of feedback students receive during structured practice has much to do with their later success. Feedback helps students find out how well they understand the new material and what their errors are. To be effective, feedback must be academic, corrective, respectful, and deserved.

The need for students to be given thorough explanations and structured practice with feedback before they begin their seatwork seems obvious. However, it is clear both from the research and from the authors' own experiences that students are often asked to work from their texts or workbooks with almost no explanation and/or practice. Students need to have a high degree of success when they are engaged in seatwork. In order for this to occur, they should move from structured practice to seatwork only when they have achieved about 90 percent accuracy on the structured-practice examples.

In the average classroom, students spend between 50 percent and 75 percent of their time working alone on seatwork (Rosenshine, 1985). If this large amount of time is to be productively directed toward learning, then students need to remain engaged in the learning task. What helps most toward engagement is being well prepared, before beginning seatwork, by the teacher's presentation and by teacher-led practice. Seatwork that is directly related to the presentation and that occurs right after teacher-led practice, facilitates student engagement. It is also helpful for the teacher to circulate during seatwork, monitoring individual students with relatively short contacts (Rosenshine, 1985).

PRACTICE THEORY

As its name implies, the "heart" of this teaching strategy is its practice activities; three phases of the model deal with practice under varying conditions of assistance. Over the years considerable research has been devoted to studying the role of practice in the acquisition of new knowledge and the conditions of practice which facilitate retention of information. From this literature we have identified six principles of effective practice.

The first principle is that of shaping. The goal of all practice is mastery, the ability to perform a skill independently and without error. When the principle of *shaping* is adhered to, the teacher *moves the student through practice with different levels of assistance*: lock-step or structured, semi-independent or guided, and independent or homework. This practice progression ensures appropriate support for the student to experience success at each practice level until independence is achieved.

The three levels of practice function in the following manner: When the students are first introduced to a new skill or concept, the teacher leads the group through each step in working out the problem. This lock-step method ensures that few errors are produced in the initial learning stages, when memory is most vulnerable to remembering incorrect practice and when errors reinforce incorrect information. After lock-step or structured practice, the students practice on their own at their seats while the teacher monitors. During this time the teacher provides corrective feedback for any errors produced as well as reinforcement for correct practice. When students are able to practice with accuracy, they are ready for independent practice—that is, for practice under conditions when assistance is not available in the environment. Homework is an example of independent practice. This last step in the practice progression is the mastery level; students are performing the skill independently with minimal error.

The second practice principle has to do with the length of each practice session. Research indicates that, on the whole, the more a person practices a skill, the longer it takes him or her to forget it. However, this relationship is affected by the length of time recommended for practice. The general principle guiding the length of time recommended for practice is: *Short, intense, highly motivated practice periods produce more learning than fewer but longer practice periods.* For example, with younger students, short, 5- to 10-minute practice sessions interspersed over the day or a series of days will be more effective than long 30- to 40-minute sessions. Older students have longer attention spans and are able to handle longer practice sessions; however, all practice sessions should be monitored so that boredom and apathy do not undercut their effectiveness.

The third principle is the need to *monitor the initial stage of practice* because incorrect performance at this stage will interfere with learning. Students need corrective feedback to prevent incorrect procedures from becoming embedded in their memories. Immediate corrective feedback (i.e., information on how to perform correctly) will reverse misconceptions early in the instructional process. It also reduces performance anxiety because students practice with the assurance of immediate feedback. In addition to catching incorrect performance in the early stages, it is also important to reinforce correct performance. This gives students the knowledge of results that stabilizes the new learning more quickly.

Having students achieve an 85 to 90 percent *level of accuracy* at the current practice level before going to the next level is the fourth practice principle. Paying attention to accuracy rates ensures that students experience success and do not practice errors.

The fifth principle is that of *distributed practice*, or multiple practice sessions spread out over a period of time. Research shows that without practice to reinforce it 80 percent of new information is forgotten within 24 hours. With periodic reviews spread out over an extended period of time, such as four or five months, nearly all new information can be retained. The effect is cumulative: The more information a person has stored in memory, the easier it is for him or her to learn new information. This is because more items of information are available from which to form memory connections. People with fewer items of information in memory have less capacity to remember new information.

The last principle addresses the issue of the optimal *amount of time between practice sessions*. The general guideline is that practice periods should be close together at the beginning of learning; once learning is at an independent level, then the practice sessions can be spaced farther and farther apart. Thus, guided practice sessions should occur immediately after new learning has been introduced and should continue frequently until independence is achieved. When this has occurred, independent practice sessions can be distributed farther apart—that is, 1, 2, 6, and then 15 days apart.

To summarize, successful practice is founded upon six principles: shaping, short and intense practice sessions, monitoring of practice, requisite accuracy level of 85 to 90 percent, distribution of practice, and appropriate length of time between practice. A practice plan designed upon these principles greatly enhances the chances for mastery of new learning.

THE MODEL OF TEACHING

SYNTAX

The direct instruction model consists of five phases of activity: orientation, presentation, structured practice, guided practice, and independent practice (see Figure 15-1 on page 317). However, the use of this model should be preceded by effective diagnosis of students' knowledge or skills to be sure that they have the prerequisite knowledge or skills to achieve high levels of accuracy in the different practice conditions.

SUMMARY CHART ► **BASIC PRACTICE MODEL**

Phase One: Orientation
Teacher establishes content of the lesson.
Teacher reviews previous learning.
Teacher establishes lesson objectives.
Teacher establishes the procedures for the lesson.

Phase Two: Presentation
Teacher explains/demonstrates new concept or skill.
Teacher provides visual representation of the task.
Teacher checks for understanding.

Phase Three: Structured Practice
Teacher leads group through practice examples in lock step.
Students respond to questions.
Teacher provides corrective feedback for errors and reinforces correct practice.
Teacher refers to VRT.

Phase Four: Guided Practice
Students practice semi-independently.
Teacher circulates, monitoring student practice.
Teacher provides feedback through praise, prompt, and leave.
Teacher refers student to VRT as a resource.

Phase Five: Independent Practice
Students practice independently at home or in class.
Feedback is delayed.
Independent practices occur several times over an extended period.

Phase one is the orientation phase in which a framework for the lesson is established. During this phase the teacher's expectations are communicated, the learning task is clarified, and student accountability is established. Three steps are particularly important in carrying out the intent of this phase: (1) the teacher provides the objective of the lesson and the level of performance; (2) the teacher describes the content of the lesson and its relationship to prior knowledge and/or experience; and (3) the teacher discusses the procedures of the lesson—that is, the different parts of the lesson and students' responsibilities during those activities.

Phase two is the presentation phase, in which the teacher explains the new concept or skill through demonstrations and examples. If the material is a new concept, it is important that the teacher discuss the characteristics (or *attributes*) of the concept, the rule or definition, and several examples. If the material is a new skill, it is important to identify the steps of the skill with examples of each step. In either case, it is helpful to convey this information both orally and visually so that students will have the visual representation as a reference in the early stages of learning. The latter is sometimes called a *visual representation of the task* (VRT). Another part of this phase is checking to see that students have understood the new information before they apply it in the practice phases. Can they recall the attributes of the concept that the teacher has explained? Can they recall the number and list of steps in the skill they have just been shown? Checking for understanding (CFU) requires that students recall or recognize the information that they have just heard. Next, in structured practice, they will apply it. Several techniques can be used to check for understanding: *sampling*, questions directed toward the entire group but responses given by only a sample of students; *signaling*, questions directed toward the entire group with responses from everyone through signaling agreement or disagreement; *individual private response*, questions directed to everyone with instructions to write responses, then students' responses checked privately. A clear, thorough explanation is crucial to students' success in applying the new information. Explaining, illustrating, and producing knowledge about understanding make up sequence.

Structured practice is phase three of the strategy. In structured practice the teacher leads students through practice examples working in lock-step fashion through each step of the problem as it appears on the VRT. The students practice as a group, offering to write answers. A good way to accomplish the lock-step technique is to use an overhead projector, doing practice examples on a transparency so that all students can see the generation of each step. The teacher's role in this phase is to give feedback on the students' responses, to reinforce accurate responses, and to correct errors. The VRT is available. In referring to it while working the practice examples, the teacher is ensuring that students understand it so that they can use it as a resource during their semi-independent practice phase.

Phase four, guided practice, presents students the opportunity to practice on their own while the teacher is still in the environment. Most of us recognize this activity as seatwork. Guided practice enables the teacher to make an assessment of the students' abilities to perform the learning task by assessing the amount and types of errors the students are making. The teacher's role in this phase is to monitor students' work, providing corrective feedback when necessary. Although this function might seem self-explanatory, research studies have shown that some teachers perform this role more effectively than others. Common but not optimal monitoring practices include having students come to the teacher and/or having the teacher move around, but help only a few students—the ones who typically get most of the help. A better way to monitor is to use a specific corrective feedback technique called "praise, prompt, and leave." In this technique the teacher moves around the room systematically and efficiently, checking students' work. The teacher tells *each* student whether he or she has done an item or part of a practice correctly; if there are errors, the teacher reteaches to *one* error and refers the student to the VRT. The corrective feedback interaction lasts about half a minute or less. In a class of 30 students and a practice activity of 30 minutes, every student can receive feedback at least twice!

Independent practice is the last phase of the direct instruction model. It begins when students have achieved an accuracy level of 85 to 90 percent in guided practice. The purpose of independent practice is to reinforce the new learning to ensure retention as well as to develop fluency. In independent practice, students practice on their own without assistance and with delayed feedback. This can be done in the classroom, if the teacher is not involved, but it is usually done at home. The teacher's role in this phase is to make sure the independent practice work is reviewed soon after completion to assess if the students' accuracy level has remained stable and to provide corrective feedback for those who need it. An independent-practice activity can be short in length of time and number of practice

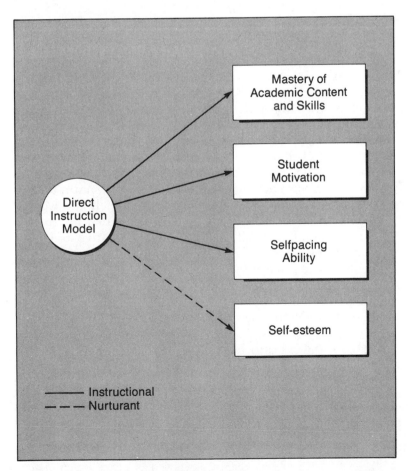

FIGURE 15–1 Instructional and nurturant effects: direct instruction model.

items; however, it should not be a one-time venture. As described earlier, five or six practice sessions distributed over a month or more will sustain retention.

DIRECT AND NURTURANT EFFECTS

The model is, as the name applies, "direct". It approaches academic content systematically. Its design is shaped to generate and sustain motivation through pacing and reinforcement. Through success and positive feedback, it tries to enhance self-esteem. The social system is highly-structured. The principles of reaction are governed by the need to provide knowledge of results, help students pace themselves, and the need for reinforcement. (See the discussion of social learning theory, below.) The support system includes sequenced learning tasks, sometimes as elaborate as the sets developed by the individually prescribed instruction team.

APPLICATION

The evidence and examples of direct instruction come from several sources, including the studies of effective teachers mentioned earlier as well as educational programs specifically designed on a direct-instruction model. The evaluation of Project Follow Through, a federal program which extended Head Start into the elementary grades, has much to tell us about the relative effectiveness of different approaches for students from disadvantaged backgrounds. When the evaluation was complete, two programs stood out as promoting greater achievement in reading and math. Both of these programs were based on a direct-instruction approach and we will describe one of these here. The University of Oregon's direct instruction model, produced more significant differences on both cognitive and affective measures than any of the other eight major programs (Becker, 1977). Overall, the students in this program went from being well below the 25th percentile in reading, math, and spelling before starting the program, to being in the 50th percentile or above (the national norm) by the third grade. Becker offers the following description of the Oregon program:

> The major goal of the Direct Instruction Model is to improve basic education of children from economically disadvantaged backgrounds and thus increase their life options. Developed by Bereiter and Becker, the model has its roots in Bereiter and Engelman's experimental preschool and in Becker's behavioral research on classroom management. The model emphasizes small-group, face to face instruction by a teacher using carefully sequenced, daily lessons in reading, arithmetic and language. The lessons utilize modern learning principles and advanced programming strategies (Becker, Engelmann & Thomas, 1975a, 1975b). . . . A positive self-concept was viewed as a by-product of good

teaching rather than as a goal to be achieved in the abstract. (Becker, 1977, pp. 921–922)

The University of Oregon model reflects nearly all the elements of the basic practice model discussed earlier. Highly structured teacher-directed lessons begin the learning. Before new material is introduced, previous material is reviewed and/or checked. To ensure appropriate sequencing of material and selection of examples, the teacher presentations have been scripted. Thus, the quality of explanation and the nature and length of structured practice are regulated. Visual representations (VRTs in our terminology) are provided as part of the script with instructions on how and when to use these cues to prompt students' responses. During structured practice students give a group (or choral) response, alternating occasionally with individual responses. The program outlines specific correction procedures and provides additional teaching (reteaching) material. The main guidelines are to teach new material in small steps, practice to the point of overlearning, and reteach, if necessary.

Student materials form the basis for guided practice. Published under the trade name DISTAR the student materials coordinate with the teacher materials. They are composed of nine curricular strands covering the areas of reading, mathematics, and language.

Three other elements of direct instruction stand out in the University of Oregon model: reinforcement and review and assessment. Positive reinforcement is strongly encouraged to enhance student motivation; negative behavior is ignored. Generally, reinforcement is in the form of praise, attention, or success; however, if necessary at the beginning of instruction, a token system may be used and later phased out. Becker and his associates have developed training manuals on the principles and procedures of reinforcement.

Periodic review and recycling of instruction are also part of the model, as are continuous progress tests. The latter are used to produce biweekly reports of students' progress in reading, math, and language. These reports form the basis for change in students' instructional groups.

Social learning theory and conventional wisdom

CASES OF "AT-RISK" APPLICATIONS

The practical reason to develop educational research and theory is to help us reach beyond our boundaries as educators—to find tools and solutions to problems that will surprise us. It is inevitable that the products of research and reflection will collide with conventional wisdom or practice, since that is precisely what is supposed to happen. Which is not to suggest that the theory-generating activity will always be productive, that research will always be helpful, or that any given model of teaching is always going to achieve its goals or even do half as well as the effort of an innovative practitioner. It does mean that there will be occasions when important developments will receive little attention because it is hard to discern them through the forest of accepted ideas.

Conventional wisdom is bonded to us by social acceptability and can be difficult to question. Once we have decided, as a society, what is "true," we simply "know" it. To question it, even vaguely, appears deviant. It is hard to change practices which are virtually laminated to our social selves.

Our difficulty becomes clear when some brash innovator generates a solution to a very difficult problem and then can only stand by while we ignore the solution and continue to employ practices that do not get the job done. One example is the application of social learning theory to the problem of overcoming the deficit that accrues to the children of poverty in the United States. The problem has received considerable attention for the last 35 years and has some fairly clear parameters.

First, the children of economically poor people have a considerable disadvantage in profiting from mainstream educational practices. The average poor child does poorly in school, is more likely to drop out, and suffers a gradual decline in aptitude, relative to wealthier age-mates. (In other words, the deficit in achievement is accompanied by an increasing deficit in academic ability.) With passing years the educational deficit compounds, with dreadful consequences to the children's chances for reasonable quality of life or for adequate educational opportunity as adults.

American society has responded with a number of federal and state initiatives. These have included efforts to ensure that the educational resources are equalized; that, for example, the poor do not go to schools with poorer school libraries. Others have generated varieties of social services to provide food (generally in the form of subsidized lunches) and clothing. The main initiatives, however, have been in educational programming. Chapter One and other programs have generated programs using smaller classes and the services of specially trained teachers. "At-risk" programs have been named after a federal report blaming the educational system. A variety of "special education" programs have addressed what are assumed to be background-related learning problems.

It is clear by now that most of these programs have not succeeded in reducing the magnitude of the problem for which they were intended (Anderson & Leonard, 1990). Yet, their structure for 25 years has, in most school districts, been fairly consistent, following conventional thought about how to conduct such programs. Generally they:

Provide highly-structured programs for the children, prescribing what they should do.
Provide highly-individualized programs, especially ones where the students work alone at prescribed tasks.

Emphasize remediation in school subjects, especially in language and arithmetic, with much attention to formal grammar and elementary arithmetic.

Group the students together for remedial instruction.

Concerned with disciplinary problems, the programs tend to emphasize 1) aversive social control (punishment), 2) the use of academic achievement measures for control, and 3) isolation to reduce disruptive behavior (Anderson & Leonard, 1990). There are exceptions to these norms, of course, but there is much evidence that many programs conform to them.

Now, there is not much question about whether the average "compensatory" education program has been successful in alleviating the disadvantages toward which it was aimed. It has not. In fact, the problem has become worse since the initiatives were generated.

However, there have been a number of examples of programs that have applied educational research successfully to treat the problem. One such is the Durham EIP project (Spaulding, 1970) which combined a number of models, with social learning theory as the centerpiece, and achieved considerable success. The program goals were: to increase the student's capacity to take charge of their education and their social behavior, thus enabling them to operate productively and integratively in school settings; to teach them to think productively, thus increasing their aptitude to learn; and to increase their achievement, making it indistinguishable from that of their wealthier counterparts.

Spaulding's application of social learning theory was almost the inverse of the typical "at-risk" or "compensatory" program. He could not avoid grouping the students together for logistical reasons, although segregating the economically disadvantaged students is generally disadvantageous (Joyce & Wolf, 1991). He did not manipulate class size, which is, generally, a low payoff variable, despite conventional wisdom. He built a program on the following principles.

The first was that students' were to take increased responsibility for their own education and self-control was essential. It would be accomplished by making them responsible for responding to opportunities for self-direction and control and by rewarding independent, responsible behavior rather than punishing off-task behavior. (Mild, off-task (inappropriate) behavior would be ignored, rather than being an occasion for the getting of attention by these children who desperately needed it.) Behavior disruptive of others' productive activity would be treated as unacceptable and responded to calmly by providing "time-out" periods of no more than five minutes in neutral environments. Aversive (punitive) sanctions would be avoided because they provide attention and the aversion attaches to productive school activities.

The students would construct their schedules from a menu that required productive work within a variety of structures ranging from the highly sequenced to those requiring self-control and self-direction. Thus, the students would be "weaned" from dependence to self-direction.

Activities requiring social cooperation would be blended with individual activities, providing the opportunity for the development of social skills. Interdependence would receive praise.

The curricular activities would emphasize productive thinking, so that the students would be directly taught to think—to build concepts and skills rather than receiving them.

Essentially, the students would be taught how to think and learn, rather than being placed in a situation that reduced responsibility and emphasized "catching up."

Gradually, the students learned to develop their daily schedules, to cooperate with their fellow students, to take responsibility for their own behavior. They became less dependent and more responsible for their own education.

Gradually, their aptitude rose, reversing the typical declining posture. Scores on tests of academic ability rose, while the students in ordinary compensatory programs remained about the same in academic ability.

Their achievement in typical school subjects rose more gradually, but slowly reversed the customary downward trend and began to gain against the socioeconomic disadvantage.

Here is a clear case where the application of the theory from one of the families of models of teaching generated a strategy almost the inverse of conventional wisdom and succeeded in its goals. Also, it is interesting in that behavioral-systems approaches are sometimes assumed to lead to the same type of individualistic, step-by-step approaches that fit the conventional wisdom. Spaulding's overriding goals were to help students take command of their education and increase their power as learners. He shaped the program to shape the behavior of his students to achieve those goals.

As we reflect on the translation of theory into practice, we need to deal with our conventional wisdom. If we think we know how to educate because the road is obvious, then we have difficulty incorporating the messages of research-based theories, and this is just what has happened in the case of Spaulding's work, which has not been incorporated into the early-childhood intervention programs.

Phase One: Orientation
Teacher establishes content of the lesson.
Teacher reviews previous learning.
Teacher establishes lesson objectives.
Teacher establishes the procedures for the lesson.

Phase Two: Presentation
Teacher explains/demonstrates new concept or skill.
Teacher provides visual representation of the task.
Teacher checks for understanding.

Phase Three: Structured Practice
Teacher leads group through practice examples in lock step.
Students respond to questions.
Teacher provides corrective feedback for errors and reinforces correct
    practice.
Teacher refers to VRT.

Phase Four: Guided Practice
Students practice semiindependently.
Teacher circulates, monitoring student practice.
Teacher provides feedback through praise, prompt, and leave.
Teacher refers student to VRT as a resource.

Phase Five: Independent Practice
Students practice independently at home or in class.
Feedback is delayed.
Independent practices occur several times over an extended period.

CHAPTER 16

LEARNING SELF-CONTROL
Using Feedback to Modify Behavior

John is a bright, verbal, second-grader who is perhaps slightly hyperactive. He is popular with his classmates and entertains them with endless stories, some true and some slightly exaggerated. John does pretty well in his studies. He is a good reader but has difficulty with math. For the past few months Jean Meades, John's teacher, has been struggling to encourage John to persist in his schoolwork. John is always up, wandering around the room or going to the pencil sharpener, aquarium, or hamster cage. More often, he is distracting another student. The problem is that when John comes to a math problem he does not understand, he complains out loud: "I don't understand," or "This doesn't make sense." Then he calls out for Jean, "Ms. Meades, I don't get this." If Jean is not at his side promptly, showing John how to do the problem, he flips his pencil in the air, whistles, and gazes at the ceiling for awhile, coming to rest by engaging his neighbor in conversation. If that does not work, he is off to the aquarium.

Jean would like John to make more of an attempt to stick with a math problem longer before he calls for assistance. Although John's jumping up and calling for assistance occur throughout the whole day, Jean decides to concentrate on the math situation.

During math the students are grouped roughly according to their abilities. Each child has a set of worksheets. Generally the children work alone more or less at their own pace. A few times each week Ms. Meades or the teacher's aide instructs the group in a new concept or principle. When the students have finished designated segments, their work is checked.

For a few days Ms. Meades pays close attention to John's behavior during math. She observes that on the average he calls out or comes up to her or the aide about 10 times during the 40-minute work period. He devotes about 10 minutes to actual work on his own. Knowing that John needs and wants a lot of adult reinforcement, Jean makes a deal with him.

She explains her observations to John and says she wants to work out a new system. She asks John to try at least three problems before asking for help. When he does need help he should raise his hand, and either Jean or the aide will come as soon as she can. In the meantime, John can work on a drawing (he is a very good artist and enjoys doodling). Every time John follows the procedure he gets a point. If he actually completes the three problems correctly, he gets two points. At the end of the week John's points are totaled. Depending on the number accumulated, he gets to select activities of his choice. Initially, Jean insists that John work on math for only part of the math period, or on nine problems. As time goes on, she adjusts the reward schedule to increase his work time and accomplishment.

Before beginning the program Jean worked with John on how to approach an unfamiliar problem. She gave him a general, three-step sequence to follow for any math problem. One of John's difficulties is that he looks at a problem, goes blank, and gives up. Jean tries to increase his capacity for reflective thought by giving him a general problem-solving approach. In addition, each step in the sequence has a corresponding color-numbered block. For a while John uses these to remind him to do the steps. He starts out with the blocks on the right side, and as he takes each step he moves the block over to the left. The manipulative activity helps ease the anxiety generated by the "blank mind"; it literally takes his mind off his feelings and onto his math and his hands.

Jean does one more thing. She makes sure that at first either she or the aide frequently passes by John's desk to compliment him for attempting the problems (if he is) and to check his work without his asking.

The contingency management program is instituted. It takes a few days for John to follow the procedures agreed upon, but Jean and the aide are very consistent in reminding him of the rules. After a while the distractibility (and distracting) becomes less frequent. John's ability to try problems and continue to work at them markedly improves, so much, in fact, that within a few weeks the number of problems solved before John needs assistance increases to five. In addition, when John does need assistance, he is not so helpless. He can tell Jean the steps he followed, what he had figured out, and where he is stuck. Jean also notices that John's attention span and ability to sit quietly without talking is maintained in other activities, not just math.

Jean alerts John's parents to the plan so that at the end of the week he will report to them his point count and the rewards. The program gives John's parents a nice way to follow his progress and talk to him about the school day.

Contingency management, which has been used in educational settings more than other applications of behavior theory, can be found in the con-

ceptualizations of entire classroom environments and educational programs, such as Pittsburgh's Primary Education Project, which stresses the
behavioral analysis of learning tasks (Resnick, 1967), Bereiter and Englemann's DISTAR program (Bereiter and Englemann, 1966; Englemann, Osborn, and Englemann, 1972), and Bushell's behavior analysis Follow-
Through classrooms (Bushell, 1970). In these instances all aspects of the
learning environment—physical, material, interactive—are perceived and
planned for in terms of behavioral principles. Other applications of behavior theory focus on specific individuals within a classroom and the identification and treatment of specific maladaptive responses. In these instances contingency management stresses tailoring its programs to
individuals, placing particular emphasis on reinforcement. Programmed
learning is a third application of behavioral theory and emphasizes control of the learning stimuli, which are carefully sequenced in relatively
small steps. Finally, the use of contingency management for the self-control of behavior is a fourth and increasingly popular use.

ORIENTATION TO THE MODEL

CONCEPTS

Behavior theorists perceive human behavior as a function of the immediate environment—specifically, an eliciting stimulus and a reinforcing
stimulus. The essential feature is the relationship between the response
and reinforcing stimuli. If the reinforcement is presented when and only
when the response appears, we say it is *contingent*. *Contingency management*, then, is the systematic control of reinforcing stimuli such that it is
presented at selected times and only after the desired response has been
given. People who set up contingency management programs must be
aware of desirable responses as well as undesirable responses. They also
must take into account the eliciting stimuli, carefully observing what trig-
gers maladaptive responses. Often the environment can be arranged so
that undesirable *cues* are minimized, and cues that facilitate desirable behaviors are enhanced. For example, people who overeat know that they
are asking for trouble when they balance their checkbooks in the kitchen.
Similarly, teachers know that play stimuli can be distracting to some students while they are accomplishing work-oriented tasks, so they remove
these stimuli from the immediate surroundings. Students who need more
attention are instructed in smaller groups. Teachers also take advantage
of positive cuing when they nonverbally remind students of the appropriate responses. A friend of ours wears a yellow scarf when she is in a bad
mood, alerting her husband that this is not a good time to make demands
or ask favors.

Contingency management is based on the operant principle that behavior is influenced by the consequences that follow. For an operant or contingent relationship to be established, *reinforcing consequences* must follow. If a behavior is not reinforced, it will become extinct. A *reinforcer*, then, is a consequence that increases the probability of a particular response. Desirable responses can be strengthened through both *positive* and *negative* reinforcements. A reinforcement is positive if its addition to the environment—such as a smile, a hug, or a deadline—produces the adaptive responses. A reinforcement is negative if its removal from the situation following a response produces the desirable behavior. Yelling, threatening, and nagging are examples of negative reinforcers. They do work. After a while most of us will respond to requests if only to stop these aversive stimuli. The problem with negative reinforcers, or *punishment*, is that the effects are less predictable than those of positive reinforcement. While they might produce impressive changes at the beginning, the side effects are often undesirable, such as hating school, disliking the punisher, or developing a poor self-concept. Programs based on behavior theory emphasize positive reinforcement, specifically discouraging the use of negative or aversive stimuli except in rare instances (Rimm and Masters, 1974).

Reinforcers can be social, material, and activity. Many of these reinforcers occur naturally in the environment, although not systematically and often in response to undesirable behavior. For instance, even though as teachers we have been told not to respond in a particular way, we still laugh at the showoff, scowl at the bully, and acknowledge the student who speaks out the quickest and loudest, often ignoring the ones who raise their hands.

Most reinforcing events are social—a smile, a hug, praise, attention, approval, or physical contact. Social reinforcers work especially well with young children. Few children are totally unresponsive to social stimuli, but some are less responsive than others. In his research using contingency management with autistic children, Lovaas has demonstrated that such asocial individuals will gradually become more socially responsive by pairing social reinforcers with an existing material reinforcer such as candy. Not all social reinforcers are verbal praise. Facial expressions such as a wink or interested look, nearness to an important person who is sharing time and conversation, and physical contact such as walking arm in arm or sitting on the teacher's lap are all rewarding.

Material reinforcers can be toys, pictures, or music or consumable items, such as candy and other foods. Tokens, which can then be exchanged for prizes or privileges, are also given as reinforcers. Gold stars are a classic classroom reinforcer. Money, of course, is always a valued material reinforcer.

The last group of reinforcers is called activity reinforcers. In 1965 Premack made a formal principle called the Premack principle. Essentially it says that you can get people to engage in one activity if you promise them the privilege of engaging in another more desirable activity when they are finished (Premack, 1965). Teachers use this principle all the time when they give students free time after completing their work. Grownups, too, reward themselves with a big treat when they have worked hard to accomplish a difficult task. Common activity reinforcers for children include being read to, recess, games, going first, and watching television.

Choosing an appropriate reinforcer involves some careful thought and attention to individual preferences. Careful behavioral observation is an indispensable tool to identifying the best reinforcers. Often the stimulus that elicits the maladaptive behavior gives us a good clue as to the best reinforcer.

We noted earlier that for a response to be established, it must be followed by a reinforcement. However, reinforcement can be delivered on several bases. Depending on the purpose some *reinforcement schedules* are more advantageous than others. *Continuous reinforcement* is the application of reinforcement after every emission of the desirable response. Although it is often inconvenient, continuous reinforcement is the quickest way to establish a new behavior and is very useful in the initial learning phases. More than likely, reinforcement is *intermittent*—that is, it occurs reliably in relationship to the desirable response either after a period of time (interval schedule) or after a certain number of desirable responses (ratio schedule). Both types of intermittent schedules can be *fixed* or *variable.*

Most naturally occurring reinforcement schedules are variable. Teachers are aware of the student responses they want to establish and periodically reinforce them. For example, when students are completing their seatwork, teachers will often praise on-task behavior; or, when gathering a group, the teacher will acknowledge students who are seated and attentive, both reinforcing that behavior and establishing a model for other students. Variable reinforcement produces a moderate response rate, but the respondent behaviors are highly resistant to extinction. It is wise to use continuous reinforcement schedules initially in establishing a behavior and, as the behavior becomes more "intrinsic," to switch to a variable reinforcement schedule to enhance its duration.

A word of caution is in order with respect to the expectations for reinforcement. Although it is true that contingency management has had an impressive, well-documented history (probably more so than most models of instruction), with many facets of learning and many types of learners, reinforcement is not effective all the time with every student. Certain elements contribute to the success of reinforcement (Rimm and Masters, 1974, pp. 177–185). For example, younger children tend to respond more to social reinforcers than do older children or adults. The nature of the reinforcing agent is a factor: High-status adults are more effective reinforcers than low-status adults; an adult with whom someone has a good relationship is a more effective reinforcer than one with whom that person has a poor, discordant relationship. Sometimes there is simply too much reinforcement in the environment, and a saturation point is reached. People deprived of positive reinforcement tend to respond well to it. Finally, people have different personality styles; contingency-management principles may work better with some people's learning styles than with others' (Spaulding and Papageorgio, 1975).

CONTINGENCY-MANAGEMENT PROCEDURES

Contingency management, used either as a basis for organizing the learning environment or for altering the behavior of individuals, consists generally of the same procedures: (1) specifying final performance, (2) assessing entering behavior (establishing baseline), (3) formulating a contingency-management program, (4) instituting the program, and (5) evaluating the program.

Phase one, *specifying the final performance*, entails a general recognition that a behavior needs to be changed or accomplished. The behavior can involve descriptive or maladaptive habits or actions, or the acquisition of particular skills and knowledge. However, before a contingency-management program can be developed it is necessary to (1) specify precisely the behavior to be altered and the responses to be enforced (or the behavioral objectives, in the case of subject-matter acquisition) and (2) develop a procedure for measuring the behavior. Classrooms conducted on a behavioral analysis model normally use highly structured, well-defined educational programs in which progress is monitored continuously as part of the design of the curriculum. Behaviors may be measured by *specimen description*, direct observational reports in which the observer records the time and occurrence of each behavior, or by *time sampling*, observing once every time period—perhaps five minutes—and noting whether the behavior has occurred. The important point is that definition of the target behavior and evaluation (or assessment) are part of the same conceptual task.

Phase two, actual *assessment of the entering behavior*, comes after the target behavior has been identified and defined and preliminary plans for measuring it have been developed. Sometimes this phase is referred to as *establishing a baseline*. It is actual recording of the frequency of behavior; in the case of maladaptive behaviors, its purpose is to confirm the initial diagnosis and give information about the maintaining conditions and stimuli. For this reason it is important to record not only when a behavior occurs but under what conditions and to whom—for example, one might note that one child hits younger children during free play. Academic behaviors are usually assessed by tests so that students can be paced at the appropriate steps in the learning sequence for their skill levels. For example, a student may be given 15 long-division problems to complete in 15 minutes. His or her performance can be calculated in terms of the number of errors.

Baseline data are useful because they help determine where to begin instruction and the rate of progress or effectiveness of the contingency program. Once the behavior has been recorded, it is best to plot it on a graph (see Figure 16-1). In some classrooms students keep their own progress charts, a procedure that tends to be highly reinforcing.

During the first four days the student was out of his seat about seven times during each abreviation period. The graph shows the drop as the program was initiated. Using data like these is very mportant to show effects and to help the *student* understand progress.

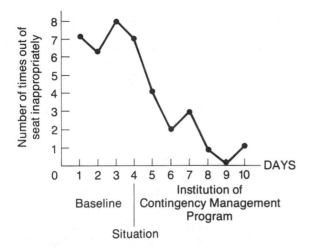

FIGURE 16–1   **Plotting baseline graph.**

The third phase is to *formulate a contingency management program* for a particular behavior or set of behaviors. This involves (1) structuring the situation, (2) selecting reinforcers, and (3) formulating behavior-shaping plans. In a classroom, attention must be given to the physical environment, the learning materials, and interactive features, all of which can facilitate the acquisition of responses. We know an enthusiastic teacher who concentrates on managing one or two hyperactive youngsters. She works hard at setting limits and reinforcing their positive behavior, but she has failed to notice that her general manner of speaking is very excitatory, almost like a spell-binding television character. She also asks many rhetorical questions to capture students' interest. When she communicates in this way, the two students become absorbed in the atmosphere and begin to talk out in response to the questions. Other youngsters are easily distracted and need the classroom arranged in a manner that minimizes such distractions.

We have already mentioned the role of some learning materials in presenting discrete, highly sequenced material with provision for immediate feedback. The selection of reinforcers is something that must be tailored for each person, though some reinforcers, particularly activity reinforcers, seem to work for most people. Finally, the planning of the contingency management program must account for gradual progress toward the terminal behavior. A procedure known as *behavior shaping* refers to the reinforcement of responses for behaviors that approximate the desired behaviors. Parents do this by rewarding beginning speech that sounds like the referent—for instance *Da* for dad. Tennis coaches reward beginners for swinging correctly or simply getting the ball over the net. Teachers praise beginning handwriting that resembles the correct letter. Even more elaborate and systematic shaping is designed for desensitization programs. Sometimes cues are used to help discriminate. One first-grade classroom has different colored lines within a single letter to remind students of the different writing strokes and which come first when they print the letter. Gradually, behavior-shaping procedures should involve the withdrawing of cues.

The fourth phase is to *institute the contingency-management program.* This includes actually arranging the environment, making the contingency announcement, and reinforcing the students' responses according to the reinforcement schedule and shaping program that have been selected.

Some behavioral practitioners do not believe it is necessary for the respondent to be aware of the target behavior and reinforcers. This is particularly true with more subtle forms of social reinforcement, such as praise for attentiveness. With other contingency-management programs it is necessary (and useful) to make the student aware of the desirable responses and reinforcers, as in a token environment or the case of free play. Many teachers prefer to have students aware of the desirable behaviors—for example, "I like the way Susan has cleared her desk and is ready for listening." or "Thank you, Brian, for waiting patiently while I helped Donald with his work." The research literature on the role of awareness is not conclusive. However, the importance of cognition in self-control and psychological development is gaining increasing respect among clinical psychologists. Many therapists have come to believe that mediating cognitive responses plays a large role in calling forth unpleasant feelings and subsequent behaviors; for example, we tell ourselves that dangerous prowlers are about and imagine such scenes, creating feelings of anxiety and avoidance of going out. When the students take exams or practice in their workbooks, they say, "I can't do it," feel discouraged, frustrated, and angry, and stop working. Our tendency is to encourage teachers to discuss the "problem-behavior sequence" with students and inform them, whenever appropriate, of the desirable response, or of the entire contingency management program. We believe that this will foster the students' own cognitive controls, both in terms of the adaptive behavior and their images of themselves. Of course, this depends on the problem behavior, the student, the relationship with the teacher, and the reinforcer. For example, teachers usually do not inform students of social reinforcers, they just supply them.

A technique that is sometimes used quite effectively, especially in the classroom, is called *time-out.* Technically this involves the withdrawal of all reinforcing consequences, usually by having the individual move to a place without objects or people. Sometimes students will ask other students to leave a group until they feel they are ready to come back. Ignoring disruptive behavior (a student who is interrupting others) or taking away a material reinforcer (a pencil with which the student is fiddling) are also forms of time-outs. In our experience this procedure gives students a chance to collect themselves and make the choice to join the group activity. It can be used very punitively and without choice, or very calmly as a mutual decision that helps students take responsibility for their behavior.

The last phase in contingency management is *evaluating the program*. Most behaviorists regard this as validating the program's success. Often this evaluation is built into the program—for example, if people are obviously not fearful in situations that previously made them fearful, or if students have maintained a high rate of progress and level of performance in a math program that has frequent evaluation measures. One of the main characteristics of behavioral-analysis environments is the deliberate structuring for and awareness of evaluation. Of course, evaluation is facilitated by initially specifying desirable behaviors in precise terms by devising or identifying measurement procedures. In some cases, particularly in behavioral research, reinforcement is discontinued for a while and then reinstated. Behavior is recorded under both conditions.

GOALS AND ASSUMPTIONS

The ultimate goal of any contingency-management program is transferability of the behaviors to similar new situations. Implicit in this goal is durability; the new adaptive behaviors will become intrinsic and under the individual's self-control and self-monitoring.

Contingency management has many uses, including reducing undesirable behaviors such as those associated with hyperdependency, aggression, passivity, depression, withdrawal, and general off-task activities. Sometimes these behaviors need removal from their reinforcing consequence. Often, however, individuals need to substitute new, more adaptive ways of behaving. Contingency management might well be used to reduce maladaptive behaviors, and other behavioral models employed to develop the new skills. However, this model is also valuable in developing new behaviors, such as academic skills, social skills, and self-management skills, and it is a valuable tool for altering emotional responses, such as reducing fears or eliminating anxiety. Finally, contingency management is effective in strengthening and maintaining existing desirable behaviors (Rimm and Masters, 1974).

THE MODEL OF TEACHING

The contingency-management model of teaching follows the five procedures discussed earlier in some detail: specifying a final performance, assessing entering behavior, formulating a program, instituting the program, and evaluating the program. The activities in each are summarized in the following section.

SYNTAX

The objective of phase one is to define the target behavior, the final behavioral outcome desired. Two activities must be accomplished at this point: (1) specifying the actual behavior outcome and (2) developing plans for measuring the behavior. Two relatively simple means of measuring and recording behavior are the *behavior specimen* and the *time sample*. A sample of a behavioral specimen from Rimm and Masters (1974) appears in Table 16-1. Another way to record is simply to observe the

TABLE 16–1 INSTANCES OF TANTRUM BEHAVIOR AND PARENTAL RESPONSES TO TANTRUM OVER A SEVEN-DAY PERIOD: SAMPLE BEHAVIOR CHART

Days	Tantrums	Duration (Minutes)	Response
1	1	4	Comforted child when he slipped and banged head during crying
2	1	5	Told child to be quiet but finally gave cookie to quiet down
	1	6	Ignored until couldn't stand it, gave cookie
3	1	5	Ignored
	2	6	Ignored
	3	8	Ignored until child took cookie himself, spanked child
4	1	4	Ignored; child stopped spontaneously
5	1	4	Company present; give child cookie to quiet him
	2	5	Ignored; finally gave in
6	1	8	Ignored, went into bathroom, had cigarette, read magazine until child quieted himself
	2	4	Ignored; just as I was about to give in, child stopped
7	1	3	Ignored, child stopped, began to play

SOURCE: David C. Rimm and John C. Masters, *Behavior Therapy: Techniques and Empirical Findings* (New York: Academic Press, Inc., 1974), p. 170.

student once every 10 minutes and to record the presence of the targeted behavior—for example, nailbiting. Modifications on the time sample may include noting the activity during the time period and noting the number of occurrences of the behavior in a particular time segment. The choice of measuring schemes depends on the behavior to be observed and other practical considerations. For instance, Rimm's example on tantrum behavior and its duration seems best suited to behavior specimen recording.

Once decisions about the target behavior and measurement have been made, the teacher can proceed with the actual assessment (phase two). Recording the frequency of the behavior creates a baseline for later comparison after the institution of the contingency managment program. It can also provide additional information about the nature and context of the behavior.

Phase three includes the final planning steps in formulating the contingency program. These are (1) structuring the situation (or environment), (2) selecting the reinforcers and reinforcement schedule, and (3) finalizing the behavior-shaping plans—that is, what will occur when.

After the first three phases have been completed, the contingency managment program can be instituted (phase four). This involves actually arranging the environment, informing the student, and maintaining the reinforcement and shaping schedules.

The final phase (five) is evaluating the program. This involves once again measuring the desired response. Some people reinstitute the old reinforcement conditions to see if the original behavior returns and then return to the contingency program.

A summary of the syntax is found in Table 16-2, p. 336.

SOCIAL SYSTEM

The social system for the particular behavior under consideration is highly structured, with the teacher controlling the reward system and the environment. Sometimes aspects of the social system can be negotiated, especially as the model moves toward contingency management for self-control. In any case, reinforcers, and occasionally the reinforcement schedule, may be negotiated with the student.

PRINCIPLES OF REACTION

The principles for reacting to the learner are based on the principles of operant conditioning and the specific contingency management that has been developed. In general, inappropriate behaviors are ignored (occasionally restructured), and appropriate ones are positively reinforced. If necessary, time-out may be used.

TABLE 16–2   SYNTAX OF THE CONTINGENCY MANAGEMENT MODEL

Phase One: Specifying a Final Performance	Phase Two: Assessing the Behavior
Identify and define target behavior. Specify desired behavioral outcome. Develop plans for measuring and recording behavior.	Observe, record frequency of behavior and, if necessary, nature and context of behavior.

Phase Three: Formulating the Contingency	Phase Four: Instituting the Program
Make decisions regarding the environment. Select the reinforcers and reinforcement schedule. Finalize behavior-shaping plans.	Arrange the environment. Inform the student. Maintain the reinforcement and behavior-shaping schedules.

Phase Five: Evaluating the Program
Measure desired response. Reinstitute old conditions, measure, and then return to contingency program (optional).

SUPPORT SYSTEM

The requirements vary with the type of contingency-management program. A simple individual behavioral program may not require any special support, or it may require material reinforcers and rearrangement of schedules or activities. A complex token economy such as the one described in the application section calls for more elaborate preparations. Programmed instructional uses require carefully sequenced material and probably an individualized learning environment. The person developing this program needs to plan carefully and must be patient and—above all—consistent.

APPLICATION

Contingency management finds educational applications in the form of programmed instruction, individual modification programs, and environmental design. Of course, the most common application is the informal use of reinforcement principles for classroom management. Descriptions of several contingency-management applications developed for the classroom are presented in the following pages. In the next section we discuss the use of similar principles for the development of self-control programs.

ENVIRONMENTAL DESIGN AND BEHAVIOR MANAGEMENT

With the assistance of two inner-city teachers, Michael Orme and Richard Purnell successfully employed contingency management procedures to modify the out-of-control behavior of 18 students in a combined third- and fourth- grade classroom. The results were reported in a 1968 study. They describe pupil behavior prior to the contingency management procedures as follows:

> Pupil behavior in the classroom was, for the most part, impulsive, aggressive and destructive. Neither T1 nor T2 was able to prevent pupils from taking apart their slatted wooden desks, tearing up classmate's papers, throwing books, yelling and singing. The noise level in the room was such [that] one could frequently hear the class from any one of the rooms in the three-story building.
>
> Aggressive pupil behavior was of central concern. In one twenty-minute period, T2 recorded aggressive acts in the classroom. She found that, while not every child had acted as an aggressor, every child in the room had been struck by another one or more times during that period. . . .
>
> Finally, the teachers were not able to stop pupils from running out of the classroom, through the halls, into other classes and offices, or outside of the school. (Orme and Purnell, 1968, p. 4)

Two of the objectives of their program were to reduce the aggressive behavior by substituting more acceptable responses and to increase the percentage of time the students spent on educationally related tasks. To accomplish these objectives, the researchers proposed to institute "total milieu control"—that is, to apply teaching techniques that manipulate multiple aspects of both the stimulus conditions and the reinforcing events. The stimulus properties they identified included the surrounding conditions of the room, the curriculum, and the teacher's verbal and nonverbal behavior. The reinforcement program included the teachers' verbal and nonverbal responses to student behavior as well as a specially designed, elaborate token (tangible) reinforcement system that was translated into instructional procedures. The next four pages describe some of the changes they made in the stimulus conditions and reinforcing events.

STIMULUS PROPERTIES

Surrounding conditions:

Physical changes in the room were made to: (1) encourage teacher movement, (2) facilitate teacher control, and (3) reduce extraneous stimulation. For example, the desks were joined together to form a U-shaped table which was strategically located to enable the teacher to control the door and also to encourage her to move from the blackboard into the U and over to the work table. All books and child art were removed from the room. They were replaced by content-relevant posters that were changed as the curriculum changed.

Teachers' verbal and nonverbal behavior:

The teachers were acquainted with the stimulus determinants of attention and were taught a variety of verbal and nonverbal techniques designed to elicit attention and curiosity, desirable behaviors that could then be reinforced. Some examples of these techniques are: presenting the content as a problem rather than a statement, rapidly shifting class focus, asking heuristic questions, enforced debates, nonverbal patterns such as silence or decisive movement patterns when shifting from one activity to another.

Curriculum:

The teachers selected content with an eye to its "control" potential. For instance, choral reading and drama were used to teach English literature. This required a relatively high level of cooperative verbal behavior by the students and provided opportunities for teacher reinforcement. Another teacher selected a math workbook which lent itself easily to token reinforcement for work completed. In another instance, a game was played with reading flashcards. This set up a quasi-competitive situation which assists in capturing student interest.

REINFORCEMENT SYSTEM

Token reinforcement

The authors provide the following description of the reinforcement system study. Unusual problems usually require unusual solutions.

To be sure, token reinforcement systems are not new ideas; they are, however, perceived as unusual by a substantial majority of educators. Like other systems, the one in this study was set up in such a way that pupils could earn points by emitting certain specified behaviors. The points or tokens earned could then be used to purchase preferred backup reinforcers from the "store." Thus, tangible reinforcers were manipulated in such a way that children's responses became contingent upon their prior behavior. The token system described here differs from those outlined in the previous literature in that the pupils shared actively in the determination of the backup reinforcers. In addition, the range of store items available went considerably beyond the usual variety of consumables and manipulables to include educationally relevant reinforcers.

In view of the strength and frequency of disruptive pupil behavior and the teachers' lack of reinforcement value in the classroom, the store included tangible items such as candy and gum. We could not be sure that the children would find more esoteric "reinforcers" reinforcing. Indeed, there was little or no evidence to indicate that they would be capable of delaying gratification long enough to accumulate any points. In anticipation of this, T2 provided herself with a liberal quantity of small candies (they were not needed, as the children immediately set their sights on items requiring fairly large numbers of points).

In addition to several kinds of candy, gum, balloons, baseball cards, and the like, the store also included items such as comics, selected novels and math puzzles, the opportunity to write poetry, a "conversation" with a computer (feed in disease symptoms for diagnosis), a short series of art lessons from a *real* artist, a model airplane together with instruction on aerodynamics, a shipbuilding project, science projects and puzzles, field trips to several types of museums and art institutions, and finally an opportunity to attend a *real* lecture at a major university. Apart from the last (for which there were no final takers), each of the "items" above were designed to provide further in-school opportunities for individual or small-group study. Thus, the student was given the opportunity to earn the right to select his or her own curriculum for a part of the school day.

All items were displayed on a table with a large white sheet of cardboard immediately above it. Trips, lessons, and projects were illustrated on colorful cards, together with their prices. Small suckers and taffy twists were priced at 15 points (the cheapest items). From there, point prices rose, with the highest priced items being the field trips and projects leading to preferred study. The latter ranged from 450 to 1,000 points.

Upon initial exposure to the room, all the pupils were given 25 points to spend immediately. This was done to impress upon them the reinforcement value of the points. Items were priced in such a way that if students purchased an item, they would still have 10 points left over. This meant they could purchase another item. This was done to avoid short-term satiation effects, and to maintain a high incentive level.

Each pupil's name was listed on the front board. The recording and decision to give points was controlled by the teacher at all times. As the children came into the room, T2 began selectively dispensing points and continued to do this throughout the experimental period.

The system was explained briefly, and the point-getting rules were outlined on the side blackboard. They were *Keep Busy All the Time, Have Good Manners,* and *Don't Bother Your Neighbor.* The teacher pointed out that these were general rules, and that the next few minutes would be devoted to allowing the pupils to suggest specific things that they thought should get points. The teacher then proceeded to list the *do* and *don't* behaviors suggested by pupils. Throughout this discussion, handraising, questioning (defining terms), and volunteered comments were reinforced verbally, nonverbally, and with points.

Both teachers were trained to emit verbal and nonverbal "reinforcement" along with points on the assumption that the teachers' reinforcement value would increase through contiguous association with the point system. At the same time they were told to reinforce only when they really felt the behavior in question was desirable or approximated some desired terminal pupil response.

Teachers' verbal and nonverbal reinforcement:

The teachers were given training in: (1) discriminating the pupil behaviors that would be reinforced (task behavior, silence, hand-raising, pupil attending to another pupil discussing lesson content, pupil-pupil cooperation); (2) providing positive and negative verbal and nonverbal gestures, teacher-change-in-position reinforcement (the teachers were directed to ignore disruptive behavior by focusing on an adjacent pupil who modeled desirable behavior); (3) manipulating schedules of reinforcement (Orme and Purnell, 1968, pp. 12–15).

The results were very encouraging. The disruptive behavior so prevalent before the behavior-shaping procedures were instituted virtually disappeared, and the pupil time spent on educationally related tasks increased from 50 percent to 80 percent.

PROGRAMMED INSTRUCTION

Programmed instruction is the most direct application of the writings of B. F. Skinner. It provides for highly systematic stimulus control and immediate reinforcement. Although Skinner's initial programmed instruction format has undergone many transformations, most adaptations retain three essential features: (1) an ordered sequence of items, either questions or statements to which the student is asked to respond; (2) the student's response which may be in the form of filling in a blank, recalling the answer to a question, selecting from among a series of answers, or solving a problem; and (3) provision for immediate response confirmation, sometimes within the program frame itself but usually in a different location, as on the next page in a programmed textbook or in a separate window in the teaching machine. (Examples of programmed material appear on the following pages.)

Recent research on programmed instruction shows that considerable deviation from these essentials can be made with no significant difference in the amount of learning that takes place. Programmed lectures with no overt student response are one example. The original linear self-instructional programs in which each student is submitted to the same material, though at his own pace, were not sufficiently individualized for some educators. Hence, "branching" programs were developed. The idea in branching is that slower students, unable to respond correctly to a particular frame or sequence of frames, may need additional information or review of background information. On the other hand, the more advanced students could benefit by additional and more difficult material. At various points the branching program directs students to the appropriate material depending on their answer to a particular frame or the number of correct responses within a particular frame sequence. Branching programs will automatically direct the student to a special section depending on his or her choice. If he or she selects any of the wrong responses, the particular mistake in reasoning is pointed out; if he or she chooses the correct response, a more difficult example may appear.

Programmed instruction has been successfully employed for a variety of subject matters, including English, math, statistics, geography, and science. It has been used at every school level from preschool through college. Programmed instructional techniques have been applied to a great variety of behaviors: concept formation, rote learning, creativity, and problem solving, for example. Some programs have even led the student to discover concepts, using a format reminiscent of inductive thinking.

How is programmed instruction different from traditional workbooks that have been used by classroom teachers for years with no startling effects? With workbooks the emphasis is on practice (response maintenance) rather than on behavioral acquisition through carefully sequenced material. Workbooks provide endless "frames" of review material. Obviously, review is of little value unless the behavior has first been successfully established; the traditional workbook is not designed to do this. Second, the reinforcing effect of continuous review is bound to suffer diminishing returns; the learner only goes over material already mastered. Lastly, most workbooks make no provision for immediate feedback, supplying the answer only in the teacher's copy!

On the following pages we have included two examples of programmed materials. The first is an excerpt from a high school English course, and the second is from an elementary school arithmetic book.

PROGRAMMED ENGLISH
M. W. Sullivan

1. Words are divided into classes. We call the largest class nouns.
   Nouns are a class of _____ .   words

2. In English the class of words called *nouns* is larger than all the other _____ .   classes
   of words combined.

3. We call the largest class of English words
   _____ .   nouns

4. You will learn a number of ways to recognize and to use the class of _____ called   words
   nouns.

5. The words in a class are all alike in some way. All the members of the _____ of words   class
   called nouns have characteristics in common.

6. You will see that nouns occur in special positions in English sentences. Any word that occurs in a noun position must be a _____ .

noun

7. Any word which fits the blank in the sentence
    "I saw the _____ ."
    occurs in the noun position.
    Can the word DOG occur in the noun position?

yes

8. Any position which is occupied by a noun in English is part of a NOUN PATTERN.
    "I saw the _____ ."
    This entire sentence is a _____ pattern.

noun

9. When a word occurs in the noun position in a noun pattern, we say that it fits the _____ pattern.

noun

10. When a word fits a noun pattern, we say that it FUNCTIONS as a noun.
    A word which does not fit the noun pattern cannot _____ as a noun.

function

11. When a word functions as a noun, we say it belongs to the class of words called _____ .

nouns

12. But a word may function as a member of several classes.
    We classify it as a noun only when it _____ as a noun.

functions

    A word functions as a noun only when it occurs in the _____ position in a noun pattern.

noun

13. A word which fits the blank in the following sentence occurs in a *noun* position
    "I saw the _____ ."
    We say that a word which occurs in a noun _____ in a noun pattern functions as a noun.

position

    Therefore we will use the above pattern as one test for _____ .

nouns

14. "I saw the *book*."
    In this pattern, the word BOOK is in a _____ position.

noun

    We therefore say that the word _____ functions as a noun.

book

15. "I saw the *airplane*."
    Here the word _____ is in a noun position.

airplane

16. Test the following words in the noun pattern to see whether or not they can function as nouns:
    desk
    "I saw the _____ ." cat
    stone
    Can these three words function as nouns?

yes

17. We use the pattern "I saw the _____ " to decide whether or not a word functions as a _____ .

noun

18. Can the word BOAT function as a noun?   yes
    We know that BOAT functions as a noun
    because we can say "_____
    _____ boat."   "I *saw the* boat."
    From now on, when several words are to be
    filled in, we will often indicate this with a
    series of dots. For example, instead of writing
    "_____ _____ _____ boat,"
    we will write
         "......... boat."
19. Give the pattern which we use to test for nouns.   "I saw the _____."
20. "I saw the _____."
    If a word fits this blank, we say that it can
    _____ as a noun.   function
21. Which of these words can function as a noun?
       chair
       cautiously   chair
22. CAUTIOUSLY does not function as a noun
    because we do not say "........."   "I saw the cautiously."
23. Which of these words can function as a noun?
       hat
       usually   hat

    (Sullivan, 1963, pp. 1–4)

INTRODUCTION TO SETS

	Some children like to collect stamps.	1
	Charles collects records. John likes to collect pictures of baseball players.	2
	Roger has a collection of model airplanes.	3
	Roger collects model planes. He has a plane	4
col*lec*tion	col_____tion.	
collec*tion*	Dick collects coins. He has a coin collec_____	5
collection	A bunch of flowers is a _____ of flowers.	6
	Another word for collection is set. A collection of	7
set	stamps is a _____ of stamps.	
set	A collection of butterflies is a _____ of butterflies.	8
collection	Set and _____ have the same meaning.	9
set	A collection of things is a _____ of things.	10
	Each thing in a set is called an element of the set. Jim has a stamp collection.	11
	His World's Fair stamp is a thing or	
element	e _____ in his collection.	
	Each roller skate in a set of roller skates is an	
element	e _____ t of that set.	12
	In John's set of train cars a flat car is an	
element	e _____ .	13
	In a set of cars, an element of this set would be a	

car	(car/thing) _____ . Choose the better answer.	14
dog	An element of the set of dogs is a(n) _____ .	15
element	A cat is a(n) _____ of the set of cats.	16
element	A funny face is a(n) _____ of the	17
set	_____ of funny faces.	
	Here is a set of kittens. Pick out an element of this set 18 by drawing a circle around this element.	
element	A cup is a(n) _____ in the set of cups.	19
	A book is an element in the set of	
books	_____ .	20
	An element is one of the things in a(n)	
set	_____ .	21

(Starr, 1965, pp. 1–3)

INSTRUCTIONAL AND NURTURANT EFFECTS

Contingency management is versatile. Teachers can use it to guide their goals in every domain and to develop their instructional materials (see Figure 16-2).

SUMMARY CHART ▶ **CONTINGENCY MANAGEMENT MODEL**

Syntax

Phase One: Specifying a Final Performance
  Identify and define target behavior.
  Specify desired behavioral outcome.
  Develop plans for measuring and recording behavior.

Phase Two: Assessing the Behavior
  Observe, record frequency of behavior and, if necessary, nature and context of behavior.

Phase Three: Formulating the Contingency
  Make decisions regarding the environment.
  Select the reinforcers and reinforcement schedule.
  Finalize behavior-shaping plans.

Phase Four: Instituting the Program
  Arrange the environment.
  Inform the student.
  Maintain the reinforcement and behavior-shaping schedules.

Phase Five: Evaluating the Program
   Measure desired response.
   Reinstitute old conditions, measure, and then return to contingency
      program (optional).

Social System

The model has high structure. The teacher controls the reward system
   and the environment. Certain aspects of the social system—for example, reinforcement and schedule—may be negotiated. Eventually,
   the model is totally in the hands of the students, especially for self-
   control.

Principles of Reactions

Follow principles of operant conditioning, including stimulus control,
   reinforcement of appropriate behavior according to the behavior-
   shaping and reinforcement schedules. Ignore inappropriate behavior
   or, when necessary, restructure and use time-out.

Support System

Support varies with the type of program, from no special support to
   elaborate support.
Material reinforcers, rearrangement of schedules, activities, seating, and
   sometimes programmed materials are needed.
The greatest human support is accuracy and consistency in applying
   contingency management.

We now move to a variation of contingency management that places
greater control in the hands of the student.

S C E N A R I O   **II**

TOWARD SELF MANAGEMENT

   Susan had been having a difficult time finishing her homework. Typically, she would relax a little after dinner, then go upstairs to her bedroom
and get her books. With her arms full of every textbook she was using that
semester and all her notebooks, she would head downstairs to the family
room and plop on the soft couch in front of the television set. Usually her
younger brother sprawled out on the mounds of pillows on the floor with
his array of school books. Together they would work on their assignments
while watching their favorite television programs, chatting, and eating
snacks. The telephone, conveniently located next to the couch, would ring

periodically. One or both of them would rush to answer it. They would carry on short conversations in the television room. If it was to be a long, private conversation they would go upstairs to the telephone extension there. Susan's grades began to drop, and one of her teachers became concerned. Jim Long, Susan's English teacher, knew she was both motivated and able to do much better work. He asked her to stay after school to speak with him.

When Jim brought the issue up to Susan, she whispered in a low careful voice, "I know. I just can't seem to concentrate on my schoolwork. I'm always rushing to get it finished and my ideas don't come easily." Mr. Long was quite familiar with the habits of teenagers (he has two boys himself). He asked Susan some questions about her study habits—where, when, and how she studied. Also, how she organized herself to get ready to study. Detail by detail Susan described her environment during study time. Mr. Long exclaimed, "No wonder you are having difficulty concentrating. You really do yourself in with all these interesting distractions. I don't think there is anything wrong with your ability to concentrate and learn. I do think you've been sabotaging yourself. Not intentionally, of course."

At first Susan thought Mr. Long was blaming her, but he explained what he has to do to get himself organized to grade English papers at night. He talked about all the things he'd rather do than grade papers. He talked about distractions and how he arranges his environment to get a little time each night to give his undivided attention to his work. Susan felt more comfortable and acknowledged that she would like to develop a better system to get her work done. Mr. Long agreed to help her design one for herself—a "self-control" project.

Before they discussed the details of the program, Mr. Long explored some of Susan's other behavior patterns—her need to talk to her friends and to watch certain television programs. He also asked her how long she could read without getting bored. Of course, her interest varied with the subject matter and type of assignment. Together they analyzed her habits

FIGURE 16–2 Instructional and nurturant effects: contingency-management model.

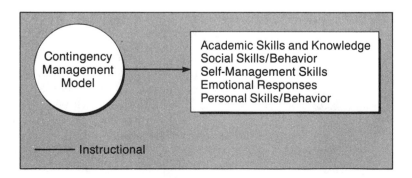

for each area. Mr. Long made it clear that Susan should take her interest and needs into account when setting up her program in order to satisfy them in a way that wouldn't interfere with her studying.

Next, Mr. Long explained to Susan some basic principles of behavior, especially how the environment influences behavior. Susan began to see that she had arranged her environment in such a way that studying was almost impossible. It wasn't a character flaw that prevented her from studying, just a normal response to immediate temptations.

Mr. Long and Susan spent several meetings setting up her program. They decided short-term goals and long-term goals. For example, each night before dinner Susan would make a list of the work to do. She would then assign priorities and decide a plan for the evening's work. After dinner Susan was to establish her bedroom desk as the place of study, away from the telephone, television, and her brother. Initially, she was to spend 20 minutes on subjects that were relatively easy to her and 15 minutes on the more difficult ones. After that time she could take a short break, either watching television or making a quick phone call. Lengthy, important calls were to be made before she began studying at 7:15 P.M., or at the end of the study period. They also worked out other details of the plan, such as what Susan would do if she got bored or frustrated. These were some of the most immediate goals. The long-term goal was to increase the length of her periods of study or amount of material covered.

As they talked, Susan made a list of the steps in her program. She purchased a special notebook in which she could keep track of her progress each day and jot down suggestions for revising the program. These notes would be the basis of her review meetings with Mr. Long. Susan and Mr. Long agreed to meet briefly twice a week for the first few weeks to discuss Susan's progress and adjust the program.

With Mr. Long's assistance, Susan applied behavioral techniques to establish self-control over her study habits. Gradually she became aware of the role the environment plays in influencing her behavior. She also became aware that she can modify the environment.

B. F. Skinner wrote *Science and Human Behavior* in 1953, inspiring the debate of mind control versus human dignity. During the next 10 years behaviorists demonstrated considerable success with the application of contingency-management techniques to previously unsolvable educational problems. Still, the community of educators seemed polarized by the freedom/control issue. By the early 1970s the social climate had changed, and behavioral scientists had published major works devoted to self-control through operant methods (Thoreson and Mahoney, 1974). Clinical psychologists moved toward behavioral techniques as a way of helping their patients quickly overcome social and emotional problems associated with self-control. It is now clear that contingency-management methods can be used successfully for such problems associated with self-control (Bandura and Perloff, 1967). Several of these methods are particularly relevant to school issues, such as study problems and social problems.

ORIENTATION TO THE MODEL

The principles of operant conditioning used in contingency management are also used here—notably, stimulus control and positive reinforcement. However, in this model these aspects are totally in the hands of the participant. One of the main reasons for moving toward a self-control model is that for many behaviors, the environment is unlikely to provide incentives at the rate and time that the individual actually needs them to establish the new behavior. Studying, exercising, practicing the piano, and more assertive social behavior toward members of the opposite sex are a few examples. Consequently, it is important that the person have ways of rewarding himself or herself. Self-control problems almost always involve situations with short-term positive gratification and long-term negative consequences. Smokers, for example, do not feel the impact of the potential long-term effects as vividly as they experience the short-term satisfaction from one more cigarette. Making people aware of the short-term and long-term response consequences that maintain their behaviors is a first step to helping them select new reinforcements.

Another critical factor hindering changes in self-control patterns is the conditions in the environment that initially stimulate the self-defeating behavior. If a student is distracted by noise but continually studies with the television on, it is likely that his or her study behavior will not be too effective. Or if a student cannot resist having a beer with the group and manages to run into them just before he or she is to go off and study, he or she is being coerced by the environmental stimuli. The ways in which people with weight problems sabotage themselves by arranging their environments with tempting food and lots of time to eat is well known. Paying attention to and deliberately arranging a better environment is a cornerstone of self-control procedures.

Often the stimulant for self-defeating behavior is covert, a thought such as "I need a little something sweet. I'll just have one cookie." "I don't think I can pass this exam." "Everyone seems to understand this material but me." It is just as possible to rearrange the stimuli in one's mental environment as in one's physical environment for the purposes of lessening the probability of such self-defeating behaviors. This is called *covert control*. In helping people establish a self-control program, it is important to check out the thoughts or images that may be part of their behavioral chains.

The key to stimulus control is *changing the environment*. This may be done through physical changes—for example, turning the television off, taking it out of the room, or selecting a different room in which to study. Narrowing the range of stimuli-eliciting behaviors is another way to control the environment. For example, a person with an eating problem may remove food from all rooms except the kitchen. Finally, the eliciting stimuli may be altered by substituting a desirable, *competing response* or thought, such as reminding oneself that he or she did well on the last exam or temporarily switching to a routine, accomplishable task instead of building up anxiety by sticking to a momentarily unsolvable problem or writing assignment. When the anxiety has subsided, the person can later come back to the problem or task.

The notion of *shaping* is applicable to self-control programs as well as to contingency management programs. Individuals often fail in their own self-control efforts because they set their goals too high and thus never obtain positive reinforcement for their efforts. They see tasks as all-or-nothing. If they "fail" one time to control the undesirable behavior, they give up, believing that the program has failed. *Changing attitudes* as to what constitutes success is a third essential feature of self-control programs. Individuals can be assisted in setting up realistic behavioral continuums in which some success is virtually assured.

THE MODEL OF TEACHING

The activities of the self-control model are similar to those of contingency management, with the major differences occurring in the orientation of the learner to the strategy and the social system—that is, in initiating and having responsibility for carrying out the model. The phases of the model include: introduction to behavioral principles, establishing the baseline, setting up the program, and monitoring and modification.

SYNTAX

In phase one the instructor introduces the self-control program, and, in particular, the self-control principles. The objective here is for the student to understand that his or her difficulty in self-control is a function of the environment, not some permanent, unalterable part of his or her character. The instructor then goes over the principles. Rimm and Masters (1974) summarize the basic operant principles with which the student should be familiar:

1. Self-control is not a matter of will power. Instead, it comes about as a result of judicious manipulation of antecedent and consequent events, in accord with established principles of learning.
2. The client should take advantage of the fact that behavior is under stimulus control by employing any of the following tactics:
   a. Physically changing the stimulus environment.
   b. Narrowing the range of stimuli eliciting undesirable behaviors.
   c. Strengthening the connection between certain stimuli and desirable behaviors.

3. The client should determine events that are potent rewards and administer them immediately after responding appropriately.

4. The client should determine which responses are competing with, and thereby inhibiting, desirable behavior, with the goal of weakening them. He should determine which responses might serve as healthy alternatives to undesirable ways of behaving, with the goal of strengthening them.

5. The client should attempt to interrupt behavior chains leading to undesirable responses as early as possible in the chain.

6. Step-wise behavior goals in a self-control program should always be easily attainable. That is, the client should deliberately plan to achieve his overall goal in a very gradual manner.
   Auxiliary Principles

7. Thoughts exert a certain amount of control over behavior. Thoughts may be thought of as internal behaviors subject to the same principles of learning applicable to overt behavior.

8. Contracts involving exchange of reinforcers may be arranged between client and therapist, or between the client and some other party. Such contracts may serve as an additional basis for motivation. (Rimm and Masters, 1974, pp. 284–285)

Of course, the introduction should be made in the context of the problem behavior and not as a formal lecture on behavioral theory. It need not be lengthy, and the manner and extent of this first phase will depend on the individual student. Obviously, the student must indicate a genuine desire to participate or at least a willingness to give it a try—a factor that must be assessed and agreed on in this first phase.

In phase two, establishing the baseline, the instructor and student agree on the procedures and schedule for collecting the baseline data about the target behavior. This should be a quantitative record including events (and thoughts) prior to and after the target behavior is emitted. The environment should also be noted. In addition to establishing a baseline, the purpose is to ascertain the controlling stimuli, reinforcing consequences, and possible adaptive and maladaptive competing responses and reinforcers. After a week or two of self-monitoring, the student will be in a position to set up a self-control program with the instructor's assistance.

Phase three is setting up the actual program, especially making decisions regarding the stimulus environment and the reinforcers. At this point both short-term and long-term goals are identified. It is important that the program be written down with each short-term goal and the target clearly specified. The instructor's role in helping the student draw up a realistic self-control program should be set up. Finally, the student should be encouraged to continue with the program even if there are behavioral lapses. At the time of the meeting, the two can review possible unanticipated problems in the original plan.

Finally, in phase four the student begins to undertake the self-control program. Initially, he or she will meet with the instructor to evaluate the progress of the program and make any modifications in schedule, reinforcement, or stimulus control that may be necessary. Gradually, as the student experiences his or her own success, instructor contact will diminish. (The syntax is summarized in Table 16-3.)

TABLE 16–3   SYNTAX OF THE SELF-CONTROL MODEL

Phase One: Introduction to Behavioral Principles	Phase Two: Establishing the Baseline
Communicate that self-control is a function of the environment. Explain specific self-control principles. Establish willingness to participate.	Specify clearly target behavior. Determine measuring procedures and schedule. Carry out measurement, noting control stimuli, reinforcing consequences, possible competing responses.

Phase Three: Setting Up the Self- Control Program	Phase Four: Monitoring and Modifying the Program
Make decisions regarding stimulus environment, reinforcers. Set up short-term and long-term goals, possible target dates. Draw up written program. Agree upon review meeting and times.	Student undertakes program. Periodic meeting with instructor to review progress and modify program as necessary.

SOCIAL SYSTEM

The structure in this model is moderate to low. Although the instructor is important in initiating the possibility of the program, the student ultimately has control over the situation and maintenance of activities, many of which are carried out independent of the joint sessions. Furthermore, all aspects of the self-control program are negotiated with the student.

PRINCIPLES OF REACTION

The instructor has a critical role to play in the success of the self-control program. First, he or she must encourage the student, reminding him or her that behavior is under environmental control and is not a function of personal weaknesses. At first, the instructor is a powerful reinforcer for the student; gradually this role will diminish. Second, he or she ensures a sense of realism (and specificity) in planning and carrying out the self-control program, seeing to it that reasonable goals are established and that perfection is not demanded. Third, the instructor offers the student intellectual guidance in applying behavioral principles and techniques.

SUPPORT SYSTEM

This model has no special support system.

APPLICATION

One of the best uses of the self-control model is toward the improvement of study habits (Rimm and Masters, 1974, pp. 292–296). Probably the biggest obstacle students have in this area is their tendency to set unrealistic goals. After a long history of failure in a subject area, they may expect themselves to do several hours or many pages of uninterrupted work. Predictably they will fail. Their frustation with the difficulty of the task will mount; and in a short time they will give up, confirming their original assumption, "I'm no good. I can't do it!" One of the most important roles of the instructor is helping the student establish a program of small goals, such as 10 to 15 minutes of study, or a few pages of the textbook. Other self-control techniques for increasing study time are: (1) changing the stimulus environment (for example, selecting a quiet place free of distractions and people); (2) cue strengthening (establishing a desk or study area used only for this purpose); and (3) reinforcement (limiting the task so that the student can experience success before boredom and frustration set in). After studying for the preselected period of time, the student should reward himself or herself. During the rest intervals, he or she may engage in the original competing behavior, such as telephoning a friend. Many people find that cleaning the house or other chores are best accomplished as a respite from studying and writing. For others, quick play periods are important. Some people need a longer break than others. In any case, the notion of rest intervals needs to be legitimated.

Besides the problem of time devoted to studying, students may have difficulty because of the quality of their habits. Various methods have been developed to improve study habits, most notably the SQ3R (Robinson, 1946; Wrenn and Larsen, 1955). Other aspects of the studying process include techniques for improving note taking (Bencke and Harris, 1972) and test taking. In the self-control model, the instructor can take the opportunity to introduce students to qualitatively different behaviors that will improve their performance.

INSTRUCTIONAL AND NURTURANT EFFECTS

This model directly instructs for the target behaviors and also eliminates maladaptive behaviors. Almost any behaviors are eligible for this model, especially those requiring large amounts of self-control. The model also has powerful nurturant effects: It teaches individuals that they can control their environments and themselves, and this enhances self-esteem. It also encourages individuals to perceive the world from a behavioral point of view, to note the stimulus and reinforcements in their interactions with people and things (Figure 16-3).

FIGURE 16–3   Instructional and nurturant effects: self-control model.

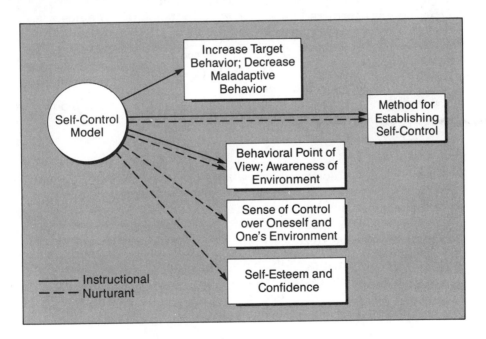

SUMMARY
CHART ▶ **SELF-CONTROL MODEL**

Syntax

Phase One: Introduction to Behavioral Principles
　Communicate that self-control is a function of the environment.
　Explain specific self-control principles.
　Establish willingness to participate.

Phase Two: Establishing the Baseline
　Specify clearly target behavior.
　Determine measuring procedures and schedules.
　Carry out measurement, noting control stimuli, reinforcing conse-
　　quences, possible competing responses.

Phase Three: Setting up the Self-Control Program
　Make decisions regarding stimulus environment, reinforcers.
　Set up short-term and long-term goals, possible target dates.
　Draw up written program.
　Agree on review meeting and times.

Phase Four: Monitoring and Modifying the Program
　Student undertakes the program.
　Periodic meeting with instructor to review progress and modify pro-
　　gram as necessary.

Social System

The model has a moderate to low structure. Instructor is a facilitator
　helping the student initiate and maintain activities. All aspects of the
　program are negotiated with the student.

Principles of Reaction

Encourage student, especially in dispelling notion of personal weakness.
　Reiterate idea of environmental control. Ensure that student's goals
　and plans are realistic. Offer knowledge and guidance in applying be-
　havioral principles and techniques.

Support System

No special support system.

CHAPTER 17

TRAINING AND SELF-TRAINING: LEARNING FROM SIMULATIONS

From the Basic Skills to the Exploration of Space

S C E N A R I O

Driver education students in a secondary school in Chicago are taking turns driving a simulated car. As the motion picture camera projects an image of the roadway ahead, obstacles appear. A child steps out from behind two parked cars; the "driver" turns the wheel and misses the child. A stop sign appears suddenly beyond a parked truck; the driver slams on the brakes. The driver makes a turn and a roadway narrows suddenly; again the driver brakes. One by one the students experience driving under simulated conditions. As students complete the "course," the instructor and the other students debrief them, questioning their reactions and their defensive driving.

In another classroom, this time in the suburbs of Boston, a class is watching a television show. The actors are portraying the members of the United States cabinet facing a crisis. After examining the issues, the class reaches a conclusion. One student reaches for the telephone in the classroom, dials a number, and speaks to the actors in the studio, suggesting how they might play their roles differently to resolve the crisis. Twenty-five other classrooms are simultaneously debating the issues seen on television and they, too, are communicating their views to the actors in the studio. The next day the show resumes. In various ways, the actors play out the suggestions made by the classes. The other members of the cabinet react. Students in the 25 classrooms not only see their ideas brought to life on the television screen, but also see the consequences of their recommendations.

In an inner-city neighborhood in Toronto, an elementary school is also watching a television screen. The announcer portrays a countdown as a rocket attempts to break free from the gravity of the moon but fails to do so. Class members then take the role of members of the spaceship crew.

Instructions from the Royal Canadian Space Administration divide them into teams, and they prepare to work together to conserve their life-support systems and to manage their relationships in the rocket ship until repairs can be made.

In San Antonio, two groups of children enter a room. One group represents the Alpha culture, the other the Beta culture. Their task is to learn how to communicate with others who have learned rules and patterns of behavior from a different society. Gradually, they learn to master communication patterns. Simultaneously, they become aware that, as members of a culture, they have inherited powerful patterns that strongly influence their personalities and their ways of communicating with other people.

In Philadelphia, a class is engaged in a caribou hunt. As they progress through the hunt, which the Netsilik Eskimos operate, they learn behavior patterns of the Netsilik and begin to compare those patterns with the ones they carry on in their everyday lives.

In a San Francisco suburb, a group of students faces a problem posed by the secretary of state. Agronomists have developed a nutrient that, when added to the food of beef cattle, greatly increases their weight. Only a limited amount of this nutrient is available, and the students must determine how the nutrient will be divided among the needy nations of the world. Congress has imposed the following restraints: The recipient nations must have a reasonable supply of beef cattle, must not be aligned with the hard-core Communist bloc of nations, must not be vegetarians, and must have a population that exceeds a certain size. The students debate the alternatives. Some countries are ruled out immediately. Of the remaining countries, some seem attractive at first, yet less attractive later. The students grapple with the problems of humanity and ideology and with practical situations. In simulation they face the problems of the committees of scientists who continually advise the U.S. government on various courses of action.

These students are all involved in simulations, playing the roles of persons engaged in real-life pursuits. Simulation allows them to face realistic conditions and develop realistic solutions. These elements of the real world are simplified and presented in a form that can be contained inside the classroom.

To progress through the tasks of the simulation, students must develop concepts and skills necessary for performance in the specified area. The young drivers have to develop concepts and skills for driving effectively. The young caribou hunters have to learn concepts about a certain culture. The young members of the cabinet need to learn about international relations and the problems of governing a major nation.

In simulation, students learn from the consequences of their actions. The driver who does not turn rapidly enough "hits" the child he or she is trying to avoid; he or she must learn to turn more quickly. Yet if the car turns too quickly, it goes out of control and veers to the other side of the street. The driver has to learn to correct the initial move while keeping his or her eyes on the road and looking for yet other obstacles. The students who do poorly in the caribou hunt learn what happens if the culture does not function efficiently, or if its members shrink from carrying out its mandates.

In this chapter we explore simulations of various kinds, some of which are goal-oriented games, such as the familiar board game, Monopoly. Monopoly simulates the activity of real estate speculators and incorporates many elements of real-life speculation. In this type of game simulation the players compete; in other simulations players attempt to reach their goals in a noncompetitive way. No score is kept, but interactions are recorded and analyzed later. An example is the Life Career game, in which the students play out the life cycle of a human being: They select mates, choose careers, decide whether to obtain various amounts of education, and learn, through the consequences of their decisions, how these choices can affect their real lives.

Unlike many other models of teaching, game simulations depend on *software*—that is, the game has paraphernalia of various kinds. Monopoly has a game board, pieces that represent the players, houses, hotels, cards that insert chance events into the situation, and paper money. Without these, the game cannot be played. Similarly, driver simulators, games involving cabinets in crises, human relations games such as Star Power, and many other simulations all require material to represent the real world to the students in a simulated form. Much of the model of teaching that we call simulation involves learning to use this software effectively. Whereas other models of teaching depend on the interpersonal skill of the teacher (understanding concepts, making skillful moves that help the students explore important ideas), the simulation model depends on the teacher's blending the already prepared game or other simulation into the curriculum, highlighting and reinforcing the learning inherent in the game. Because many people do not realize the critical role a teacher can play in enhancing learning from a simulation activity, we believe a model of teaching that describes these activities is especially useful. The game itself is essential, but the teacher's ability to make the activities truly meaningful is critical.

ORIENTATION TO THE MODEL

CYBERNETIC PRINCIPLES

Simulations have been used increasingly in education over the last 30 years, but the simulation model did not originate within the field of education. Rather, it is an application of the principles of *cybernetics*, a branch of psychology. Cybernetic psychologists, making an analogy between humans and machines, conceptualize the learner as a self-regulating feedback system. As a discipline, cybernetics "has been described as the comparative study of the human (or biological) control mechanism, and electromechanical systems such as computers" (Smith and Smith, 1966, p. 202). The central focus is the apparent similarity between the feedback control mechanisms of electromechanical system and human systems. "A feedback control system incorporates three primary functions: it generates movement of the system toward a target or defined path; it compares the effects of this action with the true path and detects error; and it utilizes this error signal to redirect the system (Smith and Smith, 1966, p. 203).

For example, the automatic pilot of a boat continually corrects the helm of the ship, depending on the readings of the compass. When the ship begins to swing in a certain direction and the compass moves off the desired heading more than a certain amount, a motor is switched on and the helm is moved over. When the ship returns to its course, the helm is straightened out again, and the ship continues on its way. The automatic pilot operates in essentially the same way as does a human pilot. Both watch the compass, and both move the wheel to the left or right, depending on what is going on. Both initiate action in terms of a specified goal ("Let's go north"), and depending on the feedback or error signal, both redirect the initial action. Very complex self-regulating mechanical systems have been developed to control devices such as guided missiles, ocean liners, and satellites.

The cybernetic psychologist interprets the human being as a control system that generates a course of action and then redirects or corrects the action by means of feedback. This can be a very complicated process—as when the secretary of state reevaluates foreign policy—or a very simple one—as when we notice that our sailboat is heading into the wind too much and we ease off on our course just a little. In using the analogy of mechanical systems as a frame of reference for analyzing human beings, psychologists came up with the central idea "that performance and learning must be analyzed in terms of the control relationships between a human operator and an instrumental situation." That is, learning was understood to be determined by the nature of the individual, as well as by the design of the learning situation (Smith and Smith, 1966, p. vii).

All human behavior, according to cybernetic psychology, involves a perceptible pattern of motion. This includes both covert behavior, such as thinking and symbolic behavior, and overt behavior. In any given situation, individuals modify their behavior according to the feedback they receive from the environment. They organize their movements and their response patterns in relation to this feedback. Thus, their own sensory-motor capabilities form the basis of their feedback systems. This ability to receive feedback constitutes the human system's mechanism for receiving and sending information. As human beings develop greater linguistic capability, they are able to use indirect as well as direct feedback, thereby expanding their control over the physical and social environment. That is, they are less dependent on the concrete realities of the environment because they can use its symbolic representations. The essence, then, of cybernetic psychology is the principle of sense-oriented feedback that is intrinsic to the individual (one "feels" the effects of one's decisions) and is the basis for self-corrective choices. Individuals can "feel" the effects of their decisions because the environment responds *in full*, rather than simply "You're right" or "Wrong! Try again." That is, the environmental consequences of their choices are played back to them. *Learning* in cybernetic terms is sensorially experiencing the environmental consequences of one's behavior and engaging in self-corrective behavior. Instruction in cybernetic terms is designed to create an environment for the learner in which this full feedback takes place.

SIMULATIONS IN EDUCATION

The application of cybernetic principles to educational procedures is seen most dramatically and clearly in the development of *simulators*. A simulator is a training device that represents reality very closely, but in which the complexity of events can be controlled. For example, a simulated automobile has been constructed in which the driver sees a road (by means of a motion picture), has a wheel to turn, a clutch and a brake to operate, a gearshift, and all the other devices of a contemporary automobile. The driver can start this stimulated automobile, and when he or she turns the key can hear the noise of a motor running. When the driver presses the accelerator the noise increases in volume, so the driver has the sensation of having actually increased the flow of gas to a real engine. As the person drives, the film shows curves in the road and, as the driver turns the wheel, he or she may experience the illusion that the automobile is turning. The simulator can present the student with learning tasks to which he or she can respond, but the responses do not have the same consequences that they would have in a real-life situation; the simulated automobile doesn't crash into anything, although it may look like it is crashing from the driver's point of view. And in the manner of training psychology, the tasks presented can be made less complex than those a driver would have to execute in the real world; this way, it is easier for the student to acquire the skills he or she will need later for actual driving. For example, in a driving simulator the student can simply practice shifting from one gear to another until he or she has mastered the task. The student can also practice applying the brakes and turning the wheel, thus developing a feel for how the automobile responds when he or she does those things.

The advantages of a simulator are several. As we noted earlier, the learning tasks can be made much less complex than they are in the real world, so that the students may have the opportunity to master tasks that would be extremely difficult when all the factors of real-world operations impinge upon them. For example, learning how to fly a complex airplane without the aid of a simulator leaves very little room for error. The student pilot has to do everything adequately the first time, or the plane is in difficulty. With the use of a simulator, the training can be staged. The trainee can be introduced to simple tasks and then more complex ones until he or she builds a repertoire of skills adequate for piloting the plane. In addition, difficulties such as storms and mechanical problems can be simulated, and the student can learn how to cope with them. Thus, by the time the student actually begins flying, he or she has built a repertoire of necessary skills.

A second advantage of simulators is that they permit students to learn from self-generated feedback. As the student pilot turns the wheel of the great plane to the right, for example, he or she can feel the plane bank and feel the loss of speed in some respects, and he or she can learn how to trim the craft during the turn. In other words, the trainees can learn through their own senses, rather than simply through verbal descriptions, the corrective behaviors that are necessary. In the driving simulation, if the driver heads into curves too rapidly and then has to jerk the wheel to avoid going off the road, this feedback permits the driver to adjust his or her behavior so that when driving on a real road he or she will turn more gingerly when approaching sharp curves. The cybernetic psychologist designs simulators so that the feedback about the consequences of behavior enables the learners to modify their responses and develop a repertoire of appropriate behaviors.

Some very elaborate applications of cybernetic psychology have been made in military training. For example, in a submarine simulator several members of the crew can communicate with one another by radio and other devices. They are able to take their "submarine" under water, maneuver it against enemy ships, raise their periscope, sight ships through it, and fire torpedoes. The simulator is constructed so it can be attacked by enemy destroyers and can emerge and engage in evasive action; the crew can hear the enemy only over sonar and other undersea listening devices.

Thus far, the application of cybernetics within normal elementary and secondary education is somewhat less spectacular. Exceptions are an urban simulator, which is being used experimentally with children from the upper elementary grades (Developed by the Washington Center for Metropolitan Studies, 1717 Massachusetts Ave., Washington, DC), and Omar Khayyam Moore's famous talking typewriter, which simulates a human being who talks back to the student as he or she presses typewriter keys representing particular words or letters. Most other applications of cybernetics to education are fairly simple. As we describe some of them here, the cybernetic principles become more explicit.

THE LIFE CAREER GAME

This game was developed to assist guidance counselors and students in their mutual task of planning for the future, a task that requires the student to consider many factors, such as job opportunities, labor-market demands, social trends, and educational requirements (Varenhorst, 1968). Vocational and educational guidance personnel seek to help students become aware of these multiple factors, evaluate their significance, and generate alternative decisions. In the *Life Career Game* students make decisions about jobs, further education or training, family life, and the use of leisure time, and they receive feedback on the probable consequences of these decisions. The environment in this case is represented by other persons or organizations. That is, the probable consequences of the students' decisions are represented by responses from persons playing the roles of teachers, college admissions officers, employers, and marriage partners. As the players move through the different environments of school, work, family, and leisure, they are able to see the interrelationships among their decisions and among the components of their lives. The game is played as follows: The Life Career Game can be played by any number of teams, each consisting of two to four players. Each team works with a profile or case history of a fictitious person (a student about the age of the players).

The game is organized into rounds or decision periods, each of which represents one year in the life of this person. During each decision period, players plan their person's schedule of activities for a typical week, allocating time among school, studying, job, family responsibilities, and leisure time activities. Most activities require certain investments of time, training, money and so on (for example, a full-time job takes a certain amount of time and often has some educational or experience prerequisites as well; similarly, having a child requires a considerable expenditure of time, in addition to financial expenses), and a person clearly cannot engage in all the available activities. Thus, the players' problem is to choose the combination of activities which they think will maximize their person's present satisfaction and chances for a good life in the future.

When players have made their decisions for a given year, scores are computed in four areas—education, occupation, family life, and leisure. Calculations use a set of tables and spinners—based upon U.S. Census and other national survey data which indicate the probability of certain things happening in a person's life, given the person's personal characteristics, past experiences, and present efforts. A chance or luck factor is built into the game by the use of spinners and dice.

A game usually runs for a designated number of rounds (usually 10 to 12), and the team with the highest total score at the end is the winner.

The variations of the Life Career Game illustrate the educational features of a simulation game as well as the enormous potential of simulation for incorporating several educational objectives into the basic simulation-game design. For instance, every simulation implies a theory about behavior in the area of life being simulated. This theory is implicit in the goal-achievement rules (the objectives of the game) and the rules governing the environmental responses.

One version of the Life Career Game assumes that each person attaches a different amount of importance to the various areas of life. Following this assumption, players determine their own goals by weighing the various areas in terms of their importance to them. At the end of the game, the objective achievements in those areas are converted to subjective satisfaction by means of weighted conversion ratios selected by the player. Alternately, if one of the processes being simulated is the selection and modification of goals contingent on the consequences of one's actions, the player may be asked to weigh the different areas of life at various times during the course of the play. In both cases, the student is "playing against" the environment according to a personal criterion rather than an externally determined goal (such as gaining more points in the game than someone else).

The game may also include certain requisite skills, such as actually making formal applications for jobs, setting up interviews, or selecting courses from the college catalog. It can be conducted to allow group discussion at the end of rounds, where students can analyze and challenge each other's decisions and identify the values underlying them.

COMPUTER-BASED ECONOMICS GAMES

The Center for Educational Services and Research of the Board of Cooperative Educational Services (BOCES) in northern Westchester County, New York, has recently developed two computer-based economics games for sixth graders (Center for Educational Services and Research, Board of Cooperative Educational Services, 42 Triangle Center, Yorktown Heights, NY, 10598). The use of the computer makes it possible to individualize the simulation in terms of learning pace, scope, sequence, and difficulty of material. Aside from this feature, the properties of the simulation remain the same as in noncomputer-based simulation games.

The Sumerian Game instructs the student in the basic principles of economics as applied to three stages of a primitive economy—the prevalence of agriculture, the development of crafts, and the introduction of trade and other changes. The game is set during the time of the Neolithic revolution in Mesopotamia, about 3500 B.C. The student is asked to take the role of the ruler of the city-state of Lagash. The ruler must make certain agricultural decisions for the kingdom at each six-month harvest. For example, the ruler is presented with the following problematic situation: "We have harvested 5,000 bushels of grain to take care of 500 people. How much of this grain will be set aside for next season's planting and how much will be stored in the warehouse?" (Boocock and Schild, 1968, p. 156). The student is asked to decide how much grain to allocate for consumption, for production, and for storage.

These situations become more complex as the game continues, for the student must take into account such circumstances as changes in population, the acquisition of new land, and irrigation. Periodically, technological innovations and disasters alter the outcome of the ruler's decisions. The effect of each decision on the economic condition of the kingdom is shown in an immediate progress report. Students are apprised of certain quantitative changes—for example, in population, in the amount of harvested grain, and in the amount of stored grain—and they are furnished with some substantive analyses of their decisions—for instance, "The quantity of food the people received last season was far too little" (Boocock and Schild, 1968, p. 164). In phase two of the Sumerian Game, the student can apply his or her surplus grain to development arts & crafts.

INTERNATIONAL SIMULATION

Harold Guetzkow and his associates have developed a very complex and interesting simulation for teaching students at the high school and upper elementary levels the principles of international relations (Guetzkow and others, 1963). This international simulation consists of five "nation" units. In each of these nations, a group of participants acts as decision makers and "aspiring decision makers." The simulated relations among the nations are derived from the characteristics of nations and from principles that have been observed to operate among nations in the past. Each of the decision-making teams has available to it information about the country it represents. This information concerns the basic capability of the national economic systems, the consumer capability, force capability (the ability of the nation to develop military goods and services), and trade and aid information. Together, the nations play an international-relations game that involves trading and the development of various agreements. International organizations can be established, for example, or mutual-aid or trade agreements made. The nations can even make war on one another, the outcome being determined by the force capability of one group of allies relative to that of another group.

As students play the roles of national decision makers, they must make realistic negotiations such as those diplomats and other representatives make as nations interact with one another, and they must refer to the countries' economic conditions as they do so. In the course of this game-type simulation, the students learn ways in which economic restraints operate on a country. For example, if they are members of the decision-making team of a small country and try to engage in a trade agreement, they find that they have to give something to get something. If their country has a largely agricultural economy and they are dealing with an industrialized nation, they find that their country is in a disadvantageous position unless the other nation badly needs the product they have to sell. By receiving feedback about the consequences of their decision, the students come to an understanding of the principles that operate in international relations.

THE TEACHER'S ROLE

It is easy to assume that because the learning activity has been designed and packaged by experts, the teacher has a minimal role to play in the learning situation. People tend to believe that a well-designed game will teach itself. But this is only partly true. Cybernetic psychologists find that educational simulations enable students to learn first-hand from the simulated experiences built into the game rather than from teacher's explanations or lectures. However, because of their intense involvement, students may not always be aware of what they are learning and experiencing. Thus, the teacher has an important role to play in raising students' consciousness about the concepts and principles underpinning the simulations and their own reactions. In addition, the teacher has important managerial functions. With more complex games and issues, the teacher's activities are even more critical if learning is to occur. We have identified four roles for the teacher in the simulation model: *explaining, refereeing, coaching,* and *discussing.*

EXPLAINING

To learn from a simulation, the players need to understand the rules sufficiently to carry out most of the activities in the game and to understand the implications of each move they might make. However, it is *not* essential that the students have a complete understanding of the game at the start. As in real life, many of the rules become relevant only as the game is played. Thus, repeating the rules of the game should be kept to a minimum. Implications of various game moves are much clearer to students *after* they have played, and are best discussed then.

REFEREEING

Simulations used in the classroom are designed to provide educational benefits. The teacher should control student participation in the game to assure that these benefits are realized. Before the game is played, the teacher must assign students to teams (if the game involves teamwork), matching individual capabilities with the roles in the game to assure active participation by all students. Shy and assertive students, for example, should be mixed on teams. One pitfall the teacher should avoid is assigning the apparently more "difficult" roles to brighter students and the more passive roles to less academically talented students. Many simulations call on a broader range of personal competencies than do typical classroom tasks. Besides, the more academically proficient students have already had experience in leadership roles. Simulations offer an opportunity to distribute such experiences more widely.

The teacher should recognize in advance that simulations are *active* learning situations and thus call for more freedom of movement and more talk among students than do other classroom activities. The teacher should act as a referee who enforces game rules but does his or her best not to interfere in the game activities.

COACHING

The teacher should act as coach when necessary, giving players advice that enables them to play better—that is, to exploit the game's possibilities more fully. As a coach, the teacher should be a supportive advisor, *not* a preacher or a disciplinarian. In a game, players have the opportunity to make mistakes and take consequences—and learn. Furthermore, a coach does *not* play. The coaching role of the teacher should consist of offering (but not insisting on) advice, only when it is solicited by players, and perhaps making some unsolicited suggestions to players who seem shy.

DISCUSSING

During the game the teacher should explain, referee, and coach. After the game the teacher should be certain to lead the class in discussing how closely the game simulates the real world, what difficulties and insights the students had in the playing of the game, and what relationships can be discovered between the simulation and the subject matter that the game was meant to supplement. The class might also suggest ways to improve the game!

THE MODEL OF TEACHING

SYNTAX

The simulation model has four phases: orientation, participant training, the simulation itself, and debriefing (see Table 17-1). In the orientation (phase one), the teacher presents the topic to be explored, the concepts that are embedded in the actual simulation, an explanation of simulation if this is the students' first experience with it, and an overview of the game itself. This first part should not be lengthy but can be an important context for the remainder of the learning activity. In phase two the students begin to get into the simulation. At this point the teacher sets the scenario by introducing the students to the rules, roles, procedures, scoring, types of decisions to be made, and goals of the game. He or she organizes the students into the various roles and conducts an abbreviated practice session to ensure that students have understood all the directions and can carry out their roles.

Phase three is the actual game activity and administration. The students participate in the game or simulation, and the teacher functions in his or her role as referee and coach. Periodically the game may be stopped so that the students receive feedback, evaluate their performances and decisions, and clarify any misconceptions.

Finally, phase four consists of participant debriefing. Depending on the outcomes of the game the teacher may help the students focus on: (1) the events and their other perceptions and reactions, (2) analyzing the

TABLE 17–1   SYNTAX OF SIMULATION MODEL

Phase One: Orientation	Phase Two: Participant Training
Present the broad topic of the simulation and the concepts to be incorporated into the simulation activity at hand. Explain simulation and gaming. Give overview of the simulation.	Set up the scenario (rules, roles, procedures, scoring, types of decisions to be made, goals). Assign roles. Hold abbreviated practice session.

Phase Three: Simulation Operations	Phase Four: Participant Debriefing (Any or All of the Following Activities)
Conduct game activity and game administration. Obtain feedback and evaluation (of performance and effects of decisions). Clarify misconceptions. Continue simulation.	Summarize events and perceptions. Summarize difficulties and insights. Analyze process. Compare simulation activity to the real world. Relate simulation activity to course content. Appraise and redesign the simulation.

process, (3) comparing the simulation to the real world, (4) relating the activity to course content, and (5) appraising and redesigning the simulation.

SOCIAL SYSTEM

Because the teacher selects the simulation activity and directs the student through carefully delineated activities, the social system of simulation is rigorous. Within this structured system, however, a cooperative interactive environment can, and ideally should, flourish. The ultimate success of the simulation, in fact, depends partly on the cooperation and willing participation of the students. Working together, the students share ideas, which are subject to peer evaluation but not teacher evaluation. The peer social system, then, should be nonthreatening and marked by cooperation.

PRINCIPLES OF REACTION

The reactions of the teacher are primarily those of a facilitator. Throughout the simulation he or she must maintain a nonevaluative but supportive attitude. It is the teacher's task to first present and then facilitate understanding and interpretation of the rules of the simulation activity. In addition, should interest in the activity begin to dissipate or attention begin to focus on irrelevant issues, the teacher must direct the group to "get on with the game."

SUPPORT SYSTEM

Simulation requires support materials from simple teacher-made games to marketed games (which sell for under $10 to more than $200), to specifically designed simulators such as car-driving or airplane-navigating simulators (whose costs can mount into thousands of dollars). Simulations are gaining in popularity, and the number of published materials increases every year. The 1973 *Social Science Education Consortium Data Book* lists more than 50 simulations available for use in social studies alone. The teacher who is interested in using simulations is directed to publishers' catalogs; the aforementioned *Data Handbook* (1971, 1972, 1973); Ronald Kleitsch, *Directory of Educational Simulations, Learning Games, and Didactic Units* (1979); David Zuckerman and Robert Horn, *The Guide to Simulation Games for Education and Training* (1970); and Ron Stadsklev, *Handbook of Simulation Gaming in Social Education* (n.d.).

APPLICATION

There are two ways students learn from a simulation game. The first is a direct result of the experience in the simulation, and the second is a result of the activities or discussions that follow the game. A good point of departure for discussion is to ask the students to evaluate how their experiences in the game compare to what they believe to be true about the real world. According to William Nesbitt, the important thing is "for students to be explicit about their experience with and in the game and from there to examine their views of the real world or referent situation" (Nesbitt, 1971, pp. 38–39).

Simulation games can stimulate a variety of learning, such as learning about: (1) competition, (2) cooperation, (3) empathy, (4) the social system, (5) concepts, (6) skills, (7) efficacy, (8) paying the penalty, (9) the role of chance, and (10) the ability to think critically (examining alternative strategies and anticipating those of others) and make decisions (Nesbitt, 1971, pp. 35–53).

The simulation model is somewhat different from many other models of teaching in that it depends on the prior development of a simulation, either by research and development specialists, a commercial company, or a teacher or group of teachers. The simulation itself presents problems to the learners, and the learners deal with those problems as they carry out the simulation operations.

The number and range of simulation games is vast for both elementary and secondary students. The Social Science Education Consortium's 1973 *Databook* covers many topics—consumer education, political decision making, city planning, economics, ecology, family management and budgeting, and career planning. Over 70 games are described in that one book.

It is apparent that the simulation model can be used for a variety of teaching purposes. In the classroom, simulations are generally employed as part of a fairly extensive unit of study. They can be used to introduce a unit of work, to extend and deepen understanding as the unit progresses, or to pull ideas together and ensure their application to real-life problem situations. For example, the game of Hang Up can be used to begin a unit on personal values and racial stereotyping. Similarly, Bafá can be used to introduce the study of culture and cultural interchange. The Legislative Game can be used to bring together knowledge of the legislative process and caucusing.

Essentially, to apply simulation to a unit, the teacher must develop a plan that specifies content and scope and then must examine lists of simulations, searching for ones that might be applicable and sifting them for quality. It is wise to try a simulation with a small group of people, whether children or adults, before using it in the classroom.

Upper elementary, junior high, and high school students can be prepared for leadership roles through simulations. It is important to note, however, that if students are to be used as leaders, they have to be coached so that the essential point of the game is quite clear to them. Some game-type simulations have a tendency to go off on tangents if the leader loses focus.

Since simulations teach people to work within a system, it is important to identify the elements of the system that have to be mastered by the end of the game. Political games, for example, require the mastery of a political system, and economic games, the mastery of an economic system. This is, of course, why simulations are so good as introduction to and culminating activities of units of study.

Some simulations are good only for one operation; Bafá is such a game. Once you have learned its system, there is little incentive to learn it again. Other simulations, such as the Legislative Game, can be played more and more effectively as students acquire information—in this case, about the legislative process.

INSTRUCTIONAL AND NURTURANT EFFECTS

The simulation model, through the actual game and through discussions afterwards, nurtures and instructs a variety of educational outcomes in-

cluding: concepts and skills; cooperation and competition; critical thinking and decision-making; empathy; knowledge of political, social, and economic systems; sense of effectiveness; awareness of the role of chance; and
facing consequences (see Figure 17-1).

FIGURE 17–1   Instructional and nurturant effects: simulation model.

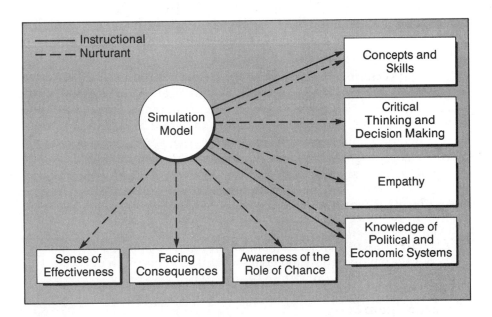

SUMMARY
CHART ► **SIMULATION MODEL**

Syntax

Phase One: Orientation
    Present the broad topic of the simulation and the concepts to be in-
    corporated into the simulation activity at hand.
    Explain simulation and gaming.
    Give overview of the simulation.

Phase Two: Participant Training
    Set up the scenario (rules, roles, procedures, scoring, types of deci-
    sions to be made, goals).
    Assign roles.
    Hold abbreviated practice session.

Phase Three: Simulation Operations
    Conduct game activity and game administration.
    Feedback and evaluation (of performance and effects of decisions).
    Clarify misconceptions.
    Continue simulation.

Phase Four: Participant Debriefing
(Any or all of the following activities:)
Summarize events and perceptions.
Summarize difficulties and insights.
Analyze process.
Compare simulation activity to the real world.
Relate simulation activity to course content.
Appraise and redesign the simulation.

Social System

The social system is structured by the teacher through selecting materials and directing the simulation. The interactive environment of the class, however, should be nonthreatening and marked by cooperation. The teacher has the role of managing the simulation (taking care of organization and logistics), explaining the game, maintaining the rules, coaching (offering advice, prompting), and conducting the debriefing discussion.

Principles of Reaction

1. Do not evaluate players' decisions and moves.
2. Facilitate student's understanding and interpretation of rules.
3. Encourage participation and help the students cope with uncertainty.
4. Tell students to "get on with the game" when necessary.

Support System

Simulation requires a carefully structured base of resource materials.

CHAPTER 18

THE CONDITIONS OF LEARNING

Focusing Instruction

One of the most important books on learning and teaching is Robert N. Gagné's *Conditions of Learning* (1965). Gagné does not provide a model of teaching as such but gives us a careful analysis of the key variables in learning and how instruction can be organized to take these variables into account. He has made a valuable contribution in developing a picture of the "varieties of chance called learning," which enables us to classify and specify learning objectives and the relationships *between* various kinds of performances.

Gagné identifies six varieties of performances that can be the result of learning:

1. Specific responding
2. Chaining
3. Multiple discrimination
4. Classifying
5. Rule using
6. Problem solving

Varieties of Performance

Specific responding is making a specific response to a particular stimulus. An example occurs when a first-grade teacher holds up a card (the stimulus) on which the word *dog* is printed and the children say "dog" (the response). Specific responding is an extremely important type of learning and is the basis for much of the information we possess. In order for the student to learn to make correct, specific responses, we must assume he or she has the ability to make connections between things. In the previous example, the printed word *dog* is associated, or connected, with the verbal statement "dog."

Chaining is making a series of responses that are linked together. Gagné uses the example of unlocking a door with a key and of translating from one language to another. Unlocking a door requires us to use a number of specific responses (selecting a key, inserting it, turning it) in an order that will get the job done. When one takes the English words "How are you?" and translates them to "Cómo está usted?" in Spanish, one is chaining by taking a series of specific responses and linking them into a phrase.

Multiple discrimination is involved in learning a variety of specific responses and chains and in learning how to sort them out appropriately. For example, one learns to associate colors with their names under very similar conditions, but then has to sort out the colors and apply them to varieties of objects under different conditions, choosing the right responses and chains. Multiple discrimination, then, involves learning to handle previously learned chains of various sorts.

Classifying is assigning objects to classes denoting like functions. Learning to distinguish plants from animals or automobiles from bicycles involves classifying. The result of this process is *concepts,* ideas that compare and contrast things and events or describe causal relations among them.

Rule using is the ability to act on a concept that implies action. For example, in spelling we learn varieties of concepts that describe how words are spelled. Then we apply those concepts in rule form in the act of spelling itself. For example, one learns that in consonant-vowel words ending in *t,* such as *sit,* the consonant is doubled when *ing* is added. This becomes a rule (double the *t*) that one usually follows in spelling such words.

Finally, *problem solving* is the application of several rules to a problem not encountered before by the learner. Problem solving involves selecting the correct rules and applying them in combination. For example, a child learns several rules about balancing on a seesaw and then applies them when moving a heavy object.

FACILITATING THE CLASSES OF LEARNING

Gagné believes that these six classes of learning form an ascending hierarchy; thus, before one can chain, one has to learn specific responses. Multiple discrimination requires prior learning of several chains. Classifying builds on multiple discrimination. Rules for action are forms of concepts learned through classification and the establishment of causal relations. Problem solving requires previously learned rules. Each level of learning requires certain conditions. The task of the instructor is to provide these conditions (by using the appropriate model of teaching).

To facilitate specific responding, a stimulus is presented to the student under conditions that will bring about his or her attention and induce a response closely related in time to the presentation of the stimulus. The response is then reinforced. Thus the teacher may hold up the word *dog*, say "dog," ask the children to say "dog," and then smile and say "good" to the students. A teacher who does this repeatedly increases the probability that the students will learn to recognize words and be able to emit the sounds associated with the symbols. The memory and training models are approaches that facilitate specific responding.

To facilitate the acquisition of chaining, a sequence of cues is offered and appropriate responses are induced. A language teacher may say, "How are you?" followed by *"Cómo está usted?"*, inviting the students to say "How are you?" and *"Cómo está usted?"* and provide sufficient repetition that the students will acquire the chain and achieve fluency. The memory model, advance-organizer, and inductive thinking models are appropriate to this area.

To facilitate multiple discrimination, practice with correct and incorrect stimuli is needed, so that the students can learn to discriminate. For example, suppose the students are learning the Spanish expressions for "How are you?", "Good morning," and "Hello"; they must learn to discriminate which one to use in a given situation. The instructor provides sets of correct and incorrect stimuli until the students learn the appropriate discrimination. Advance organizers and inductive reasoning are useful in this process.

Classification is taught by presenting varieties of exemplars and concepts so that the students can gradually learn bases for distinguishing them. Concept attainment and inductive thinking are appropriate, among others.

Rule using is facilitated by inducing the students to recall a concept and then apply it to a variety of specific applications. In the earlier spelling example, students recall the rule about doubling the final consonant when adding *ing* and are presented with examples they can practice. Inquiry training can help students move from concepts to rules.

Problem solving is largely done by the students themselves, because problem situations are unique. It can be facilitated by providing sets of problems that the students can attempt to attack, especially when the instructor knows that the students have acquired the rules needed to solve the problem. Inquiry training, group investigation, synectics, simulation, and nondirective teaching can be used for problem-solving activities.

FUNCTIONS OF THE INSTRUCTOR

Gagné emphasizes that it is the learner's activity that results in the learning. It is the function of the instructor to provide conditions that will increase the probability that the student will acquire the particular performance. Practice is extremely important so that the learner makes the necessary connections, but it is the learner who makes the connections even when they are pointed out to him or her. The instructor cannot substitute his or her own activity for that of the student. We agree completely with Gagné on this point.

Instructors (or perhaps instructional systems) operate through the following instructional functions:

1. Informing the learner of the objectives
2. Presenting stimuli
3. Increasing learners' attention
4. Helping the learner recall what he or she has previously learned
5. Providing conditions that will evoke performance
6. Determining sequences of learning
7. Prompting and guiding the learning

Also the instructor encourages the student to generalize what he or she is learning so that the new skills and knowledge will be transformed into other situations.

Informing the learner of the performance expected is critical for providing him or her with a definite goal. For example, the teacher might say, "Today we're going to try to learn about three presidents of the United States. We'll learn their names, when they lived, and what they are most known for." The teacher then presents the pictures of Washington, Lincoln, and Theodore Roosevelt. Their names are printed under the pictures. Pointing to the pictures and names, and saying the names will draw the students' attention.

To recall previous learning, the teacher may say, "Do you remember that we discussed how the country has grown and changed in various ways? Can you tell me what some of these changes were?" The students can reach into their memories and stimulate themselves with material that will later be connected to the presidents.

To induce performance, a teacher may ask the students to name the three presidents and then read printed material describing the life of each. Then the teacher can ask them to tell him or her what they have learned.

A variety of sequences can be used, depending on the type of learning and the subject matter in question. Generally, however, presenting a stimulus, evoking attention, attention, helping the learner understand the objectives, inducing performance, and then helping the learner to generalize are the major instructional tasks, which follow one another naturally.

Gagné has provided an instructional paradigm that is useful in defining learning outcomes and identifying the tasks of instruction. As indicated throughout this discussion, models of teaching, especially from the information-processing and cybernetic/behavior-modification families, can be used to design many of the conditions. Concept attainment, for example, provides ways of presenting stimuli, controlling attention, and evoking performance.

Gagné's paradigm also reminds us of a variety of important instructional functions not specifically dealt with in several of the models. For example, the importance of informing the learner of objectives and encouraging generalization is implicit in many models but is not spelled out in particular.

Although the instructional paradigm Gagné advocates is very direct and may appear at first to be highly controlling, he emphasizes that we cannot control learning but can only increase the probability that certain kinds of behavior will occur. We can present stimuli in close connection with others and ask the student to perform, but it is the *learner* who makes the connection between the printed and spoken word:

> It seems evident, then, that in controlling all of the aspects of external learning conditions described previously, instruction nevertheless can only make the occurrence of this crucial internal, idiosyncratic event more probable. So far [as] is known now, instruction cannot directly control this eternal and internal event. The careful design of instruction can surely increase its probability, and, by so doing, make the entire process of learning more sure, more predictable and more efficient. But the individual nervous system must still make its own individual contribution. The nature of that contribution is, of course, what defines the need for the study of individual differences. (Gagné, 1967, pp. 291–313)

From this point of view, a model of teaching brings structures to the student that change the probability that he or she will learn certain things. The syntax presents tasks to the student; the reactions of the teacher pull the student toward certain responses; and the social system generates a need for particular kinds of interaction with others. The net effect is to make it more likely that various kinds of learning will take place. In Table 18-1, several information-processing models and a few from other families are paired with the six varieties of performance that Gagné has identified.

The more complex models involve activities likely to increase the probability that several kinds of learning will take place. Gagné's hierarchy is useful in helping us select models appropriate for varieties of educational objectives. It also reminds us of the multiple types of learning promoted by individual models and the attention that must be given to the varieties of performance as the students engage in the study of any important topic. For example, students using inductive thinking to explore a problem in international relations, such as the balance of payments, will gather data (specific responding and chaining), organize it (multiple discrimination and classifying), and develop principles (rule using) to explore solutions to problems (problem solving).

Before beginning any extensive unit of instruction, it is worthwhile to identify the varieties of performance that will be sought, determine the appropriate models, and then analyze which kinds of learning will be emphasized in phases of the study and how they can be enhanced.

TABLE 18–1   MODELS ESPECIALLY APPROPRIATE FOR VARIETIES OF PERFORMANCE

Types of Performance	Models				
Specific responding	Memory	Phase one inductive thinking	Phase one of concept attainment	Advance organizer	Group investigation (data-gathering activities)
Chaining	Concept attainment	Inductive thinking			
Multiple discrimination	Inquiry training				
Classifying	Concept attainment	Inductive thinking	Advance organizer		
Rule using	Inquiry training	Simulation			
Problem solving	Synectics	Scientific thinking	Inquiry training	Group investigation	

THE BEHAVIORAL SYSTEMS FAMILY: ADDITIONAL NOTE ON EXPECTED EFFECTS

All models are somewhat controversial in our somewhat fractious democracy, and all have their detractors. The personal family is criticized as "soft," the social family for relying on the social skills of the immature, the information-processing family for being "academic," and the behavioral systems family for presumably being impersonal and hard-edged. As we have seen, the research provides fuel for detracting the detractors in the personal, social, and information-processing families, and this is no less true than for the behavioral systems.

It would take a book much larger than this one to describe adequately the enormous base of research on which these theorists rely and to which they contribute. Unquestionably, behavioral systems engineers can create systems that teach both simple and complex skills and knowledge. In this summary we will mention only one small piece of that research, because it strikes at the heart of an argument that highly-directive, feedback-laden instruction produces mindless activity. We refer to the summary of research on the social-learning theory based approaches of Becker and Englemann at the University of Oregon. They use one of the tightest, most highly sequenced and feedback-oriented versions of the approach. White (1986), reviewing the studies accompanying the approach, chose to focus part of his analysis on measures of ability and asked what effects the "direct instruction" approach had on ability measures with special education children. He reported that students who were exposed to the approach for three years had "learned" more ability. The effect sizes ranged from .5 to 1.0. So much for the argument that highly sequenced approaches necessarily deaden the mind. What is probably more true is that poorly designed instruction, from whatever vantage, is the real killer of intelligence.

PART V

PROFESSIONAL SKILL

In the last two chapters of the book we deal with two important aspects of professional skill. The first is the process of adding teaching skills and strategies to the teaching repertoire. The second deals with how to modulate teaching to the learning styles of the students to increase *their* learning repertoires.

Over the last 25 years, research has brought some exceedingly good news to both teacher candidates and experienced teachers. This good news is that virtually all teachers and teacher candidates who wish to can add to their repertoires any of the models of teaching described in this book or any of the research-based teaching skills that have come from other lines of research. Chapter 19 describes how this can be accomplished and provides recommendations for the design of preservice and staff development programs where the mastery of professional skills is a central goal.

During the same period of time, several lines of research have explored how students can be taught to profit from a wide range of models of teaching and learning and, again the news is good: Virtually all students can increase their learning rates dramatically if we arrange the learning environment to facilitate development. The products of these lines of research have been brought together in Chapter 20 to describe how individual differences in learning styles can be accommodated to so that students of widely differing backgrounds and skills can increase their power to educate themselves in the wide variety of ways described in this book. A major component of professional skill is the design of environments that enable students to increase their power as learners and the discussion of that skill seems a fitting way to close the book. For, after years of searching for "special" methods of education for students of particular characteristics, it appears that improving "the quality of schooling for *all* pupils may well be the most advantageous way of responding to those who come to be described as having special educational needs" (Ainscow, 1991).

CHAPTER 19

HOW TO LEARN A TEACHING REPERTOIRE
The Professional Learning Community

We are in the midst of a period where strong new efforts are being made to develop a new kind of professional community in education—one whose ethos is built around the continuous study of teaching and learning. This chapter is designed to describe the kinds of professional communities that we hope are emerging and to discuss how teachers and teacher candidates can work together to expand their teaching repertoire. Since most of you who read this book are practicing teachers or are in teacher education programs, the chapter represents advice to you about how to profit from the book, use the peer coaching guides, and learn from demonstrations of models in action, both videotaped and "live."

It is plain from the research on training that teachers can be wonderful learners. They can master just about any kind of teaching strategy or implement almost any kind of sensible curriculum—if the appropriate conditions are provided. It is also clear that those who criticize the motivations of teachers, worry about their willingness and ability to learn, or believe that the only way to improve the teaching profession is to change its personnel are fundamentally wrong. Twenty years of research on how people learn teaching skills have developed a knowledge base that can guide us as we try to expand our teaching repertoire. This knowledge can also help us deal with ourselves as we learn how to teach students to respond to a rich array of learning environments. For important new learning involves a certain amount of discomfort (see Chapter 20), and teachers and teacher-candidates are well able to withstand the pain—provided that they understand its nature and how to cope with it.

SCHOOLS AS CENTERS OF INQUIRY

The culture of most school faculties has been highly individualistic with nearly all interaction over day-to-day operations. Without collective action, schools have difficulty addressing problems that cannot be solved by individual action. Without a balance between operations and the study of teaching and curriculum, the school is liable to drift toward obsolescence and fail to adapt to the needs of the surrounding society. Reorienting school cultures toward collegial problem solving and the study of advances in research on curriculum and teaching is vitally important (Schon, 1982).

There are some powerful and visionary models for reorganizing schools to generate collegial organizations that productively address problems and study innovations in the field. For example, Robert Schaefer's marvelous 1966 essay—written at the height of the movements to improve the academic content of curriculum, involve students in driving inquiry, and develop collegial workplaces for teachers—synthesized those movements into a fresh conception of the school as a workplace. The core of the paper argued for schools that not only involve students in academic inquiry but involve the teachers in the continuous study of teaching and learning. Experimentation with teaching would be a normal and shared activity as the teachers developed new procedures and instructional materials and tried them out. Bringing together as it did a concept of a community of collaborating teachers, a recognition that educational knowledge is emergent, a belief that the future science of education would be built around clinical inquiry, and a sense of an organization whose staff is truly empowered, the essay embodied a striking vision of professionalization.

A variety of similar conceptions have been developed over the years (for example, see Goodlad, 1983, and Sizer, 1982). Various models for team teaching (for example, Joyce, Hersh, and McKibbin, 1983) have included forms of the collegial, inquiry-oriented notion. The problem is less one of conception than of implementation.

STUDY GROUPS AND COACHING TEAMS: BUILDING COMMUNITIES OF PROFESSIONAL EDUCATORS

In our work with school districts we recommend the extensive use of study teams and councils to facilitate learning. Each teacher and administrator has membership in a team whose members support one another in study. For example, each person can have membership in a coaching team of two or three. Each team is linked to one or two others, forming a study group of no more than six members. The principal and the leaders of the study groups in a school form the staff development/school improvement council of that school. A representative from each school within a district cluster (usually a high school and its feeder schools) serves on the District Cluster Network Committee, which coordinates staff development efforts between schools and the district and works directly with the director of staff development (see Figure 19-1).

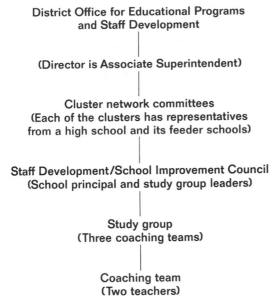

District Office for Educational Programs
and Staff Development

(Director is Associate Superintendent)

Cluster network committees
(Each of the clusters has representatives
from a high school and its feeder schools)

Staff Development/School Improvement Council
(School principal and study group leaders)

Study group
(Three coaching teams)

Coaching team
(Two teachers)

FIGURE 19–1   A district staff development governance structure

This governance structure is illustrated by the staff at the Onyx Elementary School whose faculty numbers 36. One teacher, Adrienne, has a coaching partner, Katherine. They belong to Study Group A, which has six members. Adrienne is, with five others, a member of the Onyx School staff development council. She and the principal are members of the cluster network committee which consists of representatives from one high school, two middle schools, and six elementary schools in the Opal school district. Through a council of teachers and administrators, that cluster, with the three others in the district, is linked to the District Office for Educational Programs and Staff Development. The director of that office is an associate superintendent and reports directly to the superintendent.

The coaching teams and study groups are the building blocks of the system. Team members support one another as they study academic content and teaching skills and strategies. The study groups within each school are responsible for implementing school-improvement efforts and districtwide initiatives.

Let us consider the case of a new member of the Onyx School faculty:

Sharlene Daniels is in her fifth year of teaching.

At a weekend science workshop she became acquainted with some of the members of the Onyx School faculty from another school district. She noticed that they had come to the workshop as a team and that they were gathering materials and making plans for their workshops back at Inland. They let her join them. Later, she visited the Inland school and watched that team and others at work, teaching before each other, offering advice and experimenting together.

When an opening at Onyx appeared, Sharlene applied for it on an impulse, was interviewed, and accepted. The members of the team to which she was assigned explained that she would have a "coaching partner" and that she and that partner would visit each other, watch each other teach, and give each other assistance. They also had to agree on one or two teaching strategies that they would focus on each year and make a commitment to master them and experiment with them in the classroom.

Before the first workshop, Sharlene was given curriculum materials and an explanation of the rationale behind the teaching-strategy approach that was to be used. The first workshop was devoted almost entirely to a discussion of the uses of the strategy, the theory behind it, and how various children responded to it. Sharlene was surprised, because she thought the workshop would be devoted to demonstrations. However, those were reserved for the workshop's second session: The Inland consultant demonstrated the teaching strategy, teaching the teachers the same kinds of lessons they would later be teaching to children. Several of the team members were uncomfortable with science, so the consultant decided that it was important for those persons to become familiar with the learner's role in the teaching strategy because they would soon be teaching their children these same roles. At the end of the workshop, the consultant did a careful demonstration with a group of children. She explained the teaching strategy to both the children and the teachers, and after the children had gone they discussed the lesson and how it could be adapted to various groups of children. For the next workshop, Sharlene found that *she* was expected to prepare a lesson and teach it to her fellow teachers.

At that workshop, Sharlene and the rest of her team took turns teaching one another. Thus, she got to see the other teachers practice the strategy. Her team then made plans to try a couple of prototype lessons for their students over the next two weeks. Those two weeks were very uncomfortable ones for Sharlene. Things did not go quite as planned. She found herself thinking she already had developed several fine ways of teaching and wondering why she should go to the trouble of learning these new methods, especially if it was going to be painful to learn them. Her coaching partner laughed when Sharlene shared her thoughts, and explained that everyone felt the same way. They had learned that it wasn't too hard to understand any new teaching strategy and to develop a certain skill with it, but until they had tried it a dozen or so times, they all felt varying degrees of discomfort. "The better you are," explained her partner, "the worse you feel, because you are used to having things go well. Actually, things probably are going well, but you just don't feel as comfortable as you did teaching in the ways that have become familiar to you."

Sure enough, after five or six tries with the children, Sharlene began to feel much more comfortable. She was actually able to get the children to engage in inductive thinking, and it excited them. Then the teachers began to demonstrate for one another. Soon she found herself in the library after school, teaching a group of her students and surrounded by a ring of her fellow teachers. She had watched the other teachers occupy the same position, but this was her first time, and she felt like a child on the first day of school. After the children left, she was surprised that no one made critical comments. Then she suddenly realized that none of them ever made critical comments to one another. Instead, they tried to learn from what they had just seen. More important, most of the discussion that followed came after a comment by one of the teachers whom Sharlene had felt looked the most confident and even nonchalant in the workshop settings. "You just showed me a new level of that lesson," she said. "I've been doing all right and thought I had it right, but the way you handled that teaching strategy gave me a lot of ideas that I can use to make it a lot stronger than I believed it was."

Sharlene was learning what it meant to go to a school whose faculty had learned how to train themselves to make curriculum changes for the school as a whole and to add new teaching techniques to their individual repertoires.

After a couple of months, during which each teacher tried the new strategies a dozen times or more, they began to feel "possession" of the strategies. Then initial discomfort passed to feelings of strength and power. They owned a new tool, and it became part of their "natural" repertoires.

The Onyx team is engaged in the serious study of alternative models of teaching, using training procedures that enable them to bring almost any approach to teaching within their grasp. The elements they use include:

The study of the theoretical basis or the rationale of the teaching method.

The observation of demonstrations by persons who are relatively expert in the model.

Practice in relatively protected conditions (such as trying out the strategy on each other and then on children who are relatively easy to teach).

Observing one another as they work the new model into their repertoires, providing companionship, helping one another to learn to teach the appropriate responses to their students and to figure out the optimal uses of the model in their courses, and providing one another with ideas. (The Peer Coaching Guides in the Appendix are designed to facilitate the sharing that we call "coaching.")

Continuous practice is essential to enable even *highly motivated* persons to bring additions to their repertoires under effective control.

To master a single teaching strategy, the Onyx team uses procedures that are much more complex and extensive than common staff-development procedures. Yet anything short of that effort will, for most people, fall short of its objective. Why is this so? We think the answer is in the nature of the process of transfer—of building competence in complex teaching skills to the point that they are incorporated into the teaching repertoire.

Horizontal and vertical transfer

Classically, *transfer* refers to the effect of learning one kind of material or skill, or the ability to learn something new. When practice of one kind of athletic skill increases ability to learn another, *transfer* is occurring. Teaching, by its nature, requires continuous adaptation; it demands new learning in order to solve the problems of each moment and situation. Teaching skills and strategies are designed to help teachers solve problems—to reach students more effectively. To master a new teaching strategy, a teacher needs first to develop *skill* in the strategy. This can be accomplished in a training setting, such as a workshop. Then, the teacher needs to acquire executive control over the strategy, including the ability to use it appropriately and to adapt it to the students and classroom setting. Sometimes the achievement of executive control requires extensive amounts of new learning that can only be accomplished through practice in the classroom. It is at this phase of the mastery of the new strategy that the distinction between horizontal and vertical transfer becomes important.

Horizontal transfer refers to conditions in which a skill can be shifted directly from the training situation in order to solve problems. *Vertical transfer* refers to conditions in which the new skill cannot be used to solve problems unless it is adapted to fit the conditions of the workplace—that is, an extension of learning is required *before* problems can be solved effectively. Vertical transfer is more likely when: the context of training and the conditions of the workplace are different, a given skill is different from one's existing repertoire and does not fit easily into it, or additional understanding is needed to achieve executive control over the skill.

When the work and training settings are virtually identical, a skill often can be transferred from the training setting to the workplace "as is," with little additional learning on the job (horizontal transfer). For example, carpenters who learn to use a handsaw in a woodshop can, on the job, recreate the conditions of the shop almost exactly and apply their skill very much as they learned it in the training setting. When a new technique is introduced, carpenters can add it to their repertoires without much additional learning. The chief problem is integrating the new skill into existing patterns of behavior. Vertical transfer, however, involves substantial differences in context so that new learning has to take place as the skill is transferred into the work situation. The additional learning has to occur in the work setting. In a real sense, one must repossess the skill in the work context.

The distinction between horizontal and vertical transfer refers to the amount of learning and repossession of the skill that is necessary if it is to be functional in the work situation. When the skill just "slides" from training place to workplace, we say that the process is horizontal. When additional learning is required to transfer the skill, we speak of the process as vertical.

An important factor is the degree to which the new skill disrupts existing patterns of performance. Familiarity is the key here. The greater the degree to which a new skill fits into already familiar patterns, the less adjustment is needed. For example, imagine a primary teacher who employs Cuisenaire rods to teach mathematics concepts and definitions and who organizes the students into small groups to work with the rods. If that teacher is then introduced to the use of the abacus, he or she will need much less adjustment than a teacher who never uses concrete aids. The nonuser will have fewer existing behaviors to draw on and may have to develop a new pattern of organization as well (such as organizing groups of students to use the new material). In other words, the second teacher will probably have more skills to develop and more adjustments to make in order to be able to use the skill effectively.

DEVELOPING EXECUTIVE CONTROL

The conditions of performance can be divided into two categories— those in which the circumstances of performance *demand* the utilization of the skills and those in which the skills are brought into play as a consequence of a judgment made by the performer. In military and industrial settings, considerable effort has been expended in the development of "standard operating procedures"—that is, sequences of skills that have been previously organized for each worker. For example, during the training of infantry platoons, procedures are developed for dispersing personnel, for organizing them to bring their fire to bear on given targets, for developing clear fields of fire, and for advancing on a target while keeping dispersed and under cover.

As much as possible, standard operating procedures include directions about when to bring to bear a cluster of relevant skills. In other words, a shifting and changing scene of events is reduced as much as possible to sets of operations that can be brought into play when the appropriate cues appear in the environment. General principles are formulated and taught so as to activate the skills. In training pilots, sets of skills are clustered around the elements of a flight plan and are brought to bear on demand. Entering the cockpit, the flight personnel know what to do to check out the equipment and instruments in the aircraft, communicate with the control tower, and leave the parking space. Another set of skills is brought into play to bring the aircraft to the edge of the runway, yet another to obtain clearance and propel the aircraft into flight. Other sets of closely monitored skills are brought to bear to carry out the flight plan and bring the aircraft to a safe landing.

The more closely the skills are identified and the principles governing their use defined, the less the employees are permitted to use their own discretion. For example, factory workers are frequently organized to the point where judgment is exercised as little as possible and breakdowns are referred to supervisory personnel.

Teaching personnel operate with relatively little surveillance and few standard operating procedures. For example, a teacher of English has considerable latitude about the literary works that will be studied, the concepts that will be emphasized, the relationship between the study of literature and the study of writing, the teaching strategies that will be used, and the methods of evaluation that will be exercised. As presently organized, the tasks of teaching are not composed, as are the tasks of factory workers, of sets of objective-related activities to be called up in sequence according to predetermined principles. Consequently, the content of teacher education cannot be organized just by referring to a set of standard operating procedures. When a teacher learns a range of teaching strategies and the appropriateness of those strategies to various kinds of objectives and students, the transfer of those skills into the workplace is largely under the governance of the individual teacher.

In the phases of work where competence is derived from one's judgment-controlled repertoire, the effective use of a skill depends on what we term "executive control." Executive control consists of understanding the purpose and rationale of the skill and knowing how to adapt it to students, apply it to subject matter, modify or create instructional materials attendant to its use, organize students to use it, and blend it with other instructional approaches to develop a smooth and powerful whole.

THE PROCESS OF COACHING

Setting up arrangements for the trainees to develop a self-help community to provide coaching is regarded as essential if transfer is to be achieved. Ideally, "coaching teams" are developed during training. If we had our way, *all* school faculties would be divided into coaching teams— that is, teams who regularly observe one another's teaching and learn from watching one another and the students. In short, we recommend the development of a "coaching environment" in which all personnel see themselves as one another's coaches.

What does the provision of coaching actually involve? We think it has three major functions:

1. Provision of companionship.
2. Analysis of application (extending executive control and attaining "deep" meaning).
3. Adaptation to the students.

PROVISION OF COMPANIONSHIP

The first function of coaching is to provide interchange with another adult human being over a difficult process. The coaching relationship results in the possibility of mutual reflection, the checking of perceptions, the sharing of frustrations and successes, and the informal thinking through of mutual problems. Two people watching each other try a new model of teaching for the first time will find much to talk about. Companionship provides reassurance that the problems are normal. Both find that their habitual and automatic teaching patterns create awkwardness when they practice the new procedures. Concentrating on unfamiliar moves and ideas, they forget essential little odds and ends. The companionship not only makes the training process technically easier, it enhances the quality of the experience. It is a lot more pleasurable to share a new thing than to do it in isolation. The lonely business of teaching has sorely lacked the companionship that we envision for our coaching teams.

As an aside, the chief benefit of observation accrues to the observer! The "coach" is the one doing the teaching!

ANALYSIS OF APPLICATION: EXTENDING EXECUTIVE CONTROL

Among the most important things one learns during the transfer period are when to use a new model appropriately and what will be achieved by doing so. Selecting the right occasions to use a teaching strategy is not as easy as it sounds. Nearly everyone needs help in learning to pick the right spots. Unfamiliar teaching processes also appear to have less certain outcomes than do the familiar ones. From the early trials, one often has the impression that one has "worked all day and not gotten very far." Most of us need help to find out how much we have, in fact, accomplished and how much we might accomplish by making adjustments in the way we are using the model. During training, the coaching teams need to spend a considerable amount of time examining curriculum materials and plans and practicing the application of the model they will be using later. Then, as the process of transfer begins, practice in the classroom is intensified with closer and closer attention given to appropriate use.

ADAPTATION TO THE STUDENTS

As we have already mentioned, much of the energy expended in learning to use a new model of teaching is consumed in the process of learning how to teach it to the children. Successful teaching requires successful student response. Teachers are familiar with the task of teaching students how to engage in common instructional activities. A model that is new to a group of students, however, will cause them trouble. *They* will need to learn new skills and to become acquainted with what is expected of them, how to fulfill the task demands of the new method, and how to gauge their own progress. In addition, the model of teaching needs to be adapted to fit different groups of students. More training must be provided for some, more structure for others, and so on. In the early stages, adaptation to the students is relatively difficult and usually requires a lot of direct assistance and companionship.

One of the major functions of the coach is to help the "players" to "read" the responses of the students so that the right decisions are made about what skill training is needed and how to adapt the model. This is especially important in the early stages of practice when one's hands are full managing one's own behavior and it is more difficult to worry about the students than it will be later on.

When practicing any new approach to teaching, one is surely less competent with it than with the approaches in one's existing repertoire. When trying a new model, nearly all of us fumble around. The students sense our uncertainty and let us know in not-so-subtle ways that they are *aware* we are less certain and sure-footed than usual. At such times, we tend to become easily discouraged. The expression, "I tried that method and it didn't work" refers as much to the sense of dismay we feel during the early trials as it does to the actual success or failure of the method itself.

The fact is, successful use of a new method requires practice. The early trials just are not perfect or even close to our normal standards of adequacy. One of the principal jobs of the coaching team, then, is to help its members feel good about themselves during the early trials.

Preservice teacher education is an ideal setting for the study-group relationship. Teacher candidates and cooperating teachers form natural coaching partnerships. Optimally, they study the same teaching and learning skills together, working together for support and sharing ideas.

LEARNING STYLES AND MODELS OF TEACHING
Making Discomfort Productive

In this chapter we deal explicitly with the relations between styles of learning and models of teaching. We present a general stance toward individual differences and how to teach students to learn productively from a variety of models.

Learning styles are important because they are the education-relevant expressions of the uniqueness of the individual. Individual differences are to be prized because they are the expression of the uniqueness of personalities. Individually, our configurations give us our personal identities; together, they also exemplify the richness of our society's culture.

We hope to provide our children with a common education that enhances their individuality and encourages their personalities and simultaneously passes along our culture and its tools. As teachers we need to use our teaching repertoires in such a way that we capitalize on the characteristics of our students to help them achieve increasing control over their own growth.

With respect to models of teaching, we can begin by avoiding two mistakes. The first is to assume that a model of teaching is a fixed, unadaptive formula for teaching, which should be employed rigidly for best results. The second is to assume that each learner has a fixed style of learning that is unlikely to change or grow. Both mistakes lead us into an impossible dilemma; for if unyielding teaching methods are mismatched with rigid learners, a destructive collision is inevitable. Fortunately, teaching methods have great flexibility, and students have great learning capacities and, hence, adaptability.

Consider the nature of the models of teaching we have been discussing. By its very nature, the personal family begins with the uniqueness of the learner and each personal model tries to help the students take charge of their own growth. The social models depend on the synergy caused by the interaction of heterogeneous minds and personalities. The group investigation model, for example, explicitly generates the energy for learning from different perceptions of academic and social problems. The behavioral models build into instructional sequences the ability to adjust pace and complexity of tasks to the ability and prior achievement of the student. The information-processing models provide ways of adjusting instruction to cognitive development and style.

Then—perhaps most important to this discussion—we not only employ a model to teach information, concepts, skills, the analysis of values, and other content objectives, but we also teach the students to use the strategies of each model to educate themselves. In the previous chapter we cast each model as a way of teaching students to learn particular ways of thinking. From that perspective, each model of teaching can be seen as a model of learning—a way of helping students expand their styles of approaching problems now and in their futures.

Yet, as we expose students to content and learning styles that are new to them, we will inevitably cause varying degrees of discomfort. We have to deal with this by teaching our students to manage discomfort productively. The real dilemma we have to solve is that real growth often requires us to make our learners uncomfortable, and we have to help them deal with the unfamiliar situations that we must create for them.

DISCOMFORT AND LEARNING

I would like to begin on a personal note (*I* refers to Bruce Joyce, who wrote this section) that explains why discomfort is so prominent in this discussion of learning styles and educational environments. At the University of Chicago, 20 years ago, I ended a conversation with Herbert Thelen by borrowing a copy of his *Education and the Human Quest* (1960); I spent much of the night reading the book. The next day we had a chance to talk again. Among the powerful ideas Thelen had generated, one left me most stimulated and uncomfortable: Significant learning is frequently accompanied or impelled by discomfort. Sometimes he put it pungently: "The learner does not learn unless he does not know how to respond" (Thelen, 1960, p. 61). Sometimes he put it in terms of the dynamics of the inquiry process in the approach to teaching he called "group investigation." Group investigation begins with a "stimulus situation to which students . . . can react and discover basic conflicts among their attitudes, ideas, and modes of perception" (Thelen, 1960, p. 8). Thelen challenges the effects of the "norms of comfort and accommodation" (Thelen, 1960, p. 80) that exist in so many classrooms and that mitigate against the abrasive argumentation and difficult, uncomfortable tasks that characterize effective instruction as he sees it.

My first reaction was confusion. Thelen's ideas appeared to conflict with what I had been taught regarding learners as fragile sets of concepts of self that had to be protected by a supportive environment, so that they would in fact feel *comfortable* enough to stretch out into the world. How can the learner be made comfortable and uncomfortable at the same time? I asked Thelen that question, and he only smiled and replied, "That is a puzzling situation you will have to think about."

Psychologists from otherwise different orientations have dealt with the concept of discomfort for some time, albeit not always using the term as such. Personalistic psychologists are an example. Interpreters of Carl Rogers frequently concentrate on his argument for providing a safe place for learners to explore themselves and their environments. However, Rogers also emphasizes that our natural tendency as learners is to confine ourselves to those domains in which we already feel safe. A major task of counselor/teachers is to help the learner reach into those domains that are shrouded in fear. To grow, learners have to acknowledge discomfort and set tasks to help break the barriers of fear. The educator's task is not simply to unloose the environmental bonds that constrict the learners but to help them become active seekers after new development (Rogers, 1951).

Self-actualization, as described by Maslow (1962), is a state that not only enables people to venture and take risks, but also to endure the inevitable discomfort felt when attempting to use skills foreign to customary practice. Maslow's constructs apply to adults as well as children. In a four-year study of teachers exposed to a wide variety of staff-development activities, it appeared that the teachers' self-concepts were important predictors of their abilities to use new skills and knowledge in their classroom situations (McKibbin and Joyce, 1980).

The role of discomfort and the ability to manage it productively appears in a different guise when we consider developmental stage theories (see Erikson, 1950; Harvey, Hunt, and Schroder, 1961; Piaget, 1952). Most developmental stage theories emphasize not only the naturalness of growth through the stages, but the possibility of arrestation, and the accommodation that is necessary if higher levels of development are to be reached. Consider Piaget: Interpreters of Piaget are often most impressed by the naturalness of growth described from his stance—the position that the assimilation of new information will inevitably force the accommodations that lead to the successive of stages of development. However, not everyone makes it upward through the Piagetian stages. Arrestation is possible. Accommodation sufficient to bring about the reconfiguration necessary to a new stage requires a "letting go" of the confines of one level so that the essentials of the next level can be reached. If the comfort of any given level of development is not challenged, the learner may happily forgo the important leaps in cognitive structure.

In conceptual systems theory, Hunt (1971) stresses the relationship of the environment to development. He describes stages of development and the characteristics of environments that permit people to function effectively at each stage while progression to the next stage is facilitated. The next chapter presents synopses of the stages and environments that facilitate progression.

If the environment is perfectly matched to the developmental level of the learners, the learners are likely to be arrested at that level. The very language that Hunt and his colleagues use is provocative. If the environment is too comfortable or "reliable," the learners may be satisfied at the stage of concrete thinking, where the ability to integrate new information and form new conceptual systems is limited indeed. To impel learners to diverge from the familiar sets of concepts that enable them to view the world in "black and white," the environment must be dissatisfying in some ways. Although he approaches development from a very different perspective from Thelen, Hunt (1971) states explicitly that discomfort is a precursor to growth. To stimulate development, we *deliberately* mismatch student and environment so that the student cannot easily maintain the familiar patterns but must move on toward greater complexity. (But not too much so, for we seek an optimal mismatch where the learner's conceptual systems are challenged but not overwhelmed.)

Research on teacher training has repeatedly uncovered a "discomfort factor" as teachers acquire new repertoires. Between 1968 and 1983 a series of investigations inquired into teachers' abilities to acquire the skills necessary to enable them to use widespread repertoires of teaching strategies (Joyce, Peck, and Brown, 1981; Joyce and Showers, 1981). Teachers could acquire skill by studying the theories of various models of teaching or skills, seeing them demonstrated a number of times (15 or 20, the researchers came to believe), and practicing them about a dozen times with carefully articulated feedback. However, as teachers attempted to use approaches new to them they experienced considerable discomfort. Only a small percentage (about 5 or 10 percent) of the teachers who had learned teaching strategies new to their repertoires were able to handle the discomfort without assistance. Most teachers never tried an unfamiliar strategy at all unless support personnel were available to them. Even then, during the first half-dozen trials, most teachers found the use of the new teaching strategies, whatever they were, to be extremely uncomfortable. The explanation was that the discomfort resulted in part because the teachers needed to adapt other, well-ingrained skills in order to use the new strategies; in part because students exposed to the new strategies needed to learn complementary skills so they could relate to them; and in part because the teachers felt less confident with any new strategy than they felt with their older repertoires.

The result was that many teachers would have withdrawn from the use of strategies new to them, even after their training had enabled them to produce these strategies with relative ease. However, after a number of trials with the new strategies, they became more comfortable with and developed power in their use. A major function of peer study groups is to provide the support necessary to work through the period of discomfort. Conceptual level (CL) is a predictor of the ability to acquire new repertoires. The higher-CL teachers mastered sets of new models more fully and also tended to use them more (Joyce, Weil, and Wald, 1981). The relationship between conceptual level and the ability to learn new teaching strategies is partly related to how one manages feelings of discomfort attendant to learning the new repertoire. The more conceptually flexible teachers managed the process of discomfort more effectively. They incorporated the new information from their students, accommodated the discomfort of their students, and—most important—learned how to live through their periods of learning until the new teaching strategies worked in their classrooms.

It also became apparent that a critical part of a teacher's task in learning to use a new teaching strategy has to do with helping the learners acquire the skills necessary to relate to the new approach to teaching. Hunt and his associates initiated a series of studies to investigate the process by which learners respond to unfamiliar teaching strategies (Hunt, Joyce, Greenwood, Noy, Reid and Weil, 1981). These researchers identified students of varying conceptual levels and exposed them to teaching strategies that were matched and mismatched to their levels of development. Nearly all learners were able to respond to a wide variety of teaching strategies, but there were considerable individual differences in their responses. Students with a high need for structure (low CL) were more uncomfortable with teaching strategies that provided low degrees of structure, whereas learners who preferred independent direction were more uncomfortable with teaching strategies that provided higher structure.

Moreover, the students "pulled" the behavior of the teachers toward their preferred styles. Those who required the higher degrees of structure "asked" for that structure, and the teachers responded by adapting the strategies to conform to the personalities of the students. Curiously, the more a given model of teaching was mismatched with the natural learning style of the student, the more it presented a challenge to the student to take an affirmative stance so as to pass through the period of discomfort and develop skills that would permit a productive relationship with the learning environment.

For example, gregarious students are initially the most comfortable with social models and can profit from them quickly. However, the less gregarious students were in the greatest need of the models least comfortable for them. Hence, the challenge is not to select the most comfortable models but to enable the students to develop the skills to relate to a wider variety of models, many of which appear, at least superficially, to be mismatched with their learning styles.

The formulation gradually developed that significant growth requires discomfort. If the environment and the student are too much in harmony, the student is permitted to operate at a level of comfort that does not require the challenge of growth. To help students grow we need to generate what we currently term a "dynamic disequilibrium." Rather than matching teaching approaches to students in such a way as to minimize discomfort, our task is to expose the students to new teaching modalities that will, for some time, be uncomfortable to them.

Marginality in Learners

Most of the literature about learners and educational environments emphasizes explicit matching, the adjustment of environments to the optimal "comfort level" of the students. The comfort-level matching concept appears frequently in most discussions of learning styles (hemispheric dominance, sensing modalities, cognitive levels, etc.). To consider the productive possibilities of discomfort, let us now discuss the "marginal" learners—students who experience great discomfort in the environments in which they find themselves.

Currently many educators are concerned with what are called "marginal" learners and are seeking ways to make the school environment more productive for the people who are regarded as marginal in the environment. If we consider the concept of marginality, we can join the issues of discomfort and growth directly. When learners relate only marginally to educational environments, we tend to change the environments and reestablish the "norms of comfort." In fact, the discomfort they feel may be a clue to how we should behave to help them reach new plateaus of growth.

Marginality is a condition that exists when a learner has difficulty relating to an educational environment and profiting from it. Learners may relate marginally to some environments but not others. The theoretically possible range of marginality is from *none* (when the learner relates productively to all of the environments to which he or she is exposed) to *all* (when the learner experiences virtually no environments that are productive for him or her). Educators create environments, but they clearly cannot do the learning—which is why the condition of the learner accounts for so much of the variance when we consider the productivity of any given environment. If the learner is marginal with respect to a particular environment, then educational productivity for that learner is likely to be depressed; worse, if the marginality is acute, serious side effects are likely to occur. The learner becomes frustrated and, very likely, "learns" that he or she cannot be productive in that environment. If the learner generalizes from enough frustrating experiences, a likely derivative lesson may be that the process of education is hopeless (from the perspective of that particular person).

ASSUMPTIONS ABOUT LEARNERS

ENCULTURATION

The first assumption is that our learner has been enculturated to a certain degree, having been exposed to the behavior patterns, artifacts, and cognitions that make up American culture. The learner may (or may not) have a smaller vocabulary than the average person but does possess a vocabulary, has internalized the basic linguistic properties of our language, has been a participant in the cultural process, and has been an observer of adults as they behave in our society. In other words, our learner is not culturally different from the rest of us, although, within the cultural boundaries, the learner may be relatively unsophisticated. This may seem like an obvious point, but much language about marginal learners connotes, if it does not actually denote, that the people who relate marginally to the common educational environments are essentially members of a subculture so different from the mainstream that they have to be treated as foreigners. That is rare indeed. Human beings are born with the capacity to learn a culture, and it is the rare person who develops cultural patterns that do not in some way match the major configurations of his or her society.

INTELLECTUAL CAPACITY AS A TEMPORAL FACTOR

Second, the position about intellectual differences articulated by Carroll (1971) and Bloom (1971) has considerable validity. Specifically, this position is that differences in intellectual ability as we currently measure them translate substantially into temporal differences with respect to the mastery of particular learning objectives. This second assumption relates to the first, for one way of restating Carroll and Bloom's position is that the less "intelligent" learner is not culturally different with respect to what can be learned but may require more time, perhaps *considerably* more time, to acquire a particular cognition that resides within the culture. In other words, the learner is one of us. Some of us are slower than others to acquire some of the elements of the culture in given educational situations. We can make the optimistic assumption that our marginal learner is capable of learning but may require more time than some people do, given the situation.

STIGMATIZATION

A third assumption is that the inability to relate to a given educational environment productively has social stigma attached to it. The learner who does not fit in will be socially stigmatized by other people and, probably more damaging, will internalize the norms of the culture; failing to fit in with these norms, the learner will stigmatize him- or herself. Education, as manifested in formal institutions, is largely a public activity, and the full power of the society comes down on the learner when a marginal condition exists—hence, the latent side effects. The marginal learner is punished twice; first by being frustrated, and second by being stigmatized by others (or by self-stigmatization).

LEARNERS ARE FLEXIBLE

A final assumption about learners is that learners are flexible. They are not fixed, but they are growing entities and have considerable adaptive capabilities. Nearly all learners have the potential to relate to a wide variety of learning environments, provided they are not made *too* uncomfortable and that they are assisted in relating productively to any given environment.

ASSUMPTIONS ABOUT LEARNING ENVIRONMENTS

ENVIRONMENTS AS WITHIN-CULTURE VARIATIONS

Learning environments, viewed from a cultural perspective, are variations on our basic cultural theme. That is, all of the approaches to teaching that have dominated our literature for the last 25 years have had their origins in Western societies. They belong well within the cultural mainstream. Put another way, all of our models of teaching represent variety within the culture, but they are not culturally different. They have originated with scholars and teachers who belong not only to the same genus and species but to the same normative configuration. Thus, both teaching models and learners have the same cultural roots.

INDIVIDUATION AND ENVIRONMENTS

Every learning environment produces a range of responses by students, expressed in terms of the efficiency and comfort with which the learners are able to interact with the environment. Loosely speaking, we can say that learning styles and environments designed to produce learning will interact differentially. No given learning environment will produce exactly the same effects on all students.

ENVIRONMENTS CAN BE ADAPTIVE

Learning environments can be adaptive, potentially at least, if we design them with flexibility in mind. An appropriate model of teaching does not simply bore into the learner in an unyielding and unforgiving fashion. Properly constructed, a learning environment fits soft rather than hard metaphors. It curls around the students, conforming to their characteristics just as, properly treated, learners also better fit soft rather than hard metaphors and can curl around the features of the learning environment.

ALTERNATIVE ENVIRONMENTS AND EDUCATIONAL OUTCOMES

Finally, there exist a good number of approaches to teaching (the construction of learning environments) that are likely to produce different effects on learners. Certain approaches to teaching increase the probability that certain kinds of learning outcomes will eventuate and, probably reciprocally, decrease the probability that others will happen. For example, contrast the role-playing model with the inquiry training model. Shaftel's model of role playing (Shaftel and Shaftel, 1967) is designed to enable students' values to become available for examination by those students. Suchman's (1962) model of inquiry training is designed to increase the probability that students will build capability to make causal inferences. As such, all things being equal, if Shaftel's model is used to design a learning environment, it will increase the probability that students' social values will be made available to them. Suchman's model will increase the probability that the students will become more able to reason causally. We are not dealing with an orthogonal world, however. The examination of values *can* improve causal reasoning, and, vigorously conducted, *ought* to do so. Similarly, there is no law that dictates that Suchman's model cannot be used to increase the ability to reason causally about values. At any given moment it is conceivable that Shaftel's model might be more effective in teaching causal reasoning than Suchman's or that Suchman's might be more effective as an approach to social values. Over the long term, however, each model is more likely to pay off in the direction for which it was designed. Thus, it is wise for educators to have in their repertoires the models of choice for given learning objectives.

DEALING WITH MARGINALITY

Returning now to marginal learners, our problem is to consider what to do when a learner has a marginal reaction to any given learning environment. To keep the discussion within some kind of boundaries, let us imagine two learners who are exposed to Shaftel's and Suchman's models. Each learner responds positively to one environment and not to the other. What do we do?

In this example, both learners are marginal in one environment but not in the other. We can predict that one will engage in the study of values in a relatively comfortable way and that the other will increase the capability to engage in causal reasoning. If we do nothing, the differences between the two learners will probably increase. One will get better and better at the study of values and the other better and better in reasoning ability.

For the time being, let us put aside the question of explanation—that is, let us not begin by sorting out the reasons *why* each learner responds to one environment and not to the other; instead, let us concentrate on what we can do.

SOLUTIONS FOR CORRECTING MARGINALITY

First, we reject the "do-nothing" approach. We do not want to leave either of our learners in an unproductive, frustrating, and, perhaps, phobia-producing situation. A second approach is to remove the learner from the offending environment, thus eliminating the frustration. For each learner we identify the models of comfort. For each learner we eliminate the models of discomfort and choose the ones of greatest comfort. On the positive side, enough models of teaching exist that we can be relatively sure that almost any learner can relate productively to some of them. In our example we already have an initial diagnosis.

THE INDUSTRIAL SOLUTION

In what Hunt (1971) calls the "industrial" solution, we search for the approaches to teaching in which our learners are least marginal, and then we employ them. This approach makes a certain amount of pragmatic sense. Its obvious difficulty is that it eliminates for certain learners the instructional models of choice for the achievement of various kinds of objectives. Consider the case of our two learners. Since Shaftel's model is elegantly constructed to promote the study of values, eliminating it for the learner who is marginal in it means that we are going to have to use a model less elegantly appropriate for the study of values. For any given learner that might be only a moderate loss of efficiency, but if we consider large numbers of learners over a long period of time, the industrial solution has a built-in deficit.

However, this is certainly a more efficient solution than ignoring the problem. It also reduces the likelihood that the most damaging side effects of mismatching will occur. The success of the industrial model depends on the assumption that we can find enough industrial models that accommodate both our students and our objectives.

ADAPTATION OF THE MODELS OF CHOICE

Another solution is to adapt the models to conform to the characteristics of the learners. We identify the reasons why a given learner has trouble relating to a particular learning environment and then modulate the features of that environment to make it easier for the learner to fit in. For example, suppose that we are using inquiry training in elementary science. It is possible that our learner who is not comfortable with the model may be reacting to the ambiguity of inductive reasoning. Our learner may like a direct route to the correct answer and may be uncomfortable asking questions that may be wrong and that, surely, do not provide quick resolution. We could moderate the task complexity of the inquiry training exercises by providing puzzlements for which there are plainly only two or three possible avenues of inquiry and to which the learner can bring considerable knowledge.

Our learner who has trouble relating to role playing may be somewhat embarrassed during the enactments of the puzzling situations, may have difficulty taking the role of the "other," or may find the discussion of values to be uncomfortable. To compensate we can guide the enactments to make them relatively simple and straightforward, or we can provide practice in the skills necessary to analyze values. Hunt (1971) has pointed out that if we "drill" a model "through" the learner we exacerbate our problem. If we take the trouble to find out what is bothering the learner, we have many options for modifying the environment. We can increase the structure of unstructured models, decrease the structure of highly structured ones, modulate the degree of learner control, manipulate task complexity, and in other ways make the learning environment a safe one for the person who would otherwise be marginal in it.

The merits of this solution are that it permits us to continue to use the "models of choice" for given objectives—that is, the ones likely to produce certain kinds of learning—and that it reduces the likelihood that the student will be acutely uncomfortable. It depends on the assumption that the natural mismatch between the learner and the model is not too great to overcome. Because learners are members of the same culture from which the models of teaching came, we can have some confidence that they will bring some developed tools to the environment. Relatively few learners lack the capacity to function within a fairly wide range of models.

Much research is needed in this area. We need to study how to adapt a wide spectrum of models to learners who, on first contact with them, display varying degrees of marginality. Without such knowledge, we are left with uncertainty about how far we can go. One of the major findings of the match-mismatch studies mentioned earlier was the extent to which the students exerted modifying influences on the environment. Students who needed more structure asked more questions about procedures and literally forced instructors to provide them with more explicit information about what they were doing, even in the open-ended models. They required teachers to interrupt themselves periodically and to re-explain what was going on. They made teachers break up the model into bite-sized chunks that better fit their intellectual mouths. Other learners vied for control of the procedures, lowering the degree of imposed structure and actually increasing the amount of ambiguity in task complexity. I was the teacher in some of these studies, and I came away from that work with the feeling that many learners will help us out if we let them. They would like to have a productive learning environment and will work with us to adapt the environment if we will give them the opportunity.

LEARNER FLEXIBILITY TRAINING

A third solution for correcting marginality is to attempt to teach the learners to relate to a wide spectrum of learning environments. Maintaining our earlier example, we teach one learner the skills necessary to relate to inquiry training. Again, Hunt's (1971) experiments with direct model-relevant skills training have contributed significantly to our knowledge in this area. To provide skill training requires diagnosing what it is about the learner that makes for a marginal relationship to the instructional model. This training is provided to help that learner become more powerful in that kind of environment. Some of the recent studies in teacher training are instructive on this point. The more a model of teaching is different from the developed and customary teaching style of given teachers, the more uncomfortable they are when beginning to use it. Practice with the model combined with model-relevant skill training appears to make a difference. As we coach teachers who are trying to learn a new model, they identify the particular areas where they are having difficulty, and we provide direct training adapted to their particular learning problems (Showers, 1982a).

We need to learn much about helping learners develop environment-relevant skills. It is interesting to observe students in schools that have distinctive approaches to learning and that pay attention to helping their learners become effective in the environments they are creating. Schools that emphasize self-directed activity need to teach students how to engage in self-direction. Learning laboratories with highly sequenced activities need to help students learn to receive diagnoses and prescriptions and relate to those highly sequenced activities. Again, some of my own clinical experience is relevant. When I was the director of the laboratory at Teachers College, Columbia University, we built a set of learning centers that operated on very different models, and the students contracted for activities within those centers. We became convinced that nearly all of our learners were increasing their capabilities to learn in a variety of ways and that they adapted their learning styles to the requirements of the different centers to which they were exposed (Joyce and Morine, 1977).

If we take the skill-training approach seriously, then we devote substantial energy to teaching students to relate to an appropriate variety of learning environments. We help them master the skills of learning that will enable them to master facts, concepts, and skills, and to solve problems collectively. We include the skills of learning as basic skills in the curriculum, and we measure our success as teachers partly by our abilities to help the students become more effective as learners.

From this perspective, we see individual differences in relating to learning environments in a fresh light. When a learner is uncomfortable with a particular learning environment, we know we have identified an objective—to help the learner become competent to relate to that environment. Rather than giving up, we proceed to give that learner protected practice and the special help necessary for a productive relationship to develop between learner and environment. Thus, our learner who has trouble relating to role playing is not viewed as being immutably unable to study values using that technique but as someone who, through practice, can develop competence. We also modify pace, using Carroll's (1971) and Bloom's (1971) formulations as a heuristic. We assume that all learners can become able to profit from a variety of environments but that some need more time than others to become productive in specific environments. One reason learners become marginal is because they are asked to work at a faster pace than will permit them mastery of the environment. Even though most of the applications of mastery learning have been within the basic skill areas of the elementary school, we suggest that the principles would apply to the ability to master all manner of learning objectives. Hence, some learners will be slower profiting from a Rogerian environment. Others will be slower working their way through the models that are appropriate to divergent thinking. Others will be slower attaining concepts with the models appropriate to concept learning.

There are no special models for marginal learners. All learners are part of this culture and practically all can learn to relate to a considerable array of environments, provided that the environments are adapted to the learners' characteristics and that we pay attention to teaching them how to learn more effectively. Experience with persons with very severe sensory handicaps provides us with a case in point. From a models-of-teaching point of view, there are no special models for the blind or the deaf. They can learn to relate to a great variety of environments and, more importantly, to profit from them. To fail to help them do this productively is to deny them opportunities for growth in many areas. Learning to relate to an increasing variety of environments is, in itself, growth. That kind of growth leads to a pyramiding array of possibilities for more learning.

THE INTELLIGENCE OF GROWTH

Our nature as learners contains an interesting contradiction: Important growth requires change. We have to give up our comfortable ways of thinking and survive the buffets of taking on unfamiliar ideas, skills, and values. The need to grow is built into the fiber of our being. We are impelled upward in a developmental sense. Paradoxically, however, we have an ingrained tendency to conserve our beings as they are or were. Nostalgia is, in fact, a yearning not to have grown or changed. We would like to go on and see things the way we could when we were young and untutored. Curiously, the answer is to produce disequilibrium—to create environments that impel us to change, not discarding what we were at any given stage, but learning to build on it productively. Thelen's advice to us is correct: The learner needs to confront problems and diverse opinions in order to reach beyond the present stage and develop the constructs that will sustain growth at another level.

When we are infants, the process of change is built into us. We do not intend to learn language but we do so, and in so doing we change. We do not expect to walk, but walking leads us where we could not go before. Not very many years later we learn our culture and begin to function at a level so satisfying that we can stay there forever. The purpose of education is to generate the conditions that will enable us to acknowledge the disequilibrium of change as a fundamental of the continuance of growth, so that we can reach beyond ourselves toward richer understanding and accept the wisdom that lies within ourselves—that discomfort is our lot if we are not to be arrested along our road.

APPENDIX

PEER COACHING GUIDES

The following pages contain peer coaching guides for eight of the most commonly used and applicable models of teaching. These forms facilitate planning and communication between members of study groups who observe one another and try to profit from the observational experience.

The forms can also be used to facilitate sharing of ideas by study group members whether or not observation of one anothers' teaching is included.

Hence, they are addressed to both parties in the peer coaching process: the teacher who is planning and directing the teaching episode and the partner who is operating as a peer coach. Both parties are involved in a continuing experiment on teaching. Even has the same purpose, which is to increase their ability to analyze the transactions between teacher and student, and their ability to teach students how to learn information and concepts. The guide is used both to assist the planning of the teaching episode and in focusing the observation on key features of the model. The teacher prepares the observer by filling out the entries where indicated. The observer fills in the observation checklist and communicates the result to the teacher. Both parties will profit most by making a partnership that studies the student responses and plans how to help the students learn more effectively. The observer is *not* present to advise the teacher on how to teach better but, rather, to learn by observing and help the teacher by providing information about the students' responses.

The communication of the analysis should be conducted in a neutral tone, proceeding matter-of-factly through the phases of the model. The guide draws attention to the syntax of the model—the cognitive and social tasks that are presented to the students and how the students respond, and the principles of reaction—the guidelines for reacting to the students as they try to attain the concept. The teacher may want to orient the coaching partner to look closely at a specific phase of the model, such as student response to a particular cognitive or social task, or reactions to student responses. The coaching partner should avoid giving gratuitous advice. Normally, the communications should be completed in five minutes or less. For self-coaching, teachers should use videotape when possible and, during playback, enter the role of coaching partner, analyzing the transactions as dispassionately as possible.

Peer Coaching Guide: Advance Organizer

Teacher: Do you want to suggest a focus for the analysis? If so, what is it?

_____

_____

THE TEACHING PROCESS

Most teaching episodes have both content and process objectives. The content objectives include the information, concepts, theories, ways of thinking, values, and other substance that the students can be expected to learn from the experience that results. The process objectives are the ways of learning—the conduct of the social and intellectual tasks that increase the power to learn. In the case of a model of teaching, the process objectives are those that enable the students to engage effectively in the tasks presented when the model is being used.

CONTENT OBJECTIVES

Teacher: Please state the concepts and information that are the primary objectives of this teaching episode. What kind of information will be presented to the student? What concepts will be presented to organize the information? Are the concepts or information new to the students?

_____

_____

PROCESS OBJECTIVES

Teacher: Please state any process objectives that are of concern during this episode. For example, are you trying to help the students learn how to comprehend and use organizers, how to relate material to the conceptual structure, how to tie new material to the organizers, how to apply what is learned to new information and skills?

_____

_____

_____

_____

Observer: Please comment on the students' familiarity with the model, referring especially to any of the process objectives mentioned above.

PHASE ONE: PRESENTATION OF THE ORGANIZER

The key aspect of the model is the use of organizing ideas to induce students to operate conceptually on the material they are trying to master. The teacher organizes the material with an "intellectual scaffolding" of concepts and presents those concepts to the students so that they can relate the new information to it—or reorganize familiar information within a more powerful conceptual framework. While even the careful organization of information under a series of topics facilitates learning, we attempt to formulate organizing concepts that are at a higher conceptual level, so that they cause the students to process the information beyond associating it with a topic and to think about the material at a more complex level than they would operate spontaneously.

Phase One is the presentation of the organizer.

Teacher: Please describe the organizer, or system of organizers, stating it (them) if that is practical. Discuss how it (they) will help the student conceptualize the material. How will you present the organizer(s)?

Observer: Please comment on the students' response to the organizer(s). Did they appear to absorb it (them)? Did they appear to understand how organizers are to function and that their task is to learn new material and relate it to the organizer(s)?

PHASE TWO: PRESENTING INFORMATION

The purpose of the model, of course, is to facilitate the learning of material at any level of abstraction: data, concepts, theories, systems of thought—all the possibilities are there. The device is to place the student in the role of active receiver, getting information by reading, watching, or scrabbling around for information from formal resources or the environment. The information can be presented through readings, lectures, films or tapes, or any other mediated form or combination of forms.

Teacher: Please describe the content that will be presented and how it will be presented. Emphasize the content you most want to be retained and how you want it to be applied in the future.

_____

_____

_____

_____

Observer: Please comment on the student responses. Are the students clear about what they are to learn? Is it clear to you (thinking from the point of view of the students) how the organizer(s) may function in relation to the material?

_____

_____

PHASE THREE: CONNECTING THE ORGANIZER TO THE PRESENTATION

The conceptual structure defined by the organizers needs to be integrated with the information that has been presented and also reconciled with the students' personal intellectual structures. While the students, with practice, will accomplish most of these tasks by themselves, it is wise to provide activities that make the relationship between concepts and material explicit and which provide the students with an opportunity to reflect on the organizing structure.

For example, we can illustrate the connection between one of the organizers and some aspect of the information and induce the students to suggest further associations and relationships. Or we can ask the students to reformulate the organizers in their own terms and indicate relationships between them and aspects of the material.

Teacher: How will you make a presentation or provide a task to increase the possibility of the integration of the organizing structure with the students' conceptual structure and also make clear the connection between organizer and the material that has been presented?

_____

_____

_____

_____

Observer: Please comment on this phase. Do the students appear to be clear about the organizing structure and its relation to the material to be learned?

_____

_____

_____

_____

PHASE FOUR: APPLICATION

Sometimes information is presented to students as a precursor to learning a skill (we may teach musical notation to facilitate learning to sing) and sometimes to assist in solving problems (knowledge of mechanics may be applied to problems requiring leverage). We also apply what is learned in subsequent learning tasks (the general concept of *equation* is useful in mastering many mathematical topics).

Teacher: Do you wish to provide an explicit application task at this point? If so, please describe it briefly.

_____

_____

_____

_____

Observer: If an application task is presented, please comment on the students' ability to make the transfer to the new material.

_____

_____

_____

_____

Peer Coaching Guide: Cooperative Learning Organization

Unlike the other guides in this series, this form to assist in the planning and observation of teaching is not built around a model of teaching. The substance is the organization of students into study groups and partnerships. It does not deal with the specific cooperative learning strategies developed by Robert Slavin and his associates (Slavin, 1983) or Roger Johnson and David Johnson (1975), although the philosophy of the approach is similar. Nor does it deal with group investigation (Sharan and Hertz-Lazarowitz, 1980; Thelen, 1960) the major democratic-process strategy that is covered in another guide.

Rather, cooperative learning organization provides a setting for cooperative study that can be employed in combination with many approaches to teaching.

This guide describes some options and asks the teacher to select from them or to generate others. The observer analyzes the students' productivity and attempts to identify ways of helping the students engage in more productive behavior. The examples provided below are in reference to the inductive model of teaching. Using the two guides simultaneously may be useful.

When other models are used, analogous use can be made of cooperative learning.

OPTIONS FOR ORGANIZATION

Essentially, we want to organize the students so that everyone in the class has a partner with whom they can work on instructional tasks. For example, pairs of students can operate throughout the inductive model, collecting information, developing categories, and making inferences about causal relationships. The partnerships (which need not be long-term, although they can be) are collected into teams. For example, if there are 30 students in the class, there can be five teams of six. We do not recommend teams larger than six. These teams can also operate throughout the inductive model, collecting and organizing data and making inferences. The partnerships provide an easy organization through which teams can divide labor. For example, each partnership can collect information from certain sources and then the information can be accumulated into a data set for the team. Similarly, team sets can be accumulated into a class set of data. Teams can then operate on these data sets and compare and contrast the results with those of other teams.

Team membership and partnerships can be organized in a number of ways, ranging from student selection, random selection, or teacher-guided choices to maximize heterogeneity and potential synergy.

Instruction of teams can range from explicit procedures to guide them through the learning activities to general procedures that leave much of the organization to the students.

ORGANIZATION

Teacher: How will you organize the class for this teaching episode? How many groups of what sizes will be selected?

_____

_____

_____

How will memberships be determined?

_____

_____

_____

What approach to teaching/learning will be used? If you are not using a specific model of teaching, what will be your instructional strategy?

_____

_____

_____

How will cooperative groups be used throughout the teaching episode? What cooperative tasks will be given to pairs, study groups, or the whole class? For example, if this were an inductive lesson, partnerships might collect data, classify it, and make inferences. Or, partnerships might collect data, but it might be assembled by the entire class prior to the classification activity. Partnerships might study words, poems, maps, number facts and operations, or other material. What is your plan?

_____

_____

_____

Observer: After you have familiarized yourself with the plan, situate yourself in the room so that you can observe about six students closely. Throughout the teaching episode, concentrate on the behavior of those students, whether they are working in partnerships, study groups, or any other organization. Then comment on their performance.

Did they appear to be clear about the tasks they were to accomplish? If not, can you identify what they were not clear about?

_____

_____

_____

Did they appear to know how to cooperate to accomplish the tasks assigned to them? Is there anything they appear to need to know in order to be more productive?

_____

_____

_____

Do they regulate their own behavior, keeping on task, dividing labor, taking turns? Could they profit from having any aspect of group management modeled for them?

_____

_____

_____

What sort of leadership patterns did they employ? Did they acknowledge one or more leaders? Did they discuss process? Were they respectful to one another?

_____

_____

_____

_____

_____

DISCUSSION

Following the episode, discuss the operation of the groups in which the six students were members. Is their productivity satisfactory? Their relationships? If not, see if you can develop a plan for helping the students become more productive. Remember that:

1. Providing practice is the simplest and most powerful way to help students learn to work productively. This is especially true if they have not had much experience working in cooperative groups.

2. The smaller the group, the more easily students can regulate their own behavior. Reducing the size of study groups often allows students to solve their own problems.

3. Demonstration gets more mileage than exhortation. A teacher can join a group and *show* the students how to work together. In fact, the observer can be a participant in a study group in future sessions.

4. Simpler tasks are easier for students to manage. Breaking complex tasks into several smaller ones often allows students to build their skills through practice.

5. Praising appropriate behavior gets results. If two groups are performing at different levels, it often helps to praise the productive group and then quietly join the less productive one and provide leadership.

Peer Coaching Guide: Jurisprudential Model

The analysis of a jurisprudential case generally takes several class sessions, which often means that the observers will be present for only one or two phases and will have to be briefed about events that occurred during their absence. The process of teaching/learning should not be rushed in an attempt to crowd it into one or two class periods.

Teacher: Do you want to suggest a focus for the analysis? If so, what is it?

_____

_____

THE TEACHING PROCESS

Most teaching episodes have both content and process objectives. The content objectives include the information, concepts, theories, ways of thinking, values, and other substance that the students can be expected to learn from the experience that results. The process objectives are the ways of learning—the conduct of the social and intellectual tasks that increase the power to learn. In the case of a model of teaching, the process objectives are those that enable the students to engage effectively in the tasks presented when the model is being used.

CONTENT OBJECTIVE(S)

Teacher: Please describe the outcomes that have the highest priority. The variety that can be encompassed by the jurisprudential model is considerable, so priority is important. Included are information about the cases to be studied, concepts about the cases, issues, values, and policies.

_____

_____

_____

_____

PROCESS OBJECTIVE(S)

Teacher: Please describe the most important process objectives. This is a model with tasks that have both complex and social dimensions. Will some aspect of the process receive special attention during this episode?

_____

_____

_____

_____

Observer: As the episode progresses, observe the student performance, especially attending to the goals described above. Because the tasks are so complex, it is probably wise to concentrate on just one or two aspects of process for comment.

_____

_____

_____

_____

PHASE ONE: OPENING UP THE ISSUES

Generally, the model is oriented around situations that involve public policy issues. Information about these situations is usually collected in case studies describing circumstances and events. The issues involve dilemmas because there are competing values and interests that need to be reconciled. The core of the model is the identification of those values and interests and the formulation and analysis of policies that could be pursued to deal with the issues.

In phase one the students are presented with the initial case that embodies the issues. Some cases involve lengthy reading and study, even to achieve enough clarity to see what the issues are. Usually, however, a situation that highlights the issues can be presented to the students.

Teacher: Please describe the case briefly. How will you present it to the students? Will you use an enactment of a situation, describe an event or conversation, present readings?

_____

_____

_____

The situation or case is discussed by the students, who are led to identify the problems or dilemmas that inhere in the situation. At this point no attempt is made to press toward conclusions of any kind. Student opinions are identified and respected, but the strongly expressed and mildly put ideas are recorded equally for later further consideration.

Observer: Please comment on the students' reception of the case and their analysis of the problems embodied by it. Are they initiating the inquiry in a cooperative manner? Do they appear to distinguish facts from issues?

_____

_____

_____

_____

_____

PHASE TWO: ISSUES, OPTIONS, AND VALUES

The next step is to bring order to the list of issues and questions that have arisen. Typically, the initial exploration of a problem elicits combinations of statements identifying issues (conflicts of interest or values), assertions of value positions (an assertion of a value that can justify why a certain course of action should be taken), and facts or questions about facts. These need to be sorted out and labeled as issues and values.

Teacher: Please discuss how you will help the students organize the material thus far generated.

_____

_____

_____

_____

Observer: Please comment on the student response. Are they able to distinguish facts, values, issues? Can they tell where they are making assumptions and where they have sufficient information? Until students can employ the model skillfully, they will respond with a melange of opinions, assertions about values, and so on. This is to be expected, but must be noted because it gives cues about how to help them develop more skill.

_____

_____

_____

_____

A decision needs to be made now about whether the students need more information about the case before they can proceed to engage in an analysis of value alternatives. If more information is needed, then it should be provided, or the students should be organized to find it. The observer wants to watch carefully to judge whether the students know enough to proceed. The teacher may decide to provide more information or have students engage in research.

PRELIMINARY IDENTIFICATION OF VALUE POSITIONS

The discussion should now proceed to an identification of the values that are involved. The heart of the dilemma is the difficulty of finding an easy solution that accommodates more than one value. Hence, the students should make an exhaustive list of the values that are represented in the situation. They may work as individuals, small groups, or as an entirety to perform the analysis.

Teacher: How will you have the students work to perform the analysis (individuals, groups, etc.)? What instruction will you give them?

_____

_____

_____

_____

Observer: Please comment on the students' analysis of the situation. Are they able to distinguish between issues and values and to identify the values that are potentially in conflict in the situation?

_____

_____

_____

_____

FOCUSING ON AN ISSUE

Because even the simpler cases generally involve a number of potential issues, it is wise to have the students select a particular issue for the initial focus of the further dialogue, although others may be dealt with subsequently.

Hence, we ask the students to select one issue for focus and to identify the values that are in potential conflict.

Observer: Please comment on the process. Are the issue and values clear?

_____

_____

_____

_____

PHASE THREE: TAKING POSITIONS

The next task is for the students to generate positions that address the issue. The positions may favor one value over another or effect a compromise.

Teacher: Please describe the instructions you will give the students. Also, how will you organize them (individuals, groups, etc.)?

_____

_____

_____

Next, the students share the positions they have generated and indicate the social consequences of their stances.

Observer: Please comment on the products of the analysis. Are the students both able to generate policy positions and see the costs and benefits they entail? Also, are they able to place themselves in the position of their fellow students as they articulate their stances?

_____

_____

_____

_____

PHASE FOUR: EXPLORING THE POSITIONS

Now the students test their positions by discussing the consequences. They may return to the case and see what would be the outcome were each of the policy positions adopted. They should distinguish between the purely practical consequences and the effects on the values. The teacher adopts a Socratic stance, drawing the students out, inducing them to examine their arguments, and assuring fair treatment of each proposal.

Teacher: How will you put this task to the students?

_____

_____

Observer: Please comment on the dialogue. Can the students distinguish between the pragmatic and value-related consequences of their positions? Do they take one another's reasoning seriously?

_____

_____

_____

_____

PHASE FIVE: MODIFYING THE POSITIONS, MAKING RECOMMENDATIONS

What remains is to modify the positions in accordance with the previous discussion and possibly to put forward candidates or a candidate for present policy action.

Teacher: Please describe how you will place this task before the students.

_____

_____

_____

COMMENTS ON STUDENT TRAINING NEEDS

Observer: Please comment on the student responses to the model, identifying any skills that you believe need special attention to improve their performance. If they are new to the model, remember that it involves some very complex social and intellectual tasks and that practice will surely result in an increment of skill. However, are there any particular skills that stand out at this point and might receive special attention in subsequent episodes in which the jurisprudential model is used?

_____

_____

_____

_____

Peer Coaching Guide: Synectics

Teacher: Do you want to suggest a focus for the observer? If so, what is it?

_____

_____

THE TEACHING PROCESS

Most teaching episodes have both content and process objectives. Content objectives include the substance (information, concepts, generalizations, relationships, skills) to be mastered by students. Process objectives include skills or procedures the students need in order to learn productively from the cognitive and social tasks of the model.

CONTENT OBJECTIVE(S)

Teacher: Please state the content objectives of the episode. What kind of learning will come from the activity? What is the nature of the area to be explored?

_____

_____

_____

PROCESS OBJECTIVE(S)

Teacher: Are the students familiar with the model? Is there some aspect of its process where they need practice or instruction, and will you be concentrating on it in this lesson?

_____

_____

_____

Observer: Please comment on the students' response to the model. Do they appear to need specific help with some aspect of the process?

_____

_____

_____

PHASE ONE: THE ORIGINAL PRODUCT

Commonly synectics is used to generate fresh perspectives on a topic or problem either for clarification or to permit alternative conceptions or solutions to be explored. Thus it generally begins by soliciting from students a product representing their current thinking. They can formulate the problem, speak or write about the topic, enact a problem, draw a representation of a relationship—there are many alternatives. The function of this phase is to enable them to capture their current thoughts about the subject at hand.

Teacher: Please describe how you will elicit the students' conceptions of the area to be explored. What will you say or do to orient them?

_____

_____

Observer: Please comment on the students' response to the originating task. What is the nature of their conceptions?

_____

_____

_____

_____

PHASE TWO: DIRECT AND PERSONAL ANALOGIES

The core of the model requires the development of distance from the original product through exercises inducing the students to make comparisons between sets of stimuli that are presented to them (direct analogy exercises) and to place themselves, symbolically, in the position of various persons, places, and things (personal analogy exercises). The analogistic material generated in these exercises will be used later in the creation of further analogies called "compressed conflicts."

Teacher: What stimuli will you use to induce the students to make the direct and personal analogies? Please describe the material and the order in which you will proceed to stretch the students toward the more unusual and surprising comparisons.

_____

_____

_____

Observer: Please comment on the stimuli and the student responses. Did the students get "up in the air" metaphorically and generate less literal and more analogistic comparisons?

_____

_____

PHASE THREE: COMPRESSED CONFLICTS AND OXYMORONIC ANALOGIES

The next task is to induce the students to operate on the material generated in phase two and create compressed conflicts. You need to be prepared to define compressed conflict, even if the students have familiarity with the model and to continue eliciting material until a number of examples clearly contain the logical (illogical?) tension that characterizes a high-quality oxymoron.

Teacher: Please describe how you will initiate phase three and how you will explain compressed conflict if you need to.

_____

_____

_____

_____

Observer: Please comment on the student response to the task. How rich was the product?

_____

_____

_____

Now we ask the students to select some pairs that manifest great tension and to generate some analogies that represent the tension. For example, we might ask them to provide some examples of "exquisite torture."

Teacher: Please describe briefly how you will present these tasks to the students.

_____

_____

_____

Observer: Please discuss the students' understanding of the concept "compressed conflict" and their ability to select the higher quality ones. Also, comment on the product of their attempt to generate oxymoronic analogies.

_____

_____

_____

PHASE FOUR: GENERATING NEW PRODUCTS

The compressed conflicts and the analogies to them provide material from which to revisit the original problem or topic. Sometimes we select or have the students select just one analogy with which to revisit the original material. At other times multiple perspectives are useful. What course to take depends on a combination of the complexity of the original problem or concept and the students' ability to handle new perspectives. For example, if a secondary social studies class has been trying to formulate potential solutions to a problem in international relations, we are dealing with a very complex problem for which multiple analogies are probably both appropriate and necessary. However, the task of helping the students share and assess a variety of analogies that can be used to redefine the problem and generate alternative solutions is complex, indeed.

Teacher: Please describe how you will present the task of revisiting the original product. What will you ask the students to do?

_____

_____

_____

_____

Observer: Please comment on the student products. What do you think has been the effect of the metaphoric exercises?

_____

_____

Now, the new product needs to be examined. If the students worked as individuals or subgroups, the separate products need to be shared. If a problem is to be solved, new definitions and solutions need to be arranged. If written expression emerged, possibly it needs further editing. Unless the teaching episode is the conclusion of a topic of study, it generally leads to further study.

Teacher: Please describe how the synectics products are to be shared and used. Will they lead to further reading and writing, data collection, or experimentation?

_____

_____

_____

_____

Observer: Please comment on the use of the new products. Are the students able to see the effects of the metaphoric activity? If they are asked to participate in further activities or to generate them, are they bringing to those tasks a "set" toward the development of alternative perspectives or avenues?

_____

_____

_____

COMMENTS ON STUDENT TRAINING NEEDS

It is the student who does the learning, and the greater the skill of the student in responding to the cognitive and social tasks of the model, the greater the learning is likely to be. Practice alone will build skill, and we want to provide plenty of it. After students are thoroughly familiar with the structure of the model, we can begin to develop specific training to improve their ability to perform.

Observer: Please comment on the skills with which the students engaged in the activities and suggest any areas where you believe training might be useful. Think especially of their ability to make comparisons, their ability to take the roles required to make "personal analogies," and their understanding of the structure of compressed conflicts and how to use them. Thinking back on the entire experience, is there any area where specific process training should be considered?

_____

_____

_____

_____

Peer Coaching Guide: Concept Attainment

The guide is designed to assist peer coaching of the concept attainment model of teaching. When planning questions, skip through the guide to the entries marked "Teacher" and fill them in as needed. They will guide you through the model. Observers can use the guide to familiarize themselves with the plans of the teacher and to make notes about what is observed. Please remember, observers, that your primary function is not to give "expert advice" to your colleague, but to observe the students as requested by the teacher and to observe the whole process so that you can gain ideas for your own teaching. The teacher is the coach in the sense that he or she is demonstrating a teaching episode for you. When you teach and are observed, you become the coach.

Teacher: Do you want to suggest a focus for the analysis? If so, what is it?

_____

_____

THE TEACHING PROCESS

Most lessons have both content and process objectives. Content objectives identify subject matter (facts, concepts, generalizations, relationships) to be mastered by students, while process objectives specify skills and procedures students need in order to achieve content objectives or auxiliary social objectives (e.g., cooperation in a learning task).

CONTENT OBJECTIVE

Teacher: Please state the concept that is the objective of the lesson. What are its defining attributes? What kind of data will be presented to the students? Is the information or concept new to the students?

_____

_____

PROCESS OBJECTIVE

Teacher: Are the students familiar with the model? Do they need special assistance or training with respect to any aspect of the process?

_____

_____

PHASE ONE: FOCUS

The focus defines the field of search for the students. It may eliminate nonrelevant lines of inquiry. Often it is pitched at a level of abstraction just above the exemplars (i.e., "a literary device" might serve as a focus for the concept of metaphor).

Teacher: Please write the focus statement here.

_____

_____

Observer: Did the teacher deliver the focus statement?

Yes [ ]   No [ ]

In your opinion, was it clear to the students and did it function to help them focus on the central content of the lesson?

Completely [ ]   Partially [ ]   No [ ]

PHASE TWO: PRESENTING THE DATA SET

The data set should be planned in pairs of positive and negative exemplars, ordered to enable the students—by comparing the positive exemplars and contrasting them with the negative ones—to distinguish the defining attributes of the concept.

Teacher: Please describe the nature of the exemplars. (Are they words, phrases, document, etc? For example: "These are reproductions of nineteenth-century paintings. Half of them are from the Impressionists [Renoir, Monet, Degas] and the other half are realistic, romantic, or abstract paintings.")

_____

_____

THE SET

Observer:
Were approximately equal numbers of positive and negative exemplars presented?

Yes [ ]   No [ ]

Were the early positive exemplars clear and unambiguous?

Yes [ ]   No [ ]

Did the data set contain at least 15 each of positive and negative exemplars?

Yes [ ]   No [ ]

How was the set presented?

A labeled pair at a time? _____
All at once, with labels following? _____
Other (please describe)

_____

_____

Did the teacher provide the labels for the first 8 or 10 pairs before asking the students to suggest a label?

Yes [ ]   No [ ]

DEVELOPING HYPOTHESES ABOUT THE NATURE OF THE CONCEPT

As the students work through the data set, they are to examine each exemplar and develop hypotheses about the concept. They need to ask themselves what attributes the positive exemplars have in common. It is those attributes that define the concept.

Teacher: How are you going to do this?

_____

_____

Observer: Were the students asked to generate hypotheses but to avoid sharing them?

Yes [ ]   No [ ]

Sometimes students are asked to record the progression of their thinking.

Teacher: Do you want to do this?

_____

Observer: Were the students asked to record their thinking as the episode progressed?

Yes [ ]   No [ ]

As the lesson progresses, we need to get information about whether the students are formulating and testing ideas.

Teacher: How will you do this? _____

_____

_____

_____

Observer: As the episode progressed, did the teacher gather information about whether the students were able to generate hypotheses?

Yes [ ]   No [ ]

Observer: Were the students asked to compare the positives and contrast them with the negatives?

Yes [ ]   No [ ]

PHASE THREE: SHARING THINKING AND HYPOTHESES

When it appears that the students have developed hypotheses that they are fairly sure of, they are asked to describe the progression of their thinking and the concept they have arrived at.

Teacher: When to do this is a matter of judgment. How will you decide, and what will you say?

_____

_____

_____

Observer:
Did the teacher ask the students to share their thinking?

Yes [ ]   No [ ]

Were the students able to express their hypotheses?

Yes [ ]   No [ ]

If there were several hypotheses, could the students justify or reconcile them?

Yes [ ]   No [ ]

PHASE FOUR: NAMING AND APPLYING THE CONCEPT

Once concepts have been agreed on (or different ones justified), they need names. After students have generated names, the teacher may need to supply the technical or common term (i.e., "We call this style 'Impressionism'"). Application requires that students determine whether further exemplars fit the concept and, perhaps, find examples of their own.

Teacher: Is there a technical or common term the students need to know? How will you provide further experience with the concept?

_____

_____

_____

Observer:

Were the students able to name the concept?

Yes [ ]   No [ ]

Was a technical or common term for the concept supplied (if needed)?

Yes [ ]   No [ ]

Were additional exemplars provided?

Yes [ ]   No [ ]

Were the students asked to supply their own?

Yes [ ]   No [ ]

As the students examined new material, supplying their own exemplars, did they appear to know the concept?

Yes [ ]   No [ ]

An assignment to follow the lesson often involves the application of the concept to fresh material. For example, if the concept of "metaphor" had been introduced, the students might be asked to read a literary passage and identify the uses of metaphor in it.

Teacher: Are you planning such an assignment? If so, please describe it briefly.

_____

_____

_____

_____

COMMENTS ON STUDENT TRAINING NEEDS

In order to improve student performance, the first option we explore is whether it will improve with practice. That is, simple repetition of the model gives the students a chance to learn to respond more appropriately. Second, we directly teach the students the skills they need to manage the cognitive and social tasks of the model.

You might discuss:

HOW THE STUDENTS RESPONDED TO PHASE ONE

Did they pay close attention to the focus statement and apply it to the examination of the exemplars? If not, is it worthwhile to give specific instruction and what might that be?

_____

_____

_____

HOW THE STUDENTS RESPONDED TO PHASE TWO

Did they compare and contrast the exemplars? Did they make hypotheses with the expectation that they might have to change them? Were they using the negative exemplars to eliminate alternatives? Is it worthwhile to provide specific training, and what might that be?

_____

_____

_____

HOW THE STUDENTS RESPONDED TO PHASE THREE

Were they able to debrief their thinking? Were they able to see how different lines of thinking gave similar or different results? Were they able to generate labels that express the concept? Do they understand how to seek exemplars on their own and apply what they have learned? Is it worthwhile to provide specific training, and what might that be?

_____

_____

_____

Peer Coaching Guide: Inquiry Training

Teacher: Do you want to suggest a focus for the analysis? If so, what is it?

THE TEACHING PROCESS

Most lessons have both content and process objectives. Content objectives identify subject matter (facts, concepts, generalizations, relationships) to be mastered by students, while process objectives specify skills and procedures students need in order to achieve content objectives or auxiliary social objectives (e.g., cooperation in a learning task).

The content objectives for inquiry training reside in the information, concepts, and theories embedded in the problem or puzzling situation that is presented to the students. They have to discover the information, form the concepts, and develop the theories. The skills to do those things are the process objectives, as are the social skills of cooperative problem solving.

CONTENT OBJECTIVE(S)

Teacher: What do you want students to gain from this task? What information, concepts, and theories do you wish them to learn?

_____

_____

_____

_____

PROCESS OBJECTIVE(S)

Teacher: Are the students familiar with the model? Do they need special assistance or training with respect to any aspect of the process? (For example, do they know how to obtain information through questioning? Can they work cooperatively with partners on a problem-solving task?)

_____

_____

_____

Observer: Was the process of the model familiar to the students? Do they need help with any aspect of the model?

_____

_____

PHASE ONE: ENCOUNTER WITH THE PROBLEM

The primary activity of phase one of the inquiry training model is the presentation of the problem.

Teacher: Please describe the problem to be used in this lesson and how you will present it.

_____

_____

_____

Observer: Did the students understand the problem and find it puzzling? Were they able to ask questions to clarify it, and could they summarize it when asked to?

_____

_____

_____

PHASE TWO: DATA GATHERING AND VERIFICATION

In this phase the students ask questions to gather information about the problem.

Observer: In your opinion, did the students understand the procedures they were to employ during this phase? Did they ask fact-oriented questions, and were they able to respond when the teacher modeled how to ask them? Could they distinguish between fact and theory-oriented questions? How well could they "caucus" and summarize what they had learned and plan sets of questions to ask? Did they listen to each other?

_____

_____

_____

PHASE THREE: EXPERIMENTATION

If the students do not do so spontaneously, the teacher will introduce this phase by instructing them to begin to develop causal hypotheses.

Observer: Please comment on the students' ability to organize the information and build hypotheses. Describe their social behavior as well as their ability to respond to the cognitive tasks.

_____

_____

_____

PHASE FOUR: FORMULATION OF LIKELY EXPLANATIONS

Now the students weigh the hypotheses and assess what are the most likely explanations of the phenomena. If this does not happen spontaneously the teacher initiates the phase.

Teacher: Please rehearse how you will initiate the phase.

_____

_____

_____

_____

Observer: Discuss the students' response to this task. Were they able to state hypotheses clearly, summarize the evidence, and, where appropriate, weigh competing explanations?

_____

_____

If students were successful in making inferences and conclusions about their data, the teacher may wish to push them a step further and ask them to predict consequences from their data by asking "What would happen if . . ." kinds of questions.

Teacher: Please write one or two examples of hypothetical questions you might ask students about these data.

_____

_____

_____

Observer: Were students able to make logical predictions based on the forgoing categorization and discussion?

_____

_____

_____

PHASE FIVE: ANALYSIS OF THE INQUIRY PROCESS

In phase five the students are led to analyze their inquiry process and contemplate how to improve it. This activity provides the teacher with the opportunity to coach the students, explaining and even modeling how they can work together to collect and verify data, build concepts, and develop hypotheses and test them.

COMMENTS ON STUDENT TRAINING NEEDS

In order to improve student performance, the first option we explore is whether it will improve with practice. That is, simple repetition of the model gives the students a chance to learn to respond more appropriately. Second, we directly teach the students the skills they need to manage the cognitive and social tasks of the model. How to improve student response is the focus of the discussion following the episode.

Observer: Please comment on the skills with which the students engaged in the activities and suggest any areas where you believe training might be useful.

_____

_____

_____

Peer Coaching Guide: Assists to Memory

During the last 15 years there has been renewed research and development on strategies for assisting students to master and retain information. The science of mnemonics, as it is called, has produced some dramatic results (Pressley, Levin, and Delaney, 1981).

Rote repetition (rehearsing something over and over until it is retained) has until recently been the primary method taught to students for memorizing information and the primary method used by teachers as they interact with students. In fact, rote methods have become so used that they have become identified in many people's minds with the act of memorization. To memorize, it is often thought, is to repeat by rote.

MEMORIZATION STRATEGIES

However, although rehearsal of material continues to be one aspect of most mnemonic strategies, a number of other procedures are employed that greatly increase the probability that material will be learned and retained. These procedures are combined in various ways, depending on the material to be learned. Most of the procedures help build associations between the new material and familiar material. Some of the procedures include:

ORGANIZING INFORMATION TO BE LEARNED

Essentially, the more information is organized, the easier it is to learn and retain. Information can be organized by categories. The concept attainment, inductive, and advanced organizer models assist memory by helping students associate the material in the categories. Consider the following list of words from a popular spelling series, in the order the spelling book presents them to the children:

soft	plus	cloth	frost	song
trust	luck	club	sock	pop
cost	lot	son	won	

Suppose we ask the students to classify them by beginnings, endings, and the presence of vowels. The act of classification requires the students to scrutinize the words and associate words containing similar elements. They can then name the categories in each classification (the "c" group and the "st" group), calling further attention to the common attributes of the group. They can also connect words that fit together ("pop song," "soft cloth," etc.). They can then proceed to rehearse the spellings of one category at a time. The same principle operates over other types of material—say, number facts, etc. Whether categories are provided to students or whether they create them, the purpose is the same. Also, information can be selected with categories in mind. The above list is, to outward appearances, almost random. A list that deliberately and systematically provides variations would be easier to organize (it would already have at least implicit categories within it).

ORDERING INFORMATION TO BE LEARNED

Information learned in series, especially if there is meaning to the series, is easier to assimilate and retain. For example, if we wish to learn the names of the states of Australia it is easier if we always start with the same one (say, the largest) and proceed in the same order. Historical events by chronology are more easily learned than events sorted randomly. Order is simply another way of organizing information. We could have the students alphabetize their list of spelling words.

LINKING INFORMATION TO FAMILIAR SOUNDS

Suppose we are learning the names of the states. We can connect *Georgia* to *George, Louisiana* to *Louis, Maryland* to *Marry* or *Merry*, and so on. Categorizing the names of the states or ordering them by size, or ordering them within region, provides more associations.

LINKING INFORMATION TO VISUAL REPRESENTATIONS

Maryland can be linked to a picture of a marriage, Oregon to a picture of a gun, Maine to a burst water main, and so forth. Letters and numerals can be linked to something that evokes both familiar sounds and images. For example, *one* can be linked to *bun* and a picture of a boy eating a bun, *b* to *bee* and a picture of a bee. Those links can be used over and over again. "April is the cruelest month, breeding lilacs out of the dead land" is easier remembered thinking of an ominous spring, bending malevolently over the Spring flowers.

LINKING INFORMATION TO ASSOCIATED INFORMATION

A person's name, linked to information such as a well-known person having the same name, a sound-alike, and some personal information, is easier to remember than the name rehearsed by itself. Louis (Louis Armstrong) "looms" over Jacksonville (his place of birth). Learning the states of Australia while thinking of the points of the compass and the British origins of many of the names (New South Wales) is easier than learning them in order alone.

MAKING THE INFORMATION VIVID

Devices that make the information vivid are also useful. Lorayne and Lucas favor "ridiculous association," where information is linked to absurd associations. ("The silly two carries his twin two on his back so they are really four." and such). Others favor the use of dramatization and vivid illustrations (such as counting the basketball players on two teams to illustrate that 5 and 5 equal 10).

REHEARSING

Rehearsal (practice) is always useful, and students benefit from knowledge of results. Students who have not had past success with tasks requiring memorization will benefit by having relatively short assignments and clear, timely feedback as they have success.

PLANNING WITH MEMORIZATION IN MIND

The task of the teacher is to think up activities that help the students benefit from these principles.

A teaching episode or learning task that can be organized at least partly by these principles contains information to be learned. Both teacher and students should be clear that a very high degree of mastery is desired. (The students need to be trying to learn all the information and to retain it permanently.)

Teacher: Please identify the information to be learned by your students in some curriculum area within a specified period of time.

_____

_____

_____

_____

Which principles will you emphasize in order to facilitate memorization?

_____

_____

_____

Will these principles be used as the information is presented to the students? If yes, how?

_____

_____

_____

_____

Which principles will be used as the students operate on the information? How?

_____

_____

_____

_____

How will rehearsal and feedback be managed?

_____

_____

_____

_____

Observer: During the teaching/learning episode, situate yourself so that you can observe the behavior of a small number of children (about a half-dozen). Concentrate on their response to the tasks that are given.

Comment on their response to the tasks. Do they appear to be clear about the objectives? Do they engage in the cognitive tasks that have been provided to them? Can they undertake these tasks successfully? Do they appear to be aware of progress?

_____

_____

_____

_____

_____

DISCUSSION

The observer should report the results of the observation to the teacher. Then, the discussion should focus on how the students responded and ways of helping them respond more effectively if that is desirable.

Practice frequently enables students to respond more productively without further instruction. Where instruction is needed, demonstration is useful. That is, the teacher may lead the students through the tasks over small amounts of material.

Tasks can be simplified in order to bring them within the reach of the students. We want the students to develop a repertoire of techniques that enable them to apply the mnemonic principles to learning tasks. Making the process conscious is a step toward independence, so we seek ways of helping the students understand the nature of the tasks and why these should work for them.

Peer Coaching Guide: Role Playing

Teacher: Do you want to suggest a focus for the analysis? If so, what is it?

_____

_____

_____

_____

THE TEACHING PROCESS

Most lessons have both content and process objectives. Content objectives identify subject matter (facts, concepts, generalizations, relationships) to be mastered by students, while process objectives specify skills and procedures students need in order to achieve content objectives or auxiliary social objectives (e.g., cooperation in a learning task).

CONTENT OBJECTIVE

Teacher: Please state the objective of the lesson. What problem will be presented to the students, or in what domain will they construct a problem? Is the problem or domain of values new to the students?

_____

_____

_____

PROCESS OBJECTIVE

Teacher: Are the students familiar with the model? Do they need special assistance or training with respect to any aspect of the process?

_____

_____

_____

PHASE ONE: WARMING UP

Role playing begins with a social problem. The problem may be from a prepared study of a human-relations situation or an aspect of human relations may be presented to the students so they can generate situations involving it. Possibly the problem is one in their lives that simply needs recapitulation.

Teacher: How will you present the problem to the students or help them develop it?

_____

_____

_____

Observer: In your opinion, was the problem clear to the students? Were they able to understand the nature of the problem and the type of human-relations problem it represents? Could they identify the players in the situation and how they act? Can they see the several sides of the problem?

_____

_____

_____

PHASE TWO: SELECTING THE PARTICIPANTS (ROLE PLAYERS AND OBSERVERS)

Teacher: Please describe how the participants will be selected.

_____

_____

_____

_____

PHASE THREE: CREATING THE LINE OF ACTION FOR THE FIRST ENACTMENT

Teacher: How are you going to do this? Do you wish the first enactment to highlight certain aspects of values?

_____

_____

_____

Observer: Were they able to generate a plausible and meaningful story line? Please note any difficulties they had.

_____

_____

_____

PHASE FOUR: PREPARING THE OBSERVERS

Once the characters have been identified and the story line generated, the observers are prepared.

Teacher: What will you ask the observers to focus on?

_____

_____

_____

_____

Sometimes the observers (students) are asked to record the progression of their impressions.

Teacher: Do you want to do this?

_____

PHASE FIVE: THE ENACTMENT

Now the students enact the problem for the first time.

Observer: How well did the students enact the roles? Did they appear to empathize with the positions they were to take? Were the observers attentive and serious? Comment on any problems either role players or observers had.

_____

_____

_____

PHASE SIX: DISCUSSION

Observer: Were the students able to analyze the nature of the conflict and the values that were involved? Did they reveal their own value positions? Did they have any confusion about tactics of argumentation, skill, and values?

_____

_____

_____

_____

From this point, phases one to three are repeated through several enactments. The teacher guides the students to ensure that the value questions are brought out.

Observer: Please comment on the student performance in the ensuing cycles of enactments and discussions. Did the students increasingly become able to distinguish value positions?

_____

_____

_____

PHASE SEVEN: ANALYSIS

When the teacher judges that sufficient material has been generated, a discussion is held (a cooperative learning format can be used for this phase to maximize participation, if desired) to ensure that the value positions are brought out and to put forth positions about what can be done to deal with the particular type of problem from a valuing basis rather than one involving adversarial uses of argumentation and conflict.

Teacher: Please prepare the instructions you will give the students to inaugurate phase four.

_____

_____

_____

_____

Observer: Please comment on the student's ability to handle the tasks involved in phase four.

_____

_____

_____

_____

DISCUSSION

Following the teaching episode, the coaching partners might discuss ways of helping the students respond more effectively to the model. Remember that the early trials are bound to be awkward and that practice often does the trick. Also, problems can be adjusted to simplify the issues that have to be dealt with at any one time. Demonstrating the phases of the model to the students is also useful. The coaching partners can play the role of observer or even role player to give the students a model. Or the two teachers can demonstrate together.

Please summarize the results of the discussion—the one or two chief conclusions you have reached to guide what you will next do as you use the model.

_____

_____

Peer Coaching Guide: Inductive Thinking

Teacher: Do you want to suggest a focus for the analysis? If so, what is it?

_____

_____

THE TEACHING PROCESS

Most lessons have both content and process objectives. Content objectives identify subject matter (facts, concepts, generalizations, relationships) to be mastered by students, while process objectives specify skills and procedures students need in order to achieve content objectives or auxiliary social objectives (e.g., cooperation in a learning task).

The content objectives for inductive thinking reside in the information and concepts embedded in a data set. Students categorize items in the data set by attributes held in common by subsets of items. For example, if the data set consisted of a collection of plants, students might classify plants by types of leaves (size, texture, patterns of veins, shape, connection of leaves to stems, etc.). Content objectives for this data set might include both information about specific plants and the building of a typology. Process objectives might include learning the scientific skill of the discipline (observation and classification) as well as the social skills of cooperative problem solving.

CONTENT OBJECTIVE(S)

Teacher: What do you want students to gain from this classification task? What, in your opinion, are the critical attributes of the data set? What categories do you bring to the set?

_____

_____

_____

_____

PROCESS OBJECTIVE(S)

Teacher: Are the students familiar with the model? Do they need special assistance or training with respect to any aspect of the process? (For example, do students understand how to group items by common attributes? Can they work cooperatively with partners on a classification task?)

_____

_____

_____

PHASE ONE: DATA COLLECTION/PRESENTATION

The primary activity of phase one of the inductive thinking model involves collection or presentation of a data set. The teacher may provide a data set or instruct students to collect the data that will be categorized. The data that will be scrutinized by the students are extremely important, for they represent much of the information the students will learn from the episode. The choice between data collection or presentation is also important. To continue the above example, if students collect leaves, a different set of data will result than if they had been presented with them. Once a data set has been collected by or presented to students, the teacher may want to set parameters for the classification activity by orienting students to relevant attributes. For example, if the data are plants, the teacher may wish to narrow the field of observation by having students classify by "types of leaves." On the other hand, the teacher may wish to leave the parameters open and simply instruct students to classify by common attributes. Generally speaking, the more open-ended the instructions, the better the results.

Items from a data set may be included in only one category or in multiple categories. You may want to experiment with different instructions regarding the classification of data and observe differences in the categories that result. Generally speaking, leaving open the possibility of multiple category membership for items from the data set provides the most energy.

Teacher: Please describe the data set to be used in this lesson. Will you provide the data set or have students collect data? If the latter, what will be the sources of information they will use?

_____

_____

_____

ENUMERATION

Data are easier to group if enumerated. Continuing with our example of plants, the teacher might place a numbered card under each plant so that students may discuss plants 1, 4, 7, and 14 as sharing a common attribute rather than by plant names (which students may not yet know).

Observer: Did the teacher/students enumerate the data before attempting to categorize it?

Yes [ ]   No [ ]

PHASE TWO: CONCEPT FORMATION

Once a data set is assembled and enumerated and students have been instructed on procedures for grouping the data, the teacher will need to attend to the mechanics of the grouping activity. Students may work alone, in pairs, in small groups, or as one large group. Working alone requires the least social skill, and working in small groups the greatest social skill. If one objective is to develop students' abilities to work cooperatively, assertively defending their groupings but compromising when appropriate for group consensus, then students will need instruction and practice to develop these skills. If the teacher chooses to work with the entire class as a single group for the categorizing activity, he or she will need to exercise caution so that categories are not inadvertently provided for the students. Structuring students into pairs for the categorizing activity is the simplest way to have all students actively engaged in the task, although the teacher must again use considerable skill in keeping everyone involved while recording and synthesizing reports from the pairs. Teachers will probably want to experiment with different ways of structuring this activity, and pros and cons of each process can be discussed and problem-solved with peer coaches.

Teacher: Please describe how you will organize students for the categorizing activity.

_____

_____

_____

Teacher: Please describe how you will instruct the students to classify the data that you have provided or that they have collected.

_____

_____

_____

Observer: In your opinion, did the students understand the criteria and procedures they were to employ during the categorizing activity? Did the teacher inadvertently give clues about what the "right" groups would be?

_____

_____

_____

Observer: Did the students work productively on the categorizing activity?

Yes [ ]   No [ ]   Partially [ ]

If the teacher had the students work in pairs or small groups, did the students listen as other groups shared their categories?

Yes [ ]   No [ ]   Partially [ ]

Were students able to explain the attributes on which they grouped items within categories?

Yes [ ]   No [ ]   Partially [ ]

Were students able to provide names for their groups which reflected the attributes on which the groups were formed?

Yes [ ]   No [ ]

The names or labels students attach to groups of items within a data set will often accurately describe the group but not coincide with a technical or scientific name. For example, students may label a group of leaves "jagged edges" while the technical term would be "serrated edges." The teacher may choose to provide technical or scientific terms when appropriate, but not before students have attempted to provide their own labels.

For some lessons, the content objectives will be accomplished at the conclusion of phase two. When the teacher wishes to have students learn information by organizing it into categories and labeling it in order to gain conceptual control of the material, he or she may choose to stop here. Or when the objective is to learn what students see within a data set and what attributes they are unaware of, the grouping activity will accomplish that objective. When, however, the objective is the interpretation and application of concepts that have been formed in phase two, the remainder of the inductive thinking model is appropriate. The final phases of the model result in further processing of the information and concepts embedded in the data set and should usually be completed.

PHASE THREE: INTERPRETATION OF DATA

The purpose of phase three is to help students develop understanding of possible relationships between and among categories that they have formed in phase two. The class will need a common set of categories in order to work productively in this kind of discussion. Working off the descriptions of individual groups students have generated in phase two, the teacher asks questions that focus students' thinking on similarities and differences between the groups. By asking "why" questions, the teacher attempts to develop cause-effect relationships between the groups. The success of this phase depends on a thorough categorizing activity in phase two, and the length of phase three is relatively short compared with the time required by phase two.

Teacher: Although you will not know during your planning what groups the students will form, make a guess about possible categories they might construct, and then write two sample questions that would explore cause-effect relationships between those groups.

_____

_____

_____

_____

Observer: Were the students able to discuss possible cause-effect relationships among the groups?

Yes [ ]   No [ ]   Partially [ ]

Did the teacher ask the students to go beyond the data and make inferences and conclusions regarding their data?

Yes [ ]   No [ ]

If yes, were the students able to do so?

Yes [ ]   No [ ]

If students were unable to make inferences or conclusions, can you think of any ideas to share with your partner that might help them do so?

_____

_____

_____

If students were successful in making inferences and conclusions about their data, the teacher may wish to push them a step further and ask them to predict consequences from their data by asking "What would happen if . . ." kinds of questions.

Teacher: Please write one or two examples of hypothetical questions you might ask students about this data set.

_____

_____

_____

Observer: Were students able to make logical predictions based on the foregoing categorization and discussion?

Yes [ ]   No [ ]

Did the teacher ask the students to explain and support their predictions?

Yes [ ]   No [ ]

If students were unable to make logical predictions based on their previous work with their categories, can you think of questions or examples that might assist students in doing so?

_____

_____

_____

For Teacher and Observer Discussion: Are there writing assignments or other activities that would be appropriate extensions of this lesson?

COMMENTS ON STUDENT TRAINING NEEDS

In order to improve student performance, the first option we explore is whether it will improve with practice. That is, simple repetition of the model gives the students a chance to learn to respond more appropriately. Second, we directly teach the students the skills they need to manage the cognitive and social tasks of the model.

Observer: Please comment on the skills with which the students engaged in the activities and suggest any areas where you believe training might be useful. Think especially of their ability to group by attributes, to provide labels for groups that accurately described the groups or synthesized attributes characteristic of a given group, their understanding of possible cause-effect relationships among groups, and their ability to make inferences or conclusions regarding their categories.

_____

_____

_____

_____

REFERENCES

Acheson, K. (1967). The effects of feedback from television recordings and three types of supervisory treatment on selected teacher behaviors. Unpublished doctoral dissertation, Stanford University.

Adkins, D. C., Payne, F. D., & O'Malley, J. M. (1974). Moral development. *Review of Research in Education* eds. Kerlinger, F. N. and Carroll, J. B. Itasca, Ill.: F. E. Peacock Publishers, Inc.

Adler, M. J. (1982). *The Paideia proposal: an educational manifesto.* New York: Macmillan.

Ainscow, Mel (1991). Preface in Ainscow, Mel, ed. *Effective Schools for All.* London: David Fulton, Publishers.

Alberti, R. E. & Emmons, F. (1978). *Your perfect right: A guide to assertive behavior* (3rd ed.). San Luis Obispo, Calif.: Impact Publishers.

Almy, M. (1970). *Logical thinking in second grade.* New York: Teachers College Press.

Anderson, H. & Brewer, H. (1939). Domination and social integration in the behavior of kindergarten children and teachers. *Genetic Psychology Monograph, 21,* 287–385.

Anderson, L. M., Evertson, C. M., & Brophy, J. E. (1979). An experimental study of effective teaching in first grade reading groups. *The Elementary School Journal,* 79(4), 191–223.

Anderson, L. W. & Pellicer, L. O. (1990). Synthesis of research on compensatory and remedial education. *Educational Leadership, 48* (1), 10–16.

Anderson, L. W., Scott, C. & Hutlock, N. (1976). The effect of a mastery learning program on selected cognitive, affective, and ecological variables in grades 1 through 6. Paper presented at the annual meeting of the American Educational Association, San Francisco.

Apple, M. (1979). *Ideology and curriculum.* London: Routledge and Kagan Paul.

Aquinas, T. *The city of God*. (J. Healy, Trans.). (1931). London: J. M. Dent.

Argyis, C., & Schon, E. (1974). *Theory into practice: Increasing professional effectiveness*. San Francisco: Jossey Bass.

Aristotle (1912). *The works of Aristotle*. Oxford: Clarendon Press. (Smith J. A., & Ross, W. D., eds.).

Arlin, M. (1984). Time variability in mastery learning. *American Educational Research Journal. 21*, 4, 103–20.

Arlin, M., & Webster, J. (1983). Time costs of mastery learning. *Journal of Educational Psychology. 75*, 3, 187–96.

Aronson, E., Blaney, N., Stephan, C., Sikes, J., & Snapp, M. (1978). *The jigsaw classroom*. Beverly Hills: Sage.

Aspy, D. N., & Roebuck, F. (1973). An investigation of the relationship between student levels of cognitive functioning and the teacher's classroom behavior. *Journal of Educational Research*, 65, 6, 365–368.

Aspy, D. N., Roebuck, F., Willson, M., & Adams, O. (1974). *Interpersonal skills training for teachers*. (Interim report #2 for NIMH Grant #5PO 1MH 19871.) Monroe, La.: Northeast Louisiana University.

Atkinson, J. W. (1966). *Achievement Motivation*. New York: John Wiley & Sons, Inc.

Atkinson, R. C. (1975). Mnemotechnics in second language learning. *American Psychologist*, 30, 821–828.

Ausubel, D. P. (1960). The use of advance organizers in the learning and retention of meaningful verbal material. *Journal of Educational Psychology. 51*, 267–272.

Ausubel, D. P. (1963). *The psychology of meaningful verbal learning*. New York: Grune and Stratton, Inc.

Ausubel, D. P. (1968). *Educational psychology: A cognitive view*. New York: Holt, Rinehart & Winston.

Ausubel, D. P. (1977). *Behavior modification for the classroom teacher*. New York: McGraw-Hill.

Ausubel, D. P. (1980). Schemata, cognitive structure, and advance organizers: A reply to Anderson, Spiro, and Anderson. *American Educational Research Journal*, 17, 3, 400–404.

Ausubel, D. P., & Fitzgerald, J. (1962). Organizer, general background and antecedent learning variables in sequential verbal learning. *Journal of Educational Psychology. 53*, 243–249.

Ausubel, D. P., Stager, M. and Gaite, A. J. H. (1968). Retroactive facilitation of meaningful verbal learning. *Journal of Educational Psychology*, 59, 250–255.

Baker, E., & Saloutas, A. (1974). *Evaluating instructional programs*. Washington, D.C.: Department of Health, Education, and Welfare, National Institute of Education.

Baker, R. G. (1983). The contribution of coaching to transfer of training: An extension study. Doctoral dissertation, University of Oregon.

Baker, R. G. & Showers, B. (1984). The effects of a coaching strategy on teachers' transfer of training to classroom practice: A six-month followup study. Paper presented at the annual meeting of the American Educational Research Association, New Orleans, La.

Baldridge, V. & Deal, T. (1975). *Managing change in educational organizations.* Berkeley: McCutchan.

Baldridge, V., & Deal, T., eds. (1983). *The dynamics of organizational change in education.* Boston: Addison-Wesley.

Ball, S. & Bogatz, G. A. (1970). *The first year of Sesame Street.* Princeton, N.J.: Educational Testing Service.

Bandura, A. (1969). *Principles of behavior modification.* New York: Holt, Rinehart & Winston.

Bandura, A. (1971a). Psychotherapy based on modeling principles. *Handbook of psychotherapy and behavior change.* Bergin, A. S. and Garfield, S. L., Eds. New York: John Wiley & Sons, Inc.

Bandura, A. (1971b). *Social learning theory.* New York: General Learning.

Bandura, A., & Perloff, B. (1967). Relative efficacy of self-monitored and externally imposed reinforcement systems. *Journal of Personality and Social Psychology,* 7, 111–116.

Bandura, A., & Walters, R. (1963). *Social learning and personality.* New York: Holt, Rinehart & Winston.

Bangert, R. L., & Kulik, J. A. (1982). Individualized systems of instruction: A meta-analysis of findings in secondary schools. Paper presented at the annual meeting of the American Educational Research Association, New York.

Bangert-Drowns, R. L. (1986). A review of developments in meta-analytic method. Paper presented at the annual meeting of the American Educational Research Association, San Francisco.

Bany, M., & Johnson, L. V. (1964). *Classroom group behavior: Group dynamics in education.* New York: Macmillan, Inc.

Barnes, B. R., & Clausen, E. U. (1973). The effects of organizers on the learning of structured anthropology materials in the elementary grades. *Journal of Experimental Education,* 42, 11–15.

Barnes, B. R. & Clausen, E. U. (1975). Do advance organizers facilitate learning? Recommendations for further research based on an analysis of 32 studies. *Review of Educational Research, 45* (4), 637–659.

Barron, F. (1963). *Creativity and psychological health: Origins of personal vitality and creative freedom.* Princeton: Von Nostrand.

Barron, R. R. (1971). The effects of advance organizers upon the reception, learning, and retention of general science concepts. DHEW Project No. IB-030 ERIC Document Reproduction Service, ED 061554.

Barth, R. (1980). *Run, school, run.* Cambridge, Mass.: Harvard University Press.

Baveja, B., Showers, B., and Joyce, B. (1985). An experiment in conceptually-based teaching strategies. Eugene: Booksend Laboratories.

Beck, A. T. (1976). *Cognitive therapy and the emotional disorders.* New York: International Universities Press.

Becker, W. (1975). *Classroom management.* Chicago: Science Research Associates.

Becker, W. (1977). Teaching reading and language to the disadvantaged—What we have learned from field research. *Harvard Educational Review, 47,* 518–543.

Becker, W., & Carnine, D. (1980). Direct instruction: An effective approach for educational intervention with the disadvantaged and low performers, in *Advances in Child Clinical Psychology,* eds. B. Lahey and A. Kazdin. (pp. 429–473). New York: Plenum.

Becker, W., Englemann, S., Carnine, D., and Rhine, W. (1981) in Rhine, W. Ray, ed. *Making schools more effective.* New York: Academic Press.

Becker, W. & Gersten, R. (1982). A followup of follow through: The later effects of the direct instruction model on children in the fifth and sixth grades. *American Educational Research Journal, 19* (1), 75–92.

Bencke, W. N., & Harris, M. B. (1972). Teaching self-control of study behavior. *Behavior Research and Therapy, 10,* 35–41.

Bennett, B. (1987). *The effectiveness of staff development training practices: a meta-analysis.* PhD thesis, University of Oregon.

Bennis, W. G., & Shepard, H. A. (1964). Theory of group development, in *The planning of change: Readings in the applied behavioral sciences,* eds. W. G. Bennis, K. D. Benne, and R. Chin. New York: Holt, Rinehart & Winston.

Bentzen, M. (1974). *Changing schools: The magic feather principle.* New York: McGraw-Hill.

Bereiter, C. (1984). How to keep thinking skills from going the way of all frills. *Educational Leadership, 42,* 1.

Bereiter, C. and Englemann, S. (1966). *Teaching the culturally disadvantaged child in the preschool.* Englewood Cliffs, N.J.: Prentice-Hall, Inc.

Bereiter, C. & Kurland, M. (1981–82). Were some follow through models more effective than others? *Interchange, 12,* 1–22.

Berger, P., & Luckman, T. (1966). *Social construction of reality.* Garden City, N.Y.: Doubleday & Co., Inc.

Berman, P., & Gjelten, T. (1983). *Improving school improvement.* Berkeley, Calif.: Berman, Weiler Associates.

Berman, P., & McLaughlin, M. (1975). *Federal programs supporting educational change, Vol. IV: The findings in review.* Santa Monica, CA: The Rand Corporation.

Beyer, Barry. (1988). *Developing a thinking skills program.* Boston: Allyn Bacon.

Black, J. (1989). Building the school as a center of inquiry: A whole-school approach oriented around models of teaching. Ph.D. thesis, Nova University.

Blatt, B., ed. (1980). *Providing leadership for staff development.* Syracuse: National Council for the States in Inservice Education.

Block, J. W. (1971). *Mastery learning: Theory and practice.* New York: Holt, Rinehart, and Winston.

Block, J. W. (1980). Success rate in *Time to learn,* Eds. C. Denham and A. Lieberman. Washington, D.C.: Program on Teaching and Learning, National Institute of Education.

Block, J. W., & Anderson, L. W. (1975). *Mastery learning in classrooms.* N.Y.: Macmillan.

Bloom, B. S. (1971). Mastery learning. In J. H. Block (Ed.), *Mastery learning: Theory and practice.* New York: Holt, Rinehart & Winston.

Bloom, B. S. (1974). Time and learning. *American Psychologist, 29,* 682–688.

Bloom, B. S. (1976). *Human characteristics and school learning.* New York: McGraw-Hill.

Bloom, B. S. (1981). The new direction in educational research and measurement: Alterable variables. Paper presented at the annual meeting of the American Educational Research Association, Los Angeles, CA.

Bloom, B. S. (1982). *Human characteristics and school learning.* New York: McGraw-Hill.

Bloom, B. S. (1984). The search for methods of group instruction as effective as one-to-one tutoring. *Educational Leadership, 41,* 4–17.

Bloom, B. S. et al. (1956). *Taxonomy of educational objectives. Handbook I: Cognitive domain.* New York: David McKay Co.

Bode, B. (1927). *Modern educational theories.* New York: Macmillan, Inc.

Boocock, S. S. (1973). The school as a social environment for learning social organization and micro-social process in education. *Sociology of Education.*

Boocock, S. S., & Schild, E. (1968). Simulation games in learning. Beverly Hills: Sage Publications, Inc.

Borg, W. R., Kallenbach, W., Morris, M., & Friebel, A. (1969). Videotape feedback and microteaching in a teacher training model. *Journal of Experimental Research, 37,* 9–16.

Borg, W. R., Kelley, Langer, P., & Gall, M. (1970). *The minicourse.* Beverly Hills, Ca.: Collier-Macmillan.

Boutwell, C. (1972). *Getting it all together.* San Rafael, Calif.: Leswing Press.

Braden, V., & Bruns, B. (1977). *Vic Braden's tennis for the future.* Boston: Little, Brown & Company.

Bradford, L. P., Gibb, J. R., & Benne, K. D. (Eds.). (1964). *T-Group theory and laboratory method.* New York: John Wiley & Sons, Inc.

Brandt, R. (1982). Overview. *Educational Leadership, 40* (4), 3.

Brandt, R. (1987). On cooperation in schools: A conversation with David and Roger Johnson. *Educational Leadership, 45,* 3, 14–19.

Brashear, R. M., & Davis, O. L. (1970). The persistence of teaching laboratory effects into student teaching: A comparative study of verbal teaching behaviors and attitudes. Paper presented at the annual meeting of the American Educational Research Association.

Bredderman, T. (1981). *Elementary school process curricula: A meta-analysis.* ERIC Ed. 170-333.

Bredderman, T. (1983). Effects of activity-based elementary science on student outcomes: A quantitative synthesis. *Review of Educational Research, 53* (4), 499–518.

Brookover, W., Schwitzer, J. H., Schneider, J. M., Beady, C. H., Flood, P. K., & Wisenbaker, J. M. (1978). Elementary school social climate and school achievement. *American Educational Research Journal, 15* (2), 301–318.

Brophy, J. E. (1973). Stability of teacher effectiveness. *American Educational Research Journal,* 10, 245–252.

Brophy, J. E. (1981). Teacher praise: A functional analysis. *Review of Educational Research,* 51, 5–32.

Brophy, J. E., & Evertson, C. (1974). *The Texas teacher effectiveness project: Presentation of non-linear relationships and summary discussion.* Austin, Tex.: Research and Development Center for Teacher Education, University of Texas.

Brophy, J. E., & Good, T. (1986). Teacher behavior and student achievement. In Merlin Wittrock (Ed.), *Handbook of research on teaching, 3rd edition,* pp. 328–375. New York: Macmillan Publishing Co.

Broudy, H. (1963). Historic exemplars of teaching methods. In N. L. Gage (Ed.), *Handbook of Research on Teaching.* Chicago: Rand McNally & Company.

Brown, C. (1967). A multivariate study of the teaching styles of student teachers. PhD dissertation. New York: Teachers College, Columbia University.

Brown, C. (1981). The relationship between teaching styles, personality, and setting. In Joyce, Peck, and Brown, eds., 94–100.

Brown, G. (1968). Humanistic education. Report to the Ford Foundation on the Ford-Esallen project: A pilot project to explore ways to adapt approaches in the affective domain to the school curriculum.

Brown, G. (1971). *Human teaching for human learning.* New York: Viking Penguin, Inc.

Bruner, J. (1961). *The process of education.* Cambridge, Mass.: Harvard University Press.

Bruner, J., Goodnow, J. J., & Austin, G. A. (1967). *A study of thinking.* New York: Science Editions, Inc.

Bruno, J. E., & Ellett, F. S. (1986). A core-analysis of meta-analysis. Paper presented at the annual meeting of the American Educational Research Association, San Francisco.

Burgess, E. W., & Bogue, D. J. (1962). The delinquency research of Clifford R. Shaw and Henry D. McKay and Associates. In *Urban Sociology,* ed. Burgess. Chicago: University of Chicago Press.

Bushell, D., Jr. (1970). *The behavior analysis classroom.* Lawrence, Kan.: University of Kansas Dept. of Human Development.

Butts, D. P. (1969). *Designs for progress in science education.* Washington, D.C.: National Science Teachers Association.

Canfield, L. H., & Wilder, H. B. (1966). *The making of modern America.* Boston: Houghton Mifflin Co.

Canter, L., & Canter, M. (1976). *Assertive discipline: A take-charge approach for today's educator.* Seal Beach, Calif.: Canter and Associates.

Carroll, J. B. (1963). A model of school learning. *Teachers College Record, 64,* 722–733.

Carroll, J. B. (1964). *Language and thought.* Englewood Cliffs, N.J.: Prentice-Hall.

Carroll, J. B. (1971). Problems of measurement related to the concept of learning for mastery. In J. H. Block (Ed.), *Mastery learning: Theory and practice.* New York: Holt, Rinehart & Winston.

Carroll, J. B. (1977). A revisionist model of school learning. *Review of Education, 3,* 155–167.

Center for Research on Elementary and Middle Schools. (1989). *Success for all.* CREMS, February, 1989.

Chamberlin, C., & Chamberlin, E. (1943). *Did they succeed in college?* New York: Harper and Row.

Charles, C. M. (1985). *Building classroom discipline: From models to practice.* White Plains, N.Y.: Longman Inc.

Chesler, M., & Fox, R. (1966). *Role-playing methods in the classroom.* Chicago: Science Research Associates, Inc.

Clark, C. & Peterson, P. (1986). Teachers thought processes. In Merlin Wittrock (Ed.), *Handbook of research on teaching,* pp. 225–296. New York: Macmillan Publishing Co.

Clark, C., & Yinger, R. (1979). *Three studies of teacher planning* (Research Series #55). East Lansing: Michigan State University.

Clauson, E. V., & Barnes, B. R. (1973). The effects of organizers on the learning of structured anthropology materials in the elementary grades. *Journal of Experimental Education, 42,* 11–15.

Clauson, E. V., & Rice, M. G. (1972). The changing world today. *Anthropology Curriculum Project Publication 72–1.* Athens, Ga.: The University of Georgia.

Codianni, A. V., & Wilbur, G. (1983). *More effective schools: From research to practice.* New York: Columbia University Teachers College Press.

Cogan, M. (1973). *Clinical supervision.* Boston: Houghton Mifflin.

Cohen, E. (1986). *Designing groupwork.* New York: Teachers College Press.

Cohen, J. (1977). *Statistical power analysis for the behavioral sciences* (rev. ed.). New York: Academic Press.

Cohen, M. (January/February 1982). Effective schools: Accumulating evidence. *American Education*, pp. 13–16.

Coleman, J. S., Campbell, E. Q., Hobson, C. J., McPortland, J., Mood, A. M., Weinfield, E. D., & York, R. L. (1966). *Equality of educational opportunity*. Washington, D.C.: Government Printing Office.

Collins, K. (1969). The importance of strong confrontation in an inquiry model of teaching. *School Science and Mathematics, 69*(7), 615–617.

Collins standard dictionary. (1978). New Delhi: Oxford and IBH Publishing Co.

Cook, L., & Cook, E. (1954). *Intergroup education*. New York: McGraw-Hill.

Cook, L., & Cook, E. (1957). *School problems in human relations*. New York: McGraw-Hill.

Cook, T., & Leviton, L. (1980). Reviewing the literature: A comparison of traditional methods with metaanalysis. *Journal of Personality, 48*(4), 449–472.

Cook, W., Leeds, C. H., & Callis, R. (1951). *The Minnesota teacher attitude inventory*. New York: Psychological Corporation.

Cooper, H. M. (1982). Scientific guidelines for conducting integrative research reviews. *Review of Educational Research, 52*, 291–302.

Cooper, H. M. (1984). *The integrative research review: A systematic approach*. Beverly Hills, Calif.: Sage.

Cooper, H. M., & Arkin, R. (1981). On quantitative reviewing. *Journal of Personality, 49*, 225–230.

Cooper, H. M., & Rosenthal, R. (1980). Statistical versus traditional procedures for summarizing research findings. *Psychological Bulletin, 87*(3), 442–449.

Cooper, L., Johnson, D. W., Johnson, R., & Wilderson, F. (1980). The effects of cooperative, competitive, and individualistic experiences on interpersonal attraction among heterogeneous peers. *The Journal of Social Psychology, 111*, 243–252.

Copeland, W. D. (1975). The relationship between micro teaching and student teacher classroom performance. *The Journal of Educational Research, 68*, 289–293.

Coppel, C., & Sigel, I. E. (1981). *Educating the young thinker: Classroom strategies for cognitive growth*. Krieger.

Costa, A. (1985). *Developing minds: A resource book for teaching thinking*. Alexandria, Va.: Association for Supervision and Curriculum Development.

Counts, G. (1932). *Dare the school build a new social order?* New York: The John Day Company.

Courmier, S., & Hagman, J., eds. (1987). *Transfer of learning*. San Diego: Academic Press.

Crandall, D. et al. (1982). *People, policies, and practices: Examining the chain of school improvement*. Vols. I–X. Andover, Mass.: The Network, Inc.

Crawford, J., Gage, N., Corno, L., Stayrook, N., Mittman, A., Schunk, D., Stallings,

J., Baskin, E., Harvey, P., Austin, D., Cronin, D., & Newman, R. (1978). *An experiment on teacher effectiveness and parent-assisted instruction in the third grade.* (3 vols.) Stanford, Calif.: Center for Educational Research at Stanford, Stanford University.

Crosby, M. (1965). *An adventure in human relations.* Chicago: Follet Corporation.

Cruickshank, D. R. (1986). Simulations and games: An ERIC bibliography. Washington: The ERIC Clearinghouse on Teacher Education.

Cuban, L. (1984). *How teachers taught.* White Plains, N.Y.: Longman, Inc.

Cuban, L. (1986). *Classroom use of technology since 1920.* New York: Teachers College Press.

Cummings, C. B. (1985). The effect of training on interactive and classroom management in non-volunteer teacher behavior. Paper presented at the American Educational Research Association, Chicago.

Dalton, M. (1986). The thought processes of teachers when practicing two models of teaching. Ph.D. Thesis, University of Oregon.

Dalton, M. & Dodd, J. (1986). Teacher thinking: The development of skill in using two models of teaching and model-relevant thinking. Paper presented at the annual meetings of the American Educational Research Association, San Francisco.

Damon, W. (1977). *The social world of the child.* San Francisco: Jossey-Bass.

Data Handbook. (1971, 1972, 1973). Boulder, Colo.: Social Science Consortium.

Deal, T. E., & Kennedy, A. A. (1984). *Corporate cultures: The rites and rituals of corporate life.* Boston: Addison-Wesley.

Dean, V. M. (1960). *The nature of the non-Western world.* New York: New American Library of World Literature, Inc.

Decker, R. E., & Alperin, R. (n.d.) *Emotional rating supplement.* Palo Alto, Calif.: Unpublished manual.

Denham, C., & Liederman, A., (Eds.) (1980). *Times to learn.* Washington, D.C.: Program on Teaching and Learning, National Institute of Education.

Derry, S. J., & Murphy, D. A. (1986). Designing systems that train learning ability: From theory to practice. *Review of Educational Research. 56,* 1–40.

Devaney, K., & Thorn, L. (1975). *Exploring teacher centers.* San Francisco: Far West Laboratory for Educational Research and Development.

Dewey, J. (1910). *How we think.* Boston: Heath.

Dewey, J. (1916). *Democracy in education.* New York: Macmillan, Inc.

Dewey, J. (1920). *Reconstruction in philosophy.* New York: Henry Holt.

Dewey, J. (1937). *Experience and education.* New York: Macmillan, Inc.

Dewey, J. (1956). *The school and society.* Chicago: University of Chicago Press.

Dewey, J. (1960). *The child and the curriculum.* Chicago: University of Chicago Press.

Downey, L. (1967). *The secondary phase of education.* Boston: Ginn and Co.

Dreikurs, R. (1968). *Psychology in the classroom.* New York: Harper and Row.

Dreikurs, R., Grunwald, B., & Pepper, F. (1982). *Maintaining sanity in the classroom.* (2nd ed.). New York: Harper and Row.

Dunn, R., Beaudry, J., & Klavas, A. (1989). Survey of research on learning styles. *Educational Leadership, 46,* 6, pp. 50–58.

Dunn, R. & Dunn, K. (1975). *Educator's self-teaching guide to individualizing instructional programs.* West Nyack, N.Y.: Parker.

Dunn, R., Dunn, K. & Price, G. E. (1989). The learning styles inventory. Lawrence, Kan.: Price Systems.

Edmonds, R. (1979). Some schools work and more can. *Social Policy, 9*(5), 28–32.

El-Nemr, M. A. (1979). Meta-analysis of the outcomes of teaching biology as inquiry. Unpublished doctoral dissertation, University of Colorado, Boulder.

Elefant, Emily. (1980). Deaf children in an inquiry training program. *The Volta Review, 82,* 271–279.

Eliot, T. S. The waste land. In *Collected Poems* 1909–1962. New York: Harcourt, Brace Jovanovich, Inc.

Ellis, A., & Harper, R. (1975). *A new guide to rational living.* Englewood Cliffs, N.J.: Prentice-Hall, Inc.

Elmore, R. (1990). On changing the structure of public schools. In Richard Elmore (Ed.), *Restructuring schools.* Oakland, Calif.: Jossey-Bass.

Emmer, E., & Evertson, C. (1980). *Effective classroom management at the beginning of the year in junior high school classrooms.* Austin, Texas: The Research and Development Center for Teacher Education, The University of Texas, Report No. 6107.

Emmer, E., Evertson, C., & Anderson, L. (1980). Effective classroom management at the beginning of the school year. *The Elementary School Journal, 80,* 219–231.

Englemann, S., & Osborn, J. (1972). *DISTAR language program.* Chicago: Science Research Associates, Inc.

Erikson, Erik. (1950). *Childhood and society.* New York: Norton.

Estes, W. E. (Ed.). (1976). *Handbook of learning and cognitive processes, Vol. IV: Attention and memory.* Hillsdale, N.J.: Lawrence Erlbaum Associates.

Evans, M., & Hopkins, D. (1988). School climate and the psychological state of the individual teacher as factors affecting the use of educational ideas following an inservice course. *British Educational Research Journal, 14* (3), 211–230.

Evertson, C. (1982). Differences in instructional activities in higher- and lower-achieving junior high English and math classes. *The Elementary School Journal, 82* (4), 329–350.

Evertson, C., Anderson, C., Anderson, L., & Brophy, J. (1980). Relationships between classroom behaviors and student outcomes in junior high mathematics and English classes. *American Educational Research Journal, 17* (1), 43–60.

Eysenck, H. J. (1978). An exercise in mega-silliness. *American Psychologist, 33* (5), 517.

Feeley, Theodore. (1972). The concept of inquiry in the social studies. Ph.D. thesis, Stanford University.

Fensterheim, H., & Baer, J. (1975). *Don't say yes when you want to say no.* New York: Del Publishing Co., Inc.

Festinger, C. L. (1964). Behavior support for opinion change. *Public Opinion Quarterly.* 28, 404–417.

Fisher, C. W., Berliner, D. C., Filby, N. N., Marliave, R., Ghen, L. S., & Dishaw, M. M. (1980). Teaching behaviors, academic learning time, and student achievement: An overview. In C. Denham and A. Lieberman (Eds.), *Time to learn.* Washington, D.C.: National Institute of Education.

Flanders, N. (1970). *Analyzing teaching behavior.* Reading, Mass.: Addison-Wesley.

Flavell, J. H. (1963). *The developmental psychology of Jean Piaget.* Princeton, N.J.: Van Nostrand Reinhold.

Flesch, Rudolph. (1955). *Why Johnny can't read.* New York: Harper Brothers.

Flint, Shirley. (1965). The relationship between the classroom verbal behavior of student teachers and the classroom verbal behavior of their cooperating teachers. PhD dissertation. New York: Teachers College, Columbia University.

Fromm, E. (1941). *Escape from freedom.* New York: Farrar and Rinehart.

Fromm, E. (1955). *The sane society.* New York: Rinehart.

Fromm, E. (1956). *The art of loving.* New York: Harper.

Fullan, M. (1982). *The meaning of educational change.* New York: Teachers College Press.

Fullan, M. (1983). Evaluating program implementation: What can be learned from follow through. *Curriculum Inquiry, 13* (2), 215–227.

Fullan, M. (1990). Staff development, innovation, and institutional development. In Bruce R. Joyce (Ed.), *ASCD yearbook on staff development.* Alexandria, Va.: The Association for Supervision and Curriculum Development.

Fullan, M., Miles, M., & Taylor, G. (1980). Organization development in schools: The state of the art. *Review of Educational Research, 50* (1), 121–184.

Fullan, M., & Park, P. (1981). *Curriculum implementation: A resource booklet.* Toronto: Ontario Ministry of Education.

Fullan, M., and Pomfret, A. (1977). Research on curriculum and instruction implementation. *Review of Educational Research, 47* (2), 335–397.

Fullan, M. G., Bennett, B., & Bennett, C. R. (1990). Linking classroom and school improvement. *Educational Leadership, 47* (8), 13–19.

Furth, H. G. (1969). *Piaget and knowledge.* Englewood Cliffs, N.J.: Prentice-Hall.

Gage, N. L. (1963). Paradigms for research on teaching. In N. L. Gage (Ed.), *Handbook of research on teaching,* pp. 94–141. Chicago: Rand McNally & Company.

Gage, N. L. (1979). *The scientific basis for the art of teaching.* New York: Teachers College Press.

Gage, N. L., & Berliner, D. (1983). *Educational psychology.* Boston: Houghton Mifflin.

Gagné, R. (1962a). Military training and principles of learning. *American Psychologist, 17,* 46–67.

Gagné, R. (1962b). *Psychological principles in system development.* New York: Holt, Rinehart, and Winston.

Gagné, R. (1965a). *The conditions of learning.* New York: Holt, Rinehart, and Winston.

Gagné, R. (1965b). The learning of concepts. *The School Review,* 75, 187–196.

Gagné, R. (1967). Instruction in the conditions of learning. In Laurence Siegel (Ed.), *Instruction: Some contemporary viewpoints.* New York: Harper & Row, Publishers, Inc.

Gagné, R., & Briggs, L. (1979). *Principles of instructional design.* New York: Holt, Rinehart and Winston.

Gagné, R., et al. (1962). *Psychological principles in systems development.* New York: Holt, Rinehart & Winston.

Gall, M. D. (1983). Using staff development to improve schools. *Research and Development Perspectives,* 1–6.

Gall, M. D. & Gall, J. (1976). The discussion method. *The Psychology of Teaching Methods.* The seventy-fifth yearbook of the National Society for the Study of Education. Chicago: University of Chicago Press, pp. 166–216.

Gall, M. D., Haisley, F. B., Baker, R. G., & Perez, M. (1982). *The relationship between inservice education practices and productivity of basic skills instruction.* Eugene: University of Oregon, Center for Educational Policy & Management.

Gall, M. D., & Renchler, R. S. (1985). *Effective staff development practices: A research-based model.* Eugene, Ore.: University of Oregon, Center for Educational Policy & Management. (ERIC Document Reproduction Service No. Ed 017 615).

Gallway, W. T. (1977). *Inner skiing.* New York: Random House, Inc.

Gardner, J. (1978). *Excellence and education.* New York: Harper & Row.

Garmston, R. J., & Eblen, D. R. (1988). Visions, decisions, and results: Changing school culture through staff development. *The Journal of Staff Development, 9* (2), 22–29.

Gentile, J. R. (1988). *Instructional improvement: Summary and analysis of Madeline Hunter's essential elements of instruction and supervision.* Oxford, Oh.: National Staff Development Council.

Gideonse, H. D. (1982). The necessary revolution in teacher education. *Phi Delta Kappan, 64* (1), 15–18.

Gilbert, J. P., McPeek, B., & Mosteller, P. (1977). Statistics and ethics in surgery and anesthesia. *Science, 198,* 684–689.

Glaser, R. (Ed.). (1962). *Training research and education.* Pittsburgh: University of Pittsburgh Press.

Glass, G. V. (1975). Primary, secondary, and meta-analysis of research. *Educational Researcher, 7* (3).

Glass, G. V. (1982). Meta-analysis: An approach to the synthesis of research results. *Journal of Research in Science Teaching, 19* (2), 93–112.

Glass, G. V., Cahan, L. S., Smith, M. L., & Filby, N. N. (1982). *School class size: Research and Policy.* Beverly Hills, Calif.: Sage.

Glass, G. V., McGaw, B., & Smith, M. L. (1981). *Meta-analysis in social research.* Beverly Hills, Calif.: Sage.

Glassbury, S., & Oja, S. N. (1981). A developmental model for enhancing teachers' personal and professional growth. *Journal of Research and Development in Education, 14* (2), 59–70.

Glasser, W. (1965). *Reality therapy.* New York: Harper & Row, Publishers, Inc.

Glasser, W. (1969). *Schools without failure.* New York: Harper and Row.

Glasser, W. (1984). *Take effective control of your life.* New York: Harper and Row.

Glasser, W., & Powers, William T. (1981). *Stations of the mind: New directions for reality therapy.* New York: Harper and Row.

Glickman, C. D. (1985). The supervisor's challenge: Changing the teachers' work environment. *Educational Leadership, 42,* 4, 38–40.

Glickman, C. D. (1989). Has Sam and Samantha's time come at last? *Educational Leadership, 46* (8), 4–9.

Gliessman, D. H., & Pugh, R. C. (1978). Acquiring teacher behavior concepts through the use of high-structure and low-structure protocol films. *Journal of Educational Psychology, 70* (5), 779–787.

Gnott, H. (1971). *Teacher and child.* New York: Macmillan.

Golemiewski, R. T., & Blumberg, A. (1970). *Sensitivity training and the laboratory approach.* Itaska, Ill.: F. E. Peacock Publishers, Inc.

Good, T. & Brophy, G. (1974). An empirical investigation: Changing teacher and student behavior. *Journal of Educational Psychology, 66,* 399–405.

Good, T. & Grouws, D. (1977). Teaching effects: A process-product study in fourth grade mathematics classrooms. *Journal of Teacher Education, 28,* 49–54.

Good, T., Grouws, D., & Ebmeier, H. (1983). *Active mathematics teaching.* New York: Longman, Inc.

Goodlad, J. (1983). *A place called school.* New York: McGraw-Hill.

Goodlad, J., & Klein, F. (1970). *Looking behind the classroom door.* Worthington, Oh.: Charles A. Jones.

Goodman, P. (1964). *Compulsory miseducation.* New York: Horizon Press.

Gordon, W. J. J. (1952). The integration of creative persons. Paper delivered to Sloan Fellows, MIT.

Gordon, W. J. J. (December 1955). Some environmental aspects of creativity. Paper delivered to the Department of Defense, Fort Belvior, Va.

Gordon, W. J. J. (1956a). Creativity as a process. Paper delivered at the First Arden House Conference on Creative Process.

Gordon, W. J. J. (1956b). Operational approach to creativity. *Harvard Business Review, 34,* (6), 41–51.

Gordon, W. J. J. (1957). The role of irrelevance in art and invention. Paper delivered to the Third Arden House Conference on Creative Process.

Gordon, W. J. J. (1961). *Synectics.* New York: Harper & Row.

Gordon, W. J. J. (November 4, 1961). Director of research. *The New Yorker.*

Gordon, W. J. J. (May 1962). The Pures. *The Atlantic Monthly.*

Gordon, W. J. J. (August 1962). The Nobel prizewinners. *The Atlantic Monthly.*

Gordon, W. J. J. (March 1963). How to get your imagination off the ground. *Think* (IBM Press).

Gordon, W. J. J. (April 1963). Mrs. Schyler's plot. *The Atlantic Monthly.*

Gordon, W. J. J. (1965). The metaphorical way of knowing. In Gyorgy Kepes (Ed.), *Education of vision.* New York: George Braziiller.

Gordon, W. J. J. (1970). The metaphorical development of man. In Chandler McC. Brooks (Ed.), *The changing world and man.* New York: NYU Press.

Gordon, W. J. J. (1971). Architecture—The making of metaphors. *Main Currents in Modern Thought, 28*(1).

Gordon, W. J. J. (Spring 1972). Use of metaphor increases creative learning efficiency. *Trend,* 11–14.

Gordon, W. J. J. (1974). Some source material in discovery-by-analogy. *Journal of Creative Behavior, 8,* (4), 239–257.

Gordon, W. J. J. (1975). Training for creativity. *International Handbook of Management Development and Training.* London: McGraw-Hill.

Gordon, W. J. J. (1977a). Connection-making is universal. *Curriculum Product Review, 9*(4).

Gordon, W. J. J. (1977b). Toward understanding 'the moment of inspiration'. Paper delivered at the Creativity Symposium for the American Association for the Advancement of Science.

Gordon, W. J. J. (with Jerome Bruner). (May 1957). Motivating the creative process. Paper delivered at the Second Arden House Conference on Creative Process.

Gordon, W. J. J. (Poze, T., Project Director). (1968). *Making it strange: Books 1 and 2.* Evanston: Harper & Row.

Gordon, W. J. J. (Poze, T., Ed.). (1969). *Making it strange: Books 3 and 4.* Evanston: Harper & Row.

Gordon, W. J. J., & Poze, T. (1971a). *The art of the possible.* Cambridge: Porpoise Books.

Gordon, W. J. J., & Poze, T. (1971b). *The basic course in synectics*. Cambridge: Porpoise Books.

Gordon, W. J. J., & Poze, T. (1971c). *Facts and guesses*. Cambridge: Porpoise Books.

Gordon, W. J. J., & Poze, T. (1971d). *Invent-o-rama*. Cambridge: Porpoise Books.

Gordon, W. J. J., & Poze, T. (1971e). *Making it whole*. Cambridge: Porpoise Books.

Gordon, W. J. J., & Poze, T. (1971f). *The metaphorical way of learning and knowing*. Cambridge: Porpoise Books.

Gordon, W. J. J. (Poze, T., Ed.). (1971g). *What color is sleep?* Cambridge: Porpoise Books.

Gordon, W. J. J., & Poze, T. (1972a). *Activities in metaphor*. Cambridge: Porpoise Books.

Gordon, W. J. J., & Poze, T. (1972b). *Introduction to synectics (Problem-solving)*. Cambridge: Porpoise Books.

Gordon, W. J. J., & Poze, T. (1972c). *Strange and familiar, Book VI*. Cambridge: Porpoise Books.

Gordon, W. J. J., & Poze, T. (1972d). *Teaching is listening*. Cambridge: Porpoise Books.

Gordon, W. J. J. (1973). On being explicit about creative process. *Journal of Creative Behavior, 6*(4), 295–300.

Gordon, W. J. J., & Poze, T. (1974a). Creative training in an occupational context. *Technical Education Reporter, 1*(1), 52–57.

Gordon, W. J. J., & Poze, T. (1974b). *From the inside*. Cambridge: Porpoise Books.

Gordon, W. J. J., & Poze, T. (1974c). Learning is connection-making. *Professional Report* (Croft Publications).

Gordon, W. J. J., & Poze, T. (1975a). *Strange and familiar: Book I*. Cambridge: Porpoise Books.

Gordon, W. J. J., & Poze, T. (1975b). *Strange and familiar: Book III*. Cambridge: Porpoise Books.

Gordon, W. J. J., & Poze, T. (1976). *The art of the possible*. Cambridge: Porpoise Books.

Grant, G. (1988). The world we created at Hamilton High. Cambridge: Harvard University Press.

Graves, N., & Graves, T. (1990). Cooperative learning: A resource guide. Santa Cruz: The International Association for the Study of Cooperation in Education.

Gregorc, A. F. (1982). *An adult's guide to style*. Maynard, Mass.: Gabriel Systems.

Griffin, G. A. (1983). *Staff development: Eighty-second yearbook of the National Society for the Study of Education*. Chicago, Ill.: University of Chicago Press.

Griffin, G. A., & Barnes, S. (1984). School change: A craft-derived and research-based strategy. *Teachers College Record, 86*(1), 103–123.

Griffin, G. A., & Lieberman, A. (1974). *Behavior of innovative personnel*. Washington, D.C.: ERIC Clearinghouse on Teacher Education.

Guetzkow, H., et al. (1963). *Simulation in international relations*. Englewood Cliffs, N.J.: Prentice-Hall, Inc.

Guetzkow, H., & Valdez, J. J. (Eds.) (1966). *Simulated international processes: Theories and research in global modeling*. Beverly Hills, Calif.: Sage Publications.

Guskey, T. (1986). Staff development and the process of change. *Educational Researcher, 15* (5), 5–12.

Hall, G. (1986). Skills derived from studies of the implementation of innovations in education. A paper presented at the annual meetings of the American Educational Research Association, San Francisco.

Hall, G., & Loucks, S. (1977). A developmental model for determining whether the treatment is actually implemented. *American Educational Research Journal, 14* (3), 263–276.

Hall, G., & Loucks, S. (1978). Teacher concerns as a basis for facilitating and personalizing staff development. *Teachers College Record, 80*(1), 36–53.

Halpin, A. W. (1966). *Theory and research in administration*. New York: Macmillan.

Hansen, C. (1962). *Amidon*. Englewood Cliffs, N.J.: Prentice-Hall, Inc.

Hargreaves, A., & Dawe, R. (1989). Coaching as unreflective practice. Paper presented at the American Educational Research Association.

Harvey, O. J., Hunt, D., & Schroeder, H. (1961). *Conceptual systems and personality organization*. New York: Wiley.

Hawkes, E. (1971). The effects of an instruction strategy on approaches to problem-solving. Unpublished doctoral dissertation, Teachers College, Columbia University.

Heard, S., & Wadsworth, B. (1977). The relationship between cognitive development and language complexity. Unpublished paper, Mount Holyoke College.

Hedges, L. V., & Olkin, I. (1986). Meta-analysis: A review and a new view. *Educational Researcher, 15*(8), 14–21.

Hersh, R. H. (1984). *What makes some schools and teachers more effective?* Eugene: Center for Educational Policy and Management, University of Oregon.

Hoetker, J., & Ahlbrand, W. (1969). The persistence of the recitation. *American Educational Research Journal, 6*, 145–167.

Holloway, S. D. (1988). Concepts of ability and effort in Japan and the United States. *Review of Educational Research, 58*(3), 327–345.

Holms, T. H., & Rahe, R. H. (1967). The social readjustment rating scale. *Journal of Psychomatic Research, 11*, 213–18.

Hooper, F. H. (1974). An evaluation of logical operations in instruction in the preschool. In R. K. Parker (Ed.), *The preschool in action: Exploring early childhood education programs*, (pp. 134–86). Boston: Allyn & Bacon.

Hopkins, D. (1990). Integrating staff development and school improvement: a study of teacher personality and school climate. In Joyce, Bruce, ed. *Changing school culture through staff development*. 1990 Yearbook of the Association for Supervision and Curriculum Development. Alexandria, Va.: ASCD.

Hopkins, I. (1982). The unit of analysis: Group means versus individual observations. *American Educational Research Journal, 19,* 5–18.

Howey, K., Yarger, S., & Joyce, B. (1978). *Improving teacher education*. Washington: Association for Teacher Education.

Huberman, A. M., & Crandall, D. P. (1983). *A study of dissemination efforts supporting school improvement: Implications for action* (Vol. 9). Andover, Mass.: The Network.

Huberman, M., & Miles, M. (1984). *Innovation up close*. New York: Plenum.

Hullfish, H. G., & Smith, P. G. (1961). *Reflective thinking: The method of education*. New York: Dodd, Mead & Company.

Human relations laboratory training student notebook. (1961). Washington, D.C.: U.S. Office of Education. ED 018 834.

Hunt, D. E. (1970a). Adaptability in interpersonal communication among training agents. *Merrill Palmer Quarterly, 16,* 325–344.

Hunt, D. E. (1970b). A conceptual level matching model for coordinating learner characteristics with educational approaches. *Interchange: A Journal of Educational Studies, 1*(2), 1–31.

Hunt, D. E. (1971). *Matching models in education*. Toronto: Ontario Institute for Studies in Education.

Hunt, D. E. (1975a). The B-P-E paradigm in theory, research, and practice. *Canadian Psychological Review, 16,* 185–197b.

Hunt, D. E. (1975b). Person-environment interaction: A challenge found wanting before it was tried. *Review of Educational Research,* 45, 209–230c.

Hunt, D. E. (1975c). Teachers' adaptation to students: Implicit and explicit matching. Stanford, Calif.: Research and Development Memorandum No. 139, SCRDT.

Hunt, D. E. (1976). Teachers are psychologists, too: On the application of psychology to education. *Canadian Psychological Review.*

Hunt, D. E., Butler, L. F., Noy, J. E., & Rosser, M. E. (1978). *Assessing conceptual level by the paragraph completion method*. Toronto: Ontario Institute for Studies in Education.

Hunt, D. E., Greenwood, J., Brill, R., & Deineka, M. (1972). From psychological theory to educational practice: Implementation of a matching model. Symposium presented at the annual meeting of the American Educational Research Association, Chicago.

Hunt, D. E., & Hardt, R. H. (1967). The role of conceptual level and program structure in summer Upward Bound programs. Paper presented to the Eastern Psychological Association, Boston.

Hunt, D. E. & Joyce, B. (1967). Teacher trainee personality and initial teaching style. *American Educational Research Journal,* 4, 253–259.

Hunt, D. E., Joyce, B., & Del Popolo, J. (1964). An exploratory study of the modification of student teachers' behavior patterns. Syracuse University, unpublished paper.

Hunt, D. E., Joyce, B., Greenwood, J., Noy, J., Reid, R., & Weil, M. (1981). Student conceptual level and models of teaching. In Joyce, Bruce, Peck, Lucy, & Brown, Clark. *Flexibility in teaching*. White Plains, N.Y.: Longman, Inc.

Hunt, D. E., & Sullivan, E. V. (1974). *Between psychology and education*. Hinsdale, Ill.: Dryden.

Hunt, J. McV. (1961). *Intelligence and experience*. New York: Ronald Press.

Hunter, I. M. L. (1964). *Memory*. Middlesex, England: Penguin Books.

Hunter, J. E., Schmidt, F. L., & Jackson, G. B. (1982). *Meta-analysis: Cumulating research findings across studies*. Beverly Hills, Calif.: Sage.

Hunter, M. (1980). Six types of supervisory conferences. *Educational Leadership, 37*, 408–412.

Hunter, M., & Russell, D. (1981a). Increasing your teaching effectiveness. Palo Alto, Calif.: Learning Institute.

Hunter, M., & Russell, D. (1981b). Planning for effective instruction: Lesson design. In *Increasing your teaching effectiveness*. Palo Alto, Calif.: Learning Institute.

Hunziker, J. C. (1972). The use of participant modeling in the treatment of water phobias. Unpublished Master's thesis, Arizona State University.

"Individually Prescribed Instruction," Philadelphia: Research for Better Schools. Unpublished manuscripts, 1966.

Ivany, G. (1969). The assessment of verbal inquiry in elementary school science. *Science Education, 53* (4), 287–293.

Jackson, G. B. (1980). Methods for integrative reviews. *Review of Educational Research, 50*, 438–460.

Jackson, P. W. (1966). *The way teaching is*. Washington: National Education Association.

Jackson, P. W. (1968). *Life in classrooms*. New York: Holt, Rinehart and Winston.

Jacobson, E. (1979). *Progressive relaxation*. Chicago, University of Chicago Press.

James, H. H. (1971). Attitude and attitude change: Its influence upon teaching behavior. *Journal of Research in Science Teaching, 8*, 234–249.

Jencks, C., Smith, M., Acland, H., Bane, M. J., Cohen, D., Gintis, H., Hayns, B., & Michelsohn, S. (1972). *Inequality: A reassessment of the effect of family and schooling in America*. New York: Basic Books.

Johnson, D. W., & Johnson, R. T. (1974). Instructional goal structure: Cooperative, competitive, or individualistic. *Review of Educational Research, 44*, 213–240.

Johnson, D. W., & Johnson, R. T. (1975a). *Circles of learning*. Englewood Cliffs: Prentice Hall.

Johnson, D. W., & Johnson, R. T. (1975b). Learning together and alone. Englewood Cliffs, N.J.: Prentice Hall, Inc.

Johnson, D. W., & Johnson, R. T. (1979). Conflict in the classroom: Controversy in learning. *Review of Educational Research, 49*(1), 51–70.

Johnson, D. W., & Johnson, R. T. (1981). Effects of cooperative and individualistic learning experiences on inter-ethnic interaction. *Journal of Educational Psychology, 73*(3), 444–449.

Johnson, D. W., & Johnson, R. T. (1990). *Cooperation and competition: Theory and research.* Edina, Minn.: Interaction Book Company.

Johnson, D. W., Johnson, R. T., Johnson, J., & Anderson, D. (1976). The effects of cooperative vs. individualized instruction on student prosocial behavior, attitudes toward learning, and achievement. *Journal of Educational Psychology, 68,* 446–452.

Johnson, D. W., Johnson, R. T., & Scott, L. (1978). The effects of cooperative and individualized instruction on student attitudes and achievement. *Journal of Social Psychology, 104,* 207–216.

Johnson, D. W., Johnson, R. T., & Skon, L. (1979). Student achievement on different types of tasks under cooperative, competitive, and individualistic conditions. *Contemporary Educational Psychology, 4,* 99–106.

Johnson, D. W., & Johnson, S. (1972). The effects of attitude similarity, expectation of goal facilitation, and actual goal facilitation on interpersonal attraction. *Journal of Experimental Social Psychology, 8,* 197–206.

Johnson, D. W., Maruyana, G., Johnson, R., Nelson, D., & Skon, L. (1981). Effects of cooperative, competitive, and individualistic goal structures on achievement: A meta-analysis. *Psychological Bulletin, 89* (1), 47–62.

Johnson, J. L., & Sloat, K. M. (1980). Teacher training effects: Real or illusory. *Psychology in the Schools Journal, 17* (1), 109–114.

Joyce, B. R. (1975). The models of teaching community: What have we learned? *Texas Tech Journal of Education, 22,* 95–106.

Joyce, B. (Ed.). (1978). *Involvement: A study of shared governance of teacher education.* Washington, D.C.: ERIC Clearinghouse on Teacher Education.

Joyce, B. (1978–79). Toward a theory of information processing in teaching. *Educational Research Quarterly, 3* (4), 66–77.

Joyce, B. (1980). *Teacher innovator system: Observer's manual.* Eugene, Ore.: Booksend Laboratories.

Joyce, B. (1987). Essential reform in teacher education. In Linda Newton, Michael Fullan, & John W. MacDonald (Eds.), *Rethinking teacher education,* pp. 1–27. Toronto: Ontario Institute for Studies in Education.

Joyce, B. (1991a). Common misconceptions about cooperative learning and gifted students. *Educational Leadership, 48* (6), 72–74.

Joyce, B. (1991b). Doors to school improvement. *Educational Leadership, 48* (8), 59–62.

Joyce, B., Bush, R., & McKibbin, M. (1982). *The California staff development study: The January 1982 report.* Palo Alto, Calif.: Booksend Laboratories.

Joyce, B. & Clift, R. (1983). Generic training problems: Training elements, socialization, contextual variables, and personality disposition across occupational categories that vary in ethos. Paper presented at the annual meetings of the American Educational Research Association, Montreal.

Joyce, B., & Clift, R. (1984). The phoenix agenda: Essential reform in teacher education. *Educational Researcher, 13* (4), 5–18.

Joyce, B., & Harootunian, B. (1967). *The structure of teaching.* Chicago: Science Research Associates.

Joyce, B., Hersh, R., & McKibbin, M. (1983). *The structure of school improvement.* New York: Longman.

Joyce, B., Howey, K., & Yarger, S. (1975). *Issues to face.* Syracuse, N.Y.: National Dissemination Center, Syracuse University.

Joyce, B., Howey, K., & Yarger, S. (1976). *Issues to face, report one: Inservice teacher education.* Palo Alto, Calif.: Educational Research & Development Center.

Joyce, B. R., McKibbin, M., & Bush, N. (1983). The seasons of professional life: The growth states of teachers. Paper presented at the annual meeting of the American Education Research Association, Montreal.

Joyce, B., McKibbin, M., & Bush, R. (1984). Predicting whether an innovation will be implemented: Four case studies. Paper presented at the annual meeting of the American Educational Research Association, New Orleans.

Joyce, B. & Morine, G. (1977). *Creating the school.* Boston: Little Brown.

Joyce, B., Murphy, C., Showers, B., & Murphy, J. (1989). School renewal as cultural change. *Educational Leadership, 47* (3), 70–78.

Joyce, B., Peck, L., & Brown, C. (1981). *Flexibility in teaching.* New York: Longman, Inc.

Joyce, B., & Showers, B. (1980). Improving inservice training: The message of research. *Educational Leadership, 37,* 163–172.

Joyce, B. R., & Showers, B. (1981). Teacher training research: Working hypothesis for program design and directions for further study. Paper presented at the annual meeting of the American Education Research Association, Los Angeles.

Joyce, B., & Showers, B. (1981). Transfer of training: The contribution of coaching. *Journal of Education, 163,* 163–172.

Joyce, B., & Showers, B. (1982). The coaching of teaching. *Educational Leadership, 40* (1), 4–10.

Joyce, B., & Showers, B. (1983). *Power in staff development through research on training.* Washington: Association for Supervision and Curriculum Development.

Joyce, B. R., & Showers, B. (1984). Persuasion-oriented studies of teaching. Paper presented at the annual meeting of the American Educational Research Association, New Orleans, April 23–27.

Joyce, B., & Showers, B. (1986). Peer coaching guides. Eugene, Ore.: Booksend Laboratories.

Joyce, B., & Showers, B. (1988). *Student achievement through staff development.* White Plains: Longman, Inc.

Joyce, B., Showers, B., Beaton, C., & Dalton, M. (1984). The search for validated objectives of teacher education: Teaching skills derived from naturalistic and persuasion oriented studies of teaching. Paper presented at the annual meeting of the American Educational Research Association, New Orleans.

Joyce, B., Showers, B., & Bennett, B. (1987). Synthesis of research on staff development: A framework for future study and a state-of-the-art analysis. *Educational Leadership, 45* (3), 77–87.

Joyce, B., Showers, B., Dalton, M., & Beaton, C. (1985). Theory-driven and naturalistic research as sources of teaching skills: A classification. Paper presented at the annual meeting of the American Educational Research Association, Chicago.

Joyce, B., Showers, B., Murphy, C. & Murphy, J. (1989). Reconstructing the workplace: School renewal as cultural change. *Educational Leadership* (in press).

Joyce, B., & Weil, M. (1980). *Models of teaching* (2nd ed.). Englewood Cliffs, N.J.: Prentice-Hall.

Joyce, B., & Weil, M. (1986). *Models of teaching* (3rd ed.). Englewood Cliffs, N.J.: Prentice-Hall.

Joyce, B., Weil, M., & Wald, R. (1981). Can teachers learn repertoires of models of teaching? In Joyce, Peck, & Brown, 141–156.

Judd, C. H. (1934). *Education and social progress.* New York: Harcourt Brace Jovanovich, Inc.

Judge, H. G. (1982). *American graduate schools of education: A view from abroad.* New York: Ford Foundation.

Kagan, S. (1990). *Cooperative learning resources for teachers.* San Juan Capistrano, Calif.: Resources for Teachers.

Kahn, S. B., & Weiss, J. (1973). The teaching of affective responses. In R. M. W. Travers (Ed.), *The second handbook of research on teaching.* Chicago: McNally & Company.

Kamii, C., & DeVries, R. (1974). Piaget-based curricula for early childhood education. In Ron Parker (Ed.), *The preschool in action.* Boston: Allyn & Bacon, Inc.

Kenworthy, L. S. (1955). *Introducing children to the world.* New York: Harper.

Kerman, S. (1979). Teacher expectations and student achievement. *Phi Delta Kappan, 60* (10), 716–718.

Kilpatrick, W. H. (1919). *The project method.* New York: Teachers College Press.

Kincaid, E. (1959). *In every war but one.* New York: W. W. Norton, Inc.

Klausmeier, H. J. (1980). *Learning and teaching concepts.* New York: Academic Press.

Klausmeier, H. J., & Harris, C. W. (1966). *Analysis of concept learning.* New York: Academic Press, Inc.

Klausmeier, H. J., & Hooper, F. H. (1974). Conceptual development on instruction. In Fred N. Kerlinger & John B. Carroll (Eds.), *Review of Research in Education*, (pp. 3–54). Itasca, Ill.: F. E. Peacock Publisher, Inc.

Kleitsch, R. G. (1969). *Directory of educational simulations, learning games, and didactic units*. St. Paul, Minn.: Instructional Simulations.

Klinzing, G., & Klinzing-Eurich, G. (1985). Higher cognitive behaviors in classroom discourse: Congruencies between teachers' questions and pupils' responses. *Australian Journal of Education, 29* (1), 63–74.

Knowles, M. (1978). *The adult learner: A neglected species* (2nd ed.). Houston: Gulf Publishing Co.

Kohlberg, L. (1966). Moral education and the schools. *School Review, 74,* 1–30.

Kohlberg, L. (1976). The cognitive developmental approach to moral education. In D. Purpel & K. Ryan (Eds.), *Moral education . . . It comes with the territory*. Berkeley, Calif.: McCutchan Publishing Corporation.

Kohlberg, L. (Ed.). (1977). *Recent research in moral development*. New York: Holt, Rinehart & Winston.

Kohlberg, L. (1981). *The philosophy of moral development*. Harper & Row.

Kohlberg, L. (1983). *The psychology of moral development*. Harper & Row.

Koran, M. L., Snow, R. E., & McDonald, F. J. (1971). Teacher aptitude and observational learning of a teaching skill. *Journal of Educational Psychology, 62* (3), 219–228.

Kourilsky, M. (1974). *Beyond simulation: The mini-society approach to education and other social sciences*. Los Angeles: Educational Research Associates.

Kuhn, D., Amsel, E., & O'Loughlin, M. (1988). *The development of scientific thinking skills*. New York: Academic Press.

Kulik, C. C., Kulik, J. A., & Bengert-Drowns, R. L. (1990). Effectiveness of mastery learning programs: a meta-analysis. *Review of Educational Research. 60,* 265–299.

Lavatelle, C. (1970). *Piaget's theory applied to an early childhood education curriculum*. Boston: American Science and Engineering.

Lawson, A. E. et al. (1984). Proportional reasoning and linguistic abilities required for hypothetico-deduct reasoning. *Journal of Research in Science Teaching, 21* (4), 377–384.

Lawton, J. T. (1977a). Effects of advance organizer lessons on children's use and understanding of the causal and logical 'Because'," *Journal of Experimental Education, 46,* 1, 41–6.

Lawton, J. T. (1977b). The use of advance organizers in the learning and retention of logical operations in social studies concepts. *American Educational Research Journal, 14* (1), 24–43.

Lawton, J. T., & Wanska, S. K. (1977). Advance organizers as a teaching strategy: A reply to Barnes and Clawson. *Review of Educational Research, 47* (1), 233–244.

Lawton, J. T., & Wanska, S. K. (1977). The effects of different types of advance organizers on classification learning. *American Educational Research Journal, 16,* 3, Summer, 223–239.

Lazarus, A. A., (1971). *Behavior therapy and beyond.* New York: McGraw-Hill.

Lederman, J. (1973). *Anger and the rocking chair.* New York: The Viking Press.

Leithwood, K. (1990). The principal's role in teacher development. In Bruce Joyce (Ed.), *ASCD Yearbook on Staff Development.* Alexandria, Va.: The Association for Supervision and Curriculum Development.

Leithwood, K., & Montgomery, D. (1982). The role of the elementary school principal in program improvement. *Review of Educational Research, 52,* 309–339.

Leithwood, K., Montgomery, D. (1983). Assumptions and uses of a procedure for evaluating the nature and degree of program implementation. Paper presented at the annual meeting of the American Educational Research Association. San Francisco.

Levin, J. R., McCormick, C., Miller, H., and Berry, J. (1982). Mnemonic versus nonmnemonic strategies for children. *American Educational Research Journal, 19* (1), 121–136.

Levin, Joel, Shriberg, L., & Berry, J. (1983). A concrete strategy for remembering abstract prose. *American Educational Research Journal, 20* (2), 277–290.

Levin, M. E., & Levin, J. R. (1990). Scientific mnemonics: Methods for maximizing more than memory. *American Educational Research Journal, 27,* 301–321.

Levy, D. V., & Stark, J. (1982). Implementation of the Chicago mastery learning reading program at inner-city elementary schools. Paper presented at the annual meeting of the American Educational Research Association, New York.

Lewis, H., and Streitfeld, H. (1970). *Growth games.* New York: Harcourt Brace Jovanovich, Inc.

Lindvall, C. M., & J. O. Bolvin. (1966). The project for individually prescribed instruction. Oakleaf Project. Unpublished manuscript, University of Pittsburgh, Learning Research and Development Center.

Lippitt, R., Fox, R., & Schaible, L. (1969a). Cause and effect: *Social science resource book.* Chicago: Science Research Associates, Inc.

Lippitt, R., Fox, R., & Schaible, L. (1969b). *Social science laboratory units.* Chicago: Science Research Associates.

Little, J. W. (1982). Norms of collegiality and experimentation: Workplace conditions of school success. *American Educational Research Journal, 19* (3), 325–340.

Little, J. W. (1986). The persistence of privacy: Autonomy and initiative in teachers' professional opportunities. Paper presented at the American Educational Research Association.

Little, J. W. (1989). *The persistence of privacy: Autonomy and initiative in teachers' professional relations.* A paper presented at the annual meeting of the American Educational Research Association, San Francisco, CA.

Little, J. W., et al. (1987). Staff development in California. San Francisco: Far West Laboratories.

Locke, J. (1927). *Some thoughts concerning education*, Ed. R. H. Quick. Cambridge: Cambridge University Press.

Lorayne, H., & Lucas, J. (1966). *The memory book*, Briercliff Manor, N.Y.

Lortie, D. (1975). *Schoolteacher.* Chicago: The University of Chicago Press.

Loucks, S. F., Newlove, B. W., & Hall, G. E. (1975). *Measuring levels of use of the innovation: A manual for trainers, interviewers, and raters.* Austin: Research and Development Center for Teacher Education, The University of Texas.

Louis, K. S., & Miles, M. B. (1990). *Improving the urban high school.* New York: Teachers College Press.

Lucas, S. B. (1972). The effects of utilizing three types of advance organizers for learning a biological concept in seventh grade science, Doctoral Dissertation, Pennsylvania State University.

Ludlum, R. P., et al. (1969). *American government.* Boston: Houghton Mifflin Company.

Luiten, J., Ames, W., and Ackerson, G. A. (1980). A meta-analysis of the effects of advance organizers on learning and retention. *American Educational Research Journal, 17,* 211–218.

Lundquist, G., and G. Parr. (1978). Assertiveness training with adolescents. *Technical Journal of Education, 5,* 37–44.

Madaus, G. F., Arasian, P. W., and Kellaghan, T. (1980). *School effectiveness: A review of the evidence.* New York: McGraw-Hill.

Madden, N. A., & Slavin, R. E. Cooperative learning and social acceptance of mainstreamed academically handicapped students, *Journal of Special Education, 17,* 1983, 171–182.

Mahoney, M., & Thorensen C. (1972). Behavioral self-control—power to the person, *Educational Researcher, 1,* 5–7.

Mandeville, G. K., & Rivers, J. L. (1989). Effects of South Carolina's Hunter-based PET program. *Educational Leadership, 46* (4), 63–66.

Marcuse, H., *Eros and Civilization.* Boston: Beacon Press, 1955.

Marzano, R., Brandt, R. Hughes, C., Jones, B., Presseisen, B., Rankin, S., & Suhor, C. (1987). *Dimensions of thinking.* Alexandria, Va.: Association for Supervision and Curriculum Development.

Maslow, A. (1962). *Toward a psychology of being.* New York: Van Nostrand.

Massialas, B., and Cox, B. *Inquiry in social studies.* New York: McGraw-Hill, 1966.

Mayer, R. F., (1979). Can advance organizers influence meaningful learning? *Review of Educational Research, 49* (2), 371–83.

McCarthy, B. (1981). *The 4mat system: Teaching to learning styles with right/left mode techniques.* Barrington, Ill.: Excel, Incorporated.

McClelland, D. C., *The achievement motive*. (1953). New York: Appleton-Century-Crofts.

McDonald, F. J., & Elias, P. (1976a). Beginning teacher evaluation study: Phase II, 1973–74. Executive Summary Report. Princeton, N.J.: Educational Testing Service.

McDonald, F. J., & Elias, P. (1976b). *Executive summary report: beginning teacher evaluation study, phase two*. Princeton, NJ: Educational Testing Service.

McKibbin, M. & Joyce, B. (1980). Psychological states and staff development. *Theory into Practice, 19* (4), 248–255.

McKinney, C., Warren, A., Larkins, G., Ford, M. J., & Davis, J. C. III (1983). The effectiveness of three methods of teaching social studies concepts to fourth-grade students: An aptitude-treatment interaction study, *American Educational Research Journal, 20,* 663–670.

McLaughlin, M., Pfeifer, R. S., Swanson-Owens, D., & Yee, S. (1986). Why teachers won't teach. *Phi Delta Kappan, 67* (6), 420–426.

McNair, K. (1978–1979). Capturing in-flight decisions. *Educational Research Quarterly, 3* (4), 26–42.

Medley, D. (1977). *Teacher competence and teacher effectiveness*. Washington, D.C.: American Association of Colleges of Teacher Education.

Medley, D. M. Teacher effectiveness. (1982). In H. Mitzel (ed.). *Encyclopedia of educational research, 1894–1903.*

Medley, D. M., Coker, H., Coker, J. G., Lorentz, J. L., Soar, R. S., & Spaulding, R. L. (1981). Assessing teacher performance from observed competency indicators defined by classroom teachers. *Journal of Educational Research, 74,* 197–216.

Medley, D. M., & Mitzel, H. (1958). A technique for measuring classroom behavior. *Journal of Educational Psychology, 49,* 86–92.

Medley, D. & Mitzel, H. (1963). Measuring classroom behavior by systematic observation. In N. L. Gage (Ed.) *Handbook of research on teaching* (pp. 247–328). Chicago: Rand McNally and Co.

Medley, D., Soar, R. & Coker, H. (1984). *Measurement-based evaluation of teacher performance*. New York: Longman.

Melamed, B., & Siegel, L. (1973). Reduction of anxiety in children facing hospitalization and surgery by use of filmed modeling. *Journal of Consulting and Clinical Psychology, 43,* 511–520.

Merrill, M. D., & R. D. Tennyson, *Concept teaching: An instructional design guide*, Englewood Cliffs, N.J.: Educational Technology, 1977.

Meyer, L., (1984). Long-term academic effects of the direct instruction project follow through, *Elementary School Journal, 84,* 380–394.

Michaelis, J. U., *Social studies for children in a democracy*. Englewood Cliffs, N.J.: Prentice-Hall, Inc., 1963.

Miel, A., and P. Bregan (1957). *More than social studies: A view of social learning in the elementary school.* Englewood Cliffs, N.J.: Prentice-Hall, Inc.

Miles, M. (1981). *Learning to work in groups.* New York: Teachers College Press.

Miles, M. (1981). Mapping the common properties of schools. In R. Lehming & M. Kane (Eds.), *Improving schools: Using what we know,* pp. 42–114. Beverly Hills, Calif.: Sage.

Miles, M. (1986). Research findings on the stages of school improvement. Conference on Planned Change, The Ontario Institute for Studies in Education.

Miles, M. & Huberman, M. (1984). *Innovation up close.* New York: Praeger.

Mitchell, L. S. (1950). *Our children and our schools.* New York: Simon & Schuster, Inc.

More, T. (1965). *Utopia.* New York: E. P. Dutton & Co., Inc.

Murphy, C. & Sudderth, C. (1990). Winning in the classroom. Augusta, Ga.: Richmond County Public Schools.

Myers, I. B. (1962). *The Myers-Briggs type indicator.* Palo Alto, Calif.: Consulting Psychologists Press.

National Council for the Social Studies. (1964). The Glen Falls story. Washington, D.C.: National Education Association.

National Institutes of Education (1975). *National conference on studies in teaching, Vols. 1–10.* Washington, DC: U. S. Department of Health, Education and Welfare.

Neill, A. S. (1960). *Summerhill.* New York: Holt, Rinehart, and Winston.

Nelson, J. (1971). Collegial supervision in multi-unit schools. Ph.D. Thesis, University of Oregon.

Nesbitt, W. A. (1971). *Simulation games for the social studies classroom.* New York: Foreign Policy Association.

New Webster's dictionary of the English language. (1981). (Deluxe Encyclopedia Edition). United States of America: Delair Publishing Co., Inc.

Nicholson, A. M., & Joyce, B. (with D. Parker & F. Waterman). (1976). *The literature on inservice teacher education. ISTE Report III.* Syracuse, N.Y.: The National Dissemination Center, Syracuse University.

Nucci, L. P., ed. (1989). *Moral development and character education.* Berkeley, McCutchan.

Oakes, J. (1986). *Keeping track: how schools structure inequality.* New Haven: Yale University Press.

Oliver, D. W., & Newman, F. (1967). *Taking a stance: A clear guide to discussion of public issues.* Middletown, Conn.: American Education Publishers.

Oliver, D., & Shaver, J. P. (1966). *Teaching Public Issues in the High School.* Boston: Houghton Mifflin Company.

Oliver, D. W., & Shaver, J. P. (1968). The effect of student characteristics and teaching method interactions on learning to think critically. Paper presented to the American Educational Research Association.

Oliver, D. W., & Shaver, J. P. (1971). *Cases and controversy: A guide to teaching the public issues series.* Middletown, Conn.: American Education Publishers.

Olson, D. R. (1970). *Cognitive development: The child's acquisition of diagonality.* New York: Academic Press, Inc.

Orme, M., & Purnell, R. (1968). Behavior modification and transfer in an out-of-control classroom. Monograph publ. by Harvard R & D Center on Educational Differences.

Ornstein, R. (1972). *The psychology of consciousness.* New York: The Viking Press.

Palomares, U., Ball, G., & Bessell, H. (1976). Magic circle: human development program. La Mesa, Calif.: Human Development Institute.

Pavlov, I. (1927). *Conditioned reflexes: An investigation of physiological activity of the cerebral cortex.* Trans. G. V. Anrep. London and New York: Oxford University Press.

Perkins, D. N. (1984). Creativity by design. *Educational Leadership, 42* (1), 18–25.

Perls, F. (1968). *Gestalt therapy verbatim.* Lafayette, Calif.: Real People Press.

Persing, P., Bailey, W. C., and Kleg, M. (1969). Life-Cycle. Anthropology Curriculum Project, Publication 49. Athens, Ga.: The University of Georgia.

Peterson, P., & Clark, C. (1978). Teachers reports of their cognitive processes while teaching. *American Educational Research Journal, 15* (4), 555–565.

Peterson, P., Marx, R., & Clark, C. (1978). Teacher planning, teacher behavior, and student achievement. *American Educational Research Journal, 15* (4), 417–432.

Phenix, P. (1961). *Education and the common good.* New York: Harper.

Phi Delta Kappa. (1985). *Exemplary practice series.* Bloomington, Ind.: Phi Delta Kappa.

Phi Delta Kappa. (1983). *Improving your own instruction: Self-assessment and peer review.* Bloomington, IN: Phi Delta Kappa.

Piaget, J. (1952). *The origins of intelligence in children.* New York: International University Press.

Piaget, J. (1960). *The child's conception of the world.* Atlantic Highlands, N.J.: Humanities Press, Inc.

Plato, *The Republic.* (1945). Trans. McDonald Cornford. New York: Oxford University Press, Inc.

Pollack, G. K. (1975). *Leadership of discussion groups.* Jamaica, N.Y.: Spectrum Publications.

Premack, D. (1965). Reinforcement theory. In Nebraska Symposium on Motivation, ed. D. Levine. Lincoln, Neb: University of Nebraska Press.

Pressley, M. (1977). Children's use of the keyword method to learn simple Spanish vocabulary words. *Journal of Educational Psychology, 69* (5), 465–472.

Pressley, M., Levin, J. R. (1978). Developmental constraints associated with children's use of the keyword method of foreign language learning. *Journal of Experimental Child Psychology, 26* (1), 359–372.

Pressley, M., Levin, J. R., and Delaney, H. D. (1982). The mnemonic keyword method. *Review of Educational Research, 52* (1), 61–91.

Pressley, M. and Dennis-Rounds, J. (1980). Transfer of a mnemonic keyword strategy at two age levels. *Journal of Educational Psychology, 72* (4), 575–582.

Pressley, M., Levin, J., & Ghatala, E. (1984). Memory-strategy monitoring in adults and children. *Journal of Verbal Learning and Verbal Behavior, 23* (2), 270–288.

Pressley, M., Levin, J. R., and McCormick, C. (1980). Young children's learning of foreign language vocabulary; A sentence variation of the keyword method. *Contemporary Educational Psychology. 5*(1), 22–29.

Pressley, M., Levin, J., & Miller, G. (1981a). How does the keyword method affect vocabulary, comprehension, and usage? *Reading Research Quarterly, 16,* 213–226.

Pressley, M., Levin, J., & Miller, G. (1981b). The keyword method and children's learning of foreign vocabulary with abstract meanings. *Canadian Psychology, 35* (3), 283–287.

Pressley, M., Samuel, J., Hershey, M., Bishop, S., & Dickinson, D. (1981). Use of a mnemonic technique to teach young children foreign-language vocabulary. *Contemporary Educational Psychology, 6,* 110–116.

Preston, R. C., *Improving the teaching of world affairs.* (1956). Englewood Cliffs, N.J.: Prentice Hall, Inc.

Purkey, S. & Smith, M. (1983). Effective schools: A review. *Elementary School Journal, 83* (4), 427–452.

Purpel, D., & Ryan, K., eds. (1976). *Moral education: It comes with the territory.* Berkeley: Macutchan.

Ralph, J., & Fennessey, J. (1983). Science or reform: Some questions about the effective schools model. *Phi Delta Kappan, 64* (10), 689–694.

Rauth, M., Biles, B., Billups, L., & Veitch, S. (1983). *Educational research and dissemination program.* Washington, D.C.: American Federation of Teachers.

Resnick, L. B. (1967). *Design of an early learning curriculum.* Pittsburgh, Pa: University of Pittsburgh Learning Research and Development Center, 1967.

Resnick, L. B. (1987). *Education and learning to think.* Washington, D.C.: Academic Press.

Rhine, W. Ray (Ed.). (1981). *Making schools more effective: New directions from follow through.* New York: Academic Press.

Richardson, V. (1990). Significant and worthwhile change in teaching practice. *Educational Researcher, 19,* 7, 10–18.

Rimm, D. C., & Masters, J. C. (1974). *Behavior therapy: Techniques and empirical findings.* New York: Academic Press, Inc.

Ripple, R., & Drinkwater, D. (1981). Transfer of learning. In H. E. Mitzel (Ed.)

Encyclopedia of educational research, Vol. 4, pp. 1947–1953. New York: The Free Press, Macmillan Publishing Company.

Roberts, J. (1969). Human relations training and its effect on the teaching-learning process in social studies. Final Report, New York State Education Department, Division of Research, Albany, New York.

Robinson, F. P. (1946). *Effective study*. New York: Harper and Bros.

Roebuck, F., Buhler, J., & Aspy, D. (1976). A comparison of high and low levels of humane teaching/learning conditions on the subsequent achievement of students identified as having learning difficulties. Final Report: Order No. PLD 6816-76 re. the National Institute of Mental Health. Denton, Texas: Texas Woman's University Press.

Rogers, C. (1961). *On becoming a person*. Boston: Houghton Mifflin.

Rogers, C. (1969). *Freedom to learn*. Columbus: Charles E. Merrill.

Rogers, C. (1971). *Client centered therapy*. Boston: Houghton Mifflin Co.

Rogers, C. (1981). *A way of being*. Boston: Houghton Mifflin.

Rogers, C. (1982). *Freedom to learn for the eighties*. Columbus: Charles E. Merrill.

Rolheiser-Bennett, C. (1986). Four models of teaching: A meta-analysis of student outcomes. Ph.D. thesis, University of Oregon.

Romberg, T. A., and Wilson, J. (1970). The effect of an advance organizer, cognitive set, and post organizer on the learning and retention of written materials. Paper presented at the annual meeting of the American Educational Research Association, Minn.

Roper, S., Deal, T., & Dornbusch, S. (1976). Collegial evaluation of classroom teaching: Does it work? *Educational Research Quarterly*, Spring, 56–66.

Rosenholtz, S. J. (1989). *Teachers' workplace: The social organization of schools*. White Plains, N.Y.: Longman.

Rosenshine, B. (1970). The stability of teacher effects upon student achievement. *Review of Educational Research, 40*, 647–662.

Rosenshine, B. (1971). *Teaching behaviours and student achievement*. London: National Foundation for Educational Research.

Rosenshine, B. (1985). Direct instruction. *International Encyclopedia of Education*, Eds. Torsten Husen and T. Neville Postlethwaite. Oxford: Pergamon Press, Vol. 3, 1395–1400.

Rosskopf, M. (1971). *Piagetian cognitive development research in mathematical education*. Washington, D.C.: National Council of Teachers of Mathematics.

Rousseau, J. J. (1983). *Emile*, New York: E. P. Dutton.

Rowe, M. B. (1969). Science, soul and sanctions. *Science and Children, 6* (6), 11–13.

Rowe, M. B. (1974). Wait-time and rewards as instructional variables, their influence on language, logic, and fate control. *Journal of Research in Science Teaching, 11*, 81–94.

Rowen, B., Bossert, S. T., & Dwyer, D. C. (1983). Research on effective schools: A cautionary note. *Educational Researcher, 12* (4), 24–31.

Rutter, M., Maughan, R., Mortimer, P., Oustin, J., & Smith, A. (1979). *Fifteen thousand hours: Secondary schools, and their effects on children.* Cambridge, Mass.: Harvard University Press.

Salter, A. (1964). The theory and practice of conditioned reflex therapy. In *Conditioning therapies: The challenge in psychotherapy,* Eds. A. Salter, J. Wolpe, and L. J. Reyna. New York: Holt, Rinehart & Winston.

Salter, A., Wolpe, J., & Reyna, J., (Eds.). (1964). *The conditioning therapies: The challenge in psychotherapies.* New York: Holt, Rinehart & Winston.

Sanders, D. A., & Sanders, J. A. (1984). *Teaching creativity through metaphor.* New York: Longman.

Sarason, S. (1982). *The culture of the school and the problem of change,* 2nd ed. Boston: Allyn & Bacon.

Scanlon, R., & Brown, M. (1969). In-service education for individualized instruction. Philadelphia: Research for Better Schools. Unpublished manuscript.

Schaefer, R. (1967). *The school as a center of inquiry.* New York: Harper & Row.

Schein, E. H., & Bennis, W. G. (1965). *Personal and organizational change through group methods.* New York: John Wiley & Sons, Inc.

Schiffer, J. (1980). *School renewal through staff development.* New York: Teachers College Press.

Schmuck, R. A., & Runkel, P. J. (1985). *The handbook of organizational development in schools* (3rd ed.). Palo Alto, Calif.: Mayfield Press.

Schmuck, R. A., Runkel, P. J., Arends, R., & Arends, J. (1977). *The second handbook of organizational development in schools.* Palo Alto, Calif.: Mayfield Press.

Schon, D. (1982). *The reflective practitioner.* New York: Basic Books.

Schrenker, G. (1976). The effects of an inquiry-development program on elementary school children's science learning. Ph.D. thesis, New York University.

Schroder, H. M., Driver, M. J., & Streufert, S. (1967). *Human information processing: Individuals and groups functioning in complex social situations.* New York: Holt, Rinehart & Winston.

Schroder, H. M., Karlins, M., & Phares, J. (1973). *Education for freedom.* New York: John Wiley.

Schutz, W. (1967). *Joy: Expanding human awareness.* New York: Grove Press, Inc.

Schutz, W. (1982). *Firo.* New York: Holt, Rinehart & Winston.

Schutz, W., & Turner, E. (1983). *Body fantasy.* Irvington, IL: Irvington Press.

Schwab, J. (1965). *Biological sciences curriculum study: Biology teachers' handbook.* New York: John Wiley and Sons, Inc.

Schwab, J. (1982). *Science, curriculum, and liberal education: Selected essays.* Chicago: University of Chicago Press.

Schwab, J., & Brandwein, P. (1962). *The teaching of science.* Cambridge, Mass.: Harvard University Press.

Seperson, M. (1970). The relationship between the teaching styles of student teachers and those of their cooperating teachers. PhD dissertation. New York: Teachers College, Columbia University.

Seperson, M., & Joyce, B. (1981). The relationship between the teaching styles of student teachers and those of their cooperating teachers. In Joyce, Peck, and Brown (Eds.), 101–108.

Shaffer, J. B. P., & Galinsky, J. D. (1974). *Models of group therapy and sensitivity training.* Englewood Cliffs, N.J.: Prentice-Hall.

Shaftel, F., & Shaftel, G. (1967). *Role playing of social values: Decision making in the social studies.* Englewood Cliffs, N.J.: Prentice-Hall.

Shaftel, F., & Shaftel, G. (1982). *Role playing in the curriculum.* Englewood Cliffs, N.J.: Prentice-Hall.

Shane, H. (1977). Curriculum change: Toward the 21st century. Washington, D.C.: National Education Association.

Sharan, S. (1980). Cooperative learning in small groups: Recent methods and effects on achievement, attitudes, and ethnic relations. *Review of Educational Research, 50* (2), 241–271.

Sharan, S. (1990). *Cooperative learning: Theory and research.* New York: Praeger.

Sharan, S., & Hertz-Lazarowitz, R. (1980a). Academic achievement of elementary school children in small group versus whole-class instruction. *Journal of Experimental Education, 48* (2), 120–129.

Sharan, S., & Hertz-Lazarowitz, R. (1980b). A group investigation method of cooperative learning in the classroom. In Sharan, S., Hare, P., Webb, C., & Hertz-Lazarowitz, R. (Eds.), *Cooperation in education* (pp. 14–46). Provo, UT: Brigham Young University Press.

Sharan, S., & Hertz-Lazarowitz, R. (1982). Effects of an instructional change program on teachers' behavior, attitudes, and perceptions. *The Journal of Applied Behavioral Science, 18* (2), 185–201.

Sharan, S., & Shachar, H. (1988). *Language and learning in the cooperative classroom.* New York: Springer-Verlag.

Sharan, S., & Shaulov, A. (1990). Cooperative learning, motivation to learn, and academic achievement. In Sharan, Shlomo, (Ed.), *Cooperative learning: Theory and research.* New York: Praeger, 173–202.

Sharan, S., Slavin, R., & Davidson, N. (1990). The IASCE: An agenda for the 90's. *Cooperative Learning, 10,* 2–4.

Shavelson, R., & Dempsey-Atwood, M. (1976). Generalizability of measures of teacher behavior. *Review of Educational Research, 46* (4), 553–611.

Shaver, J. P., Davis, O. L., & Helburn, S. W. (1978). *An interpretive report on the status of pre-college social studies education based on three NIE-funded studies.* Washington, DC: National Council for the Social Studies.

Shaver, J. P., & Strong, W. (1982). *Facing value-decisions: Rationale-building for teachers*. New York: Teachers College Press.

Shepard, H. A. (1964). The T-Group as training in observant participation. In W. G. Bennis, K. D. Benne, & R. Chin (Eds.), *The planning of change: Readings in the applied behavioral sciences*. New York: Holt, Rinehart & Winston.

Showers, B. (1980). Self-efficacy as a predictor of teacher participation in school decision-making. Ph.D. thesis. Stanford University.

Showers, B. (1982a). A study of coaching in teacher training. Eugene: University of Oregon, Center for Educational Policy & Management.

Showers, B. (1982b). *Transfer of training: The contribution of coaching*. Eugene, OR: Center for Educational Policy and Management.

Showers, B. (1984). Peer coaching and its effect on transfer of training. Paper presented at the annual meeting of the American Educational Research Association, New Orleans.

Showers, B. (1985). Teachers coaching teachers. *Educational Leadership, 42* (7), 43–49.

Showers, B. (1989). *Implementation: Research-based training and teaching strategies and their effects on the workplace and instruction*. Paper presented at the annual meeting of the American Educational Research Association, San Francisco (March).

Showers, B., Joyce, B., & Bennett, B. (1987). Synthesis of research on staff development: A framework for future study and a state-of-the-art analysis. *Educational Leadership, 45* (3), 77–87.

Shulman, L. S., & Keislar, E. R. (Eds.). (1966). *Learning by discovery: A critical appraisal*. Skokie, Ill.: Rand McNally & Company.

Siegel, I. E. (1984). *Advances in applied developmental psychology*. New York: Ablex.

Sigel, F. E. (1969). The Piagetion system and the world of educational studies. In David Elkind & John Flavell (Eds.). *Cognitive development*. New York: Oxford University Press.

Sigel, I. E., & Hooper, F. H. (1968). *Logical thinking in children*. New York: Holt, Rinehart, & Winston.

Simon, A., & Boyer, E. G. (1967). *Mirrors for behavior: An anthology of classroom observation instruments*. Philadelphia: Research for Better Schools, Inc.

Sizer, Theodore R. (1984). *Horace's compromise: The dilemma of the American high school*. Boston: Houghton Mifflin.

Skinner, B. F. (1953). *Science and human behavior*. New York: Macmillan, Inc.

Skinner, B. F. (1957). *Verbal behavior*. New York: Appleton-Century-Crofts.

Skinner, B. F. (1968). *The technology of teaching*. Englewood Cliffs, N.J.: Prentice-Hall, Inc.

Skinner, B. F. (1971). *Beyond freedom and dignity*. New York: Knopf.

Skinner, B. F. (1978). *Reflections on behaviorism and society*. Englewood Cliffs, N.J.: Prentice-Hall.

Slavin, R. E. (1977a). Classroom reward structure: An analytic and practical review. *Review of Educational Research, 47* (4), 633–650.

Slavin, R. E. (1977b). How student learning teams can integrate the desegregated classroom. *Integrated Education, 15* (6), 56–58.

Slavin, R. E. (1977c). Student learning team techniques: Narrowing the achievement gap between the races. Center for Social Organization of Schools: The Johns Hopkins University, Report No. 228.

Slavin, R. E. (1977d). A student team approach to teaching adolescents with special emotional and behavioral needs. *Psychology in the Schools, 14* (1), 77–84.

Slavin, R. E. (1978a). Separating incentives, feedback, and evaluation: Toward a more effective classroom system. *Educational Psychologist, 13,* 97–100.

Slavin, R. E. (1978b). Student teams and achievement divisions. *Journal of Research and Development in Education, 12,* 39–49.

Slavin, R. E. (1983). *Cooperative learning.* New York: Longman, Inc.

Slavin, R. E. (1986). The Napa evaluation of Madeline Hunter's ITIP: Lessons learned. *The Elementary School Journal, 87* (2), 165–171.

Slavin, R. E. (1989). PET and the pendulum: Faddism in education and how to stop it. *Phi Delta Kappan, 70* (10), 752–758.

Slavin, R. E. (1990a). Achievement effects of ability grouping in secondary schools. *Review of Educational Research, 60* (3), 471–500.

Slavin, R. E. (1990b). Mastery learning reconsidered. *Review of Educational Research, 60,* 300–302.

Slavin, R. E. (1991). Are cooperative learning and "untracking" harmful to the gifted? *Educational Leadership, 48,* 6, 68–70.

Slavin, R. E., Madden, N. A., Karweit, N., Livermon, B. J., & Dolan, L. (1990). Success for all: First-year outcomes of a comprehensive plan for reforming urban education. *American Educational Research Journal, 27,* 255–278.

Smith, K., & Smith, M. (1966). *Cybernetic principles of learning and educational design.* New York: Holt, Rinehart, and Winston.

Smith, L., & Keith, P. (1971). Anatomy of an innovation. New York: Wiley.

Smith, M. L. (1980). Effects of aesthetics educations on basic skills learning. Boulder, Colo.: Laboratory of Educational Research, University of Colorado.

Snow, R. (1982). Intelligence, motivation, and academic work. Paper presented for a symposium on "The student's role in learning," conducted by the National Commission for Excellence in Education, U.S. Department of Education, San Diego, Calif.

Soar, R. S. (1973). Follow through classroom process measurement and pupil growth (1970–71): Final Report. Gainesville: College of Education, University of Florida.

Soar, R. S., Soar, R. M., & Ragosta, M. (1971). *Florida Climate and Control System: Observer's Manual.* Gainesville: Institute for Development of Human Resources, University of Florida.

Spaulding, R. L., & Papageorio, M. R. (1975). Observation of the coping behavior of children in elementary schools. Unpublished manuscript, San Jose State University.

Spaulding, R. L. (1974). *CASES Manual.* San Jose, Calif.: San Jose State University.

Spaulding, R. L. (1978). *STARS Manual.* San Jose, Calif.: San Jose State University.

Sprinthall, M. A., & Thies-Sprinthall, L. (1983). Teachers as adult learners. In The eighty-second yearbook of the National Society for the SRI International. (1982). Evaluation of the implementation of Public Law 94-142. Menlo Park, Calif.: SRI International.

Stadsklev, R. (n.d.). Handbook of simulation gaming in social education: I (Textbook) and II (Directory). Tuscaloosa: University of Alabama, Institute of Higher Education Research and Services.

Stallings, J. (1975). Implementation and child effects of teaching practices in follow through classrooms. *Monographs of the Society for Research in Child Development*, 4D 17-8, Serial No. 163.

Stallings, J. (1979). *How to change the process of teaching reading in secondary schools.* Menlo Park, Calif.: SRI International.

Stallings, J. (1980). Allocating academic learning time revisited: Beyond time on task. *Educational Researcher, 9*, 11–16.

Stallings, J. (1985). A study of implementation of Madeline Hunter's model and its effects on students. *Journal of Educational Research, 78*, 325–337.

Stallings, J., & Kaskowitz, D. (1972–73). *Follow through classroom observation evaluation.* Menlo Park, Calif.: SRI International.

Stallings, J., Needels, P., & Stayrook, N. (1979). *The teaching of basic reading skills in secondary schools: Phase Two and Phase Three.* Menlo Park, Calif.: SRI International.

Stanford Program on Teaching Effectiveness. (1976). A factorially designed experiment on teacher structuring, soliciting, and reacting. Stanford, Calif.: Stanford Center for Research and Development in Teaching.

Starr, J. (1965). *Programmed modern arithmetic: Introduction to sets.* Boston: D. C. Heath and Company.

Stephens, W. B. (1972). The development of reasoning, moral judgment and moral conduct in retardates and normals: Phase II. Unpublished manuscript, Temple University.

Sternberg, R. (1986). *Intelligence applied: Understanding and increasing your intellectual skills.* San Diego: Harcourt Brace Jovanovich.

Sternberg, R. J. (1986). Synthesis of research on the effectiveness of intellectual skills programs. *Educational Leadership, 44*, 60–67.

Sternberg, R., & Bahna, K. (1986). Synthesis of research on the effectiveness of intellectual skills programs: Snake-oil remedies or miracle cures? *Educational Leadership, 44* (2), 60–67.

Stevenson, H. W., Lee, S., & Stigler, J. W. (1986). Mathematics achievement of Chinese, Japanese, and American children. *Science, 231*, 693–699.

Stone, C. L. (1983). A meta-analysis of advance organizer studies. *Journal of Experimental Education, 51* (4), 194–199.

Suchmán, R. J. (1962). The elementary school training program in scientific inquiry. Report to the U.S. Office of Education, Project Title VII. Urbana: University of Illinois.

Suchman, R. J. (1964). Studies in inquiry training. In R. Ripple and V. Bookcastle (Eds.), *Piaget reconsidered.* Ithaca, NY.: Cornell University Press.

Suchman, R. J. (1981). *Idea book for geological inquiry.* Trillium Press.

Sullivan, E. (1967). Piaget and the school curriculum: A critical appraisal. *Bulletin No. 2.* Toronto: Ontario Institute for Studies in Education.

Sullivan, E. V. (1984). *A critical psychology: Interpretations of the personal world.* Plenum.

Sullivan, M. S. (1963). *Programmed English: A modern grammar for high school and college students.* New York: Macmillan Publishing Co., Inc.

Taba, H. (1966). *Teaching strategies and cognitive functioning in elementary school children.* (Cooperative Research Project 2404.) San Francisco: San Francisco State College.

Taba, H. (1967). *Teacher's handbook for elementary school social studies.* Reading, Mass.: Addison-Wesley Publishing Co., Inc.

Taber, J., Glaser, R., & Halmuth, H. S. (1967). *Learning and programmed instruction.* Reading, Mass.: Addison-Wesley Publishing Company, Inc.

Taylor, C., (Ed.). (1964). *Creativity: Progress and potential.* New York: McGraw-Hill.

Tennyson, R. D., & Cocchiarella, M. (1986). An empirically based instructional design theory for teaching concepts. *Review of Educational Research, 56,* 40–71.

Thelen, H. (1954). *Dynamics of groups at work.* Chicago: University of Chicago Press.

Thelen, H. (1960). *Education and the human quest.* New York: Harper and Row.

Thelen, H. (1967). *Classroom grouping for teachability.* New York: John Wiley and Sons, Inc.

Thelen, H. (1981). *The classroom society: The construction of education.* Halsted Press.

Thorndike, E. L. (1911). Animal intelligence: An experimental study of the associative process in animals. In *Psychological Review,* Monograph Supplement 2, no. 8. New York: Macmillan, Inc.

Thorndike, E. L. (1913). *The psychology of learning, Vol. II: Educational psychology.* New York: Teachers College.

Tinsman, S. (1981a). The effects of instructional flexibility training on teaching styles and controlled repertoire. PhD dissertation. New York: Teachers College, Columbia University.

Tinsman, S. (1981b). The effects of instructional flexibility training on teaching styles and controlled repertoire. In B. Joyce, C. Brown, & L. Peck (Eds.), *Flexibility in teaching.* New York: Longman.

Tobin, K. (1986). Effects of teacher wait time on discourse characteristics in mathematics and language arts classes. *American Educational Research Journal, 23* (2), 191–200.

Torrance, E. P. (1962). *Guiding creative talent.* Englewood Cliffs, N.J.: Prentice-Hall, Inc.

Torrance, E. P. (1965). *Gifted children in the classroom.* New York: Macmillan, Inc.

Torrance, E. P. (1966). *Torrance Tests of Creative Thinking.* Normal Annual, Research Edition. Princeton, N.J.: Personnel Press.

Tyler, R. W. (1950). *Basic principles of curriculum and instruction.* Chicago: University of Chicago Press.

"The Urban Simulator." Washington, D.C.: Washington Center for Metropolitan Studies, 1972.

U. S. Department of Education. (1986). *What works: Research about teaching and learning.* Washington, D.C.: U. S. Department of Education.

Vance, V. S., & Schlechty, P. C. (1982). The distribution of academic ability in the teaching force: Policy implications. *Phi Delta Kappan, 64* (1), 22–27.

Varenhorst, B. B. (1968). The life career game: Practice in decision-making. In S. Boocock & E. O. Schild (Eds.), *Simulating games in learning.* Beverly Hills, Calif.: Sage Publications, Inc.

Voss, B. A. (1982). *Summary of research in science education.* Columbus, Oh.: ERIC Clearinghouse for Science, Mathematics, and Environmental Education.

Wadsworth, B. (1978). *Piaget for the classroom teacher.* New York: Longman, Inc.

Walberg, H. J. (1985). *Why Japanese educational productivity excels.* Paper presented at the annual meeting of the American Educational Research Association, Chicago.

Walberg, H. J. (1986). What works in a nation still at risk. *Educational Leadership, 44* (1), 7–11.

Walberg, H. J. (1990). Productive teaching and instruction: Assessing the knowledge base. *Phi Delta Kappan, 71* (6), 70–78.

Walker, J. (1977). *The flying circus of physics.* New York: Wiley.

Wallace, R. C., Lemahieu, P. G., & Bickel, W. E. (1990). The Pittsburgh experience: Achieving commitment to comprehensive staff development. In Bruce Joyce (Ed.), *Changing school culture through staff development.* Alexandria, Va.: Association for Supervision and Curriculum Development.

Wallace, R. C., Young, J. R., Johnston, J., Bickel, W. E., & LeMahieu, P. G. (1984). Secondary educational renewal in Pittsburgh. *Educational Leadership, 41* (6), 73–77.

Warren, M. (1966). The classification of offenders as an aide to efficient management and effective treatment: Community treatment project. Prepared for the President's Commission on Law Enforcement and the Administration of Justice, Task Force on Corrections.

Waterman, F. (1977). *Interviews: ISTE 4th Report.* Syracuse: Syracuse University National Dissemination Center in Education.

Watson, J. B. (1916). The place of conditioned reflex in psychology. *Psychological Review, 23,* 89–116.

Watson, J. B., & Rayner, R. (1921). Conditioned emotional reactions. *Journal of Experimental Psychology, 3,* 1–14.

Webster's new collegiate dictionary. (1975). Springfield, Mass.: G. & C. Merriam Company.

Weikart, D., et al. (1971). The cognitively oriented curriculum: A framework for pre-school teachers. Washington, D.C.: National Association for Education of Young Children.

Weil, M. (1973). Deriving teaching skills from models of teaching. Paper delivered to the annual meeting of the American Educational Research Association, New Orleans.

Weil, M., Joyce, B., & Kluwin, B. (1978). *Personal models of teaching.* Englewood Cliffs, N.J.: Prentice-Hall, Inc.

Weil, M., Marshalek, B., Mittman, A., Murphy, J., Hallinger, P., & Pruyn, J. (1984). Effective and typical schools: How different are they? Paper presented at the annual meeting of the American Educational Research Association, New Orleans.

Weiler, H. (1983). Hunter's model and its effects on students. *Journal of Educational Research, 78,* 325–337.

Weinstein, G., & Fantini, M. (Eds.). (1970). *Toward humanistic education: A curriculum of affect.* N. Y.: Praeger, Inc.

Weiss, I. R. (1978). *Nineteen seventy-seven national survey of science, social science, and mathematics education.* National Science Foundation. Washington, DC: U. S. Government Printing Office.

Wertheimer, M. (1945). *Productive thinking.* New York: Harper.

Wilson, C. (1971). The open-access curriculum. Boston: Allyn Bacon.

Wing, R. (1965). Two computer-based economic games for sixth graders. Yorktown Heights, N.Y.: Center for Educational Services and Research, Board of Cooperative Educational Services.

Wittrock, M. C., & Alesandrini, K. (1990). Generation of summaries and analogies and analytic and holistic abilities. *American Educational Research Journal, 27,* 3, 489–502.

Wolpe, J. (1958). *Psychotherapy by reciprocal inhibition.* Stanford, Calif.: Stanford University Press.

Wolpe, J. (1969). *The practice of behavior therapy.* Oxford: Pergamon Press.

Wolpe, J., & Lang, P. Fear survey schedule. San Diego: Educational and Industrial Testing Service.

Wolpe, J., & Lazarus, A. (1966). *Behavior therapy techniques: A guide to the treatment of neuroses.* Oxford: Pergamon Press, Inc.

Wolpe, J., & Wolpe, D. (1981). *Our useless fears*. Boston: Houghton Mifflin.

Worthen, B. (1968). A study of discovery and expository presentation: Implications for teaching. *Journal of Teacher Education, 19*, 223–242.

Wrenn, C. G., & Larsen, R. P. (1955). *Studying effectively*. Stanford, Calif.: Stanford University Press.

Young, D. (1971). Team learning: An experiment in instructional method as related to achievement. *Journal of Research in Science Teaching, 8*, 99–103.

Zaltman, G., Duncan, R., & Holberg, J. (1973). *Innovation and organization*. New York: John Wiley.

Ziegler, S. (1981). The effectiveness of cooperative learning teams for increasing cross-ethnic friendship: Additional evidence. *Human Organization, 40*, 264–268.

Zuckerman, D. W., & Horm, R. E. (1970). *The guide to simulation Games for Education and Training*. Cambridge, Mass.: Information Resources, Inc.

Zumwalt, K. (Ed.). (1986). *Improving teaching: 1986 Yearbook of the Association for Supervision and Curriculum Development*. Washington, D.C.: Association for Supervision and Curriculum Development.

INDEX

UNIVERSITY OF WOLVERHAMPTON
LEARNING RESOURCES

ACKNOWLEDGMENTS

Excerpts from *Teaching Strategies and Cognitive Functioning in Elementary School Children* by Hilda Taba, 1966, San Francisco State College, Cooperative Research Project No. 2404, San Francisco. Reprinted by permission. Excerpts from *Elementary School Training Program in Scientific Inquiry* by J. Richard Suchman, on pp. 58-60, © 1962 by The University of Illinois. Excerpts from *The Changing World Today* by Elmer V. Clauson and Marion G. Rice, The University of Georgia, 1972. Excerpts from *The Memory Book* by Harry Lorayne and Jerry Lucas, copyright © 1974 by Harry Lorayne and Jerry Lucas. Reprinted with Permission of Stein and Day Publishers. Excerpts from "Piaget and the School Curriculum: A Critical Appraisal" by Edmund Sullivan, Bulletin No. 2 of the Ontario Institute for studies in education (Toronto, 1967). Reprinted by permission. Excerpts from *Piaget for the Classroom Teacher* by Barry J. Wadsworth, © 1978 by Longman Inc. Excerpts from *Moral Education: It Comes with the Territory* by David and Kevin Kohlberg et al., Berkeley, McCutchan Publishing Corporation © 1976. Permission granted by the publisher. Excerpts from *BSCS, Biology Teacher's Handbook* (New York: John Wiley and Sons, Inc. 1965) reprinted by permission of the Biological Sciences Curriculum Study. Excerpts from Carl Rogers, *Freedom to Learn*, (Columbus, Ohio: Charles E. Merrill Co., 1969). Reprinted by permission of Charles E. Merrill. Excerpts from *The Structure of School Improvement* by Bruce R. Joyce, Richard H. Hersh and Michael McKibbon, copyright © 1983 by Longman Inc. Excerpts from William J. J. Gordon, *Metaphorical Way of Learning and Knowing* (Cambridge, Mass: S.E.S. Press, 1970). Excerpts from *Growth Games* by Howard Lewis and Harold Strietfield, reprinted by permission of Harcourt, Brace, Javonovich, Inc. Excerpts from George Brown, *Humanistic Education Report to Ford Foundation* on the Ford-Esalen Project, "A Pilot Project to Explore Ways to Adapt Approaches in the Affective Domain to the School Curriculum," 1968. Excerpts from Herbert Thelen, *Education and the Human Quest* (New York: Harper & Row, Publishers, Inc., 1960). Excerpts from Fannie R. Shaftel, George Shaftel, *Role-Playing for Social Values: Decision-Making in the Social Studies*, © 1967, pp. 67, 69, 71. Reprinted by permission of Prentice-Hall, Englewood Cliffs, New Jersey. Excerpts from Donald W. Oliver and James P. Shaver, *Teaching Public Issues in the High School*, Logan, UT: Utah State University Press, 1974 (first edition published by Houghton Mifflin, 1966). Excerpts from *Models of Group Therapy and Sensitivity Training* by John B. Shaffer and M. David Galinsky reprinted by permission of Prentice-Hall © 1974, pp. 194-95. Excerpts from *Inquiry in Social Studies* by Byron Massialas and Benjamin Cox. Copyright 1966, by McGraw-Hill Book Company. Used by permission of McGraw-Hill Company. Excerpts from Leon H. Canfield and Howard B. Wilder. *The Making of Modern America*. Copyright © 1966, 1950 by Houghton Mifflin Company. Reprinted by permission of the publisher. Excerpts from *The Nature of the Non-Western World* by Vera Micheles Dean. Copyright © 1957, 1963, 1966 by Vera Micheles Dean. Reprinted by arrangement with The New American Library, Inc., New York, NY. *Behavior Modification and Transfer in an out-of-control Classroom* by Orme and Purnell, used with permission of the Center for Research and Development on Educational Differences, Harvard University, Cambridge, MA. *Programmed English* by M. W. Sullivan, reprinted with permission of Macmillan Publishing Company. Copyright © by M. W. Sullivan Associates 1963. Excerpts from *Human Information Processing* by Harold M. Schroder, Michael J. Driver, and Siegfried Streufert. Copyright © 1967 by Holt, Rinehart & Winston, Inc. Reprinted with permission of CBS College Publishing. Excerpts from David C. Rimm and John C. Masters, *Behavior Therapy: Techniques and Empirical Findings* (New York: Academic Press, Inc., 1974), pp. 284-85. Excerpts from George Brown, *Human Teaching for Human Learning*, pp. 143-45, 150-51. Copyright 1971 by George Brown, An Esalen Book. All rights reserved. Reprinted with permission of Viking Press, Inc. Excerpts from *The Structure of School Improvement* by Bruce R. Joyce, Richard H. Hersh and Michael McKibbon. Copyright © 1983 by Longman Inc.